The Ancient Synagogue from its Origins to 200 C.E.

A Source Book

by

Anders Runesson, Donald D. Binder
and Birger Olsson

BRILL

LEIDEN • BOSTON
2008

In some cases it has not been possible, despite every effort, to locate those with rights to material that may still be in copyright. The publisher would be glad to hear from anyone who holds such rights, in order that appropriate acknowledgement can be made in future editions.

This book is printed on acid-free paper.

Library of Congress Cataloging-in-Publication Data

A C.I.P. record for this book is available from the Library of Congress.

ISSN 1871-6636
ISBN 978 90 04 16116 0

Copyright 2008 by Koninklijke Brill NV, Leiden, The Netherlands.
Koninklijke Brill NV incorporates the imprints Brill, Hotei Publishing,
IDC Publishers, Martinus Nijhoff Publishers and VSP.

PRINTED IN THE NETHERLANDS

The Ancient Synagogue
from its Origins to 200 C.E.

Ancient Judaism and Early Christianity

Arbeiten zur Geschichte des antiken Judentums und des Urchristentums

VOLUME 72

For Rachel, Noah, Rebecca and Anna,
Mary,
and Martin,
in thanksgiving

CONTENTS

FOREWORD

This book had its beginnings in a multidiscplinary research project on ancient synagogues at Lund University in Sweden. Initiated and led by Birger Olsson, the project was conducted between 1997 and 2001. It resulted in the publication of several monographs and articles on the origin, nature, architecture, hermeneutics, and language of the synagogue, as well as analyses of the process of separation between Jews and Christians.

In addition to these, it was clear from the very outset, not least in view of recent scholarly debates, that a collection of relevant sources on the synagogue was a desideratum. It was also evident that the best way to proceed in realising such a source book was through teamwork, not only in order to be able to treat the vast number of diverse sources within a reasonable time frame, but also to ensure that the attendant interpretations and comments embodied a wider view than a single scholar could provide. The present volume represents the culmination of many years of work on ancient synagogues, and we are pleased to be able to present to the reader the results of our common efforts.

Colleagues have generously shared their time and expertise in different ways, and for this we are very greatful. Especially, we would like to thank (in alphabetic order), Douglas Edwards, Claude Eilers, Jim Eisenbraun, Lee Levine, Peter Richardson, Anna Runesson, Eileen Schuller, and Peter Widdicombe. Our research assistants at McMaster University have been invaluable: doctoral students Wayne Baxter, Jonathan Bernier, and Nick Meyer worked on preparing texts and indices. A special thanks to Nick for his indefatigable work on the penultimate draft of the manuscript. Any remaining errors are, of course, our own.

For generous finacial support we would like to acknowledge the Bank of Sweden Tencentenary Foundation, the Segelberska Foundation (Sweden), the Arts and Research Board of McMaster University, Canada, and the Social Sciences and Humanities Research Council (Canada).

Last but not least, we want to express our gratitude to our editors at Brill, Louise Schouten and Ivo Romein, for their enthusiastic support and patience, and to the editors of the *Ancient Judaism and Early Christianity Series*, for accepting our book in this fine series.

Anders Runesson, Donald D. Binder, Birger Olsson
Hamilton, ON—Mt. Vernon, VA—Lund
June 2007

CHAPTER ONE

INTRODUCTION

1.1   *The Synagogue in Ancient Writings and Modern Studies*

Ancient synagogues, the institutional matrixes in which two world religions were born, have been discussed and debated by scholars of Early Judaism and Christianity since modern historical research entered the world of academics around the 16th century. The Enlightenment, however, did not mark the beginning of learned interest in the early synagogue. As is evident in the works of Philo and Josephus, ideas and assumptions about the origin and nature of these institutions flourished already in the first century c.e.

Since then, "the synagogue" has been used in the narrative worlds of academic essays of various types and for different reasons, strikingly few of which have had anything to do with an interest in the institutions themselves. In fact, most often claims about, descriptions of, and references to "the synagogue" and its activities comment on Judaism as a religious or ethnic tradition rather than inform the reader about institutional realities in any given century. "The synagogue" has, in such discourses, acquired a metaphorical life of its own, becoming a monolithic representative, used positively or negatively, of a religious tradition and its adherers, especially defining their relationship to other religions, cultures and peoples (Graeco-Roman and/or Christian).

Even a cursory reading of Philo, Josephus, the New Testament Gospels and Acts or, to take more recent examples, a multitude of 19th and 20th century academic studies on ancient Judaism and Christianity, indicate that "the synagogue" is a powerful and important discursive category that has helped those from different perspectives define inter-action between socio-ethnic and religious groups.

Among first century Diaspora Jews, "the synagogue," and specifically the activity of reading and teaching Torah publicly each Sabbath, could be referred to in order to seek understanding and evoke friendly attitudes from Graeco-Roman neighbours and rulers interested in maintaining law and order. Early followers of Jesus, on the other hand, would often focus on intra-Jewish interaction, both friendly and hostile, within synagogues. By contrast, later non-Jewish Christians moulded a thoroughly negative and stereotyped portrayal of "the synagogue," which came to stand for everything considered to be opposed to "Christianity." "Church" and "synagogue" became, after centuries of religious rhetoric and art, irreconcilable rivals; ultimate truth could only abide within one of the institutions, as proclaimed by its appointed leaders.[1]

As the Roman Empire gradually transformed itself into a (non-Jewish) Christian mono-religious culture, such unsympathetic and totalising discourses of distance and contempt travelled from the political margins to the centre and eventually became mainstream. The earlier Graeco-Roman respect for ancient Jewish institutional traditions to which Philo and Josephus could refer in times of trouble was replaced by religio-political intolerance. Unavoidably, marginalisation followed for the Jews as a people. Anti-synagogue legislation began appearing in the fifth century when Theodosius in 438 c.e. prohibited the construction of new synagogues (although he did allow for the repair of already existing buildings). Later, in the sixth century, Justinian reinforced and expanded such legislation aimed at circumscribing Jewish communal life (545/553 c.e.).[2]

Backed by political interests, this situation became cemented in Christian Europe. In the East, with the arrival of Islam in the seventh century, such developments were halted and Christian anti-Jewish rhetoric was prevented from entering the echelons of political power. With Islam dictating the dominant vision of a just religious society, neither the synagogue nor the church had access to the political influence needed to marginalise the other. By this time, however, the social reality of synagogue and church as two distinct and independent (religious) institutions had already been firmly established, although it is possible that some Christ-believing Jewish groups still existed. If so, by their very existence, they challenge any over-simplification of the institutional situation even in the seventh century.[3]

---

[1] Such rhetoric is prevalent in the writings of the Church Fathers; while not fully developed, one of the first examples of such a use of "the synagogue" as metaphor is found in Justin Martyr: for examples, see the relevant section below. For representations of "synagogue" and "church" in art, see, e.g., Heinz Schreckenberg, *The Jews and Christian Art: An Illustrated History* (New York: Continuum, 1996).

[2] For Roman legislation on Jews and Judaism, see Amnon Linder, *The Jews in Roman Imperial Legislation* (Detroit: Wayne State University Press, 1987), which contains all relevant documents, with translations and commentary.

[3] Cf. Paula Fredriksen, "What Parting of the Ways? Jews, Gentiles, and the Ancient Mediterranean City," in *The Ways that Never Parted: Jews and Christians in Late Antiquity and the Early Middle Ages* (ed. Adam Becker and Annette Yoshiko Reed; Tübingen: Mohr Siebeck, 2003), 35–63.

This development in the West led to the formation within mainstream culture of two basic assumptions about the synagogue, assumptions that have persisted into our own time, even within the scholarly community. The first is that "synagogue" has always, from the first century onwards, referred to an institution separate from the "church." Thus attitudes that developed in the second century and later among elite non-Jewish Christians have been retrojected back onto the first century. This has resulted in scholarly misconceptions about first-century synagogues, perpetuating the view of "synagogue" and "church" as binary opposites in constant conflict. This last constitutes the second assumption.

Despite the prevalence of these notions, the first-century institutional realities behind the "synagogue" do not allow for such a polarisation of categories; neither is the idea of consistent conflict warranted. From an institutional perspective, the conflicting and totalising language of some Christian authors beginning in the second century should not be read as reflecting a first-century situation. Nor should it provide a point of departure for analysing "Jewish and Christian interaction" in "New Testament times" as has so often been done.

Even today, different kinds of religious conflicts in antiquity are frequently "re-termed" as a conflict between "Jesus and the synagogue," or between "synagogue and church."[4] Indeed, repeatedly in the scholarly literature "synagogue" seems to be used as a synonym for "Pharisees," the group (incorrectly) assumed to have provided the leadership in first-century synagogues before being replaced by the rabbis in the late first to early second centuries.[5] Primary sources reveal, however, that synagogue leadership was diverse, consisting of people representing different religio-political outlooks. Not a few leaders were priests—a fact that in itself challenges the common assumption of a dichotomy

---

[4] This is especially frequent in studies on the so-called parting(s) of the ways of Judaism and Christianity, but we find the same assumptions and terminology in many New Testament studies on the Gospels and Paul. The terminological problematic is related to a similar use of "Judaism" and "Christianity" when describing first-century realities; the diversity of the first century hardly allows, however, the use of such distinct and homogenous categories.

[5] Pharisaic or rabbinic leadership in the ancient synagogue has been rejected by most synagogue scholars (so, e.g., Shaye Cohen, Lee I. Levine). Today, the emerging consensus is that the rabbis became influential in Jewish society only in the fourth–fifth centuries or later, and had little influence in the synagogue before this time. Seth Schwartz, *Imperialism and Jewish Society: 200 B.C.E. to 640 C.E.* (Princeton: Princeton University Press, 2001), argues for an even later date. We shall return to this below.

between temple and synagogue in terms of influence and leadership in Jewish society.[6]

It seems that such reconstructions of "synagogue" and "church" as institutional opposites rest not only on the retrojection of modern institutions upon the past, but also on culturally conditioned readings of isolated passages from the New Testament or rabbinic literature. The persuasiveness of such reconstructions lies in the fact that they "make sense" within our own cultural context; by appealing to common sense, they are easily perpetuated in popular and scholarly writings. Nonetheless, as is widely agreed, "common sense" is not enough for historical analysis and may indeed be misleading, since every time-period and culture operates with its own definition of what constitutes collective wisdom.[7] Consequently, re-thinking long-held assumptions about antiquity and its institutions (both scholarly and popular) has gradually become a desideratum within historical studies.

If scholarly ideas and theories about interactions between Jews, Christians, and Graeco-Romans have been founded upon anachronistic or unwarranted assumptions about ancient synagogues, then changes in the understanding of these institutions will undoubtedly lead to changes in the perception of the interaction between socio-religiously defined groups, Jewish, Christian, or other.

Turning to the field of synagogue research, such changes in the understanding of ancient synagogues have been underway for some time now. Today, most of the traditional views have been dismantled by an unprecedented surge of specialist studies in the field. The ground is being prepared for a renewed understanding of the most important institutional settings of nascent Judaism and Christianity, with far-reaching implications for our understanding of the formative period of these religions.

---

[6] See, e.g., Donald D. Binder, *Into the Temple Courts: The Place of the Synagogues in the Second Temple Period* (SBLDS 169; Atlanta: Society of Biblical Literature, 1999), 355ff. Contrary to popular contemporary views, in the first century (and earlier) the priests dominated leadership groups both nationally and locally, and they were regarded as the teachers of Israel: cf., e.g., 2 Chr 19:5–11; Sir 45:17; 1 Macc 14:44; Josephus, *A. J.* 9.4; The Theodotos inscription (*CIJ* 2.1404) mentions three generations of synagogue leaders (*archisynagōgoi*) who were priests. See also Lee I. Levine, *The Ancient Synagogue: The First Thousand Years* (New Haven: Yale University Press, 2005), 519–29, for a discussion of post-70 material. For comprehensive discussions of different synagogue functionaries and leaders, see Binder, *Temple Courts*, 343–87, and Levine, *Ancient Synagogue*, 412–53.

[7] See, e.g., Matthew Johnson, *Archaeological Theory: An Introduction* (Oxford: Blackwell, 1999), 1–33; Anders Runesson, *The Origins of the Synagogue: A Socio-Historical Study* (Stockholm: Almqvist & Wiksell International, 2001), 27.

1.2   The Current State of Research

The interest in ancient synagogues has increased dramatically over the last 20 years or so, and researchers from different fields are now involved in renewed attempts to unveil the many mysteries that surround the origins and development of these institutions. Even if the exploration of the early life of the synagogue has attracted scholars' attention since the dawn of modern historical studies,[8] with major contributions published in the early 20th century,[9] the recent publication of two wide-ranging collections of essays,[10] and nine comprehensive monographs on the topic—and a tenth forthcoming 2007[11]—is unparalleled in the history of scholarship. Indeed, the surge of synagogue studies moved Lee Levine to quickly revise and update his 748-page magnum opus, *The Ancient Synagogue*, originally published in 2000: the second, 796-page edition of this seminal work appeared a mere five years later. As Levine notes in the second edition, "This explosion of synagogue-related research persists to this very day."[12]

The contemporary scholarly enthusiasm for and engagement in the study of ancient synagogues may partly be explained by the fact that the institution was a central part of Jewish life in antiquity and therefore important for the study of Jewish history generally. More significantly, synagogues provided the socio-political and religious setting without

---

[8] Carolus Sigonius, *De republica Hebraeorum libri VII* (Colonie, 1583); Campegius Vitringa, *De synagoga vetere libri tres* (Franequeræ: Typis & Impensis Johannis Gyzelaar, 1696).

[9] Ishmar Elbogen, *Jewish Liturgy: A Comprehensive History.* (Philadelphia: The Jewish Publication Society, 1993); Samuel Krauss, *Synagogale Altertümer* (Berlin-Wien: Verlag Benjamin Harz, 1922).

[10] Dan Urman and Paul V. M. Flesher, *Ancient Synagogues: Historical Analysis and Archaeological Discovery* (2 vols.; Leiden: Brill, 1995). Birger Olsson and Magnus Zetterholm, eds., *The Ancient Synagogue From Its Origins Until 200 C.E.: Papers Presented at an International Conference at Lund University, October 14–17, 2001* (Stockholm: Almqvist & Wiksell International, 2003).

[11] Rachel Hachlili, *Ancient Jewish Art and Archaeology in the Land of Israel* (Handbuch der Orientalistik, Abt. 7. Bd 1. Abschnitt 2. B. Lief. 4. Leiden: Brill, 1988); eadem, *Ancient Jewish Art and Archaeology in the Diaspora* (Handbuch der Orientalistik, Abt. 1, Bd 35. Leiden: Brill, 1998); Steven Fine, *This Holy Place: On the Sanctity of the Synagogue during the Greco-Roman Period* (Notre Dame, Indiana: University of Notre Dame Press, 1997); Binder, *Temple Courts*; Levine, *Ancient Synagogue*; Runesson, *Origins*; Carsten Claußen, *Versammlung, Gemeinde, Synagoge: Das hellenistisch-jüdischen Umfelt der früchristlichen Gemeinden* (Göttingen: Vandenhoeck & Ruprecht, 2002); Philip Harland, *Associations, Synagogues, and Congregations* (Minneapolis: Fortress Press, 2003); David Milson, *Art and Architecture of the Synagogue in Late Antique Palestine: In the Shadow of the Church* (Leiden: Brill, 2007); Stephen K. Catto, *Reconstructing the First-Century Synagogue: A Critical Analysis of Current Research* (T & T Clark, 2007, forthcoming).

[12] Levine, *Ancient Synagogue*, 14.

which the formative stages of Judaism and Christianity can hardly be understood. Exploring the nature and origin of ancient synagogues thus becomes crucial not only to scholars working within the fields of early Jewish and Christian history respectively, but also to researchers interested in the so-called "parting of the ways" between Judaism and Christianity—an interest that is itself popular both inside and outside the academy.

However, these concerns and interests of scholars are not enough to explain the stream of synagogue studies that have recently poured over academic libraries in the form of articles, monographs and edited volumes. Rather, the explanation for this development is found in the recent loss of major scholarly consensuses in academia, a phenomenon not limited to synagogue studies.

Since the 1970s and 1980s, many long-held ideas about the nature and origin of the synagogue—such as the claim that the institution had its beginnings in the Babylonian exile as a replacement for the lost temple cult (Sigonius 1583), or that synagogue architecture displays certain stylistic patterns that indicate stages of development—have been rejected by synagogue scholars. New archaeological discoveries and the use of new methods and perspectives in reinterpreting known sources have been at the forefront of this movement.

Consequently, we are currently experiencing a new process of consensus formation, in which a multitude of diverse theories compete to attract the approval of the majority of researchers. The increasingly international scope of this debate, moreover, means that more approaches, perspectives, and ideas share the stage and have to be taken into account when historical judgments are made. Such a variety of alternatives and opportunities for divergent interpretations make consensus formation more difficult to achieve now than ever before.[13] In addition—and as a consequence of the aforementioned situation—the fields of research related to ancient synagogues continue to multiply, making the task of reconstructing these institutions more complex. The study of ancient synagogues is indeed, by necessity, an interdisciplinary endeavour.

---

[13] We may note, e.g., that, from the first to the seventeenth century, Moses was generally seen as the creator of the synagogue; Sigonius' criticism of this consensus in the late 16th century, and his suggestion of a Babylonian origin for the synagogue slowly gained followers and then held sway until the 1970s. Indeed, although outdated, one may still see this hypothesis in popular books on the synagogue and in studies by scholars from adjacent fields. See the discussion in Runesson, *Origins*, 110–23.

1.3 Topics in Synagogue Research

It is an admittedly difficult task to present an overview of synagogue studies while correlating the research of so many diverse subfields. Nevertheless, most of the various aspects and approaches to synagogue research may be generally categorized within one of four broad aspects: Spatial, liturgical, non-liturgical, and institutional.

a) *Spatial aspects* concern not only analyses of archaeological remains and architecture, but also wider studies of Jewish art and iconography as they relate to synagogues. Contributions within this field consist of studies on specific synagogue remains, as well as attempts at integrating the evidence into more holistic interpretations. The problems of methodology and dating have been crucial in recent research, particularly as they apply to the interpretation of art within a Jewish building. Recent comparative analyses have focussed upon the relationship between the synagogues and Graeco-Roman temples, the Jerusalem temple, Christian house churches, and Graeco-Roman voluntary associations (*collegia*). Among the contributors to this area of research are, e.g., Donald Binder, Philippe Bruneau, Marilyn Chiat, Virgilio Corbo, Steven Fine, Gideon Foerster, Erwin Goodenough, Shmaryahu Gutman, Rachel Hachlili, Alf Thomas Kraabel, Carl Kraeling, Lee I. Levine, Stanislao Loffreda, Jodi Magness, Zvi Ma'oz, Eric M. Meyers, Ehud Netzer, Peter Richardson, Anders Runesson, Leonard Victor Rutgers, Maria Floriani Squarciapino, James Strange, Eleazar Sukenik, Danny Syon, Monika Trümper, L. Michael White, Yigael Yadin, and Boaz Zissu.

b) *Liturgical aspects* of the ancient synagogues is another intensely researched subfield in synagogue studies. What religious activities took place within the early synagogues? The public reading of Torah is well attested,[14] but was prayer also included in early synagogue

---

[14] The following sources mention Torah reading, teaching, or the presence of Torah scrolls in synagogues: Philo, *Somn.* 2.127; *Opif.* 128; *Hypoth.* 7:11–13; *Legat.* 156, 157, 311–313; *Mos.* 2.215–216; *Spec.* 2.60–62; *Contempl.* 30–31 (cf. 28); *Prob.* 80–83; Josephus, *B. J.* 2.289–92; *A. J.* 16.43–45, 164; *C. Ap.* 2.175; Mark 1:21, 39; 6:2; Matt 4:23; 9:35; 13:54; Luke 4:15, 16–30, 31–33, 44; 6:6; 13:10; Acts 9:20; 13:5, 14–16; 14:1; 15:21; 17:2–3, 10–11, 17; 18:4–6, 26; 19:8; John 6:59; 18:20; *CIJ* 1404. Cf. 1 Tim 4:13. Note that when teaching is mentioned without readings in connection with a synagogue, readings or quotations from the Torah may nevertheless be assumed, since there was hardly more than one copy of the law in each synagogue; cf. Acts 17:3. Even if Torah reading could take place on any weekday (Philo, Contempl. 28; Acts 17:11), the Sabbath was specifically dedicated for this purpose: see, e.g., Josephus, A. J.

worship?[15] In what ways, if any, were public fasts and festivals observed within the synagogues? How were the various rituals performed, and who performed them? The liturgical material from Qumran has become increasingly important for the study of synagogue worship. To these more traditional research topics we may now add questions concerning Jewish magic and mysticism as they relate to the synagogue and its activities.[16] Scholars involved in addressing these and similar questions include, e.g., Paul Bradshaw, Ester Chazon, Ismar Elbogen, Esther Eshel, Daniel Falk, Steven Fine, Ezra Fleisher, Lawrence Hoffman, Pieter van der Horst, Reuven Kimelman, Lee I. Levine, Heather McKay, William O. E. Oesterly, Charles Perrot, Stefan Reif, Richard Sarason, Eileen Schuller, and Eric Werner.

c) *Non-liturgical aspects*, sometimes referred to as the *social aspects* of the synagogue, have hitherto been less explored than the previous two areas. However, in recent years, this lacuna has been noted, and major work has been done to widen the understanding of this important aspect of the synagogue. Contrary to popular belief, "synagogues" (as referenced in antiquity by a number of terms; see below) served a variety of functions that contemporary western culture would regard as properly belonging to municipal institutions. These included council halls, law courts, schools, treasuries, and public archives.[17] One of the first scholars to call attention to such non-liturgical practices of the synagogue (particularly as they relate to synagogue origins) was Leopold Löw (1884), followed by Mendel Silber (1915), and Sidney B. Hoenig (1979).[18] While Richard Horsley has emphasised the communal aspect of ancient synagogues, today Lee Levine is the strongest proponent for an understanding of the earliest synagogue based on non-liturgical activities.

16.43; *C. Ap.* 2.175; Philo, Opif. 128; Hypoth. 7.11–13; Contempl. 30–31; Mark 1:21; Luke 4:16; Acts 15:21.

[15] Cf., e.g., Josephus, *A. J.* 14.260; *Vita* 295; *C. Ap.* 1.209; Philo, *Spec.* 3.171; Matt 6:5). Public fasts, which included prayer rituals, could also take place in synagogues (e.g., Josephus, *Vita* 290), as could communal meals (Josephus, *A. J.* 14.216).

[16] Cf. Levine, *Ancient Synagogue*, 17.

[17] Judicial proceedings (e.g., Mark 13:9); council halls (*CJZ* 70); archives (apart from copies of the Torah [Josephus, *B. J.* 2.291], records of manumissions were kept in these buildings; *IJO* 1, BS5); treasuries (Philo, *Spec.* 1.77–78; Josephus, *A. J.* 16.164; cf. Matt 6:2); manumissions (*IJO* 1, BS6, BS7, BS9, BS17, BS18, BS19, BS24). An oft-cited example of political meetings in a *proseuchē*, is the Tiberias incident recounted by Josephus, *Vita* 277ff. Travellers could find lodging for the night in at least some synagogues (*CIJ* 2.1404).

[18] See Binder, *Temple Courts*, 204–26.

d) *Institutional aspects* refer to a variety of characteristics related to synagogue leadership and operations. Understanding the former of these is essential for understanding the place of synagogues in Jewish society. Did any particular party, such as the Pharisees, control the synagogues, or were synagogue hierarchies open to a variety of people regardless of group identity? What were the roles of priests in a synagogue setting? Recent research has convincingly argued that Pharisees did not have more influence in synagogues than any other group—nor was it uncommon for priests (regardless of religio-political affiliation) to be leaders (Shaye Cohen, Lee Levine). Ancient synagogues clearly had an elaborate hierarchy: already by the first century c.e. (and perhaps earlier), officials were given formal titles. It is still debated, however, to what degree (if at all) the hierarchies of the synagogue were modelled after that of the Jerusalem temple.

One of the increasingly studied aspects regarding leadership concerns the role of women.[19] This topic is related to that of synagogue benefactors, since there are examples of several women acting in this capacity. Here, it seems clear that Diaspora synagogues were involved in the same system of benefaction as other Graeco-Roman associations, and that both Jews and non-Jews were among the benefactors (Philip Harland 2003).

The presence of non-Jews among these benefactors may lead to a favourable verdict regarding the existence of the so-called God-fearers within the synagogues. While non-Jewish worshippers of the God of Israel were no doubt part of some, or even most, Diaspora synagogues, evidence suggests that not all non-Jewish benefactors to these institutions were. The larger question of who was part of synagogue communities needs to be addressed within an overall understanding of institutional realities in the Graeco-Roman world. Functionary aspects of ancient synagogues with specific focus on their connection to early Christ-believing communities have been studied by James Burtchaell.

---

[19] See especially the work of Bernadette Brooten and Lee Levine: Bernadette J. Brooten, *Women Leaders in the Ancient Synagogue: Inscriptional Evidence and Background Issues* (Brown Judaic Studies 36; Chico, Calif.: Scholars Press, 1982); eadem, "Female Leadership in the Ancient Synagogue," in *From Dura to Sepphoris: Studies in Jewish Art and Society in Late Antiquity* (ed. Lee I. Levine and Z. Weiss; Ann Arbor: Journal of Roman Archaeology Supplementary Series, 2000), 215–23; Levine, *Ancient Synagogue*, 499–518. See also Binder, *Temple Courts*, 372–79; Runesson, "Women Leadership in the Early Church: Some Examples and an Interpretive Frame," *STK* 82.4 (2006): 173–83 (Swedish; English summary).

Several scholars have made substantial specialist contributions to more than one of the four areas. In addition to some of the researchers already mentioned, the contributions of the following scholars have been influential: Doron Chen, Carsten Claußen, Paul Flesher, Joseph Gutmann, Martin Hengel, Richard Oster, Jacob Petuchowski, Tessa Rajak, Ronny Reich, Rainer Riesner, Shmuel Safrai, Paul Trebilco, Dan Urman, and Solomon Zeitlin.

Important inscriptional work, which is, by nature, covering or having implications for several of the areas mentioned, has been done by E. Leigh Gibson and Irina Levinskaya (especially on manumissions), Jean Baptiste Frey, William Horbury, G. H. R. Horsley, Pieter van der Horst, Frowald Hüttenmeister, Laurence Kant, Aryeh Kasher, John S. Kloppenborg, Baruch Lifshitz, Gert Lüderitz, David Noy, Andrew Overman, and Avigdor Tcherikover.

In addition to the above four areas of inquiry into which synagogue research may be divided, there are two problems related to the ancient synagogues that need to take into account all four areas: the origins and the nature of ancient synagogues.

The question of synagogue origins is a classic problem that has been addressed in a multitude of articles and book sections, as well as in a couple of monographs. Discussions have often focussed on one or two of the above four subfields, usually the spatial or the liturgical. A comprehensive analysis of the state of research is given in Runesson (2001).[20]

These studies seek to answer questions such as: When and where do we find the earliest signs of the institutions that by the first century were labelled *synagōgē*, *proseuchē*, and several other names?[21] Was prayer one of

---

[20] Runesson, *Origins*, 67–168. See also Samuel Krauss, *Synagogale Altertümer* (Berlin: Hildesheim, 1922), 52–66; H. H. Rowley, *Worship in Ancient Israel: Its Forms and Meaning* (London: S.P.C.K., 1967), 213–45; Heather McKay, "Ancient Synagogues: The Continuing Dialectic Between Two Major Views," *CR:BS* 6 (1998): 103–42. Lee Levine has discussed recent contributions in "The First Century Synagogue: Critical Reassessments and Assessments of the Critical," in *Religion and Society in Roman Palestine: Old Questions: New Approaches* (ed. Douglas R. Edwards; New York: Routledge, 2004), 70–102; see also idem, *Ancient Synagogue*, 22–28.

[21] What in English is translated "synagogue" went under several different names in antiquity (in Greek, Latin and Hebrew): *synagōgē*, *proseuchē*, *ekklēsia*, *oikos*, *topos*, *hagios topos*, *hieros peribolos*, *hieron*, *synagōgion*, *sabbateion*, *semneion*, *didaskaleion*, *amphitheatron*, *eucheion*, *proseuktērion*, *thiasos*, *templum*, *proseucha*, *bet moʿed*, *bet ha-Torah*, *bet ha-kneset*. For *naos* (*A. J.* 19.305) and *andrōn* (*A. J.* 16.164) as possible synagogue terms, see Per Bilde, "Was hat Josephus über die Synagoge zu sagen?" in *Internationales Josephus-Kolloquium Brüssel 1998* (ed. J. U. Kalms and F. Siegert; Münster: Lit. Verlag, 1999), 15–35, 17. Other terms discussed include *bet hishtahavot* and *bet ha-midrash*. The diversity in synagogue terminology has implications not least for how early Christ-believing communities organised themselves. For example, the term *ekklēsia*, which is commonly translated

the earliest synagogue functions? What activity, liturgical or non-liturgical, should be understood as defining the earliest synagogues? Where and when were the first synagogue buildings constructed?

In response to the most basic of these questions, nearly every region of the Mediterranean world has been proposed as the birthplace of this institution, as has every time period, from the age of the Patriarchs to the Late Roman period.

Lurking behind all of these proposals lies one of the most difficult questions to answer: "Why?" That is to say, just what historical, social, economic, political, and religious mechanisms gave rise to the institutional realities we refer to as "the synagogue"? Regardless of the theory preferred, the conundrum of synagogue origins is entangled in complex and hard-to-resolve methodological problems, which need to be explicitly addressed in all future research on the topic.

As to the nature of the ancient synagogue institutions, this much-debated problem is closely related to the origins quest, though it moves beyond the basic question. As with the origins problem, however, any theory on the nature of the synagogue needs to take into account all the available literary, epigraphic, and archaeological evidence, as well as to integrate all the areas of research listed above, including the origins question. It goes without saying that this complex task has generated a multitude of suggested solutions.

How should we best describe the synagogue of, say, the first century c.e.? As an informal gathering of people (Kee 1990)?[22] As a public formal gathering, but not in specific purpose-built edifices (Horsley 1999)?[23] As a public assembly in a purpose-built edifice (Oster 1993)?[24] Was the Jewish home the primary model giving the synagogue its unique character (Claußen 2002)?[25] Or are we dealing with a semi-public,

---

"church," was in fact used for synagogues around the first century c.e. (see the index for examples of sources). It is thus not possible to argue that when a group of Christ-believers use *ekklēsia* to designate their institution (e.g., Matt 16:18; 18:17; cf. also 3 John, and comments below on Jas 2:2–4) they are departing from either "the Jewish community," from "Jewishness," or from Jewish organisational forms, as has so often been assumed. Only at a much later time was *ekklēsia* used exclusively for Christian churches, as opposed to Jewish synagogues.

[22] Howard Clark Kee, "The Transformation of the Synagogue after 70 c.e.: Its Import for Early Christianity," *NTS* 36 (1990): 1–24.

[23] Richard Horsley, "Synagogues in Galilee and the Gospels," in *Evolution of the Synagogue: Problems and Progress* (ed. Howard Clark Kee and Lynn H. Cohick; Harrisburg: Trinity Press, 1999), 46–69.

[24] Richard E. Oster, "Supposed Anachronism in Luke-Acts' Use of ΣΥΝΑΓΩΓΗ: A Rejoinder to Howard Clark Kee," *NTS* 39 (1993): 178–208.

[25] Claußen, *Versammlung*.

voluntary association, similar to, or indeed within the same category as the Graeco-Roman *collegia* (Hengel 1971, Richardson 2004, Harland 2003)?[26] Did the synagogue parallel Graeco-Roman temples—but without animal sacrifices (Flesher 2001)?[27] Or was the Jerusalem temple the blueprint for the institution, the latter functioning as a (non-sacrificial) extension of and supplement to the former (Binder 1999)?[28] Did the Egyptian *Per Ankh*, an institution closely related to both temples and associations, stand as a model for the synagogue (Griffiths 1995)?[29] Or should we rather focus on local administration, viewing the first century synagogue as a communal institution with a religious dimension (Levine, 2004)?[30] Or again, does the evidence lead us to the conclusion that synagogue terms could refer to two types of institutions—both public communal assemblies *and* Jewish voluntary associations—and that, consequently, the meaning of "synagogue" was still fluid at this time (Runesson 2001)?[31]

When posing these and related questions, one also needs to ask: from whose perspective? It is one thing to claim that the Romans understood and categorised Diaspora synagogues as *collegia*, quite another to assert that this was also how the Jews themselves understood the nature of their institution. The same goes for the temple-suggestion. In both cases, agreement between different perspectives is possible, but needs to be argued.

Which of these suggestions can best explain the diverse source material? While recent research has ruled out the suggestion of informal gatherings, there are good arguments in favour of several of the other theories.

---

[26] Martin Hengel, "Proseuche und Synagoge: jüdische Gemeinde, Gotteshaus und Gottesdienst in der Diaspora und in Palästina," in *Tradition und Glaube: Das fruehe Christentum in seiner Umwelt* (ed. Gert Jeremias et al.; Gottingen: Vandenhoeck & Ruprecht, 1971), 157–184; Peter Richardson, *Building Jewish in the Roman East* (Waco: Baylor University Press, 2004); Harland, *Associations*.

[27] Paul Virgil McCracken Flesher, "Prolegomenon to a Theory of Early Synagogue Development," in *Judaism in Late Antiquity*, Part III: *Where We Stand: Issues and Debates in Ancient Judaism* (vol. IV of *The Special Problem if the Synagogue*; ed. by A. J. Avery-Peck and Jacob Neusner; Leiden: Brill, 2001).

[28] Binder, *Temple Courts*.

[29] Gwyn J. Griffiths, "Egypt and the Rise of the Synagogue," in *Ancient Synagogues: Historical Analysis and Archaeological Discovery* (vol. 1; ed. Dan Urman and Paul Virgil McCracken Flesher; New York: Brill, 1995): 3–16.

[30] Levine, "Critical Reassessments."

[31] Runesson, *Origins*.

Whatever final verdicts are reached, they are sure to have an impact on related fields of historical study. Returning to remarks made earlier— that conclusions about the synagogue would affect how we understand the foundational period of Judaism and Christianity—we may take the *collegia*-theory as an example. For such a socio-institutional setting as the *collegia* may well shed new light on certain theological texts: the fact that men and women, slaves and free, Jews and non-Jews could interact more freely in many *collegia* than most elsewhere in Graeco-Roman society suggests a socio-institutional interpretive frame for understanding Paul's salvation-inclusive theological message to his diaspora community in Gal 3:28.[32]

1.4   Tools for Synagogue Studies

Although methodological reflection is of outmost importance in the present state of research on ancient synagogues, having immediate access to all the relevant sources is, of course, crucial. Until now, such sources have been scattered across a multitude of publications. Moreover, when collections of primary sources have been produced (often with an aim broader than the synagogue itself), they have frequently been limited to a single type, e.g., archaeological or epigraphic. From among these, the following publications may be considered essential:

Archaeological: Chiat;[33] Hachlili;[34] Saller;[35] Ilan;[36] *NEAEHL*;[37] Hütten-meister and Reeg.[38]

---

[32] Cf. Runesson, "Women Leadership," 182.

[33] Marilyn Joyce Segal Chiat, *Handbook of Synagogue Architecture* (Brown Judaic Studies 29; ed. Jacob Neusner; Chico: Scholars Press, 1982).

[34] Hachlili, *Israel*; eadem, *Diaspora*.

[35] Sylvester J. Saller, *The Second Revised Catalogue of the Ancient Synagogues of the Holy Land* (Jerusalem: Franciscan Printing, 1972).

[36] Z. Ilan, *Ancient Synagogues in Israel* (Tel Aviv: Ministry of Defence, 1991 [in Hebrew]).

[37] Ephraim Stern, *The New Encyclopedia of Archaeological Excavations in the Holy Land* (4 vols.; Jerusalem: Carta, 1993).

[38] Frowald Hüttenmeister and Gottfried Reeg, *Die antiken Synagogen in Israel: Die judischen Synagogen, Lehrhäuser und Gerichtshöfe* (Wiesbaden: Dr. Ludwig Reichert Verlag, 1977). In addition to these studies and catalogues, a helpful introduction to architectural terminology is found in Ruth Jacoby and Rina Talgam, *Ancient Jewish Synagogues: Architectural Glossary* (Jerusalem: Centre for Jewish Art, Hebrew University of Jerusalem, 1988).

Inscriptions: JIGRE;[39] *JIWE* (2 vols.);[40] *IJO* (3 vols.);[41] *CIJ* (2 vols.);[42] Lifshitz;[43] Lüderitz;[44] Scheiber;[45] Naveh;[46] Roth-Gerson.[47] A useful tool when studying and interpreting inscriptions is Kant.[48]

Papyri: Tcherikover (3 vols.).[49] A fine introduction to the use of papyri in history writing is found in Bagnall.[50]

Legal: Imperial Roman legislation explicitly related to ancient synagogues is collected in Linder,[51] but does not appear until the fifth century c.e., and is thus beyond the chronological scope of the present study.

Literary sources (Philo, Josephus, The Qumran texts, Pseudo-Philo, the New Testament, Cleomedes, Artemidorus, Tacitus, Juvenal, the Mishnah) have never been collected and published in a single volume.

---

[39] William Horbury and David Noy, *Jewish Inscriptions of Greco-Roman Egypt: With an Index of the Jewish Inscriptions of Egypt and Cyrenaica* (Cambridge: Cambridge University Press, 1992).

[40] David Noy, *Italy (Excluding the City of Rome), Spain and Gaul* (vol. 1 of *Jewish Inscriptions of Western Europe*; Cambridge, New York: Cambridge University Press, 1993); idem, *The City of Rome* (vol. 2 of *Jewish Inscriptions of Western Europe*; Cambridge, New York: Cambridge University Press, 1995).

[41] David Noy, Alexander Panayotov, and Hanswulf Bloedhorn, eds., *Eastern Europe* (vol. 1 of *Inscriptiones Judaicae Orientis*; Texts and Studies in Ancient Judaism 101; Tübingen: Mohr Siebeck, 2004); Walter Ameling, ed., *Kleinasien* (vol. 2 of *Inscriptiones Judaicae Orientis*; Texts and Studies in Ancient Judaism 99; Tübingen: Mohr Siebeck, 2004); David Noy, Hanswulf Bloedhorn, eds., *Syria and Cyprus* (vol. 3 of *Inscriptiones Judaicae Orientis*; Texts and Studies in Ancient Judaism 102; Tübingen: Mohr Siebeck, 2004).

[42] Jean Baptiste Frey, ed., *Corpus Inscriptionum Judaicarum* (2 vols.; vol. 1, rev. ed.; 1975; Rome: Poniticio Instituto di Archeologia Christiana, 1936–52).

[43] Baruch Lifshitz, *Donateurs et fondateurs dans les synagogues juives: répertoire des dédicaces grecques relatives à la construction et à la réfection des synagogues* (Paris: Gabalda, 1967). See also his *"Prolegomenon,"* in *Corpus of Jewish Inscriptions: Jewish Inscriptions from the Third Century B.C. to the Seventh Century* a.d. (ed. Jean Baptiste Frey; New York: Ktav Publishing House, 1975).

[44] Gert Lüderitz, *Corpus jüdischer Zeugnisse aus der Cyrenaika* (Beihefte zum Tübinger Atlas des vorderen Orients B 53; Wiesbaden: Dr. Ludwig Reichert Verlag, 1983).

[45] Alexander Scheiber, *Jewish Inscriptions in Hungary, from the 3rd Century to 1686* (Leiden: Brill, 1983).

[46] Joseph Naveh, *On Stone and Mosaic: The Aramaic and Hebrew Inscriptions from Ancient Synagogues* (Jerusalem: Israel Exploration Society & Carta, 1978 [Hebrew]).

[47] Lea Roth-Gerson, *The Greek Inscriptions from the Synagogues in Eretz-Israel* (Jerusalem: Yad Izhak Ben-Zvi, 1987 [Hebrew]); eadem, *The Jews in Syria as Reflected in the Greek Inscriptions* (Jerusalem: Shazar Centre Historical Society of Israel, 2001 [Hebrew]).

[48] Laurence H. Kant, "Jewish Inscriptions in Greek and Latin," in *Aufstieg und Niedergang der romischen Welt: Geschichte und Kultur Roms im Spiegel der neueren Forschung* (ed. Wolfgang Haase; New York: W. de Gruyter, 1987), 671–713.

[49] Avigdor Tcherikover, Alexander Fuks, and Menahem Stern, *Corpus Papyrorum Judaicarum* (3 vols.; Cambridge: Harvard University Press, 1957–64).

[50] Roger S. Bagnall, *Reading Papyri, Writing Ancient History* (London: Routledge, 1995).

[51] Linder, *Imperial Legislation.*

However, Tzvee Zahavy has gathered and interpreted references to the synagogue in the Mishnah (and the Tosefta and the Jerusalem Talmud) in his *Jewish Prayer*.[52]

The present source book, covering the earliest material with an upper limit of 200 c.e., is meant to fill this void by gathering all types of sources into one single volume, presenting them, as far as possible, according to geographical location.

1.5 *The Organization and Aim of the Present Collection of Synagogue Sources*

The present source book is the first of its kind, including all available evidence pertaining to the earliest synagogues in the land of Israel and the Diaspora: literary sources, papyri, inscriptions, and archaeological remains. Any source book needs to limit its scope in some way, however, and to constrain its contents chronologically. We have chosen the parameters of the present volume in the following way.

With respect to chronological restrictions, at first glance, the upper time limit of 200 c.e. might seem arbitrary. Most recent studies have focussed on 70 c.e.—and there may well be good reasons for doing so. For the present volume, however, we have viewed such a limitation as both methodologically and pedagogically problematic.

First, there is still an ongoing debate about the significance of the fall of the Jerusalem temple for the early development of the synagogue. By moving well beyond this date, the present volume avoids taking a stance in this dispute and allows the reader to decide for him or herself what conclusions seem reasonable on the basis of the sources themselves.

Second, while anachronistic readings of earlier material from the perspective of later sources have been especially frequent in synagogue studies, those who are interested in Second Temple synagogues may benefit from knowing what happened during the following century. Correctly used, later developments give perspective on earlier phenomena that are otherwise lost. Further, the second century is, from an archaeological perspective, distinct from the first century due to the relative lack of structures in the land of Israel. Beginning in the third

---

[52] Tzvee Zahavy, *Studies in Jewish Prayer* (Lanham: University Press of America, 1990).

century, several structures identified as synagogues again surface.[53] The second century situation is thus somewhat anomalous, a fact that still awaits a convincing explanation.

Finally, an upper limit of 200 C.E. allows us to include the earliest rabbinic source, the Mishnah. This evidence, which sometimes purports to describe earlier periods, informs us of how a specific Jewish group related to the synagogue institution and understood its functions.[54] Drawing the line at 200 C.E. keeps the focus on the earliest developments and, at the same time, avoids the wealth of material surfacing in later rabbinic writings, which would make the book much too large and inconvenient to use: this later material is reserved for a second volume.[55]

If 200 C.E. is the upper limit and our aim is to cover all the material from the inception of the institution, why do we not include material older than the third century B.C.E.? After all, even some recent researchers have claimed that the public institution of the synagogue had its origins in the Persian period, and that some texts in the Hebrew Bible include important information supporting this theory.[56] While such theories trace activities found in the first century synagogue back in time, they do so before the first mention of synagogue terms known from later periods.

In this book, however, we have chosen to limit the material to sources explicitly mentioning terms that are known to have been used for syna-

---

[53] Some of the structures originally dated to the third century are now being re-dated to the fifth century. This discussion is, however, beyond the scope of the present volume; a future volume covering synagogue remains from 200 C.E. to the Islamic conquest needs to take this into account.

[54] There is today a growing consensus that the rabbis did not become influential in Jewish society until the fourth or fifth century (see Günter Stemberger, *Jews and Christians in the Holy Land: Palestine in the Fourth Century* [Edinburgh: T & T Clark, 2000], 269–97 on the position of the rabbis in Jewish society, and Levine, *Ancient Synagogue*, 412–98, who focusses specifically on the synagogue), or even later (Schwartz, *Imperialism*). This means that the researcher needs to treat this evidence not as representative of how Jews generally related to the synagogue during this time, but as one example of a Jewish perspective. This is important not least when considering the later architectural and liturgical development of the synagogue in the period when the rabbis actually achieved this general influence. Again, however, this is beyond the scope of the present volume.

[55] On the invitation of Brill, we are currently considering such a second volume.

[56] Passages from the Hebrew Bible that have been part of the scholarly discussion on synagogues include, e.g., Deut 31:9–13; Josh 22:10–34; 2 Chr 17:7–9; Ezra 7:25; Neh 8–9; Ps 74:8; Ezek 11:16.

gogues in or around the first century c.e.[57] This does not mean that
all synagogue researchers would agree that, e.g., *proseuchē*, a term we
translate as "prayer hall," always referred to synagogue-like institutions
in the earliest evidence.[58] Nor does it mean, obviously, that we sub-
scribe to the methodologically questionable assumption that the earliest
mention of any such term would indicate the origin of the synagogue.
Rather, by providing all sources that explicitly mention terms used in
connection with the synagogue prior to the third century c.e., we invite
the reader to pursue an independent study of this topic, making use
of additional sources that may have a bearing on an understanding of
the institution during its formative period.[59]

Regarding the archaeological material, we have aimed at including
site remains that have been identified as synagogue buildings by a
majority of scholars. We have also incorporated entries for several more
recent discoveries judged to have the potential for being recognised by
a majority as synagogue buildings. However, the catalogue also contains
a few sites that we believe should be removed from the lists of ancient
synagogues. In each case, comments have been provided directing
the reader to the relevant studies and discussions. In general, we have
tried to err on the side of inclusion, while commenting upon points of
current debate for individual entries, as applicable.

Finally, a few words about sources on Jewish temples outside Jerusalem. Most theories on ancient synagogues involve, in one way or the
other, references to the Jerusalem temple. More rarely have temples outside Jerusalem been taken into account; indeed, often it seems as if this
material is either not known to the authors, or simply ignored. Because
of the importance of this material for the formation of synagogue

---

[57] There are some exceptions to this rule. Because of the frequent mention in synagogue studies of the "chair of Moses," and the interpretation of some archaeological
remains as examples of such a seat of honour (e.g., the Delos synagogue) we have
included the earliest text mentioning this expression (Matt 23:2) despite the fact that no
synagogue term is used. In the same way, a few texts mentioning public Torah reading
on Sabbaths, without using synagogue terminology, have been included.

[58] Runesson, for example, would argue that this term was originally a temple term
and only later used to connote a synagogue institution; see *Origins*, 429–36. Cf. Joseph
Gutmann, "Ancient Synagogues: Archaeological Facts and Scholarly Assumpion," *BAI*
9 (1997): 226–27.

[59] Other such sources, not included in this volume due to the lack of an explicit
mention of a synagogue term but which may be of importance for the reconstruction
of different aspects of the ancient synagogue include, e.g., *Let. Arist.* 308–10; see also
some of the sources mentioned above, n. 14.

theories, we have chosen to include a final chapter listing the most important evidence.[60]

We have sought to arrange the volume in a user-friendly fashion, and to take into consideration the varying needs of both scholar and layman within the comments offered for each entry in the catalogue.

The basic criterion for ordering the material is geographical, with the major divisions being the Land of Israel (chapter 2) and the Diaspora (chapter 3). Within these, locations are sorted alphabetically, facilitating searches for evidence relating to a specific place. Those sources that could not be located exactly are listed according to region (e.g., Judaea, or Galilee) or as non-specific allusions. Chapter 4 contains general evidence that could not be fixed specifically within either of the major divisions.

Each entry is numbered for easy reference. Those containing primary texts are presented in both their original language and in English translation. Unless otherwise noted, all inscriptions and papyri have been freshly translated. Biblical texts are rendered in the NRSV if not otherwise noted. For Philo, translations of *Legat.* are from Smallwood, for *Flacc.* from van der Horst, and for *Opif.* from Runia; all other translations of Philo take Colson's translation (LCL) as point of departure. Josephus has, if not otherwise noted, been translated anew. Translations of the Mishnah are by Blackman. Most translations mentioned above have been modified by the authors, with a special focus on synagogue terminology; discussions or alternative translations are also given in comments, or, in some cases, footnotes.

Catalogue entries also include both hermeneutical comments and bibliographic suggestions for further exploration. Mindful of the breadth of scholarly opinion in this field, we have sought to present these features as even-handedly as possible. The fact that even the co-authors do not agree on the interpretation of every source should suggest to the reader that comments and secondary literature listings have been thoroughly discussed in order to do justice to a wide range of interpretive positions.

---

[60] Excluded from this chapter are the oldest references in Egyptian inscriptions to *proseuchai*, which some scholars interpret as evidence of Jewish temples in Egypt (e.g., Gutmann, "Scholarly Assumpion"; Runesson, *Origins*, 429–54); these sources have instead been included in chapter 3.1.6.

For readers interested in specific subjects, texts, or terminology, extensive indices have been included, covering literary texts, inscriptions, and papyri.

In closing, we hope that this source book will provide scholars and students easy access to the diverse source material relating to synagogues from the third century B.C.E. to 200 C.E., facilitating direct interaction with the primary materials both in their original language and in translation. This, we believe, will benefit synagogue research specifically, and studies on ancient Judaism and Christianity more generally.

CHAPTER TWO

THE LAND OF ISRAEL

2.1 *Identified Locations*

2.1.1 *Caesarea*

No. 1

Source: *Literary.* Josephus, *B. J.* 2.285–92.

Date: *Bellum Judaicum* consists of seven books and was published in the late 70s. The event described is said to have taken place just before the first Jewish war broke out, i.e., ca. 65/66 c.e.

[285] πρὸς δὲ τὸ μέγεθος τῶν ἐξ αὐτοῦ συμφορῶν οὐκ ἀξίαν ἔσχεν πρόφασιν· οἱ γὰρ ἐν Καισαρείᾳ Ἰουδαῖοι, συναγωγὴν ἔχοντες παρὰ χωρίον, οὗ δεσπότης ἦν τις Ἕλλην Καισαρεύς, πολλάκις μὲν κτήσασθαι τὸν τόπον ἐσπούδασαν τιμὴν πολλαπλασίονα τῆς ἀξίας διδόντες· [286] ὡς δ᾽ ὑπερορῶν τὰς δεήσεις πρὸς ἐπήρειαν ἔτι καὶ παρῳκοδόμει τὸ χωρίον ἐκεῖνος ἐργαστήρια κατασκευαζόμενος στενήν τε καὶ παντάπασιν βιαίαν πάροδον ἀπέλειπεν αὐτοῖς, τὸ μὲν πρῶτον οἱ θερμότεροι τῶν νέων προπηδῶντες οἰκοδομεῖν ἐκώλυον. [287] ὡς δὲ τούτους εἶργεν τῆς βίας Φλῶρος, ἀμηχανοῦντες οἱ δυνατοὶ τῶν Ἰουδαίων, σὺν οἷς Ἰωάννης ὁ τελώνης. πείθουσι τὸν Φλῶρον ἀργυρίου ταλάντοις ὀκτὼ διακωλῦσαι τὸ ἔργον. [288] ὁ δὲ πρὸς μόνον τὸ λαβεῖν ὑποσχόμενος πάντα συμπράξειν, λαβὼν ἔξεισιν τῆς Καισαρείας εἰς Σεβαστὴν καὶ καταλείπει τὴν στάσιν αὐτεξούσιον, ὥσπερ ἄδειαν πεπρακὼς Ἰουδαίοις τοῦ μάχεσθαι.

[289] Τῆς δ᾽ ἐπιούσης ἡμέρας ἑβδομάδος οὔσης τῶν Ἰουδαίων εἰς τὴν συναγωγὴν συναθροισθέντων στασιαστής τις Καισαρεὺς γάστραν καταστρέψας καὶ παρὰ τὴν εἴσοδον αὐτῶν θέμενος ἐπέθυεν ὄρνεις. τοῦτο τοὺς Ἰουδαίους ἀνηκέστως παρώξυνεν ὡς ὑβρισμένων μὲν αὐτοῖς τῶν νόμων, μεμιασμένου δὲ τοῦ χωρίου. [290] τὸ μὲν οὖν εὐσταθὲς καὶ πρᾷον ἐπὶ τοὺς ἡγεμόνας ἀναφεύγειν ᾤετο χρῆναι, τὸ στασιῶδες δὲ καὶ ἐν νεότητι φλεγμαῖνον ἐξεκαίετο πρὸς μάχην. παρεσκευασμένοι δὲ εἰστήκεσαν οἱ τῶν Καισαρέων στασιασταί, τὸν γὰρ ἐπιθύσοντα προπεπόμφεσαν ἐκ συντάγματος, καὶ ταχέως ἐγένετο συμβολή. [291] προσελθὼν δὲ Ἰούκουνδος ὁ διακωλύειν τεταγμένος ἱππάρχης τήν τε γάστραν αἴρει καὶ καταπαύειν ἐπειρᾶτο τὴν στάσιν. ἡττωμένου δ᾽

αὐτοῦ τῆς τῶν Καισαρέων βίας Ἰουδαῖοι τοὺς νόμους ἁρπάσαντες ἀνεχώρησαν εἰς Νάρβατα· χώρα τις αὐτῶν οὕτω καλεῖται σταδίους ἑξήκοντα διέχουσα τῆς Καισαρείας. [292] οἱ δὲ περὶ τὸν Ἰωάννην δυνατοὶ δώδεκα πρὸς Φλῶρον ἐλθόντες εἰς Σεβαστὴν ἀπωδύροντο περὶ τῶν πεπραγμένων καὶ βοηθεῖν ἱκέτευον, αἰδημόνως ὑπομιμνήσκοντες τῶν ὀκτὼ ταλάντων. ὁ δὲ καὶ συλλαβὼν ἔδησεν τοὺς ἄνδρας αἰτιώμενος ὑπὲρ τοῦ τοὺς νόμους ἐξενεγκεῖν τῆς Καισαρείας.

[285] The ostensible pretext for war was out of proportion to the magnitude of the disasters to which it led. The Jews in Caesarea had a synagogue [*synagōgē*] adjoining a plot of ground owned by a Greek of that city; this site they had frequently endeavoured to purchase, offering a price far exceeding its true value. [286] The proprietor, disdaining their solicitations by way of insult further proceeded to build upon the site and erect workshops, leaving the Jews only a narrow and extremely awkward passage. Thereupon, some of the hot-headed youths proceeded to set upon the builders and attempted to interrupt operations. [287] Florus having put a stop to their violence, the Jewish notables, with John, the tax collector, having no other expedient, offered Florus eight talents of silver to procure the cessation of the work. [288] Florus, with his eye only on the money, promised them every assistance, but, having secured his pay, at once quitted Caesarea for Sebaste,[1] leaving a free field to sedition, as though he had sold the Jews a license to fight the matter out.

[289] On the following day, which was a Sabbath, when the Jews assembled at the synagogue [*synagōgē*], they found that one of the Caesarean mischief-makers had placed beside the entrance a pot, turned bottom upwards, upon which he was sacrificing birds. This spectacle of what they considered an outrage upon their laws and a desecration of the spot enraged the Jews beyond endurance. [290] The steady-going and peacable members of the congregation were in favour of immediate recourse to the authorities; but the factious folk and the passionate youth were burning for a fight. The Caesarean party, on their side, stood prepared for action, for they had, by a concerted plan, sent the man on to the mock sacrifice; and so they soon came to blows. [291] Jucundus, the cavalry commander commissioned to intervene, came up, removed the pot and endeavoured to quell the riot, but was unable

---

[1] The Greek name for Samaria.

to cope with the violence of the Caesareans. The Jews, thereupon, snatched up their copy of the Law and withdrew to Narbata, a Jewish district sixty furlongs distant from Caesarea. [292] Their leading men, twelve in number, with John at their head, waited upon Florus at Sebaste, bitterly complained of these proceedings and besought his assistance, delicately reminding him of the matter of the eight talents. Florus actually had them arrested and put in irons on the charge of having carried off the copy of the Law from Caesarea.[2]

Literature: Oster, "Supposed Anachronism," 188–89; Bilde, "Synagoge" 31–32; Binder, *Temple Courts*, 101–2, 156; Levine, *Ancient Synagogue*, 68; Runesson, *Origins*, 369.

Comments: The incident in the synagogue (*synagōgē*) at Caesarea is described by Josephus as the very cause for the first Jewish war (66–70 C.E.). While this is certainly an attempt by Josephus to avoid mentioning for his Roman readers the full range of the disastrous situation in the land that led to the revolt, the passage provides several details of importance for the understanding of ancient synagogues. "Synagogue" here clearly refers to a building, one in which assemblies were held on the Sabbath. Furthermore, Torah scrolls were kept inside. The edifice must have been regarded as having some level of sanctity, since the mock sacrifice of the birds was seen as desecrating (*miainō*) the building. In addition, the bribe to Florus of eight talents of silver was an enormous sum, implying that the structure was a monumental building that could not easily be relocated. Finally, the centrality of the Torah scrolls is evident from the fact that they were taken out of the synagogue and brought to where the Jews were fleeing. Florus' arrest of the Jews who removed the scrolls from the synagogue likewise underscores their great worth.

2.1.2   *Cana*

No. 2
Source: *Literary.* John 2:6
Date: Ca. 90–100 C.E.

[6] ἦσαν δὲ ἐκεῖ λίθιναι ὑδρίαι ἓξ κατὰ τὸν καθαρισμὸν τῶν Ἰουδαίων κείμεναι, χωροῦσαι ἀνὰ μετρητὰς δύο ἢ τρεῖς.

[6] Now standing there were six stone water jars for the Jewish rites of purification, each holding twenty or thirty gallons.

---

[2] Adapted from Thackeray (LCL).

Literature: As a general reference to commentaries, see Brown, Moloney and Thyen, *Comm., ad loc.* Deines, *Steingefässe*, 245–75, Olsson, *Structure and Meaning*, 26–27, 47–53, 105–7; Runesson, *Water and Worship.*

Comments: While there is no direct reference to a synagogue in the Cana story, verse 6 functions as an interpretative element in the story as a whole, with its association to Jewish purification rituals and perhaps also to the number six. Moreover, interpretative elements in the Gospel of John have in general concrete correspondences in the real world. Within the narrative, the reference to the location of the jars is very vague, and the man responsible for the marriage did not see what the servants were doing. The mention of stone vessels large enough to hold ca. 100 litres each argues for a fixed place in a building rather than portable vessels. In addition, the stated use of the vessels ("for the Jewish rites of purification") calls to mind the *miqweh* or ritual bath, which needed ca. 500 litres. Where in a small village would one find such an arrangement of purification vessels? Perhaps in a synagogue. Most wedding feasts were celebrated outdoors. Purification rituals were necessary for visiting not only a temple but also a synagogue. Thus the above passage may have envisioned the wedding feast being set near a synagogue at Cana, a town that possibly also served as the seat of one of the 24 priestly divisions.

No. 3
Source: *Archaeological.*
Date: Late first to second century C.E.

Literature: Edwards, "Khirbet Qana"; idem "Recent Work in Galilee"; Rech et al., "Direct dating of plaster and mortar"; Richardson, *Building Jewish*, 55–71; 91–107; idem, "Khirbet Qana," 136–140, 144.

Comments: Khirbet Qana has recently been identified as the site of Cana of the New Testament (see above, No. 2). Excavations under the direction of Douglas R. Edwards, University of Puget Sound, are not yet completed, but significant reports and articles have been published.

The main hall of the building measures 10×15 m. The edifice had columns, each of which sat on three dressed foundation stones. Floors in the aisles were plastered, but the nave's floor is dressed bedrock. Furthermore, the main hall contained a discontinuous bench of various widths, lining three of the walls. To the east, there was a smaller room, measuring 3×4 m; this room also had a single low bench on three sides, with a bedrock floor. While this may have been a study room (so Richardson, *Building Jewish*, 66), the term *bet ha-midrash* should be avoided, since it may lead to the faulty impression that the rabbis were heavily involved in the early synagogue. The building is dated to the late first or early second century C.E. (Rech et al. 2003).

While it is too early to draw any firm conclusions regarding the edifice, it is clear that we are dealing with a public building, and it seems likely that Edward's and Richardson's assessment is correct, i.e., that this building should

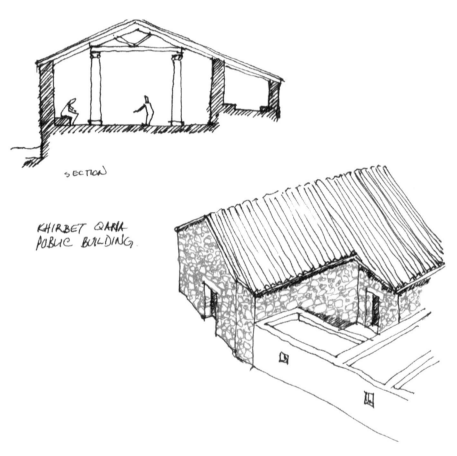

SECTION

KHIRBET QANA
PUBLIC BUILDING.

Figure 1. Reconstruction of the public building/synagogue in Cana

be identified as a synagogue. The question of identification is, of course, dependent on the definition of "synagogue." From the perspective of Runesson's distinction between public and semi-public institutions, the evidence as described in the reports and articles so far seems to indicate a public institution housed in a public building.

2.1.3   *Capernaum*

No. 4
Source: *Literary.* Mark 1:21–29
Date: Ca. 70 C.E.

[21] Καὶ εἰσπορεύονται εἰς Καφαρναούμ· καὶ εὐθὺς τοῖς σάββασιν εἰσελθὼν εἰς τὴν συναγωγὴν ἐδίδασκεν. [22] καὶ ἐξεπλήσσοντο ἐπὶ τῇ διδαχῇ αὐτοῦ· ἦν γὰρ διδάσκων αὐτοὺς ὡς ἐξουσίαν ἔχων καὶ οὐχ ὡς οἱ γραμματεῖς. [23] Καὶ εὐθὺς ἦν ἐν τῇ συναγωγῇ αὐτῶν ἄνθρωπος ἐν πνεύματι ἀκαθάρτῳ καὶ ἀνέκραξεν [24] λέγων· τί ἡμῖν καὶ σοί, Ἰησοῦ Ναζαρηνέ; ἦλθες ἀπολέσαι ἡμᾶς; οἶδά σε τίς εἶ, ὁ ἅγιος τοῦ θεοῦ. [25] καὶ ἐπετίμησεν αὐτῷ ὁ Ἰησοῦς λέγων· φιμώθητι καὶ ἔξελθε ἐξ αὐτοῦ. [26] καὶ σπαράξαν αὐτὸν τὸ πνεῦμα τὸ ἀκάθαρτον καὶ φωνῆσαν φωνῇ μεγάλῃ ἐξῆλθεν ἐξ αὐτοῦ. [27] καὶ ἐθαμβήθησαν ἅπαντες ὥστε συζητεῖν πρὸς ἑαυτοὺς λέγοντας· τί ἐστιν τοῦτο; διδαχὴ καινὴ κατ' ἐξουσίαν· καὶ τοῖς πνεύμασι τοῖς ἀκαθάρτοις ἐπιτάσσει, καὶ ὑπακούουσιν αὐτῷ. [28] καὶ ἐξῆλθεν ἡ ἀκοὴ αὐτοῦ εὐθὺς πανταχοῦ εἰς ὅλην τὴν περίχωρον τῆς Γαλιλαίας. [29] Καὶ εὐθὺς ἐκ τῆς συναγωγῆς ἐξελθόντες ἦλθον εἰς τὴν οἰκίαν Σίμωνος καὶ Ἀνδρέου μετὰ Ἰακώβου καὶ Ἰωάννου.

[21] They went to Capernaum; and when the Sabbath came, he entered the synagogue [*synagōgē*] and taught. [22] They were astounded at his teaching, for he taught them as one having authority, and not as the scribes. [23] Just then there was in their synagogue [*synagōgē*] a man with an unclean spirit, [24] and he cried out, "What have you to do with us, Jesus of Nazareth? Have you come to destroy us? I know who you are, the Holy One of God." [25] But Jesus rebuked him, saying, "Be silent, and come out of him!" [26] And the unclean spirit, convulsing him and crying with a loud voice, came out of him. [27] They were all amazed, and they kept on asking one another, "What is this? A new teaching—with authority! He commands even the unclean spirits, and they obey him." [28] At once his fame began to spread throughout the surrounding region of Galilee. [29] As soon as they left

the synagogue [*synagōgē*], they entered the house of Simon and Andrew, with James and John.

Literature: As a general reference to commentaries see Pesch, Guelich, and Marcus, *Comm., ad loc.* Binder, *Temple Courts*, 155; Runesson, "Identity Formation."

Comments: A parallel text in Luke 4:31–38 (No. 5). See the first comment to Luke 4:16–30 (No. 33). The word synagogue in definite form, v. 21, could be interpreted as the only synagogue in this small village of Capernaum. The wording in v. 23, "their synagogue," marks a distance between Mark's Christ-believing readers and other forms of Judaism, or rather describes the synagogue only as belonging to the people just mentioned. Jesus' teaching is strongly emphasized in the story, as is often the case in the Gospel of Mark ("teach" 15 times, "teacher" 12 times, and "teaching" 5 times). The imperfect form in v. 21, *edidasken*, can also be translated as "he began to teach." The periphrastic form in v. 22, *ēn didaskōn*, in English "was teaching," expresses an ongoing activity. Jesus' teaching is characterized in three ways: "as one having authority/with authority," "not as the scribes" and "new." In the Gospel of Matthew (7:29) this may be interpreted as a teaching not dominated by references to the Scriptures and to traditional interpretations. In a Marcan context, however, the teaching is associated with God's reassertion of his royal authority in the end-time, where proclamation of the kingdom of God is combined with an exorcism. Jesus' eschatological divine power makes his synagogue teaching "a new teaching" (Marcus) that serves as a programmatic introduction of his public ministry. This kind of teaching leads to very strong reactions and long discussions in the Sabbath synagogue meeting in Capernaum. According to Mark the big eschatological battle has begun.

No. 5
Source: *Literary*. Luke 4:31–38
Date: 80–90 C.E.

[31] Καὶ κατῆλθεν εἰς Καφαρναοὺμ πόλιν τῆς Γαλιλαίας. καὶ ἦν διδάσκων αὐτοὺς ἐν τοῖς σάββασιν· [32] καὶ ἐξεπλήσσοντο ἐπὶ τῇ διδαχῇ αὐτοῦ, ὅτι ἐν ἐξουσίᾳ ἦν ὁ λόγος αὐτοῦ. [33] Καὶ ἐν τῇ συναγωγῇ ἦν ἄνθρωπος ἔχων πνεῦμα δαιμονίου ἀκαθάρτου καὶ ἀνέκραξεν φωνῇ μεγάλῃ· [34] ἔα, τί ἡμῖν καὶ σοί, Ἰησοῦ Ναζαρηνέ; ἦλθες ἀπολέσαι ἡμᾶς; οἶδά σε τίς εἶ, ὁ ἅγιος τοῦ θεοῦ. [35] καὶ ἐπετίμησεν αὐτῷ ὁ Ἰησοῦς λέγων· φιμώθητι καὶ ἔξελθε ἀπ᾽ αὐτοῦ. καὶ ῥῖψαν αὐτὸν τὸ δαιμόνιον εἰς τὸ μέσον ἐξῆλθεν ἀπ᾽ αὐτοῦ μηδὲν βλάψαν αὐτόν. [36] καὶ ἐγένετο θάμβος ἐπὶ πάντας καὶ συνελάλουν πρὸς ἀλλήλους λέγοντες· τίς ὁ λόγος οὗτος ὅτι ἐν ἐξουσίᾳ καὶ δυνάμει ἐπιτάσσει τοῖς

ἀκαθάρτοις πνεύμασιν καὶ ἐξέρχονται; [37] καὶ ἐξεπορεύετο ἦχος περὶ αὐτοῦ εἰς πάντα τόπον τῆς περιχώρου. [38] Ἀναστὰς δὲ ἀπὸ τῆς συναγωγῆς εἰσῆλθεν εἰς τὴν οἰκίαν Σίμωνος.

[31] He went down to Capernaum, a city in Galilee, and was teaching them on the Sabbath. [32] They were astounded at his teaching, because he spoke with authority. [33] In the synagogue [synagōgē] there was a man who had the spirit of an unclean demon, and he cried out with a loud voice, [34] "Let us alone! What have you to do with us, Jesus of Nazareth? Have you come to destroy us? I know who you are, the Holy One of God." [35] But Jesus rebuked him, saying, "Be silent, and come out of him!" When the demon had thrown him down before them, he came out of him without having done him any harm. [36] They were all amazed and kept saying to one another, "What kind of utterance is this? For with authority and power he commands the unclean spirits, and out they come!" [37] And a report about him began to reach every place in the region. [38] After leaving the synagogue [synagōgē] he entered Simon's house.

Literature: As a general reference to commentaries, see Fitzmyer, Schürmann and Bovon, *Comm., ad loc.* Binder, *Temple Courts*, 155; Levine, *Ancient Synagogue*, 51; Claußen, *Versammlung*, 71, 121, 168; Runesson, *Origins*, 185, 217; idem "Identity Formation."

Comments: See comments on Mark 1:21–29 (No. 4). Luke 4:33–38 is a typical exorcism story with all the characteristics of this genre. Compare 8:26–30, 9:37–43 and 11:14–15. The introductory verses 31–32 could be understood as Jesus "used to teach," *ēn didaskōn*, in Capernaum on the Sabbath(s). Luke focuses the powerful word of Jesus, *logos* and *en exousia kai dynamei* in v. 36, here translated by "utterance" and "with authority and power." Jesus is a prophet with authority from God and power from the Spirit. In Luke he is the Spirit-guided agent, 4:18, vested with the power of the Spirit, 4:14; Acts 10:38 (Fitzmyer).

No. 6
Source: *Literary.* Luke 7:1–5
Date: 80–90 c.e.

[1] Ἐπειδὴ ἐπλήρωσεν πάντα τὰ ῥήματα αὐτοῦ εἰς τὰς ἀκοὰς τοῦ λαοῦ, εἰσῆλθεν εἰς Καφαρναούμ. [2] Ἑκατοντάρχου δέ τινος δοῦλος κακῶς ἔχων ἤμελλεν τελευτᾶν, ὃς ἦν αὐτῷ ἔντιμος. [3] ἀκούσας δὲ περὶ τοῦ Ἰησοῦ ἀπέστειλεν πρὸς αὐτὸν πρεσβυτέρους τῶν Ἰουδαίων ἐρωτῶν

αὐτὸν ὅπως ἐλθὼν διασώσῃ τὸν δοῦλον αὐτοῦ. [4] οἱ δὲ παραγενόμενοι πρὸς τὸν Ἰησοῦν παρεκάλουν αὐτὸν σπουδαίως λέγοντες ὅτι ἄξιός ἐστιν ᾧ παρέξῃ τοῦτο· [5] ἀγαπᾷ γὰρ τὸ ἔθνος ἡμῶν καὶ τὴν συναγωγὴν αὐτὸς ᾠκοδόμησεν ἡμῖν.

[1] After Jesus had finished all his sayings in the hearing of the people, he entered Capernaum. [2] A centurion there had a slave whom he valued highly, and who was ill and close to death. [3] When he heard about Jesus, he sent some Jewish elders to him, asking him to come and heal his slave. [4] When they came to Jesus, they appealed to him earnestly, saying, "He is worthy of having you do this for him, [5] for he loves our people, and it is he who built our synagogue [*synagōgē*] for us."

Literature: As a general reference to commentaries, see Fitzmyer, Schürmann and Bovon, *Comm., ad loc.* Binder, *Temple Courts*, 93–6; Levine, *Ancient Synagogue*, 51–2; Runesson, *Origins*, 185, 219, 354; idem, "Identity Formation"; Riesner, "Synagogues", 203–4.

Comments: A parallel text that does not mention the synagogue is found in Matt 8:5–13, though Binder argues that Luke better preserves the underlying common source. Luke 7:1–8:3 gives us a series of episodes about the reception accorded to Jesus by various persons. "A great prophet has been raised in our midst, and God has looked favorably on his people", 7:16. The centurion in Capernaum, in Greek *hekatontarchēs*, originally an officer in charge of a company, one hundred in number, is a Gentile. Like the God-fearer Cornelius from Caesarea (Acts 9–10), who is also a centurion, this man is also a friend of the Jewish people. He respected the Jewish customs, and the elders, a group of Jewish leaders in Capernaum, highly prized him. We do not know about any Roman troops in Galilee during the time of Herod Antipas, but the centurion could have belonged to Antipas' militia. Epigraphic evidence attests Gentile contributions to early synagogues, including the donation of an entire building. See comments on No. 103.

No. 7
Source: *Literary.* John 6:59
Date: 90–100 c.e.

[59] Ταῦτα εἶπεν ἐν συναγωγῇ διδάσκων ἐν Καφαρναούμ.

[59] He said these things while he was teaching in the synagogue [*synagōgē*] at Capernaum.

Literature: As a general reference to commentaries, see Brown, Moloney and Thyen, *Comm., ad loc.* Borgen, *Bread from Heaven*, 28–98; Olsson, *In synagogues*, 220–22. Binder, *Temple Courts*, 155; Runesson, *Origins*, 185, 192, 360, 385.

Comments: See the comment to Luke 4:16–30 (No. 33). Some scholars regard this verse as a later addition to the text, but the Gospel of John has several spatial notes of this kind. The translation "in the synagogue" is the most common one, even if the article is missing. This is sometimes the case in preposition phrases and before general concepts. See also John 18:20. An alternative would be "in a gathering," "when the people had come together (in solemn assembly/to service?)," but even in this case the synagogue in Capernaum would be the natural place. The anaphoric *tauta*, translated as "these things," refers to the dialogue between Jesus and the crowd, which towards the end becomes more and more a speech. Peder Borgen compares it with a synagogue sermon using Exod 16:4, 15 as a reference to a Torah text and Isa 54:13 as a supporting text from the Prophets.

No. 8
Source: *Archaeological.*
Date: First century C.E.

Literature: Kohl and Watzinger, *Antike Synagogen*, 4–40; Corbo, "Sinagoga del primo secolo"; Loffeda, "Ceramica"; idem, "Late Chronology"; idem, *Capharnaum*, 32–49; Foerster, "Recent Excavations"; Avi-Yonah, "Some Comments"; Bloedhorn, "Capitals"; Binder, *Temple Courts*, 186–193; Zvi Uri Ma'oz, "Galilean Synagogues"; idem, "Radical Solution"; Strange, "Archaeology"; Levine, *Ancient Synagogue*, 71; Runesson, "Identity Formation." The dating of the Capernaum and other Galilean synagogues has been and still is intensely debated. For some of the more important aspects of this discussion, see the discussion between Jodi Magnes, James F. Strange, and Eric M. Meyers in Avery-Peck and Jacob Neusner (eds.) *Ancient Synagogue* (2001).

Comments: The synagogue at Capernaum has been the object of scholarly discussion for almost a century. The debate has primarily concerned the dating of the limestone synagogue (either a third century C.E. date [e.g., Foerster], or a fourth- fifth- [Loffreda] or even sixth-century date [so Magnes]), and the possible existence of a first-century synagogue beneath. The chronological limit of the present work restricts discussion to the latter.

The black basalt remains beneath the limestone synagogue, uncovered in excavations initiated in 1969, may be described as follows. The limestone synagogue was built not on virgin soil but on the remains of earlier structures. Underneath the aisles of the main hall, as well as under the porch and the eastern court, these consisted of private houses dating from the Early Roman and Late Hellenistic periods (one wall originated in the Late Bronze age). Trenches dug in the central area of the main hall, however, revealed

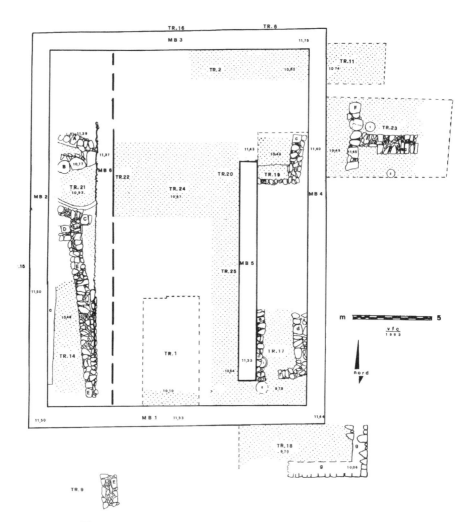

Figure 2. Plan of the first-century synagogue beneath the later limestone synagogue in Capernaum.

Figure 3. Reconstruction of the first-century synagogue in Capernaum, based on the remains

a large basalt stone pavement dated to the first century c.e. Beneath this pavement were found Hellenistic period pottery and coins. In addition, it was discovered that the limestone walls of the main hall were built on top of basalt stone walls. The same type of basalt walls were also found beneath the stylobates. In sharp contrast to the basalt foundations underneath the walls of the eastern court, which were carefully executed and cut, these basalt wall remains were of inferior quality. Further, as Loffeda puts it: "there is a shift in axiality between the 'basalt stone wall' and the outer walls of the prayer hall" (Loffreda, *Capharnaum*, 49). The basalt stone wall slopes from north to south, so that the limestone blocks had to be cut to compensate the shift in elevation in the opposite direction.

These are the facts, but how to interpret them? The excavators and several other scholars, including the authors of this volume, have concluded that the remains are best explained as belonging to an earlier public structure. However, while Corbo believes that both the basalt walls and the platform beneath the main hall were part of the first-century synagogue, Loffreda's suggestion that the walls belonged to an intermediate stage between the first-century synagogue and the later limestone synagogue deserves consideration. This is because of the discontinuity of the basalt platform underneath the aisles, where the excavators instead found remains of private houses (cf. Runesson, "Identity Formation"). In any case, the theory that the basalt remains, the walls, and the platform were newly constructed foundations for the limestone synagogue in the fifth or sixth century creates more problems than it solves; such a reconstruction must be considered unlikely. In all probability, the black basalt platform underneath the main hall of the limestone synagogue constitutes the ruins of a first-century synagogue.

2.1.4 *Chorazin*

No. 9
Source: *Archaeological.*
Date: Possibly first or second century c.e.

Literature: Chiat, *Handbook*, 97–98; Binder, *Temple Courts*, 198; Levine, *Ancient Synagogue*, 72.

Comments: The synagogue at Chorazin that visitors can see today dates to about the fourth century c.e. It was first excavated by Kohl and Watzinger in 1905, and then again by N. Makhouly and J. Ory in 1926. Of interest here is, however, an additional note by Ory, which claims that the remains of a second synagogue were found ca. 200 m west of the fourth-century structure. This synagogue has never been found again, despite several attempts. Ory's report describes this building as being similar to the fourth-century synagogue: "A square colonnaded building of small dimensions, of a position similar to the interior arrangement of the synagogue, 7 columns 3 on each side, the entrance was afforded through the east wall, were supporting the roof, and the whole space between the colonnade and the walls on three sides was occupied with sitting benches in probably 5 courses. The columns and 1–3 courses of the benches are still existing."[3] Even if taken at face value, Ory's brief note does not, of course, provide enough information for an in-depth discussion of either architectural design or date. A first-century date has been suggested, but, as Chiat notes, excavations of the site have led to the conclusion that the town was not built until after the second Jewish revolt. If indeed true—and here, mention of Chorazin in parallel accounts in Matt 11:21 and Luke 10:13 (= Q) must be noted—Ory's lost synagogue may well date to the Second century rather than the First.

2.1.5   *Gamla*

No. 10
Source: *Archaeological.*
Date: Second half of the first century B.C.E.

Literature: Gutman, *Eight Seasons of Excavations*; Gutman, "Gamla" (*NEAEHL* 2.459–63); Gutman and Raphel, *City in Rebellion*; Chiat, *Handbook*, 282–84; D. Syon, "Portrait of a Rebellion"; Binder, *Temple Courts*, 162–172; Runesson, *Origins*, 175–78, 357–58; Levine, *Ancient Synagogue*, 54–55.

Comments: The Gamla synagogue is located just by the city wall, which it antedates. It is one of the best preserved examples of a synagogue of the Second Temple period. The internal measure of the building is 20 × 16 m (floor space: 12 × 10 m), and all four walls are lined with tiers of benches. Rows of columns are located between the benches and the open space in the centre of the hall. A niche, possibly for storage, is found in the northwest corner of the hall. In the eastern aisle there is a small basin, perhaps for hand-washing. The floor of the main hall is pressed earth, except for the area of the possible peristyle, which is paved with basalt flags. At the opposite wall of the main entrance, i.e., to the northeast is a smaller room (actually part of the city wall) that also contains benches. This may have been a study room (cf. Cana, No. 3). Adjacent to the building at the southwest is a large stepped pool (4 × 4.5 m) that served as a *miqweh* or ritual bath. The *miqweh*, along with an accompanying *otzar* (storage tank) by its northern corner, postdate the construction of the synagogue and were added in the first century C.E.

---

[3] Quoted from Foerster, "Masada and Herodion" 8.

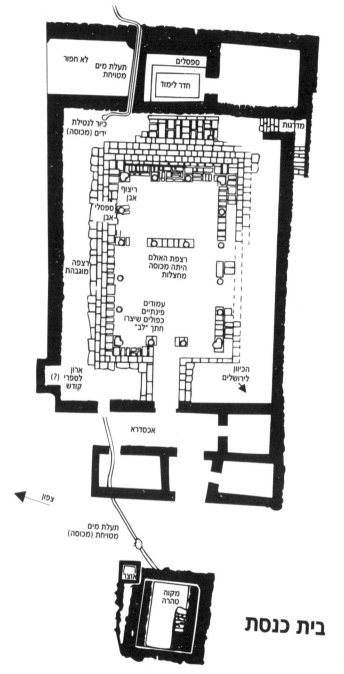

Figure 4. Plan of the Gamla synagogue and miqweh (ritual bath)

Figure 5. The Gamla remains, looking southwest

2.1.6 *Herodion*

No. 11

Source: *Archaeological.*

Date: Originally constructed in the first century B.C.E., this building was renovated for synagogue use sometime between 66 and 71 C.E.

Literature: Corbo, *Herodion*; Foerster, "Masada and Herodion", idem, "Herodium" in *NEAEHL* 2.618–21; Chiat, *Handbook*, 204–7; Netzer, "Herodian Triclinia"; Binder, *Temple Courts*, 180–85; Runesson, *Origins*, 177–78, 357–62; Levine, *Ancient Synagogue*, 63.

Comments: The edifice was originally constructed as a *triclinium* (dining hall) in Herod's fortress palace. Although Corbo has suggested a date during the Bar Kochbah revolt in the second century for the transformation of the edifice, it is more likely that the building was converted for synagogue use around the First Jewish Revolt (so Foerster, Chiat, Binder, Levine, Runesson). Benches line the four walls, and four, possibly six (Corbo; Binder) columns supported the roof and were located between the benches and the open space of the centre of the hall. The rectangular building measures 15.15 × 10.6 m, and a *miqweh* (2 × 1.5 m) is located just outside the entrance by the northern part of the wall. Identification of this building as a synagogue is based on architectural similarities to other public structures identified as synagogues, e.g., Gamla and Masada (Nos. 10, 28), as well as by the presence of a nearby *miqweh*.

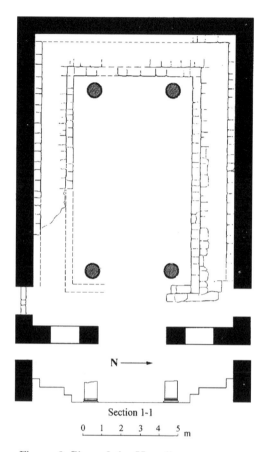

Figure 6. Plan of the Herodion synagogue

2.1.7 *Horvat 'Etri*

No. 12
Source: *Archaeological.*
Date: Late first or early second century C.E.

Literature: Zissu and Ganor, "Horvat 'Etri"; Ma'oz "Notes"; Levine, *Ancient Synagogue*, 74.

Comments: This building surfaced during excavations carried out by Zissu and Ganor in 1999–2000. The village was destroyed during the First Jewish Revolt, rebuilt, and destroyed again during the second war of 132–135 C.E. Originating sometime between the Jewish wars, the building that the excavators identified as a synagogue is a public edifice, measuring 13 × 7 m and located on the fringes of the town. It had three columns located on a row in the middle of the hall, supporting the roof. In the courtyard outside the

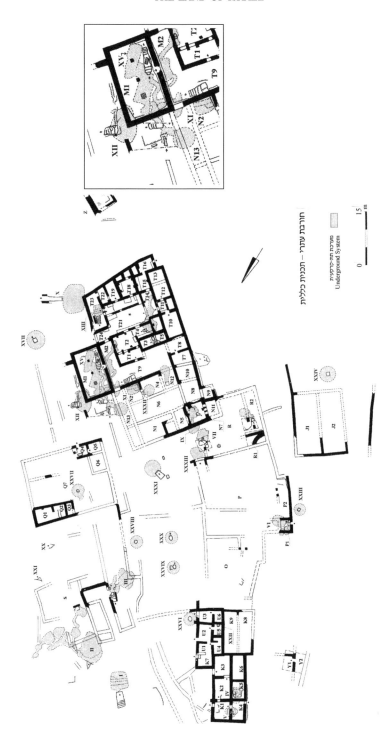

Figure 7. Plan of Horvat 'Etri. The synagogue is marked M1 and has a vestibule (M2) and a courtyard (T9) with a rock-cut miqweh (ritual bath; XI). A public hiding place (XV) rock-cut underneath M1 connects the edifice with neighbouring buildings. The underground facilities in the town are marked in grey on the plan

entrance, which was located in one of the longer walls, was a stepped basin, probably used as a *miqweh*. As with the edifices in Gamla and Jericho, the floor did not have a stone pavement. Unlike other structures identified as synagogues, however, this building did not have permanent benches, and the placement of the columns in the middle of the room also departs from the common pattern. Still, the public nature of the building cannot be doubted, which, together with the location of the edifice, makes a strong case for adding Horvat 'Etri to the list of early synagogues. If we accept this identification, the architectural variation of early synagogues has proven to be yet more diverse than previously thought.

2.1.8 *Idumea*

No. 13
Source: *Literary*. Josephus, *A. J.* 14.374
Date: *Antiquitates Judaicae* was published 93/94.

[374] Ἔπειτα δόξαν ἀναχωρεῖν ἀπῄει μάλα σωφρόνως τὴν ἐπ᾽ Αἰγύπτου. καὶ τότε μὲν ἔν τινι ἱερῷ κατάγεται, καταλελοίπει γὰρ αὐτόθι πολλοὺς τῶν ἑπομένων.

[374] Then, on deciding to retire, he very prudently took the road to Egypt. And on that occasion he lodged in a certain sanctuary [*hieron*] where he had left many of his followers.[4]

Literature: Dion, l'Égypt hellénistique," 53; Bilde, "Synagoge," 25; Binder, *Temple Courts*, 156–57; Runesson, *Origins*, 462–63; Claußen, *Versammlung*, 119–20; Levine, *Ancient Synagogue*, 46, n. 4.

Comments: The events mentioned in the passage are said to have taken place in the latter half of the first century B.C.E. Josephus reports that Herod stayed overnight in one of the *hiera* of Idumea (= *B. J.* 1.277; cf. 4.408 [Judaea]; 7.144). Several scholars, including the authors of this volume, have interpreted *hieron* here as referring to a synagogue rather than a temple. Two main reasons are cited. First, the term *hieron* was sometimes used for synagogues in the first century. Second, if indeed the reference were to a temple, it would be hard to explain the existence of a (Jewish) temple in this area at this time.

Some scholars have tried to solve this problem by suggesting that "Judaea" refers to "greater Judaea," including non-Jewish areas with non-Jewish temples (Levine; cf. Claußen). In *B. J.* 7.144, however, Josephus describes the triumph following the First Jewish Revolt, and there the burning of *hiera* is explicitly mentioned. In this context, these *hiera* could only refer to Jewish buildings.

---

[4] Adapted from Marcus' translation (LCL).

Since their depiction is clearly *not* a reference to different structures in the Jerusalem temple, it would seem that Josephus used the term *hieron* in both the description of the triumph and in the above passage. Regarding guest chambers in synagogues, cf. No. 26.

No. 14

Source: *Literary*. Josephus *B. J.* 1.277–78

Date: *De bello Judaico* consists of seven books and was published in the late 70s. The events described are said to have taken place in the second half of the first century B.C.E.

[277] Ἡρώδης μὲν δὴ πολεμίους τοὺς Ἄραβας εὑρὼν δι' ἃ φιλτάτους ἤλπισεν καὶ τοῖς ἀγγέλοις ἀποκρινάμενος ὡς ὑπηγόρευε τὸ πάθος ὑπέστρεψεν ἐπ' Αἰγύπτου. καὶ τὴν μὲν πρώτην ἑσπέραν κατά τι τῶν ἐπιχωρίων ἱερὸν αὐλίζεται τοὺς ὑπολειφθέντας ἀναλαβών, τῇ δ' ἑξῆς εἰς Ῥινοκούρουρα προελθόντι τὰ περὶ τὴν τἀδελφοῦ τελευτὴν ἀπαγγέλλεται. [278] προσλαβὼν δὲ πένθους ὅσον ἀπεθήκατο φροντίδων ᾔει προσωτέρω. καὶ δὴ βραδέως ὁ Ἄραψ μετανοήσας ἔπεμψεν διὰ τάχους τοὺς ἀνακαλέσοντας τὸν ὑβρισμένον. ἔφθανεν δὲ καὶ τούτους Ἡρώδης εἰς Πηλούσιον ἀφικόμενος, ἔνθα τῆς παρόδου μὴ τυγχάνων ὑπὸ τῶν ἐφορμούντων τοῖς ἡγεμόσιν ἐντυγχάνει· κἀκεῖνοι τήν τε φήμην καὶ τὸ ἀξίωμα τἀνδρὸς αἰδεσθέντες προπέμπουσιν αὐτὸν εἰς Ἀλεξάνδρειαν.

[277] Herod, finding the Arabs hostile to him for the very reasons which had made him look for their warm friendship, gave the messengers the reply which his feelings dictated and turned back towards Egypt. The first evening he encamped in one of the temples [*hieron*] of the country, where he picked up those of his men who had been left in the rear. The next day he advanced to Rhinocorura, where he received the news of his brother's death. [278] His load of anxiety thus replaced by as heavy a burden of grief, he resumed his march. The Arab king, now tardily repenting his conduct, dispatched messengers in haste to recall his insulted suitor; but Herod outstripped them, having already reached Pelusium. Here, being refused a passage by the fleet stationed in that port, he applied to the authorities, who, out of respect for his fame and rank, escorted him to Alexandria.[5]

---

[5] Translation by Thackeray (LCL).

Literature: See above, No. 13.

Comments: See above, No. 13.

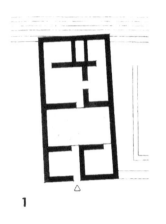
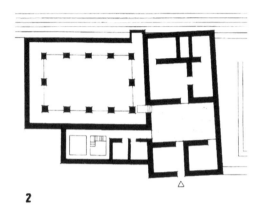

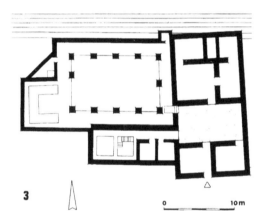

Figure 8. Schematic plans of the three stages of the synagogue in Jericho:
(1) the courtyard house, (2) addition of the main hall and miqweh (ritual
bath), (3) addition of the triclinium.

2.1.9 *Jericho*

No. 15
Source: *Archaeological.*
Date: First century B.C.E.

Literature: Netzer, "Hasmonean Period"; idem "Exist or Not?"; idem,
Hasmonean and Herodian Palaces, 159–92; Ma'oz, "Never Existed"; Binder, *Temple*

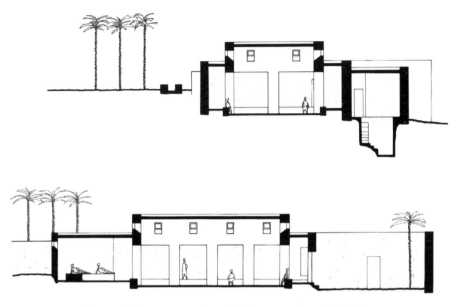

Figure 9. Reconstructions of the synagogue in Jericho,
looking east and north respectively

Courts, xiii; Runesson, *Origins*, 181–82, 359–60; idem, "1st Century Synagogue";
Strange, "Archaeology"; Levine, "Critical Reassessments" 87–89; idem, *Ancient
Synagogue*, 72–74; Rapuano, "Hasmonean Period."

Comments: This recently discovered building was intially identified as a
synagogue by the excavator, Ehud Netzer. The first publication appeared
in 1998 and was followed by discussions both critical and supportive of this
conclusion. A competing interpretation argues that the edifice was designed
as a Hellenistic-Roman villa, and thus was a private building (cf. discussion
in Levine, "Critical Reassessments").

The building developed in three main stages, and measured 28 × 20 m in
its final phase. The original edifice, dated ca. 80/74 B.C.E., did not contain the
main hall interpreted as the assembly hall. The second phase, ca. 70 B.C.E.,
added the main hall, *miqweh* and *otzar* around 70 B.C.E., while the third phase,
some ten to twenty years later, added the *triclinium* at the west end of the main
hall. The entire complex was destroyed in the earthquake of 31 B.C.E.

The main hall had 12 pillars. Somewhat unlike other buildings identified as
synagogues, there were aisles between the walls and the pillars on the southern
and eastern sides of the main hall, the benches running between the pillars; on
the western and northern sides, the benches are placed along the walls, so that
the pillars stand between the benches and the open central area, as in other
synagogue buildings. The location of the eastern and southern benches and
pillars thus meant that the pillars did not obstruct the view with regard to the

open area of the main hall, as in other early synagogues (cf. Strange, 43–44).
The floor of the main hall was pressed earth as in the Gamla synagogue. Also,
a channel carrying water from an aqueduct north of the building runs in a
north-south direction through the main hall, feeding a basin in the building
before continuing south to the otzar (cf. Gamla, No. 10).

Although the Jericho building has several architectural features in common
with other buildings identified as synagogues, one of the main arguments
against this interpretation is the location of the building, which would seem
to exclude a "synagogue community." This argument from context, however,
is based on a specific definition of a "synagogue." As Runesson ("1st Century
Synagogue") has argued, the building may have served the needs of an association synagogue (i.e., a guild house), where membership consisted of, e.g., the
staff of the nearby Hasmonean palace. While the debate will likely continue
and further discussion is needed, at this point the evidence seems to weigh in
favour of the excavator's interpretation.

2.1.10 *Jerusalem*

No. 16
Source: *Literary.* John 9:22–23
Date: Ca. 90–100 C.E.

[22] ταῦτα εἶπαν οἱ γονεῖς αὐτοῦ ὅτι ἐφοβοῦντο τοὺς Ἰουδαίους· ἤδη
γὰρ συνετέθειντο οἱ Ἰουδαῖοι ἵνα ἐάν τις αὐτὸν ὁμολογήσῃ χριστόν,
ἀποσυνάγωγος γένηται. [23] διὰ τοῦτο οἱ γονεῖς αὐτοῦ εἶπαν ὅτι
ἡλικίαν ἔχει, αὐτὸν ἐπερωτήσατε.

[22] His parents said this because they were afraid of the Jews; for the
Jews had already agreed that anyone who confessed Jesus to be the
Messiah would be put out of the synagogue [*aposynagōgos*]. [23] Therefore
his parents said, "He is of age; ask him."

Literature: As a general reference to commentaries, see Brown, Moloney
and Thyen, *Comm., ad loc.* Horst, *Birkat ha-minim*; Olsson, *In synagogues*, 218–19.
Binder, *Temple Courts*, 75–78; Levine, *Ancient Synagogue*, 193; Runesson, *Origins*,
376; Stegemann, *Synagoge und Obrigkeit*, 139–42; Horst, *Birkat ha-minim*; Olsson,
In synagogues, 218–19.

Comments: John 9:22–23, 12:42–43 and 16:2–3 are bound together by the
very uncommon word *aposynagōgos*, not attested in Greek texts before the Gospel
of John and without any clear correspondence in Hebrew or Aramaic. It is a
good Greek construction, an adjective derived from a preposition phrase (*apo
synagōgēs*), like *apodēmios*, "away from one's country, away from home, abroad,"
apophylios, "having no tribes, foreign," *apobōmios*, "far from an altar, godless," or
apoikos, "away from home, abroad." These parallels suggest a general meaning

of the word *aposynagōgos*, like "having no synagogue, away from the synagogue, synagogueless." It gives no information about how they had to leave the synagogues. The different Jewish forms of exclusion aim at reforming, converting, or winning back the person concerned. In the Gospel of John, however, *aposynagōgos* marks a serious split within the Jewish community.

The three Johannine passages are also connected in their fusion of different time horizons. The present of the narrator is combined with the past of the Jesus event. According to Raymond E. Brown the comment in 9:22 tells about "the ultimate development of the hostility that was incipient in Jesus' lifetime" (Brown, *Comm.*, *ad loc.*). The partial repetition of v. 21 in v. 23 gives the note an important role in the paragraph. The questions of discipleship, fellowship and unity are crucial in the context, 9:1–10:21, as in John 15:1–16:4a and also in John 12:37–50.

The meaning of the clause "the Jews had already decided (*synetetheinto*)" is not clear. Some scholars refer to the so-called *birkat ha-minim*, the 12th *berakhah* in the *Shemoneh Esreh*, at that time funtioning as a curse against heretics. However, the old consensus that this *berakhah* was a curse against Christians, proclaimed in the 80s by the Pharisaic or rabbinic center at Jamnia, and to be used in all synagogues, has been proved to be entirely invalid. On this, see the excellent survey of recent research in Horst, *Birkat ha-minim*, which argues: (1) that *minim* in the Tannaitic period always refers to Jews, (2) that it is extremely likely that the *birkat ha-minim* could also be applied to Christ-believing Jews, (3) that the primary purpose was to strengthen the unity and create solidarity among the Jews, not to throw (non-Jewish) Christians out of the synagogues, and (4) that, while there was increasing enimity between what later became Judaism and Christianity during the first two centuries C.E., only in Jerome's time was the word *notsrim*, in the sense of Christians in general, added to the 12th *berakhah*. With this background, the Johannine conflicts should be viewed as primarily an inner-Jewish affair, with the *berakhah* marking a later climax of tensions that began within the synagogues during the last decades of the first century. Thus, within some synagogues of that era, confessions of Jesus as Messiah, Son of God, made some Jews "synagogueless."

John 12:42–43, 16:2–3 and 9:22–23 thus offer some insights into an inner-Jewish process within the framework of the synagogue, where the Johannine Christ-believers lived together with their fellow Jews, probably for many years. Later, however, probably after the destruction of the temple, the Johannine Christ-believers were made "synagogueless," with consequences for both sides. Some Jesus-believing Jews drew back to traditional Judaism by not confessing Jesus as Messiah, others confessed him and had to leave the synagogue. The reason for this split, from the Johannine perspective, is attributed to the different confessions about Jesus. A new eagerness among early rabbis after 70 C.E. to strengthen the unity and self-consciousness of the Jews probably resulted in different forms of *birkat ha-minim* towards the end of the first century. This situation, together with inner-Johannine changes, may then provide the background for the glimpses of the Johannine community we find in these three passages (Olsson, *In synagogues*, 219).

No. 17
Source: *Literary.* John 12:42–43
Date: Ca. 90–100 C.E.

[42] ὅμως μέντοι καὶ ἐκ τῶν ἀρχόντων πολλοὶ ἐπίστευσαν εἰς αὐτόν,
ἀλλὰ διὰ τοὺς Φαρισαίους οὐχ ὡμολόγουν ἵνα μὴ ἀποσυνάγωγοι
γένωνται· [43] ἠγάπησαν γὰρ τὴν δόξαν τῶν ἀνθρώπων μᾶλλον ἤπερ
τὴν δόξαν τοῦ θεοῦ.

[42] Nevertheless many, even of the authorities, believed in him. But
because of the Pharisees they did not confess it, for fear that they would
be put out of the synagogue [*aposynagōgos*]; [43] for they loved human
glory more than the glory that comes from God.

Literature: As a general reference to commentaries, see Brown, Moloney and
Thyen, *Comm., ad loc.* Binder, *Temple Courts*, 75–78; Levine, *Ancient Synagogue*,
193; Runesson, *Origins*, 376; Stegemann, *Synagoge und Obrigkeit*, 139–42; Horst,
Birkat ha-minim; Levine, *Synagogues*, 440–60; Olsson, *In synagogues*, 213–17.

Comments: See the comments to John 9:22–23 (No. 16). "The Jews" in
9:22 often refer to Jewish leaders in the Gospel of John and are equated with
"the Pharisees" elsewhere in that chapter. This group is again referenced in
the above text. Although existing as a party in the time of Jesus, according
to some scholars the Pharisees became more influential at the end of the
first century, following the destruction of the Jerusalem temple. They became
leaders of synagogues rather late (Levine).

Two reasons are given in the context, 12:37–43, for the fact that not all
Jews believed in Jesus. The first one is more fundamental and theological
(viz., Scripture must be fulfilled) and reflects early Christian traditions (Mark
4:11–12 par.; Acts 28:26–27 and Rom 10:16; 11:8,10). The second is more
sociological (viz., the threat from leaders in some synagogues).

Some Jesus-believing Jews within the synagogues probably drew back to
traditional Judaism by not confessing Jesus, while other Jesus-believing Jews
left the synagogue. The content of the confession in 9:22—that Jesus was the
Messiah—is not explicitly mentioned, but the phrase "the glory that comes
from God" may be a reference to Jesus' divine origin. The word used for
"the authorities," *archontes*, was a common word for leaders in Jewish society.
It is also used for leaders of the synagogues. A reference to the Sanhedrin in
Jerusalem was not relevant for the time after 70 C.E.

No. 18
Source: *Literary.* Acts 6:9–10
Date: Ca. 90–110 C.E.

[9] ἀνέστησαν δέ τινες τῶν ἐκ τῆς συναγωγῆς τῆς λεγομένης Λιβερτίνων
καὶ Κυρηναίων καὶ Ἀλεξανδρέων καὶ τῶν ἀπὸ Κιλικίας καὶ Ἀσίας

συζητοῦντες τῷ Στεφάνῳ, [10] καὶ οὐκ ἴσχυον ἀντιστῆναι τῇ σοφίᾳ καὶ τῷ πνεύματι ᾧ ἐλάλει.

[9] Then some of those who belonged to the synagogue [synagōgē] of the Freedmen (as it was called), Cyrenians, Alexandrians, and others of those from Cilicia and Asia, stood up and argued with Stephen. [10] But they could not withstand the wisdom and the Spirit with which he spoke.

Literature: As a general reference to commentaries see Barrett, Fitzmyer and Jervell, *Comm., ad loc.* Binder, *Temple Courts*, 78–81, 157–58; Levine, *Ancient Synagogue*, 52–54; Claußen, *Versammlung*, 72–75, 93–95; Runesson, *Origins*, 157–58, 228–29, 354; Riesner, "Synagogues," 204–6.

Comments: Of the thirty-four references to synagogues in Luke's two books, nineteen come from Acts. Those mentioned are located in Jerusalem, Damascus, Salamis, Pisidian Antioch, Iconium, Thessalonica, Beroea, Athens, Corinth and Ephesus. Acts and the Gospel of John are the oldest biblical witnesses to synagogues in Jerusalem.

The one or more synagogues mentioned in Acts 6:9 are defined by references to different ethnic or social groups, and are reminiscent of the Graeco-Roman voluntary associations. As such, they have a semi-public character (Runesson) and function as synagogues for Greek-speaking Jews from the Diaspora, including Stephen and Paul.

Scholars have often discussed how many synagogues or synagogue assemblies are referenced in Acts 6:9. The use of the word *synagōgē* just once and in the singular has been taken as evidence for only one synagogue, regarded by a few scholars as identical to the synagogue mentioned in the Theodotos inscription (No. 26 below). Others argue that the use of *tōn… tōn* in the Greek text indicates two synagogues: "those of the synagogue called that of the Libertines, both Cyrenians and Alexandrians" and "some of those who came from Cilicia and Asia." Still others note the peculiarity of only a few named places being mentioned in the text despite the existence of many groups of Dispora Jews in Jerusalem. These scholars see this as a good argument for finding five synagogue assemblies in the text (Levine). In support of this last hypothesis, a rabbinic source, *t. Meg.* 2:17, also mentions "the synagogue of the Alexandrians."

Whatever the final verdict on this question, Luke clearly believed that there were several synagogues in Jerusalem during Paul's time (Acts 24:12; 26:9–11). These "synagogues" were smaller interpretative communities that gathered in special buildings or perhaps even in private houses.

In Greek *Libertinoi*, a transliteration of Latin *libertini*, refers to former slaves (and their subsequent offspring) who had been set free. During the first century B.C.E., many Jews had been enslaved and brought to Rome as war prisoners. Later manumitted, they became Roman citizens (Philo, *Legat.* 155, No. 182).

In the text, the Diaspora Jews "argued" (*syzētein*) with Stephen in the synagogue(s). The Greek word means "dispute, discuss" (Mark 9:14; Acts 9:29).

No. 19
Source: *Literary.* Acts 24:12
Date: Ca. 90–110 C.E.

[12] καὶ οὔτε ἐν τῷ ἱερῷ εὗρόν με πρός τινα διαλεγόμενον ἢ ἐπίστασιν ποιοῦντα ὄχλου οὔτε ἐν ταῖς συναγωγαῖς οὔτε κατὰ τὴν πόλιν.

[12] They did not find me disputing with anyone in the temple or stirring up a crowd either in the synagogues [*synagōgai*] or throughout the city.

Literature: As a general reference to commentaries see Barrett, Fitzmyer and Jervell, *Comm., ad loc.* Binder, *Temple Courts*, 158–59; Claußen, *Versammlung*, 95; Riesner, "Synagogues," 204.

Comments: See the comments on Acts 6:9–10 (No. 18) and on Acts 26:9–11 (No. 20). Acts 24:12 and Acts 26:9–11 are excerpts of rhetorical speeches composed by Luke. In the first, Paul defends himself before the Roman procurator Felix in Caesarea (Acts 24:10–21), and in the second, before the Jewish king Agrippa II (Acts 26:2–29). The context makes clear that Luke is thinking of synagogue buildings in Jerusalem. "Arguing" (*dialegesthai*) with somebody in the temple or in synagogues is here the first step towards creating a disturbance. *Dialegesthai* means "to argue about differences of opinion, to dispute, to argue" or "to address, to make a speech." Luke often uses the word when describing Paul's activities in synagogues (Acts 17:2, 17; 18:4, 19; 19:8).

No. 20
Source: *Literary.* Acts 26:9–11
Date: Ca. 90–110 C.E.

[9] Ἐγὼ μὲν οὖν ἔδοξα ἐμαυτῷ πρὸς τὸ ὄνομα Ἰησοῦ τοῦ Ναζωραίου δεῖν πολλὰ ἐναντία πρᾶξαι, [10] ὃ καὶ ἐποίησα ἐν Ἱεροσολύμοις, καὶ πολλούς τε τῶν ἁγίων ἐγὼ ἐν φυλακαῖς κατέκλεισα τὴν παρὰ τῶν ἀρχιερέων ἐξουσίαν λαβὼν ἀναιρουμένων τε αὐτῶν κατήνεγκα ψῆφον. [11]καὶ κατὰ πάσας τὰς συναγωγὰς πολλάκις τιμωρῶν αὐτοὺς ἠνάγκαζον βλασφημεῖν περισσῶς τε ἐμμαινόμενος αὐτοῖς ἐδίωκον ἕως καὶ εἰς τὰς ἔξω πόλεις.

[9] Indeed, I myself was convinced that I ought to do many things against the name of Jesus of Nazareth. [10] And that is what I did in Jerusalem; with authority received from the chief priests, I not only locked up many of the saints in prison, but I also cast my vote against them when they were being condemned to death. [11] By punishing them often in all the synagogues [*synagōgai*] I tried to force them to

blaspheme; and since I was so furiously enraged at them, I pursued them even to foreign cities.

Literature: As a general reference to commentaries see Barrett, Fitzmyer and Jervell, *Comm., ad loc.* Binder, *Temple Courts*, 158–59; 445–46; Stegemann, *Synagoge und Obrikeit*, 97–112, 114–18.

Comments: See the comments on Acts 24:12 (No. 19) and Acts 22:19 (No. 73). In these verses, Paul is the forensic subject about what *he* did in Jerusalem, not what synagogue officials did. For rhetorical reasons he clearly exaggerates his actions. "The name of Jesus of Nazareth" encompasses those who believe in Jesus and what this name says about them. Treating such persons as apostates, Paul had tried to force them to deny their belief—or, failing that, to imprison or condemn them to death, thereby "cleansing" the synagogues. According to Luke, the synagogues had no forensic competence (Stegemann). See the comments on Luke 12:11–12 (No. 70) and Luke 21:12–13 (No. 71).

No. 21
Source: *Literary.* Agatharchides ap. Josephus, *C. Ap.* 1.209–11.
Date: *Contra Apionem* was Josephus' last work; it is dated to the middle of the 90s C.E. Agatharchides of Cnidus was born ca. 215 and died after 145 B.C.E.

[209] "οἱ καλούμενοι Ἰουδαῖοι πόλιν οἰκοῦντες ὀχυρωτάτην πασῶν, ἣν καλεῖν Ἱεροσόλυμα συμβαίνει τοὺς ἐγχωρίους, ἀργεῖν εἰθισμένοι δι' ἑβδόμης ἡμέρας καὶ μήτε τὰ ὅπλα βαστάζειν ἐν τοῖς εἰρημένοις χρόνοις μήτε γεωργίας ἅπτεσθαι μήτε ἄλλης ἐπιμελεῖσθαι λειτουργίας μηδεμιᾶς, ἀλλ' ἐν τοῖς ἱεροῖς ἐκτετακότες τὰς χεῖρας [210] εὔχεσθαι μέχρι τῆς ἑσπέρας, εἰσιόντος εἰς τὴν πόλιν Πτολεμαίου τοῦ Λάγου μετὰ τῆς δυνάμεως καὶ τῶν ἀνθρώπων ἀντὶ τοῦ φυλάττειν τὴν πόλιν διατηρούντων τὴν ἄνοιαν, ἡ μὲν πατρὶς εἰλήφει δεσπότην πικρόν, ὁ δὲ νόμος ἐξηλέγχθη φαῦλον ἔχων ἐθισμόν. [211] τὸ δὲ συμβὰν πλὴν ἐκείνων τοὺς ἄλλους πάντας δεδίδαχε τηνικαῦτα φυγεῖν εἰς ἐνύπνια καὶ τὴν περὶ τοῦ νόμου παραδεδομένην ὑπόνοιαν, ἡνίκα ἂν τοῖς ἀνθρωπίνοις λογισμοῖς περι; τῶν διαπορουμένων ἐξασθενήσωσιν."

[209] "The people known as Jews, who inhabit the most strongly fortified of cities, called by the natives Jerusalem, have a custom of abstaining from work every seventh day; on those occasions they neither bear arms nor take any agricultural operations in hand, nor engage in any other form of public service, but pray with outstretched hands in

the temples [*hiera*] until the evening. [210] Consequently, because the inhabitants, instead of protecting their city, persevered in their folly, Ptolemy, son of Lagus, was allowed to enter with his army; the country was thus given over to a cruel master, and the defect of a practice enjoined by law was exposed. [211] That experience has taught the whole world, except that nation, the lesson not to resort to dreams and traditional fancies about the law, until the difficulties are such as to baffle human reason."[6]

Literature: Stern, *GLAJJ*, 1.104–8; Whittaker, *Jews and Christians*, 67–68; Cohen, "Pagan and Christian Evidence," 162–63; Bilde, "Synagoge," 26–27; Binder, *Temple Courts*, 159; Runesson, *Origins*, 346–47, 354, 377; Levine, *Ancient Synagogue*, 28.

Comments: The Greek historian Agatharchides spent most of his life in Alexandria in Egypt. Here he is quoted as describing Jewish worship customs in Jerusalem. The term he uses for the buildings in which prayers took place is *hieron*, usually translated as "temple." However, as we have seen elsewhere, while the primary meaning of *hieron* is temple or sanctuary, this term was used for synagogues as well.

Some scholars have argued that this passage describes temple worship in Jerusalem on the basis of the term used. Others have pointed to the fact that the plural *hiera* makes such an identification less likely. In addition, the context of regular Sabbath worship fits a synagogue setting better, since temple rituals were performed every day of the week.

Another detail in the text relates to a much-debated issue in synagogue studies: was prayer part of synagogue rituals before 200 C.E.? If *hiera* is understood as referring to synagogues in Jerusalem (see Nos. 18, 19, 20, 22, 26 for other sources on Jerusalem synagogues), then this passage indicates that this may have been the case (cf. No. 43 for additional evidence of prayer in a synagogue context). However, one has to take into account the possibility of provincialism, i.e., that Agatharchides' knowledge of synagogue rituals was limited to Alexandria, and that he might have read Egyptian-Jewish customs into the Jerusalem context.

While the situation Agatharchides describes refers to the time of Ptolemy I Soter (d. 301 B.C.E.), it is more likely that he describes what he knew to be true in his own time, i.e., the second century B.C.E. The possibility that Josephus has modified Agatharchides's text to fit his own late first century C.E. context exists; if this were the case, however, we might have expected a less ambiguous wording.

---

[6] Adapted from Thackeray, LCL.

No. 22
Source: *Literary.* Apion, *History of Egypt* ap. Josephus, *C. Ap.* 2.10–12
Date: *Contra Apionem* was Josephus' last work; it is dated to the middle of the 90s C.E. Apion wrote his *History* in the first half of the first century C.E.

[10] φησὶ γὰρ ἐν τῇ τρίτῃ τῶν Αἰγυπτιακῶν τάδε· "Μωσῆς, ὡς ἤκουσα παρὰ τῶν πρεσβυτέρων τῶν Αἰγυπτίων, ἦν Ἡλιοπολίτης, ὃς πατρίοις ἔθεσι κατηγγυημένος αἰθρίους προσευχὰς ἀνῆγεν εἰς οἵους εἶχεν ἥλιος περιβόλους, πρὸς ἀφηλιώτην δὲ πάσας ἀπέστρεφεν· ὧδε γὰρ καὶ Ἡλίου κεῖται πόλις. [11] ἀντὶ δὲ ὀβελῶν ἔστησε κίονας, ὑφ᾽ οἷς ἦν ἐκτύπωμα σκάφη, σκιὰ δ᾽ ἀνδρὸς ἐπ᾽ αὐτὴν διακειμένη, ὡς ὅτι ἐν αἰθέρι τοῦτον ἀεὶ τὸν δρόμον ἡλίῳ συμπεριπολεῖ." [12] τοιαύτη μέν τις ἡ θαυμαστὴ τοῦ γραμματικοῦ φράσις· τὸ δὲ ψεῦσμα λόγων οὐ δεόμενον, ἀλλ᾽ ἐκ τῶν ἔργων περιφανές· οὔτε γὰρ αὐτὸς Μωσῆς, ὅτε τὴν πρώτην σκηνὴν τῷ θεῷ κατεσκεύασεν, οὐθὲν ἐκτύπωμα τοιοῦτον εἰς αὐτὴν ἐνέθηκεν οὐδὲ ποιεῖν τοῖς ἔπειτα προσέταξεν, ὅ τε μετὰ ταῦτα κατασκευάσας τὸν ναὸν τὸν ἐν Ἱεροσολύμοις Σολομὼν πάσης ἀπέσχετο τοιαύτης περιεργίας οἵαν συμπέπλεκεν Ἀπίων.

[10] In the third book of his History of Egypt he [i.e., Apion] makes the following statement: "Moses, as I have heard from old people in Egypt, was a native of Heliopolis, who, being pledged to the customs of his country, erected prayer halls [*proseuchai*], open to the air, in the various precincts of the city, all facing eastwards; such being the orientation also of Heliopolis. [11] In place of obelisks he set up pillars, beneath which was a model of a boat; and the shadow cast on this basin by the statue described a circle corresponding to the course of the sun in the heavens." [12] Such is the grammarian's amazing statement. Its mendacious character needs no comment; it is exposed by the facts. When Moses built the first tabernacle [*skēnē*] for God, he neither placed in it himself, nor instructed his successors to make, any graven imagery of this kind. When Salomon, later on, built the temple [*naos*] at Jerusalem, he too refrained from any curiosities of art such as Apion has conceived.

Literature: Stern, *GLAJJ*, 1.389–90, 392–95; Cohen, "Pagans and Christian Evidence," 162–63; Whittaker, *Jews and Christians*, 54; Binder, *Temple Courts*, 160; Bilde, "Synagoge," 24; Runesson, *Origins*, 79, 431; Claußen, *Versammlung*, 117.

Comments: In this passage, Josephus quotes Apion as mentioning *proseuchai* (prayer halls) constructed in Jerusalem by Moses. Some scholars have interpreted this as a reference to synagogues—though they have cautioned that provincialism might have been at work in Apion's description (viz., his use of the Diapora term *proseuchē* rather than *synagōgē*). Despite the difference in terminology, these scholars argue, Apion may indeed have known about the existence of synagogues in Jerusalem.

A possible difficulty with this interpretation is that Josephus' response to Apion's description focusses on Moses' tabernacle and Salomon's temple, not synagogues. While this may be interpreted as a *maiore ad minorem* argument, another view is that *proseuchē* was understood here as a temple term by both Apion and Josephus.

If so, the following scenario could be reconstructed (following Runesson). Apion, a Greek scholar of Egyptian origin, described here first-century *proseuchai* that he knew from Egypt. They were open to the air, suggesting that these buildings were originally (Jewish) temples (cf. Nos. T2–T7). Further, he knew that Egyptian Jews, like other Jews, connected the origin of the synagogue with Moses (cf. Nos. 72, 166), so he mentioned Moses as the one initiating the building of the *proseuchai*. No doubt Apion would also have heard about the Jerusalem temple, but since he knew about several Jewish temples (*proseuchai*) in Egypt (not knowing, however, that by this time these structures functioned as synagogues), he assumed that Jerusalem also had several temples of similar form and function. Subsequently, this confused report of Jewish religious customs and buildings became an easy target for Josephus, who picked up the temple association and mentions first Moses, connecting him to the tabernacle, then Salomon, showing him to be the one erecting the temple (*naos*) in Jerusalem. He does not mention synagogues, despite the fact that the natural response might have been to point to their form and function.

Both the above interpretations, despite their differences, suggest that the *proseuchai* known by Apion were functionally synagogues. The first reading would place these synagogues in Jerusalem, while the second would emphasise Apion's possible provincial bias, understanding the passage as evidence of early first-century Egyptian synagogue institutions housed in temple-like structures.

No. 23
Source: Literary. *m. Yoma* 7:1
Date: Ca. 200 C.E.

בא לו כהן גדול לקרות. אם רצה לקרות בבגדי בוץ קורא, ואם לאו קורא באצטלית לבן משלו. חזן הכנסת נוטל ספר תורה ונותנו לראש הכנסת, וראש הכנסת נותנו לסגן, והסגן נותנו לכהן גדול. וכהן גדול עומד ומקבל וקורא עומד.

The High Priest came to read. If he wished to read in the linen vestments he could read thus, but if not he could read in his own white garment. The sexton/attendant of the synagogue [*hazzan ha-kneset*] took a scroll of the Torah and gave it to the president of the synagogue [*rosh ha-kneset*], and the president of the synagogue gave it to the prefect [*sagan*] and the prefect gave it to the high priest. And the high priest stood and received it and read standing.

Literature: Hoenig, "Temple-Synagogue"; Schürer, *HJP* 2.438; Fine, *This Holy Place*, 50; Runesson, *Origins*, 207–12; 364–65; Levine, *Ancient Synagogue*, 415–27, 437–39; cf. Binder, *Temple Courts*, 368–70; Rajak and Noy, "*Archisynagogoi*."

Comments: The high priest is here described as going into the women's court in the Jerusalem temple once a year to read on Yom Kippur. Traditional scholarship maintained that a synagogue once existed on the temple mount, an inference partially based upon references to service there by synagogue-related officials (the *hazzan ha-kneset* and the *rosh ha-kneset*). Hoenig ("Temple-Synagogue"), however, has argued forcefully against this view.

While Hoenig was correct in his analysis of the relevant Mishnaic passages (*Tamid* 4:3–5:1, *Yoma* 7:1, *Sotah* 7:8, *Sukkah* 5:1, *Ta'an.* 2:5), his definition of "synagogue" may have been too narrow (Runesson, 365). If "synagogue" is defined as a public institution in charge of municipal and other socio-religious aspects of community life, the Jerusalem temple would have provided the public space for such an institution in Jerusalem (Runesson, 207–12; cf. Levine 420–21).

The office of the *hazzan* is clearly of pre-70 origin, and has its equivalent in the Greek terms *neōkoros* (cf. *CPJ* 1.129, see No. 147) and *hypēretēs* (cf. Luke 4:20; No. 33) (Binder, 368–70; Levine, 437–39). For *Rosh ha-kneset* and its Greek equivalent *archisynagōgos*, see Levine, 415–27; cf. Rajak and Noy, "*Archisynagogoi*."

In addition to the above ceremony, the public reading of Torah in the Jerusalem temple also took place on a septennial cycle in relation to the *hakhel* ceremony on Sukkoth (see No. 25). In both cases, the reading of Torah, a defining feature of the synagogue, was administered by officials known from public synagogue contexts.

No. 24
Source: *Literary. m. Sotah* 7:7
Date: Ca. 200 C.E.

ברכות כהן גדול כיצד? חזן הכנסת נוטל ספר תורה ונותנו לראש הכנסת, וראש הכנסת נותנו לסגן, והסגן נותנו לכהן גדול, וכהן גדול עומד ומקבל, וקורא עומד.

What was the manner of the *Blessings of the High Priest?*—The minister of the Synagogue [*hazzan ha-kneset*] took a Scroll of the Law and gave it to the president of the Synagogue [*rosh ha-kneset*], and the president of the Synagogue gave it to the Prefect [*sagan*] of the priests, and the Prefect [*sagan*] of the priests gave it to the High Priest, and the High Priest stood when he received it, and read it standing.

Literature: See above, No. 23.

Comments: This passage deals with a ritual performed once a year in the Jerusalem temple on Yom Kippur. Regarding a connection to the synagogue and synagogue leadership, see comment to No. 23.

No. 25
Source: *Literary. m. Sotah* 7:8
Date: Ca. 200 C.E.

פרשת המלך כיצד? מוצאי יום טוב הראשון של חג, בשמיני, במוצאי שביעית, עושין
לו בימה של עץ בעזרה והוא יושב עליה, שנאמר, מקץ שבע שנים במועד,
ונומר. וחזן הכנסת נוטל ספר תורה ונותנו לראש הכנסת, וראש הכנסת נותנו
לסנן, והסנן נותנו לכהן נדול, וכהן נדול נותנו למלך, והמלך עומד ומקבל
וקורא יושב.

What as the manner of the *Portion of the King?*—At the conclusion of the first Holyday day of the Festival of Tabernacles, in the eighth year, after the close of the seventh year, they prepared for him in the Temple Court a platform of wood and he sat thereon, as it is said, *At the end of seven years at the appointed time, etc.* The minister of the Synagogue [*hazzan ha-kneset*] took a Scroll of the Law and gave it to the president of the Synagogue [*rosh ha-kneset*], and the president of the Synagogue gave it to the Prefect [*sagan*] of the priests, and the Prefect of the priests gave it to the High Priest, and the High Priest gave it to the king, and the king stood and received it and read it sitting.

Literature: See above, No. 23.

Comments: As they did similarly in Nos. 23 and 24, the rabbis here deal with the *hakhel* ceremony, performed every seventh year during Sukkoth. Regarding a connection to the synagogue and synagogue leadership, see comment to No. 23. The reader in this ritual is the king rather than the high priest, representing political and religious authority.

No. 26
Source: *Inscription. CIJ* 2.1404 (*SEG* 8.170)
Date: Before 70 C.E.

θ[ε]όδοτος Οὐεττήνου, ἱερεὺς καὶ
ἀ[ρ]χισυνάγωγος, υἱὸς ἀρχισυν[αγώ]-
γ[ο]υ, υἱωνὸς ἀρχισυν[α]γώγου, ᾠκο-
δόμησε τὴν συναγωγὴν εἰς ἀν[άγν]ω-
σ[ιν] νόμου καὶ εἰς [δ]ιδαχ[ὴ]ν ἐντολῶν, καὶ   5

τ[ὸ]ν ξενῶνα, κα[ὶ τὰ] δώματα καὶ τὰ χρη-
σ[τ]ήρια τῶν ὑδάτων εἰς κατάλυμα τοῖ-
ς [χ]ρήζουσιν ἀπὸ τῆς ξέ[ν]ης, ἥν ἐθεμε-
λ[ίω]σαν οἱ πατέρες [α]ὐτοῦ καὶ οἱ πρε-
σ[β]ύτεροι καὶ Σιμων[ί]δης.   10

Theodotos, son of Vettenus, priest and ruler of the synagogue [*archi-synagōgos*], son of a ruler of the synagogue [*archisynagōgos*], grandson of a ruler of the synagogue [*archisynagōgos*], built the synagogue [*synagōgē*] for the reading of the law and the teaching of the commandments, and also the guest chamber and the upper rooms and the ritual pools of water for accommodating those needing them from abroad, which his fathers, the elders [*presbyteroi*] and Simonides founded.

Literature: Weill, *La cité de David*, 98–100, 186–90, pl. XXVA; Reinach, "L'inscription," 46–56; Clermont-Ganneau, "Découverte," 190–97, pl. XVIIIA; Vincent, "Découverte," 247–77; FitzGerald, "Theodotos," 175–81; Holleau, "Une inscription," 1–57; Deissman, *Light*, 439–41, fig. 80; Sukenik, *Ancient Synagogues*, 69–72, pl. XVIa; Schwabe, "Greek Inscriptions," 362–65; *DF*, 70–71 (no. 79); Schürer, *HJP* 2.425; Hüttenmeister, *Synagogen in Israel*, 192–95; Roth-Gerson, *Greek Inscriptions*, 76–86; Myers, "Synagogue," 252; Kee, "Transformation," 8; idem, "Early Christianity," 5–6; idem, "Changing Meaning," 283; idem, "Defining," 499; Flesher, "Palestinian Synagogues," 33–34; White *Social Origins*, 2.294–95 (no. 62); Riesner, "Synagogues," 192–200; Reich, "The Synagogue," 291–92; Fine, *This Holy Place*, 30; Atkinson, "Further Defining," 491–502; Strange, "Ancient Texts," 29; Binder, *Temple Courts*, 104–9, 157; van der Horst, "Ancient Synagogue," 18–43; Runesson, *Origins*, 226–31; Claußen, *Versammlung*, 186–91; Kloppenborg Verbin, "Theodotos," 243–80; Levine, *Ancient Synagogue*, 57–59; Martin, "Interpreting," 160–81.

Comments: French archaeologist Raimund Weill discovered this most famous of early synagogue inscriptions in 1913 during his excavations of the lower eastern slope of the Ophel, the ancient City of David, which rests below the Temple Mount in Jerusalem. Recovered in a cistern about 50 metres due west of remains often identified as the Tower of Siloam, the dedication provides a valuable snapshot of a synagogue that existed in Jerusalem during the Second Temple period.

This inscription was the centre of some controversy during the 1990s when Howard Kee challenged the earlier consensus that had dated it to the first century C.E., himself assigning an origin of two to three centuries later. This suggestion led several researchers, especially Riesner and Kloppenborg Verbin, to carefully re-examine both the monument's palaeography and the archaeological context of its recovery. Their conclusions vindicated the earlier view and firmly reestablished a pre-70 dating.

Of the several remarkable features of this inscription, one of the most striking is its mention of the patron, Theodotos, as both priest and ruler of the synagogue (*archisynagōgos*). Moreover, he is described as being the son and grandson of similar office-holders for this congregation. This identification suggests not only the potential for hereditary leadership within the early synagogues, but also the possibility that priestly families commonly populated such dynasties (cf. Philo, *Hypoth.* 7.12–3, No. 162; *CJZ* 72, No. 133). The inscription also refers to "the elders" (*hoi presbyteroi*; cf. Luke 7:3–5, No. 6) as holding subsidiary leadership and patronal roles under Theodotos and his predecessors.

Vettenus, the surname of Theodotos, undoubtedly derives from either the Vetteni or Vettieni families of Rome, who are attested from the first century B.C.E. This connection has led some commentators to infer that Theodotos was their freed slave and, further, that his synagogue should be identified with the so-called "Synagogue of the Freedmen" mentioned in Acts 6:9 (No. 18). Such conjectures, however, overlook the naming conventions of the period, which indicate that Theodotos was a freeborn man who was *not* a Roman citizen (a manumitted slave of a Roman family was by law a citizen). It is thus more likely that Theodotos' father was simply named after the Vett(i)eni out of gratitude for some unspecified kindness to his family.

Nevertheless, the preceding observations suggest that Theodotos' ancestors once lived outside of Palestine and returned to their homeland around the turn of the era. This supposition is strengthened by the fact that the dedication was inscribed in Greek, not Aramaic, and many of the synagogue's ancillary functions are geared towards pilgrims from the Diaspora—although these latter could conceivably have applied to any visitor from beyond Jerusalem's immediate environs.

If the founders were indeed repatriate Jews, they did not call their building a *proseuchē*, the more common word for the synagogue in the Diaspora. Instead, they adopted the term *synagōgē*, which appears to have held the widest currency inside Palestine during the Second Temple period (e.g., Mark 1:21, No. 4; Luke 7:5, No. 6).

The dedication gives the primary purpose of the synagogue as being a place for the reading and study of Torah—the most widely attested function for synagogues during this period. The other attributes are clearly secondary and more focussed on tending to the needs of pilgrims, either out of hospitality or as a means of revenue for the congregation.

In particular, the ancillary rooms associated with these functions could have accommodated those seeking to celebrate the Jewish feasts inside Jerusalem, especially Passover in the "guest-chamber" (*xenōn . . . eis kataluma*; cf. Mark 14:14; Luke 22:11) and Sukkoth in the "upper rooms" (*dōmata*), this last probably a reference to rooftop cubicles where tents could be erected (Neh 8:16, LXX).

Similarly, the cryptic phrase *chrēstēria tōn hydatōn*—literally "oracles of water"—carries a cultic sense and thus likely refers to ritual baths that pilgrims could use for purification rites (Josephus, *C. Ap.* 2.104; Acts 21:24–6). Weill himself originally connected these with several pools unearthed near the discovery site (Weill, pl. III, P1–P6). These latter can now be more accurately identified as *miqwaoth* or ritual baths.

2.1.11   *Magdala*

No. 27
Source: *Archaeological.*
Date: First century B.C.E./first century C.E.

Literature: Corbo, "Archaeologici a Magdala"; idem, "Citta romana"; Netzer, "Springhouse"; Binder, *Temple Courts*, 193–96; Runesson, *Origins*, 175, n. 18; Levine, *Ancient Synagogue*, 71–72.

Comments: Corbo first identified this structure (8.2 × 7.2 m) as a synagogue that was subsequently transformed into a springhouse during the first century C.E. Since that time, Netzer has argued convincingly that the building was a springhouse originally, not just in its second phase. One of the main arguments in favour of Netzer's conclusion is that the water channels on three sides of the hall were part of the earliest building, not later additions. Also, Corbo's initial identification of benches in the hall was incorrect, since their size and design conform to those of a stairway (Binder). The renovation of the edifice in the first century C.E., which involved the raising and replacement of the basalt slab floor, was prompted by flooding. While some studies still include the Magdala building as a first-century synagogue, the authors of this volume believe this identification should be abandoned.

2.1.12   *Masada*

No. 28
Source: *Archaeological.*
Date: First century C.E.

Literature: Yadin, "Synagogue at Masada"; idem, "Masada" in *NEAEHL* 3.793–816; Cohen, "Masada"; Foerster, "Masada and Herodion"; Netzer, *Masada III*; Chiat, *Handbook*, 248–251; Fine, *This Holy Place*, 30–31; Binder, *Temple Courts*, 172–79; Runesson; *Origins*, 357–58; Levine, *Ancient Synagogue*, 61–62.

Comments: Initially excavated by Yigael Yadin and his team in the early 1960s, this edifice was part of Herod's desert fortress at Masada. Its inital construction is thus dated to the second half of the first century B.C.E. While the original function of the building is uncertain, renovations made during the First Jewish Revolt clearly adapted it for use as a synagogue.

After the transformation of the building, the main hall had five columns in two rows, and benches along each of the four walls. The benches are arranged in four tiers on all except the northern side, where there is only one row, as in the Gamla synagogue. The hall measures 15 × 12 m, including a small chamber (5.7 × 3.5 m) in the northern corner. The floor of the main hall was made of ash lime plaster over a layer of stones and potsherds; the chamber had a floor of pressed earth.

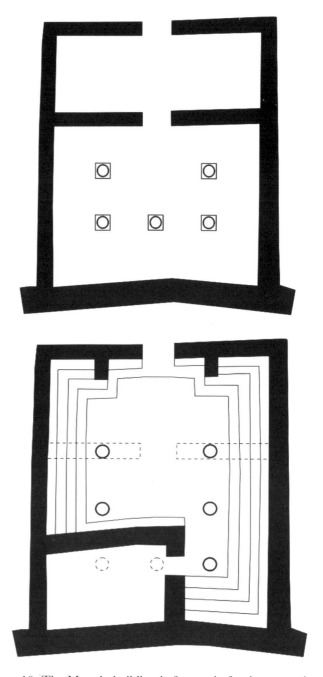

Figure 10. The Masada building before and after its renovation into a synagogue

The ancillary chamber yielded several interesting finds. The floor of the room contained an oven and bowls, while soundings beneath the floor led to the discovery of two pits. These contained parchment fragments of passages from Deuteronomy and Ezekiel. Just outside the chamber were found two ostraca inscribed with the words "priest's tithe" and "Hezekiah."

Observing that a *miqweh* was uncovered 15 meters north of the edifice, Binder suggests that it too was built by the rebels. Taken together, the evidence strongly suggests that this building should be identified as a synagogue, and few (Chiat) would doubt this today. In fact, the Masada building has served as a model for identifying other early structures as synagogues, mainly because of the convergence of several types of evidence found here, not least the fragments of Deuteronomy and Ezekiel. In addition, the ostracon mentioning the "priest's tithe" may add to other evidence supporting the theory of the priestly involvement in synagogues, as mentioned in the introduction to this volume.

2.1.13   *Modiʿin*

No. 29
Source: *Archaeological.*
Date: Hasmonean period/second half of the first century B.C.E.

Literature: Onn et al., "Khirbet Umm el-ʿUmdan"; Weksler-Bdolah et al., "Hasmonean Village" 72–76; Levine, *Ancient Synagogue*, 70; Strange, "Archaeology."

Comments: This building was discovered during excavations of the village of Modiʿin by Alexander Onn in 2000–2001. The village dates back to the Persian period, but most of the remains come from the Roman era. Among the discoveries found were a *miqweh*, a bathhouse, and a public building identified as a synagogue. The original building (11 × 6.5 m) dates back to the Hasmonean period, and the edifice may have served as a synagogue already at that time (so Levine, but cf. Onn et al., p. 66). It had a rectangular niche in the northern wall.

The second and principle phase dates to the Herodian period. The main hall measures ca. 12 × 10 m and had a floor paved with stone. Benches lined all walls, and eight columns in two rows (four each) supported the roof. Fragments of red, white and yellow painted plaster (secco), dated to the first century B.C.E., were found. Alterations were made in the building in the first century; this third phase of the edifice ended during the Bar Kochba revolt when the building was destroyed. A small room (2.5 × 2 m) was located to the northeast of the main hall, with a passageway connecting the structures. Levine notes that this synagogue is among the oldest discovered in Judaea so far, dating from about the same period as the Gamla synagogue and the early edifice mentioned in the Theodotos inscription.

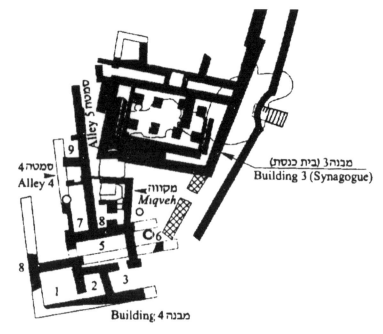

Figure 11. Plan of the synagogue at Modi'in

2.1.14   *Nabratein (Nevoraya)*

No. 30
Source: *Archaeological.*
Date: Mid-second century C.E.

Literature: Kohl and Watzinger, *Antike Synagogen*, 101–6; Meyers, Strange, and Meyers, "Second Preliminary Report"; Meyers and Meyers, "Real Lost Ark"; Meyers, "Nabratein"; Meyers, "Torah Shrine"; Meyers and Meyers, *Ancient Nabratein*; Chiat, *Handbook*, 41–45; Hachlili, *Land of Israel*, 398–99; Runesson, *Origins*, 204, 358, 361.

Comments: Located 4 kilometres north of Safed, these ruins were investigated by Kohl and Watzinger in 1905 (published in 1916), but comprehensive excavations were not undertaken until Eric M. Meyers and his team worked on the site in the early 1980s. Three buildings constructed on top of each other have been identified; the earliest is one of the few public buildings of the second century C.E. to be identified as a synagogue. The date is confirmed by coins and pottery sealed under the plaster floor or under the foundations of the walls and benches. This edifice (11.2 m × 9.35 m), which was oriented so that the broad wall with a double bema was on the south, facing Jerusalem, had four columns. At least one of the platforms probably supported a Torah shrine. The two platforms are the earliest found in any synagogue (platforms

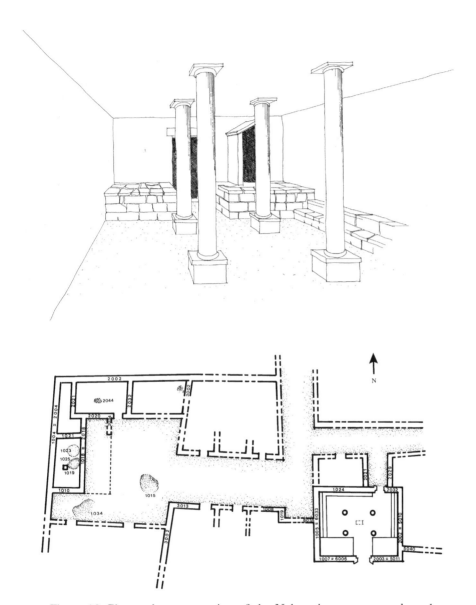

Figure 12. Plan and reconstruction of the Nabratein synagogue, phase 1

and Torah shrines became common in the fourth century c.e.). A depression in
the centre of the room may indicate the location of a reader's platform (Meyers).
Benches were found along all walls except the one facing Jerusalem.

2.1.15 *Nazareth*

No. 31
Source: Literary. Mark 6:1–6
Date: Ca. 70 c.e.

[1] Καὶ ἐξῆλθεν ἐκεῖθεν καὶ ἔρχεται εἰς τὴν πατρίδα αὐτοῦ, καὶ
ἀκολουθοῦσιν αὐτῷ οἱ μαθηταὶ αὐτοῦ. 2 καὶ γενομένου σαββάτου
ἤρξατο διδάσκειν ἐν τῇ συναγωγῇ, καὶ πολλοὶ ἀκούοντες ἐξεπλήσσοντο
λέγοντες· πόθεν τούτῳ ταῦτα, καὶ τίς ἡ σοφία ἡ δοθεῖσα τούτῳ, καὶ
αἱ δυνάμεις τοιαῦται διὰ τῶν χειρῶν αὐτοῦ γινόμεναι; [3] οὐχ οὗτός
ἐστιν ὁ τέκτων, ὁ υἱὸς τῆς Μαρίας καὶ ἀδελφὸς Ἰακώβου καὶ Ἰωσῆτος
καὶ Ἰούδα καὶ Σίμωνος; καὶ οὐκ εἰσὶν αἱ ἀδελφαὶ αὐτοῦ ὧδε πρὸς
ἡμᾶς; καὶ ἐσκανδαλίζοντο ἐν αὐτῷ. [4] καὶ ἔλεγεν αὐτοῖς ὁ Ἰησοῦς
ὅτι οὐκ ἔστιν προφήτης ἄτιμος εἰ μὴ ἐν τῇ πατρίδι αὐτοῦ καὶ ἐν τοῖς
συγγενεῦσιν αὐτοῦ καὶ ἐν τῇ οἰκίᾳ αὐτοῦ. [5] καὶ οὐκ ἐδύνατο ἐκεῖ
ποιῆσαι οὐδεμίαν δύναμιν, εἰ μὴ ὀλίγοις ἀρρώστοις ἐπιθεὶς τὰς χεῖρας
ἐθεράπευσεν. [6] καὶ ἐθαύμαζεν διὰ τὴν ἀπιστίαν αὐτῶν.

[1] He left that place and came to his hometown, and his disciples
followed him. [2] On the Sabbath he began to teach in the synagogue
[*synagōgē*], and many who heard him were astounded. They said,
"Where did this man get all this? What is this wisdom that has been
given to him? What deeds of power are being done by his hands! [3]
Is not this the carpenter, the son of Mary and brother of James and
Joses and Judas and Simon, and are not his sisters here with us?" And
they took offense at him. [4] Then Jesus said to them, "Prophets are
not without honor, except in their hometown, and among their own
kin, and in their own house." [5] And he could do no deed of power
there, except that he laid his hands on a few sick people and cured
them. [6] And he was amazed at their unbelief.

Literature: As a general reference to commentaries see Pesch, Guelich, and
Marcus, *Comm., ad loc.* Binder, *Temple Courts*, 155; Runesson, *Origins*, 214–20.

Comments: A parallel text is found in Matt 13:53–58 (No. 32; see also the
first comment to Luke 4:16–30, No. 33). Mark 6:1–6a is a kind of commentary
on what has been said about Jesus' power in words and deeds in 1:21–5:43.

The first part of this presentation of Jesus and his ministry ends with his sharp rejection by the religious authorities (3:1–6), the second part by a rejection of the people in his hometown, including his own kin (6:1–6a; cf. 3:31–35). This pericope is the last in Mark mentioning Jesus' presence and teaching in synagogues. The use of the imperfect in vv. 3c–5 could be understood as indicating that Jesus had left the synagogue scene already in v. 3c. The content of Jesus' teaching in the synagogue can surely be implied from what is said in 1:14–15 and 1:21–28, as well as in 1:21–5:43 as a whole (see the comments on 1:21–29 [No. 4] and 1:39 [No. 45]).

Jesus' appearance in the synagogue here leads to many questions, some of which reference news of his mighty deeds. Answers are implied by formulations in the text: "that has been given to him [by God]," "[God working] through his hands," and Jesus as "prophet [sent by God]." Jesus is the agent through whom God is at work in the synagogue in Nazareth.

The parallel version in Matt 13:53–58 is told in another context, and the questions have been abbreviated and arranged in a more logical form with "Where then did this man get all this" placed in the final position. The synagogue there is described as "their synagogue."

No. 32
Source: *Literary*. Matt 13:53–58
Date: Ca. 80–90 C.E.

[53] Καὶ ἐγένετο ὅτε ἐτέλεσεν ὁ Ἰησοῦς τὰς παραβολὰς ταύτας, μετῆρεν ἐκεῖθεν. [54] καὶ ἐλθὼν εἰς τὴν πατρίδα αὐτοῦ ἐδίδασκεν αὐτοὺς ἐν τῇ συναγωγῇ αὐτῶν, ὥστε ἐκπλήσσεσθαι αὐτοὺς καὶ λέγειν· πόθεν τούτῳ ἡ σοφία αὕτη καὶ αἱ δυνάμεις; [55] οὐχ οὗτός ἐστιν ὁ τοῦ τέκτονος υἱός; οὐχ ἡ μήτηρ αὐτοῦ λέγεται Μαριὰμ καὶ οἱ ἀδελφοὶ αὐτοῦ Ἰάκωβος καὶ Ἰωσὴφ καὶ Σίμων καὶ Ἰούδας; [56] καὶ αἱ ἀδελφαὶ αὐτοῦ οὐχὶ πᾶσαι πρὸς ἡμᾶς εἰσιν; πόθεν οὖν τούτῳ ταῦτα πάντα; [57] καὶ ἐσκανδαλίζοντο ἐν αὐτῷ. ὁ δὲ Ἰησοῦς εἶπεν αὐτοῖς· οὐκ ἔστιν προφήτης ἄτιμος εἰ μὴ ἐν τῇ πατρίδι καὶ ἐν τῇ οἰκίᾳ αὐτοῦ. [58] καὶ οὐκ ἐποίησεν ἐκεῖ δυνάμεις πολλὰς διὰ τὴν ἀπιστίαν αὐτῶν.

[53] When Jesus had finished these parables, he left that place. [54] He came to his hometown and began to teach the people in their synagogue [*synagōgē*], so that they were astounded and said, "Where did this man get this wisdom and these deeds of power? [55] Is not this the carpenter's son? Is not his mother called Mary? And are not his brothers James and Joseph and Simon and Judas? [56] And are not all his sisters with us? Where then did this man get all this?" [57] And they took offense at him. But Jesus said to them, "Prophets are not without honor except in their own country and in their own house." [58] And he did not do many deeds of power there, because of their unbelief.

Literature: As a general reference to commentaries, see Bonnard, Luz and Hagner, *Comm., ad loc.* Binder, *Temple Courts*, 155; Runesson, *Origins*, 355–57.

Comments: See comments on Mark 6:1–6 (No. 31). In comparison with the parallel version, Mark 6:1–6, Matthew has very much abbreviated the text and structured it into a concentric, chiastic pattern with the questions in the centre, the first and the last one beginning with "where" (*pothen*). The implicit answers given in Mark ("that has been given to him," "being done by his hands") are omitted. What has been said about Jesus' wisdom and mighty works before (Matt 9:35, No. 51) is repeated here in the context of the synagogue.

No. 33
Source: *Literary.* Luke 4:16–30
Date: Ca. 80–90 C.E.

[16] Καὶ ἦλθεν εἰς Ναζαρά, οὗ ἦν τεθραμμένος, καὶ εἰσῆλθεν κατὰ τὸ εἰωθὸς αὐτῷ ἐν τῇ ἡμέρᾳ τῶν σαββάτων εἰς τὴν συναγωγὴν καὶ ἀνέστη ἀναγνῶναι. [17] καὶ ἐπεδόθη αὐτῷ βιβλίον τοῦ προφήτου Ἡσαΐου καὶ ἀναπτύξας τὸ βιβλίον εὗρεν τὸν τόπον οὗ ἦν γεγραμμένον· [18] πνεῦμα κυρίου ἐπ' ἐμὲ οὗ εἵνεκεν ἔχρισέν με εὐαγγελίσασθαι πτωχοῖς, ἀπέσταλκέν με, κηρύξαι αἰχμαλώτοις ἄφεσιν καὶ τυφλοῖς ἀνάβλεψιν,, ἀποστεῖλαι τεθραυσμένους ἐν ἀφέσει, [19] κηρύξαι ἐνιαυτὸν κυρίου δεκτόν. [20] καὶ πτύξας τὸ βιβλίον ἀποδοὺς τῷ ὑπηρέτῃ ἐκάθισεν· καὶ πάντων οἱ ὀφθαλμοὶ ἐν τῇ συναγωγῇ ἦσαν ἀτενίζοντες αὐτῷ. [21] ἤρξατο δὲ λέγειν πρὸς αὐτοὺς ὅτι σήμερον πεπλήρωται ἡ γραφὴ αὕτη ἐν τοῖς ὠσὶν ὑμῶν. [22] Καὶ πάντες ἐμαρτύρουν αὐτῷ καὶ ἐθαύμαζον ἐπὶ τοῖς λόγοις τῆς χάριτος τοῖς ἐκπορευομένοις ἐκ τοῦ στόματος αὐτοῦ καὶ ἔλεγον· οὐχὶ υἱός ἐστιν Ἰωσὴφ οὗτος; [23] καὶ εἶπεν πρὸς αὐτούς· πάντως ἐρεῖτέ μοι τὴν παραβολὴν ταύτην· ἰατρέ, θεράπευσον σεαυτόν· ὅσα ἠκούσαμεν γενόμενα εἰς τὴν Καφαρναοὺμ ποίησον καὶ ὧδε ἐν τῇ πατρίδι σου. [24] εἶπεν δέ· ἀμὴν λέγω ὑμῖν ὅτι οὐδεὶς προφήτης δεκτός ἐστιν ἐν τῇ πατρίδι αὐτοῦ. [25] ἐπ' ἀληθείας δὲ λέγω ὑμῖν, πολλαὶ χῆραι ἦσαν ἐν ταῖς ἡμέραις Ἠλίου ἐν τῷ Ἰσραήλ, ὅτε ἐκλείσθη ὁ οὐρανὸς ἐπὶ ἔτη τρία καὶ μῆνας ἕξ, ὡς ἐγένετο λιμὸς μέγας ἐπὶ πᾶσαν τὴν γῆν, [26] καὶ πρὸς οὐδεμίαν αὐτῶν ἐπέμφθη Ἠλίας εἰ μὴ εἰς Σάρεπτα τῆς Σιδωνίας πρὸς γυναῖκα χήραν. [27] καὶ πολλοὶ λεπροὶ ἦσαν ἐν τῷ Ἰσραὴλ ἐπὶ Ἐλισαίου τοῦ προφήτου, καὶ οὐδεὶς αὐτῶν ἐκαθαρίσθη εἰ μὴ Ναιμὰν ὁ Σύρος. [28] καὶ ἐπλήσθησαν πάντες θυμοῦ ἐν τῇ συναγωγῇ ἀκούοντες ταῦτα [29] καὶ ἀναστάντες ἐξέβαλον αὐτὸν ἔξω τῆς πόλεως καὶ ἤγαγον αὐτὸν ἕως ὀφρύος τοῦ ὄρους ἐφ' οὗ ἡ πόλις ᾠκοδόμητο αὐτῶν ὥστε κατακρημνίσαι αὐτόν· [30] αὐτὸς δὲ διελθὼν διὰ μέσου αὐτῶν ἐπορεύετο.

[16] When he came to Nazareth, where he had been brought up, he went to the synagogue [*synagōgē*] on the Sabbath day, as was his custom. He stood up to read, [17] and the scroll of the prophet Isaiah was given to him. He unrolled the scroll and found the place where it was written: [18] "The Spirit of the Lord is upon me, because he has anointed me to bring good news to the poor. He has sent me to proclaim release to the captives and recovery of sight to the blind, to let the oppressed go free, [19] to proclaim the year of the Lord's favor." [20] And he rolled up the scroll, gave it back to the attendant [*hypēretēs*], and sat down. The eyes of all in the synagogue [*synagōgē*] were fixed on him. [21] Then he began to say to them, "Today this scripture has been fulfilled in your hearing." [22] All spoke well of him and were amazed at the gracious words that came from his mouth. They said, "Is not this Joseph's son?" [23] He said to them, "Doubtless you will quote to me this proverb, 'Doctor, cure yourself!' And you will say, 'Do here also in your hometown the things that we have heard you did at Capernaum.'" [24] And he said, "Truly I tell you, no prophet is accepted in the prophet's hometown. [25] But the truth is, there were many widows in Israel in the time of Elijah, when the heaven was shut up three years and six months, and there was a severe famine over all the land; [26] yet Elijah was sent to none of them except to a widow at Zarephath in Sidon. [27] There were also many lepers in Israel in the time of the prophet Elisha, and none of them was cleansed except Naaman the Syrian." [28] When they heard this, all in the synagogue [*synagōgē*] were filled with rage. [29] They got up, drove him out of the town, and led him to the brow of the hill on which their town was built, so that they might hurl him off the cliff. [30] But he passed through the midst of them and went on his way.

Literature: As a general reference to commentaries, see Fitzmyer, Schürmann and Bovon, *Comm., ad loc.* Binder, *Temple Courts*, 368–70, 400–402; Levine, *Ancient Synagogue*, 46–48; Claußen, *Versammlung*, 215–16; Runesson, *Origins*, 214–20; Riesner, "Synagogues," 202–3; Stegemann, *Synagoge und Obrigkeit*, 215.

Comments: Jesus' attendence in the synagogue on the Sabbath is an important element in the Synoptic tradition (Matt 12:1, 9; Mark 1:21; 3:2–3; 6:1; Luke 4:16, 31; 6:6; 13:10). His activity there is often described as teaching (*didaskein*) the synagogue crowd (Matt 4:23; 9:35; 13:54; Mark 1:21–22; 6:2; Luke 4:15, 16, 31; 6:6; 13:10; John 18:20).

Luke begins his account of the Galilean ministry of Jesus in 4:14 (see the comments on Luke 4:14–15, No. 53). The Lucan composition in 4:16–30, inspired by Mark 6:1–6, has a clear programmatic character, foreshadowed in 2:34 and presaging the entire ministry of Jesus. It summarizes not only Jesus' message, but also Jewish reactions to it—both reception and rejection—and announces the inclusion of Gentiles.

The historicity of the information Luke gives about the synagogue service
is much debated. Does it reflect the time of Jesus or that of Luke? With
regard to the service as a whole, Luke gives very limited information. Did it
include readings from the Torah and the Prophets, translations of the texts
into Aramaic, a sermon expounding the scriptures, recitation of the Shema,
psalms and benedictions, including some form of the *Shemoneh Esreh*? If so,
Luke remains silent about their inclusion.

Jesus is presented as taking the initiative in reading the biblical text.
Perhaps he was invited by the synagogue leader to do that, as were Paul and
Barnabas at Pisidian Antioch (Acts 13:15). The servant mentioned, a *hypēretēs*,
was some kind of assistant in the synagogue. Elsewhere, the word *hypēretēs* is
used as a title in a synagogue inscription from Egypt, probably referencing
an overseer of other synagogue servants (see the comment on *CPJ* 1.138, No.
170). The servant is said to have given Jesus a scroll of the prophet Isaiah.
Corroborating such a possibility is the discovery of a scroll from the Prophets
(Ezekiel) among the remains of the synagogue at Masada. From the text, it is
not clear if Jesus read a passage from Isaiah assigned for this service or if he
chose it himself. In either case, 11QMelch 2:16 connects the chosen passage
with the Jubilee Year.

Jesus unrolled the scroll, read it, rolled it up and gave it back to the attendant. Taken from the LXX, the text read is a combination of Isa 61:1a,b,d,
58:6d and 61:2a. Luke summarizes the ensuing sermon in a single sentence.
At first, it results in a positive reaction from the synagogue crowd. Subsequent
discussion, followed by additional teaching by Jesus, elicits a strong negative
reaction.

Thus Luke condenses his view of Jesus' entire ministry into a single synagogue episode.

2.1.16   *Qatzion*

No. 34
Source: *Archaeological; inscription.*
Date: Between 196 and 198 C.E., probably 197 C.E.

Literature: Kohl and Watzinger, *Antiken Synagogen*, 160–61; Chiat, *Handbook*;
62–63; Hachlili, *Land of Israel*, 212, 396–97; Foerster, *Galilean Synagogues*, 103–5;
Fine, "Late Antique Palestine"; Runesson, *Origins*, 175, n. 18; Levine, *Ancient
Synagogue*, 84.

Comments: Located 9 kilometres northeast of Safed, the remains of this edifice were first discovered in the 19th century. After investigations by Kohl and
Watzinger, as well as others, the site was abandoned only to be rediscovered
in the late 20th century (Hachlili). Since the building has not been completely
excavated, further investigations are crucial in order to enable well-founded
judgments regarding the nature of this structure. At the moment, the most
important find is a lintel containing a six-line Greek dedicatory inscription men-

tioning the Roman emperor Septimius Severus. It securely dates the structure
to 197 C.E. The text of the inscription is translated by Chiat as follows:

> For the salvation of the Roman Caesars,
> L[ucius] Sept[imius] Severus Pius
> Pert[inax] Aug[ustus], and M[arcus]
> Aur[elius] A[nton]inus [[and L[ucius]
> Sept[imius] G]]eta, their sons, by a
> vow of the Jews.

Dedicatory inscriptions for the health or long life of non-Jewish rulers and
emperors are well attested in Jewish inscriptions from Egypt in relation to
proseuchai (prayer halls) or specific structures within them (cf. below, Nos. 144,
150–152, 156, 158, 159). The Mindius Faustus inscription from Ostia, dating
to the second century (No. 176), is another example. The present inscription
is the only one of its kind from the land of Israel. However, it has not been
established whether the structure is in fact a synagogue (Foerster), or if the
Jews mentioned donated a non-Jewish temple to Graeco-Roman inhabitants
of the area (Kohl and Watzinger; Fine). The fact that a Jewish community
could donate a temple to non-Jews should not surprise us, since non-Jewish
donations of synagogues to Jewish Diaspora communities are well attested (cf.
No. 103, Julia Severa). Modern religious sensitivities should not be applied to
ancient social systems of benefaction. Until further excavations can determine
the nature of the edifice, it seems best to understand the remains as belonging
to a non-Jewish temple.

2.1.17   *Qiryat Sefer*

No. 35
Source: *Archaeological.*
Date: Early first century C.E.

Literature: Magen, "Kiryat Sefer," 25–32; Binder, *Temple Courts*, 197;
Runesson, *Origins*, 358–61; Levine, *Ancient Synagogue*, 69.

Comments: The village of Qiryat Sefer is located close to Modi'in, ca. 32
kilometres northwest of Jerusalem. The building, measuring 9.6 × 9.6 m, was
discovered during excavations led by Magen in 1995. Four columns with Doric
capitals were located between the open space in the centre and benches lining
three of the walls. The floor was paved with large flagstones. The façade was
constructed using hewn stones with margins typical of Herodian building style
(Levine). Given the features of the building, as well as its location in the village
at a prominent open space, the identification of this edifice as a synagogue is
highly probable. The village—and thus the synagogue—was abandoned as a
result of the Bar Kochbah revolt.

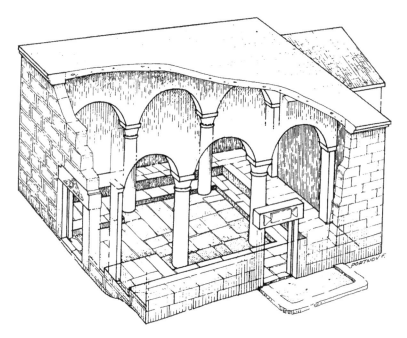

Figure 13. Reconstruction of the Qiryat Sefer synagogue

2.1.18   *Qumran*

No. 36
Source: *Literary.* CD 11.22–12.1
Date: While some parts of the document may be older, most scholars date
the final composition of the text to ca. 100 B.C.E.

21 וכל הבא אל 22 בית השתחות אל יבא טמא כבוס ובהרע החצוצרות הקהל 23
יתקדם או יתאחר ולא ישביתו את העבודה כולה [כ]י בית 12.1 קודש הוא

And everyone who enters [22] a house of prostration [*bet hishtahavot*]
should not enter with impurity requiring washing; and when the trumpets of the assembly sound, [23] he may advance or retreat, but they
should not stop the whole service, [f]or [12.1] it is a holy house.[7]

Literature: Kosmala, *Hebräer*, 353–54; Steudel, "House of Prostration"; Falk,
Prayers, 243–45; Binder, *Temple Courts*, 455; Runesson, *Origins*, 334–35; Levine,
Ancient Synagogue, 64–65.

---

[7] Translation by Martinez.

Comments: While it has been suggested that *bet hishtahavot* ("House of Prostration") refers to a synagogue building (so Steudel; cf. Levine), others have argued that what is discussed here is the Jerusalem temple (Falk; cf. Runesson). In this regard, it is of interest that the Greek translation that comes closest to this Hebrew expression is *oikos proseuchēs* (cf. Binder); this, in turn, may speak in favour of the term *proseuchē* originally having been a temple term, which, like other temple terms, came to be used for synagogues too around the turn of the era (Runesson, 335, 429–36). It is clear that the terminology used for what is today called "synagogue" in English was fluid at this time, and that, more often than not, temple and synagogue terms overlapped.

No. 37
Source: Literary. CD 20.2, 10–13
Date: While some parts of the document may be older, most scholars date the final composition of the text to ca. 100 B.C.E.

וכן המשפט [2] לכל באי עדת אנשי תמים הקדש ויקוץ מעשות פקרדי
ישרים...[10] אין להם חלק בבית התורה:
כמשפט רעיהם אשר שבו [11] עם אנשי הלאון ישפטו כי דברו תועה על
חקי הצדק ומאסו {.} בברית [12] ואמנה
אשר קימו בארץ דמשק והוא ברית החדשה: 13 ולא יהיה להם {ו}
ולמשפחותיהם חלק בבית התורה

And thus is the judgment [2] of everyone who enters the congregation of the men of perfect holiness and is slack in the fulfilment of the instructions of the upright...[10] For them there shall be no part in the house of the law [*bet ha-Torah*]. *Blank* They shall be judged according to the judgment of their companions, who turned round [11] with insolent men, for they spoke falsehood about the just regulation and despised [12] the covenant {...} and the pact which they established in the land of Damascus, which is the new covenant. [13] And neither for them nor their families shall there be a part in the house of the law [*bet ha-Torah*].[8]

Literature: Binder, *Temple Courts*, 455–56; Runesson, *Origin*, 335.

Comments: This passage from the Damascus Document may contain an expression used for synagogue: *bet ha-Torah*. We know from Philo (No. 40) that Essene synagogue rituals were focussed on the reading and discussion of Torah. While the term may have been used metaphorically, this does not

---

[8] Translation by Martinez.

exclude the possibility of its use for the space in which the group gathered (cf. the double use of *synagōgē* for both congregation and building in Berenice, No. 133; see also Zahavy, *Jewish Prayer*, 55, who refers to diverse uses of the Hebrew *bet* in relation to different institutions: the word can denote both building and assembly).

No. 38
Source: *Literary.* 1QM 3.3–4
Date: 1QM is a composite document; the parts were combined by the middle of the first century B.C.E.

ועל החצוצרות מקרא ה{ס} שרים יכתובו נשיאי אל ועל החצוצרות המסרורת
יכתובו סרך אל ועל החצוצרות אנשי 4 השם {יכתבו} ראשי אבות העדה
בהאספם לבית מועד יכתובו תעודות אל לעצת קודש

On the trumpets of muster of the commanders they shall write: "Princes of God". And on the trumpets for enlisting, they shall write "Rule of God". And on the trumpets of [4] the men of renown, {they shall write} chiefs of the fathers of the congregation, when they meet in the meeting-house (*bet moʿed*), they shall write: "God's directives for the holy council".[9]

Literature: Kosmala, *Hebräer*, 351–63; Binder, *Temple Courts*, 454–55; Runesson, *Origins*, 335.

Comments: It has been noted that while the Hebrew term *bet ha-kneset* and the Aramaic *bet knisah*, both equivalent to the Greek *synagōgē*, are not in evidence for the first century C.E., *bet moʿed* (meeting-house), which also translates well into Greek as *synagōgē*, is used in the War Scroll. It may be noted in this regard that Philo uses the term *synagōgē*, not his usual *proseuchē*, when describing the meeting place of the Essenes (No. 40). It is probable that *bet moʿed* represents the earliest known Hebrew term for synagogue. (See also the discussion of the archaeological remains, No. 41). Since we know that *synagōgē* was used widely, it cannot be excluded that *bet moʿed* was used beyond the sectarian community.

No. 39
Source: *Literary.* Josephus, *B. J.* 2.128–32
Date: *De bello Judaico* consists of seven books and was published in the late 70s.

[128] Πρός γε μὴν τὸ θεῖον εὐσεβεῖς ἰδίως· πρὶν γὰρ ἀνασχεῖν τὸν ἥλιον οὐδὲν φθέγγονται τῶν βεβήλων, πατρίους δέ τινας εἰς αὐτὸν εὐχὰς

---

[9] Translation by Martinez.

ὥσπερ ἱκετεύοντες ἀνατεῖλαι. [129] καὶ μετὰ ταῦτα πρὸς ἃς ἕκαστοι τέχνας ἴσασιν ὑπὸ τῶν ἐπιμελητῶν διαφίενται, καὶ μέχρι πέμπτης ὥρας ἐργασάμενοι συντόνως πάλιν εἰς ἓν συναθροίζονται χωρίον, ζωσάμενοί τε σκεπάσμασιν λινοῖς οὕτως ἀπολούονται τὸ σῶμα ψυχροῖς ὕδασιν, καὶ μετὰ ταύτην τὴν ἁγνείαν εἰς ἴδιον οἴκημα συνίασιν, ἔνθα μηδενὶ τῶν ἑτεροδόξων ἐπιτέτραπται παρελθεῖν· αὐτοί τε καθαροὶ καθάπερ εἰς ἅγιόν τι τέμενος παραγίνονται τὸ δειπνητήριον. [130] καὶ καθισάντων μεθ᾽ ἡσυχίας ὁ μὲν σιτοποιὸς ἐν τάξει παρατίθησι τοὺς ἄρτους, ὁ δὲ μάγειρος ἓν ἀγγεῖον ἐξ ἑνὸς ἐδέσματος ἑκάστῳ παρατίθησιν. [131] προκατεύχεται δ᾽ ὁ ἱερεὺς τῆς τροφῆς, καὶ γεύσασθαί τινα πρὶν τῆς εὐχῆς ἀθέμιτον· ἀριστοποιησάμενος δ᾽ ἐπεύχεται πάλιν· ἀρχόμενοί τε καὶ παυόμενοι γεραίρουσι θεὸν ὡς χορηγὸν τῆς ζωῆς. ἔπειθ᾽ ὡς ἱερὰς καταθέμενοι τὰς ἐσθῆτας πάλιν ἐπ᾽ ἔργα μέχρι δείλης τρέπονται. [132] δειπνοῦσι δ᾽ ὁμοίως ὑποστρέψαντες συγκαθεζομένων τῶν ξένων, εἰ τύχοιεν αὐτοῖς παρόντες. οὔτε δὲ κραυγή ποτε τὸν οἶκον οὔτε θόρυβος μιαίνει, τὰς δὲ λαλιὰς ἐν τάξει παραχωροῦσιν ἀλλήλοις.

[128] Their piety towards their deity takes a peculiar form. Before the sun is up they utter no word on mundane matters, but offer to him certain prayers, which have been handed down from their forefathers, as though entreating him to rise. [129] They are then dismissed by their superiors to the various crafts in which they are severally proficient and are strenuously employed until the fifth hour, when they again assemble in one place and, after girding their loins with linen cloths, bathe their bodies in cold water. After this purification, they assemble in a private apartment [*idion oikema*] which none of the uninitiated is permitted to enter; pure now themselves, they repair to the refectory as to some sacred shrine [*eis hagion ti temenos*]. [130] When they have taken their seats in silence, the baker serves out the loaves to them in order, and the cook sets before each one plate with a single course. [131] Before the meal the priest says a grace, and none may partake until after the prayer. When breakfast is ended, he pronounces a further grace; thus, at the beginning and at the close they do homage to God as the bountiful giver of life. Then laying aside their raiment, as holy vestments, they again betake themselves to their labours until the evening. [132] On their return they sup in like manner, and any guests who may have arrived sit down with them. No clamour or disturbance ever pollutes their dwelling; they speak in turn, each making way for his neighbour.

Literature: Binder, *Temple Courts*, 461–63; Runesson, *Origins*, 181; Levine, *Ancient Synagogue*, 65.

Comments: The description given in this passage refers to a situation before 70 C.E. If this description of Essene customs could be linked to the archaeological remains at Qumran, locus 77 is surely the best candidate for the communal dining ritual (cf. No. 41). It may even be that Josephus based his text upon his own experience when investigating the Essene way of life in his youth (*Vita* 9–12; Binder). Of interest is Josephus' description of the refectory as a "sacred shrine." Such a view of a refectory would probably have been unusual to his readers.

After purification in cold water, the distinction between the initiated and uninitiated is played out in a "private apartment" (*idion oikema*), not apparently in the communal meal, to which guests could be invited (132). If the meal was eaten in locus 77, where then did the exclusive gathering take place? Possibly in locus 4, a smaller room with benches along all four walls, though *idion oikema* may refer to the entire Essene complex.

No. 40
Source: *Literary*. Philo, *Prob.* 80–83
Date: Ca. 10–30 C.E.

[80] φιλοσοφίας τε τὸ μὲν λογικὸν ὡς οὐκ ἀναγκαῖον εἰς κτῆσιν ἀρετῆς λογοθήραις, τὸ δὲ φυσικὸν ὡς μεῖζον ἢ κατὰ ἀνθρωπίνην φύσιν μετεωρολέσχαις ἀπολιπόντες, πλὴν ὅσον αὐτοῦ περὶ ὑπάρξεως θεοῦ καὶ τῆς τοῦ παντὸς γενέσεως φιλοσοφεῖται, τὸ ἠθικὸν εὖ μάλα διαπονοῦσιν ἀλείπταις χρώμενοι τοῖς πατρίοις νόμοις, οὓς ἀμήχανον ἀνθρωπίνην ἐπινοῆσαι ψυχὴν ἄνευ κατοκωχῆς ἐνθέου. [81] τούτους ἀναδιδάσκονται μὲν καὶ παρὰ τὸν ἄλλον χρόνον, ἐν δὲ ταῖς ἑβδό-μαις διαφερόντως. ἱερὰ γὰρ ἡ ἑβδόμη νενόμισται, καθ' ἣν τῶν ἄλλων ἀνέχοντες ἔργων, εἰς ἱεροὺς ἀφικνούμενοι τόπους, οἳ καλοῦνται συναγωγαί, καθ' ἡλικίας ἐν τάξεσιν ὑπὸ πρεσβυτέροις νέοι καθέζονται, μετὰ κόσμου τοῦ προσήκοντος ἔχοντες ἀκροατικῶς. [82] εἶθ' εἷς μέν τις τὰς βίβλους ἀναγινώσκει λαβών, ἕτερος δὲ τῶν ἐμπειροτάτων ὅσα μὴ γνώριμα παρελθὼν ἀναδιδάσκει· τὰ γὰρ πλεῖστα διὰ συμβόλων ἀρχαιοτρόπῳ ζηλώσει παρ' αὐτοῖς φιλοσοφεῖται. [83] παιδεύονται δὲ εὐσέβειαν, ὁσιότητα, δικαιοσύνην, οἰκονομίαν, πολιτείαν, ἐπιστήμην τῶν πρὸς ἀλήθειαν ἀγαθῶν καὶ κακῶν καὶ ἀδιαφόρων, αἱρέσεις ὧν χρὴ καὶ φυγὰς τῶν ἐναντίων, ὅροις καὶ κανόσι τριττοῖς χρώμενοι, τῷ τε φιλοθέῳ καὶ φιλαρέτῳ καὶ φιλανθρώπῳ

[80] As for philosophy they abandon the logical part to quibbling ver-balists as unnecessary for the acquisition of virtue, and the physical to visionary praters as beyond the grasp of human nature, only retaining

that part which treats philosophically of the existence of God and the creation of the universe. But the ethical part they study very industriously, taking for their trainers the laws of their fathers, which could not possibly have been conceived by the human soul without divine inspiration. [81] In these they are instructed at all other times, but particularly on the seventh days. For that day has been set apart to be kept holy and on it they abstain from all other work and proceed to sacred spots which they call synagogues (*synagōgai*). There, arranged in rows according to their ages, the younger below the elder, they sit decorously as befits the occasion with attentive ears. [82] Then one takes the books and reads aloud and another of especial proficiency comes forward and expounds what is not understood. For most of their philosophical study takes the form of allegory, and in this they emulate the tradition of the past. [83] They are trained in piety, holiness, justice, domestic and civic conduct, knowledge of what is truly good, or evil, or indifferent, and how to choose what they should and avoid the opposite, taking for their defining standards these three, love of God, love of virtue, love of men.

Literature: Radice and Runia, *Bibliography* 1937–1986; Runia, *Bibliography* 1987–1996; Vermes and Goodman, *Essenes*, 19–22; Fine, *This Holy Place*, 31; Binder, *Temple Courts*, 103, 453–54; Runesson, *Origins*, 172, 333–34, 354; Levine, *Ancient Synagogue*, 65–66.

Comments: The essay "Every good man is free" (*Quod omnis probus liber sit*) is considered as one of Philo's earlier works. He energetically argues that only the wise man is a free man. In §§71–109, he gives examples of the virtuous, among them the Essenes in Palestine, §§75–91. §§80–83 concentrate on their devout study of the Law, especially on the Sabbath.

§80 *As for philosophy*. As often in Philo, the ethical part, "the acquisition of virtue" and "the existence of God and the creation of the universe," is the main subject of the Jewish philosophy (see comments on No. 160, §30, and No. 166, §215).... *taking for their trainers the laws of their fathers*. Or more literally, "utilizing the ancestral laws as trainers" (from *aleiptēs* "anointer, trainer, teacher"). Vermes and Goodman translate, "constantly utilizing the ancestral laws."

§81 *they are instructed*. Or "they instruct themselves" (Vermes and Goodman), or "they are taught" (Yonge). Philo uses the verb *anadidaskesthai* "to be better instructed, learn better/anew/from the beginning," in §82 in the active form about the teacher, where it may be translated as "expounds" (Colson), or "explains" (Yonge, Vermes and Goodman)....*proceed to holy spots*. The Greek verb *aphikneisthai* normally means "arrive at, come to, reach," translated as "frequent" by Yonge. The place of the synagogue is regarded as holy. According to Philo the Essenes share houses ("no house belongs to any one man") and property, §§84–86... *synagogues*. Philo uses the common word *synagōgē* for a Jewish meeting hall only here, though the related *synagōgion* appears in *Somn.* 2.127 (No. 167) and *Legat.* 311 (No. 194). For *synagōgē* as assembly, see *Post.* 67; *Agr.* 44; *QG* 2.66 and *QE* 1.19.

§82 *one takes the books and reads aloud*. See comment on No. 160, §31. Philo uses the word *biblos* "papyrus, roll of papyrus, book" (not *biblion*) often when referring to sacred writings. The meaning could be a roll of papyrus containing several writings. Yonge gives the rendering "takes up the holy volume."...*of special proficiency*. See comment on No. 162, §7.11. Other translations: "of the greatest experience" (Yonge) and "from among the more learned" (Vermes and Goodman)....*what is not understood*. More literal: "what is not discernible, what is not clear." Vermes and Goodman have "what is not easy to understand in these books" and Yonge has "what is not very intelligible." The last sentence of §82 is difficult to translate: *For most of their philosophical study takes the form of allegory*, or "for a great many precepts are delivered in enigmatical modes of expression, and allegorically" (Yonge), or "Most of the time...instruction is given them by means of symbols" (Vermes and Goodman)....*and in this they emulate the tradition of the past*, with an alternative in a note: "with ardour worthy of the men of old." Colson refers to *Plant.* 158 and *Migr.* 201 which have the same expression (*archaiotropōi zēlōsei* from *archaiotropos* "old-fashioned" and *zēlōsis*.')

§83. *They are trained in*. In Greek *paideuontai*. See comment on No. 182, §156. On training in different virtues in Philo, see comment on No. 166, §216....*taking for their defining standards these three*. Or "utilizing three standards and rules" (*horois kai kanosi trittois*). In Yonge's translation: "using a threefold variety of definitions, and rules, and criteria, namely." The threefold is very nicely expressed by Philo using the words *filotheos, filaretos, filanthrōpos*.

No. 41
Source: *Archaeological.*
Date: First century B.C.E.

Literature: Steudel, "House of Prostration"; Binder, *Temple Courts*, 459–68; Runesson, *Origins*, 179–81, 357–61; Klinghardt, "Manual of Discipline"; Weinfeld, *Organizational Pattern*; Levine, *Ancient Synagogue*, 61–66. For general description of the buildings and occupational phases at Qumran, see Magness, *Qumran*, esp. 47–72, 113–33; Roitman, *Shrine of the Book*, 16–42.

Comments: Whether there exists archaeological evidence for a synagogue at Qumran very much hinges upon one's definition of "synagogue." If a synagogue building is defined as an edifice housing a public institution such as a town assembly, one looks in vain for such a structure at Qumran since, by definition, the site is not a town, but a complex of buildings used by a specific (sectarian) Jewish group, most likely a branch of the Essenes. However, as is clear from Philo's description of an *Essene* synagogue (*synagōgē*; No. 40), if the term "synagogue" was also used for semi-public or sectarian assemblies, as well as the structures housing them, then a room used for assemblies at Qumran may indeed be defined with this term.

Figure 14. Plan of Qumran, periods 1b–2

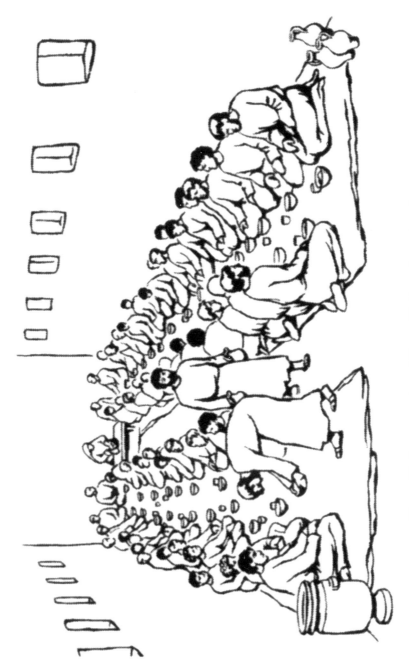

Figure 15. Reconstruction of Room 77 (the refectory) at Qumran

In this regard, several authors have broadened the definition of "synagogue" to account for this allusion. Thus Binder refers to the Essene assemblies (and their meeting halls) as "sectarian synagogues," while Runesson labels them "association synagogues." Klinghardt, on the other hand, has compared the Qumran community to Hellenistic associations (see also Weinfeld). Reading Philo with such a comparison in mind, it seems evident that, in the first century, a Jewish voluntary association may be referred to as a synagogue.

A likely place for assemblies of different kinds in Qumran is locus 77, the largest room on the site, measuring 22 × 4.5 m. A paved area was unearthed in the northeast corner of the room, where it most likely supported a wooden podium used by one of the community leaders. The room also served as a refectory, an interpretation supported by the fact that the adjacent loci (86 and 89) served as a pantry, as is evident from the stacks of dishes and bowls uncovered there. Thus, locus 77 served both as a dining room and a hall where readings and discussion of scripture took place (cf. Josephus, *B. J.* 2.128–132 [No. 39]).

Locus 4, measuring only 8 × 4 m, had benches along all four walls and likely served as an assembly room too, but not for the whole community. Perhaps the sectarian leadership gathered here for a variety of purposes. The function of the adjoining room, locus 30, was somehow linked to the production of scrolls, which took place on the floor directly above: among the roof-fall uncovered there were benches serving as tables, as well as ink wells.

In summary, the most likely setting for communal assemblies at Qumran was locus 77, where rituals and sacred meals took place. Levine notes that the fact that the same room was used for a variety of purposes makes this synagogue conform in certain ways with other (public) Judaean synagogues: liturgical activities were not separated spatially from other communal endeavours.

2.1.19   *Shuafat*

No. 42
Source: *Archaeological*.
Date: Early first century B.C.E.

Literature: Rabinovich, "Jewish Prayer Room"; Riesner, "Synagogues"; Onn and Rafyunu, "Jerusalem: Khirbeth a-ras," 61; Binder, *Temple Courts*, 196–97; Runesson, *Origins*, 175, n. 18; Levine, *Ancient Synagogue*, 72.

Comments: This settlement was founded in the second century B.C.E. and abandoned due to an earthquake in 31 B.C.E. Excavations took place in 1991 under Alexander Onn. Very little information has been published on the results of the excavations, making it extremely difficult to evaluate the identification of one of the rooms as a synagogue, or "prayer room," as it has also been labelled. Different descriptions of the remains in the various publications make the task even harder.

The room measures 5 × 4 m, and a low wall of hewn stones divided the space. While benches have been mentioned in some publications, none appear in Onn and Rafyunu's article from 1993. The room seems to have had a niche; outside the room at least one *miqweh* was discovered.

Unless further excavations or more detailed information can strengthen the case for the identification of this building as a synagogue, the authors believe the claim should be withdrawn.

2.1.20   *Tiberias*

No. 43
Source: *Literary.* Josephus, *Vita* 276–81, 294–95
Date: *Josephi vita* was published in the middle of the 90s C.E.

[276] Κἀγὼ μηδὲν ὑπονοήσας ἐς τὰς Ταριχέας ἀπῆλθον καταλιπὼν ὅμως ἐν τῇ πόλει τοὺς πολυπραγμονήσοντας, τί περὶ ἡμῶν λέγοιτο. διὰ πάσης δὲ τῆς ὁδοῦ τῆς ἀπὸ Ταριχεῶν εἰς Τιβεριάδα φερούσης ἐπέστησα πολλούς, ἵνα μοι δι᾽ ἀλλήλων σημαίνωσιν ἅπερ ἂν παρὰ τῶν ἐν τῇ πόλει καταλειφθέντων πύθωνται. [277] κατὰ τὴν ἐπιοῦσαν οὖν ἡμέραν συνάγονται πάντες εἰς τὴν προσευχὴν μέγιστον οἴκημα καὶ πολὺν ὄχλον ἐπιδέξασθαι δυνάμενον. εἰσελθὼν δὲ ὁ Ἰωνάθης φανερῶς μὲν περὶ τῆς ἀποστάσεως οὐκ ἐτόλμα λέγειν, ἔφη δὲ στραγηγοῦ κρείττονος χρείαν τὴν πόλιν αὐτῶν ἔχειν. [278] Ἰησοῦς δ᾽ ὁ ἄρχων οὐδὲν ὑποστειλάμενος ἀναφανδὸν εἶπεν· ϛάμεινόν ἐστιν, ὦ πολῖται, τέσσαρσιν ἡμᾶς ἀνδράσιν ὑπακούειν ἢ ἑνί, καὶ κατὰ γένος λαμπροῖς καὶ κατὰ σύνεσιν οὐκ ἀδόξοις.ϛ ὑπεδείκνυε δὲ τοὺς περὶ Ἰωνάθην. [279] ταῦτ᾽ εἰπόντα τὸν Ἰησοῦν ἐπήνει παρελθὼν Ἰοῦστος καί τινας ἐκ τοῦ δήμου συνέπειθεν. οὐκ ἠρέσκετο δὲ τοῖς λεχθεῖσιν τὸ πλῆθος καὶ πάντως ἂν εἰς στάσιν ἐχώρησαν, εἰ μὴ τὴν σύνοδον διέλυσεν ἐπελθοῦσα ἕκτη ὥρα, καθ᾽ ἣν τοῖς σάββασιν ἀριστοποιεῖσθαι νόμιμόν ἐστιν ἡμῖν, καὶ οἱ περὶ τὸν Ἰωνάθην εἰς τὴν ἐπιοῦσαν ὑπερθέμενοι τὴν βουλὴν ἀπήεσαν ἄπρακτοι. [280] εὐθὺς δέ μοι τούτων ἀπαγγελθέντων πρωὶ διέγνων εἰς τὴν Τιβεριέων πόλιν ἀφικέσθαι, καὶ τῇ ἐπιούσῃ περὶ τὴν ὥραν ἧκον ἀπὸ τῶν Ταριχεῶν, καταλαμβάνω δὲ συναγόμενον ἤδη τὸ πλῆθος εἰς τὴν προσευχήν· ἐφ᾽ ὅ τι δ᾽ ἦν αὐτοῖς ἡ σύνοδος οὐκ ἐγίνωσκον οἱ συλλεγόμενοι. [281] οἱ δὲ περὶ τὸν Ἰωνάθην ἀπροσδοκήτως θεασάμενοί με παρόντα διεταράχθησαν. εἶτ᾽ ἐπινοοῦσιν διαδοῦναι λόγον, ὅτι Ῥωμαίων ἱππεῖς ἐν τῇ μεθορίῳ πόρρω τριάκοντα σταδίων ἀπὸ τῆς πόλεως κατὰ τόπον λεγόμενον Ὁμόνοιαν εἰσὶν ἑωραμένοι.

[294] Τοὺς μὲν οὖν σὺν ἐμοὶ πάντας ἐκκλεῖσαι προσέταξεν Ἰησοῦς ὁ ἄρχων, αὐτὸς γὰρ ταῖς θύραις ἐφειστήκει, μόνον δ᾽ ἐμὲ μετὰ τῶν φίλων εἰσελθεῖν εἴασεν. [295] ἤδη δ᾽ ἡμῶν τὰ νόμιμα ποιούντων καὶ πρὸς εὐχὰς τραπομένων ἀναστὰς Ἰησοῦς περὶ τῶν ληφθέντων ἐκ τοῦ ἐμπρησμοῦ τῆς βασιλικῆς αὐλῆς σκευῶν τοῦ ἀσήμου ἀργυρίου

ἐπυνθάνετό μου, παρὰ τίνι τυγχάνει κείμενα. ταῦτα δ᾽ ἔλεγεν διατρίβειν τὸν χρόνον βουλόμενος, ἕως ἂν ὁ Ἰωάννης παραγένηται.

[276] So I departed for Tarichea, having suspected nothing, but all the same having left behind in the city those who would pass along anything that they may say about us. And along the entire road from Tarichea to Tiberias I set up many others, so that they could signal me via relay about whatever those left behind in the city might discover. [277] On the following day, then, everyone came together [synagō] into the prayer hall [proseuchē], the largest building and able to accommodate a large crowd. When Ionathes went in, although he did not dare to speak openly of defection, he did say that their city had need for a better general. [278] The council-president [archōn] Iesous, holding back nothing, said plainly: "It is preferable, citizens, for us to submit to four men rather than to one, especially those who are so brilliant with respect to ancestry and so renowned with respect to insight." He indicated Ionathes' group. [279] Now Iustus came forward and praised Iesous who had said these things; accordingly, he persuaded some of the populace. But the mob was not pleased with what was said. They would surely have proceeded to a riot if the meeting [synodos] had not dissolved at the arrival of the sixth hour, at which time it is lawful for us to take our luncheon on Sabbaths. Ionathes group left, unsuccessful, having held over the council until the following day. [280] When these things were immediately reported to me, I determined to go early [next day] to the city of the Tiberians. On the following day, I came at about the first hour from Tarichea and on my arrival found the mob already gathering [synagō] into the prayer hall [proseuchē]. Why there was even a meeting [synodos], those assembling [syllegō] did not know. [281] Now Ionathes' group, when they unexpectedly observed me present, were quite disturbed. At that, they schemed to disseminate word that Roman cavalry were near, on the frontier some thirty stadia away from the city: they had been discovered at a place called Homonoioa.

[294] Now the council-president Iesous, for he had posted himself by the doors, gave instructions that all the men that were with me should be kept out; he allowed only me and the friends to enter. [295] Just when we were performing our lawful duties and directing ourselves to prayer, Iesous stood up and began interrogating me about the furnishings and the uncoined silver that had been taken from the burning of the royal palace. "With whom do they happen to have been left?" He

was saying these things because he wanted to occupy the time until Iouannes came along.[10]

Literature: Binder, *Temple Courts*, 344–48, 404–15; Bilde, "Synagoge," 23–24; McKay, *Sabbath*; Runesson, *Origins*, 58, 190, 347–48, n. 355; Levine, *Ancient Synagogue*, 52–54, 162–69, 427.

Comments: This long passage, abbreviated here for brevity's sake, describes events surrounding Josephus' activities in Tiberias during the First Jewish Revolt. The edifice in which the recounted gatherings took place is here called a *proseuchē* (prayer hall), a designation more often used in a Diaspora setting than in Palestine. The building is described as being large enough to hold the entire council (*boulē*) of the city, as well as a crowd of the populace (*Vita* 284). Elsewhere, Josephus states that the Tiberian *boulē* consisted of 600 members (*B. J.* 2.641).

The text alludes to two types of public assemblies (referred to here using the verbs *synagō*, *syllegō*, or the noun *synodos*): political (§§277–280) and socio-religious (the public fast, §§294–295). The description of events during the public fast provides a rare instance of prayer taking place in a synagogue context. While this liturgy has been the object of much discussion, what cannot be doubted is that prayer took place in a synagogue building as part of a public liturgical performance prior 70 C.E.: the fact that prayer is mentioned in passing, among other things, makes it unlikely that Josephus would have introduced Diaspora practices or those from a later period into this autobiographical text.

The office of *archōn*—a title common in Graeco-Roman literature where it refers to a magistrate in a city or region (cf. No. 103)—is mentioned here in a public synagogue context. Elsewhere Josephus ascribes to Moses the appointment of seven *archontes* to administer affairs in each city of Israel (*A. J.* 4.214). During the First Jewish Revolt, Josephus himself established in Galilee a council of 70 *archontes*, assigning them public administrative tasks (*B. J.* 2.570–571). In Tiberias one *archōn*, together with ten principal councillors, led the city council (*boulē*). In the above passage, the *archōn* convened three meetings over a short period of time in the synagogue, indicating that this building was the usual venue for the exercise of this public office (Binder, 347).

No. 44
Source: *Literary. m. 'Erub.* 10:10
Date: Ca. 200 C.E.

נגר שיש בראשו נלוסטרה, רבי אליעזר אוסר ורבי יוסי מתיר. אמר רבי
אליעזר, מעשה בכנסת שבטבריא שהיו נוהגין בו היתר עד שבא רבן נמליאל
והזקנים ואסרו להן. רבי יוסי אומר, איסור נהגו בה, בא רבן נמליאל והזקנים
והתירו להן.

---

[10] Translation adapted from Mason (the Mason Josephus project).

Rabbi Eliezer forbids, but Rabbi Jose permits a door-bolt with a knob on its top. Rabbi Eliezer says: "It transpired in the synagogue (*kneset*) in Tiberias that they used one that was loose until Rabban Gamaliel and the Elders came and prohibited it for them." Rabbi Jose says: "They considered it forbidden, but Rabban Gamaliel and the Elders came and permitted it for them."

Literature: Levine, *Ancient Synagogue*, 458.

Comments: This discussion of what may or may not be permitted on the Sabbath (i.e., under which circumstances the door to a synagogue may be bolted on the Sabbath) indicates a) that a synagogue building existed in Tiberias, b) that the Jewish community in Tiberias followed local customs regarding halakhic matters in relation to their synagogue, and c) that the rabbis of the second century had an interest in how things were done locally in synagogues. Gamaliel II, whom R. Eliezer and R. Jose refer to, was a prominent leader in the late first and early second century C.E.

2.2   *General References and Unidentified Locations*

2.2.1   *Galilee*

No. 45
Source: *Literary.* Mark 1:39
Date: Ca. 70 C.E.

[39] Καὶ ἦλθεν κηρύσσων εἰς τὰς συναγωγὰς αὐτῶν εἰς ὅλην τὴν Γαλιλαίαν καὶ τὰ δαιμόνια ἐκβάλλων.

[39] And he went throughout Galilee, proclaiming the message in their synagogues [*synagōgai*] and casting out demons.

Literature: As a general reference to commentaries see Pesch, Guelich, and Marcus, *Comm., ad loc.* Binder, *Temple Courts*, 155; Runesson, *Origins*, 355–57.

Comments: Parallel texts in Matt 4:23 (No. 48) and Luke 4:44 (No. 53). See comments on Mark 1:21–29 (No. 4). This summary report of Jesus' preaching and exorcism concludes the material beginning with 1:21 and is illustrated by a new healing/exorcism in 1:40–45, the climax of the Marcan edition of 1:21–45. Here the healed person begins to take part in Jesus' proclamation of the kingdom of God. The verb "proclaiming" (*kēryssein*) corresponds to "teaching" in 1:21–28 and refers back to the preaching of the Kingdom in 1:14–15 and 1:38. In 1:21–45 Jesus is going to the people—Mark talks about "their synagogues"—and after that people are coming to Jesus. Luke (4:44) has also "proclaim," but he does not mention exorcisms and replaces Galilee with Judaea. Matt 4:23 is a typical summary report with both "teaching" and "proclaiming the good news of the kingdom" and healings among the people. As one send by God, Jesus declares, in word and deed, the fulfillment of time and the presence of God's kingdom in the Galilean synagogues (Guelich).

No. 46
Source: *Literary.* Mark 3:1–6
Date: Ca. 70 C.E.

[1] Καὶ εἰσῆλθεν πάλιν εἰς τὴν συναγωγήν. καὶ ἦν ἐκεῖ ἄνθρωπος ἐξηραμμένην ἔχων τὴν χεῖρα. [2] καὶ παρετήρουν αὐτὸν εἰ τοῖς σάββασιν θεραπεύσει αὐτόν, ἵνα κατηγορήσωσιν αὐτοῦ. [3] καὶ λέγει τῷ ἀνθρώπῳ τῷ τὴν ξηρὰν χεῖρα ἔχοντι· ἔγειρε εἰς τὸ μέσον. [4] καὶ λέγει αὐτοῖς· ἔξεστιν τοῖς σάββασιν ἀγαθὸν ποιῆσαι ἢ κακοποιῆσαι, ψυχὴν σῶσαι ἢ ἀποκτεῖναι; οἱ δὲ ἐσιώπων. [5] καὶ περιβλεψάμενος αὐτοὺς μετς· ὀργῆς, συλλυπούμενος ἐπὶ τῇ πωρώσει τῆς καρδίας αὐτῶν λέγει τῷ ἀνθρώπῳ· ἔκτεινον τὴν χεῖρα. καὶ ἐξέτεινεν καὶ ἀπεκατεστάθη ἡ χεὶρ αὐτοῦ. 6 καὶ ἐξελθόντες οἱ Φαρισαῖοι εὐθὺς μετὰ τῶν Ἡρῳδιανῶν συμβούλιον ἐδίδουν κατ᾽ αὐτοῦ ὅπως αὐτὸν ἀπολέσωσιν.

[1] Again he entered the synagogue [*synagōgē*], and a man was there who had a withered hand. [2] They watched him to see whether he would cure him on the Sabbath, so that they might accuse him. [3] And he said to the man who had the withered hand, "Come forward." [4] Then he said to them, "Is it lawful to do good or to do harm on the Sabbath, to save life or to kill?" But they were silent. [5] He looked around at them with anger; he was grieved at their hardness of heart and said to the man, "Stretch out your hand." He stretched it out, and his hand was restored. [6] The Pharisees went out and immediately conspired with the Herodians against him, how to destroy him.

Literature: As a general reference to commentaries see Pesch, Guelich, and Marcus, *Comm., ad loc.* Binder, *Temple Courts,*155; Levine, *Ancient Synagogue,* 43–45; Runesson, *Origins,* 222.

Comments: Parallel texts in Matt 12:9–14 (No. 52) and Luke 6:6–11 (No. 55). See the comment on Luke 4:16–30 (No. 33). Jesus either entered "the synagogue" or "a synagogue": two old manuscripts, Sinaiticus and Vaticanus, omit the definite article. The definite form together with "again" may be interpreted as a reference to the synagogue in Capernaum, 1:21. The first controversy story of the five found in 2:1–3:6 is situated in Capernaum, and the Sabbath in 2:23 could be the same Sabbath as in 3:1–6. The words in v. 3,

"Get up and come to the middle [of the synagogue]" (NRSV "Come forward") indicate that there was free space in the middle of the room, suggesting a room with benches along the walls. Jesus' healing activity is combined with a discussion about the Sabbath law and results in a conflict between Jesus and the Pharisees in the synagogue. The root of the conflict in the Marcan context goes to Jesus' claim of authority, clearly presented already in 1:21–28 and mentioned in 2:10. The conflict will result in Jesus' death, foreshadowed by the note at the end of the fifth controversy story.

No. 47
Source: *Literary.* Mark 5:22–23, 35–43
Date: Ca. 70 c.e.

[22] Καὶ ἔρχεται εἷς τῶν ἀρχισυναγώγων, ὀνόματι Ἰάϊρος, καὶ ἰδὼν αὐτὸν πίπτει πρὸς τοὺς πόδας αὐτοῦ [23] καὶ παρακαλεῖ αὐτὸν πολλὰ λέγων ὅτι τὸ θυγάτριόν μου ἐσχάτως ἔχει, ἵνα ἐλθὼν ἐπιθῇς τὰς χεῖρας αὐτῇ ἵνα σωθῇ καὶ ζήσῃ.

[35] Ἔτι αὐτοῦ λαλοῦντος ἔρχονται ἀπὸ τοῦ ἀρχισυναγώγου λέγοντες ὅτι ἡ θυγάτηρ σου ἀπέθανεν· τί ἔτι σκύλλεις τὸν διδάσκαλον; [36] ὁ δὲ Ἰησοῦς παρακούσας τὸν λόγον λαλούμενον λέγει τῷ ἀρχισυναγώγῳ· μὴ φοβοῦ, μόνον πίστευε. [37] καὶ οὐκ ἀφῆκεν οὐδένα μετ' αὐτοῦ συνακολουθῆσαι εἰ μὴ τὸν Πέτρον καὶ Ἰάκωβον καὶ Ἰωάννην τὸν ἀδελφὸν Ἰακώβου. [38] καὶ ἔρχονται εἰς τὸν οἶκον τοῦ ἀρχισυναγώγου, καὶ θεωρεῖ θόρυβον καὶ κλαίοντας καὶ ἀλαλάζοντας πολλά, [39] καὶ εἰσελθὼν λέγει αὐτοῖς· τί θορυβεῖσθε καὶ κλαίετε; τὸ παιδίον οὐκ ἀπέθανεν ἀλλὰ καθεύδει. [40] καὶ κατεγέλων αὐτοῦ. αὐτὸς δὲ ἐκβαλὼν πάντας παραλαμβάνει τὸν πατέρα τοῦ παιδίου καὶ τὴν μητέρα καὶ τοὺς μετ' αὐτοῦ καὶ εἰσπορεύεται ὅπου ἦν τὸ παιδίον. [41] καὶ κρατήσας τῆς χειρὸς τοῦ παιδίου λέγει αὐτῇ· ταλιθα κουμ, ὅ ἐστιν μεθερμηνευόμενον· τὸ κοράσιον, σοὶ λέγω, ἔγειρε. [42] καὶ εὐθὺς ἀνέστη τὸ κοράσιον καὶ περιεπάτει· ἦν γὰρ ἐτῶν δώδεκα. καὶ ἐξέστησαν [εὐθὺς] ἐκστάσει μεγάλῃ. [43] καὶ διεστείλατο αὐτοῖς πολλὰ ἵνα μηδεὶς γνοῖ τοῦτο, καὶ εἶπεν δοθῆναι αὐτῇ φαγεῖν.

[22] Then one of the leaders of the synagogue [*archisynagōgoi*] named Jairus came and, when he saw him, fell at his feet [23] and begged him repeatedly, "My little daughter is at the point of death. Come and lay your hands on her, so that she may be made well and live."

[35] While he was still speaking, some people came from the leader's [*archisynagōgos*] house to say, "Your daughter is dead. Why trouble the

teacher any further?" [36] But overhearing what they said, Jesus said to
the leader of the synagogue [*archisynagōgos*], "Do not fear, only believe."
[37] He allowed no one to follow him except Peter, James, and John,
the brother of James. [38] When they came to the house of the leader
of the synagogue [*archisynagōgos*], he saw a commotion, people weeping
and wailing loudly. [39] When he had entered, he said to them, "Why
do you make a commotion and weep? The child is not dead but sleeping." [40] And they laughed at him. Then he put them all outside, and
took the child's father and mother and those who were with him, and
went in where the child was. [41] He took her by the hand and said
to her, "Talitha cum," which means, "Little girl, get up!" [42] And
immediately the girl got up and began to walk about (she was twelve
years of age). At this they were overcome with amazement. [43] He
strictly ordered them that no one should know this, and told them to
give her something to eat.

Literature: As a general reference to commentaries see Pesch, Guelich, and
Marcus, *Comm., ad loc.* Binder, *Temple Courts*, 348–49; Levine, *Ancient Synagogue*,
43–45; Claußen, *Versammlung*, 256–64; Runesson, *Origins*, 174, n. 15.

Comments: Parallel texts in Matt 9:18, 23–26 and Luke 8:40–42, 49–56. This
healing story (death represents the most extreme form of illness) is situated in
Galilee, on the western side of the lake. A man with the Hebrew name Jair, in
Greek Jairos, is presented as "one of the leaders of the synagogue" which means
that he either belonged to the class of "synagogue leaders" (cf. "one of the scribes"
in 12:28–34) or was a functioning leader of a synagogue (cf. Acts 13:15). Not
all Jewish leaders in Mark have a negative attitude towards Jesus.
    A "synagogue leader" (*archisynagōgos*; the word is also used in vv. 35, 36 and
38) had responsibilities for arranging the synagogue services and overseeing the
synagogue building. It is the most common title related to the ancient synagogue. It could designate an honorary title, though in most cases it was the title
of an active functionary. In Luke the *archisynagōgos* clearly has an authoritative
function (Luke 13:14–15). The highly abbreviated story in Matthew mentions
only an anonymous leader (*archōn*), while Luke initially employs the phrase
"leader of the synagogue" (*archōn tēs synagōgēs*). For the use of *archisynagōgos* in
inscriptions, see comments on No. 116.

No. 48
Source: *Literary.* Matt 4:23
Date: 80–90 C.E.

[23] Καὶ περιῆγεν ἐν ὅλῃ τῇ Γαλιλαίᾳ διδάσκων ἐν ταῖς συναγωγαῖς
αὐτῶν καὶ κηρύσσων τὸ εὐαγγέλιον τῆς βασιλείας καὶ θεραπεύων
πᾶσαν νόσον καὶ πᾶσαν μαλακίαν ἐν τῷ λαῷ.

[23] Jesus went throughout Galilee, teaching in their synagogues [*synagōgai*] and proclaiming the good news of the kingdom and curing every disease and every sickness among the people.

Literature: As a general reference to commentaries, see Bonnard, Luz and Hagner, *Comm., ad loc.* Binder, *Temple Courts*, 155; Runesson, *Origins*, 355–57.

Comments: See the comments on Mark 1:39 (No. 45) and on Matt 9:35 (No. 51).

No. 49
Source: *Literary.* Matt 6:2
Date: Ca. 80–90 C.E.

[2] Ὅταν οὖν ποιῇς ἐλεημοσύνην, μὴ σαλπίσῃς ἔμπροσθέν σου, ὥσπερ οἱ ὑποκριταὶ ποιοῦσιν ἐν ταῖς συναγωγαῖς καὶ ἐν ταῖς ῥύμαις, ὅπως δοξασθῶσιν ὑπὸ τῶν ἀνθρώπων· ἀμὴν λέγω ὑμῖν, ἀπέχουσιν τὸν μισθὸν αὐτῶν.

[2] So whenever you give alms, do not sound a trumpet before you, as the hypocrites do in the synagogues [*synagōgai*] and in the streets, so that they may be praised by others. Truly I tell you, they have received their reward.

Literature: As a general reference to commentaries, see Bonnard, Luz and Hagner, *Comm., ad loc.* Binder, *Temple Courts*, 429–30; Levine, *Ancient Synagogue*, 372.

Comments: It is not easy to determine the concrete background behind the two examples in Matt 6:2 and 6:5, which function as parts of a longer catechetical section on "righteousness" in 6:1–18. Private almsgiving plays an important role in Jewish piety, but we do not know about a blowing of trumpets in connection with almsgiving. It could easily be interpreted metaphorically: compare such phrases as "trumpet forth," "sound one's own trumpet."

According to rabbinic sources, alms to the poor were organized by the synagogues. The givers were announced in synagogue meetings. Sirach 31:11 says: "His prosperity will be established, and the assembly will proclaim his acts of charity." The meaning of the example is clear: some pious people used public forms of almsgiving as self-glorification.

No. 50
Source: *Literary.* Matt 6:5
Date: Ca. 80–90 C.E.

[5] Καὶ ὅταν προσεύχησθε, οὐκ ἔσεσθε ὡς οἱ ὑποκριταί, ὅτι φιλοῦσιν ἐν ταῖς συναγωγαῖς καὶ ἐν ταῖς γωνίαις τῶν πλατειῶν ἑστῶτες προσεύχεσθαι, ὅπως φανῶσιν τοῖς ἀνθρώποις· ἀμὴν λέγω ὑμῖν, ἀπέχουσιν τὸν μισθὸν αὐτῶν.

[5] And whenever you pray, do not be like the hypocrites; for they love to stand and pray in the synagogues [*synagōgai*] and at the street corners, so that they may be seen by others. Truly I tell you, they have received their reward.

Literature: As a general reference to commentaries, see Bonnard, Luz and Hagner, *Comm.*, *ad loc.* Binder, *Temple Courts*, 413–14 n. 69; Levine, *Ancient Synagogue*, 38; Runesson, *Origins*, 59, 449.

Comments: See the comments on Matt 6:2 (No. 49). Prayer or benedictions may be said individually, especially in the morning, at noon, and in the evening. As a rule, the posture when praying was standing. Here "standing" has the nuance of having taken a position and continuing to stand in place in order to get attention and admiration from others (Hagner). According to this passage, private prayers were offered in the synagogues.

No. 51
Source: *Literary.* Matt 9:35
Date: Ca. 80–90 C.E.

[35] Καὶ περιῆγεν ὁ Ἰησοῦς τὰς πόλεις πάσας καὶ τὰς κώμας διδάσκων ἐν ταῖς συναγωγαῖς αὐτῶν καὶ κηρύσσων τὸ εὐαγγέλιον τῆς βασιλείας καὶ θεραπεύων πᾶσαν νόσον καὶ πᾶσαν μαλακίαν.

[35] Then Jesus went about all the cities and villages, teaching in their synagogues [*synagōgai*], and proclaiming the good news of the kingdom, and curing every disease and every sickness.

Literature: As a general reference to commentaries, see Bonnard, Luz and Hagner, *Comm.*, *ad loc.* Binder, *Temple Courts*, 155; Runesson, *Origins*, 355–57; Gerhardsson, *Mighty Acts*, 20–37.

Comments: See the comment on Matt 4:23 (No. 48). Matthew presents frequent summaries of Jesus' activity (4:23, 24–25; 8:16–17; 9:35; 12:15–21; 14:13–14, 35–36; 15:29–31; 19:1–2 and 21:14). The first two, 4:23 and 9:35, are programmatic and present him as both teaching and healing. The others concentrate on his therapeutic activity. Jesus is "teaching" (*didaskein*), preaching (*kēryssein*), and "healing" (*therapeuein*) in the synagogues (4:23, 9:35). In this context, the content of these activities is given in 4:17, 4:5–7 and 4:8–9.

The emphasis in Matthew is on teaching, while healing may be seen as a part of his teaching. The basic initiative comes from Jesus. He goes out to teach and heal all Israel, "all Galilee" in 4:23, and "all the cities and villages" in 9:35. Both activities are related to a fulfilling of the Scripture. And his activity is bound to "their synagogues," 4:23; 9:35. A break within local Jewish communities would explain the consequent description of the synagogues in Matthew as "their synagogues" (4:23; 9:35; 10:17; 12:9; 13:54; 23:34), but there are also other explanations (Runesson). Matthew uses "synagogues" only in general examples (6:2, 5; 23:6).

No. 52
Source: *Literary.* Matt 12:9–14
Date: Ca. 80–90 c.e.

[9] Καὶ μεταβὰς ἐκεῖθεν ἦλθεν εἰς τὴν συναγωγὴν αὐτῶν· [10] καὶ ἰδοὺ ἄνθρωπος χεῖρα ἔχων ξηράν. καὶ ἐπηρώτησαν αὐτὸν λέγοντες· εἰ ἔξεστιν τοῖς σάββασιν θεραπεῦσαι; ἵνα κατηγορήσωσιν αὐτοῦ. [11] ὁ δὲ εἶπεν αὐτοῖς· τίς ἔσται ἐξ ὑμῶν ἄνθρωπος ὃς ἕξει πρόβατον ἕν καὶ ἐὰν ἐμπέσῃ τοῦτο τοῖς σάββασιν εἰς βόθυνον, οὐχὶ κρατήσει αὐτὸ καὶ ἐγερεῖ; [12] πόσῳ οὖν διαφέρει ἄνθρωπος προβάτου. ὥστε ἔξεστιν τοῖς σάββασιν καλῶς ποιεῖν. [13] τότε λέγει τῷ ἀνθρώπῳ· ἔκτεινόν σου τὴν χεῖρα. καὶ ἐξέτεινεν καὶ ἀπεκατεστάθη ὑγιὴς ὡς ἡ ἄλλη. [14] ἐξελθόντες δὲ οἱ Φαρισαῖοι συμβούλιον ἔλαβον κατ᾽ αὐτοῦ ὅπως αὐτὸν ἀπολέσωσιν.

[9] He left that place and entered their synagogue [*synagōgē*]; [10] a man was there with a withered hand, and they asked him, "Is it lawful to cure on the Sabbath?" so that they might accuse him. [11] He said to them, "Suppose one of you has only one sheep and it falls into a pit on the Sabbath; will you not lay hold of it and lift it out? [12] How much more valuable is a human being than a sheep! So it is lawful to do good on the Sabbath." [13] Then he said to the man, "Stretch out your hand." He stretched it out, and it was restored, as sound as the other. 14 But the Pharisees went out and conspired against him, how to destroy him.

Literature: As a general reference to commentaries, see Bonnard, Luz and Hagner, *Comm., ad loc.* Binder, *Temple Courts*, 155–56; Runesson, *Origins*, 355–57; idem, "Re-Thinking."

Comments: See the comments on Mark 3:1–6 (No. 46). The argumentation in the synagogue is the central point in Matthew's text. It begins with an explicit question of the opponents, "Is it lawful to cure on the Sabbath?" and ends in a conclusion by Jesus, "So it is lawful to do good on the Sabbath." His arguments consist of a well-known analogy and a deduction *a fortiori*. The healing becomes of secondary importance after the climactic statements in v. 12. As to the nature of the synagogue in questions, it may have been public, but there are also arguments in favour of interpreting the institution as a Pharisaic association synagogue (cf. Runesson).

No. 53
Source: *Literary.* Luke 4:14–15
Date: Ca. 80–90 c.e.

[14] Καὶ ὑπέστρεψεν ὁ Ἰησοῦς ἐν τῇ δυνάμει τοῦ πνεύματος εἰς τὴν Γαλιλαίαν. καὶ φήμη ἐξῆλθεν καθ᾽ ὅλης τῆς περιχώρου περὶ αὐτοῦ. [15] καὶ αὐτὸς ἐδίδασκεν ἐν ταῖς συναγωγαῖς αὐτῶν δοξαζόμενος ὑπὸ πάντων.

[14] Then Jesus, filled with the power of the Spirit, returned to Galilee, and a report about him spread through all the surrounding country. [15] He began to teach in their synagogues [*synagōgai*] and was praised by everyone.

Literature: As a general reference to commentaries, see Fitzmyer, Schürmann and Bovon, *Comm., ad loc.* Binder, *Temple Courts*, 155–56; Levine, *Ancient Synagogue*, 43–45; Runesson, *Origins*, 355.

Comments: See the comment on Luke 4:16–30 (No. 33). Luke begins to describe Jesus' public ministry with a summary statement, 4:14–15, which gives an overview of his activity in Galilee, 4:14–9:50. In particular, it introduces 4:14–4:44 with its emphasis upon Jesus' teaching in synagogues. In some way 4:14–15 and 4:44 function as an inclusio. Jesus' ministry in Galilee is characterized by (1) the power of the Spirit, 1:35; 3:22; 4:14, 18, (2) teaching, 4:15, 18–19, 21, 24–27, 31–32, 43 and 44, and (3) the positive reaction from all who hear him. See also the comments to Luke 4:31–38 (No. 5). The formulation "their synagogues" may be borrowed from Mark or explained by the fact that the author was not a Jew; it could also refer to the geographical region.

No. 54
Source: *Literary.* Luke 4:44
Date: Ca. 80–90 c.e.

[44] Καὶ ἦν κηρύσσων εἰς τὰς συναγωγὰς τῆς Ἰουδαίας.

[44] So he continued proclaiming the message in the synagogues [*synagōgai*] of Judaea.

Literature: As a general reference to commentaries, see Fitzmyer, Schürmann and Bovon, *Comm., ad loc.* Binder, *Temple Courts*, 155–56; Levine, *Ancient Synagogue*, 443–45; Runesson, *Origins*, 158.

Comments: See the comments on Luke 4:14–15 (No. 53). According to the context—Jesus' Galilean ministry—"Judaea" must mean "the land of the Jews" as in 1:5, 6:17; 7:17; 23:5 and Acts 10:37. The word "proclaiming" (*kēryssein*)—not "teaching" as in 4:15—takes up the phrase "proclaim the kingdom of God" in 4:43.

No. 55
Source: *Literary.* Luke 6:6–11
Date: Ca. 80–90 c.e.

[6] Ἐγένετο δὲ ἐν ἑτέρῳ σαββάτῳ εἰσελθεῖν αὐτὸν εἰς τὴν συναγωγὴν καὶ διδάσκειν. καὶ ἦν ἄνθρωπος ἐκεῖ καὶ ἡ χεὶρ αὐτοῦ ἡ δεξιὰ ἦν ξηρά. [7] παρετηροῦντο δὲ αὐτὸν οἱ γραμματεῖς καὶ οἱ Φαρισαῖοι εἰ ἐν τῷ σαββάτῳ θεραπεύει, ἵνα εὕρωσιν κατηγορεῖν αὐτοῦ. [8] αὐτὸς δὲ ᾔδει τοὺς διαλογισμοὺς αὐτῶν, εἶπεν δὲ τῷ ἀνδρὶ τῷ ξηρὰν ἔχοντι τὴν χεῖρα· ἔγειρε καὶ στῆθι εἰς τὸ μέσον· καὶ ἀναστὰς ἔστη. [9] εἶπεν δὲ ὁ Ἰησοῦς πρὸς αὐτούς· ἐπερωτῶ ὑμᾶς εἰ ἔξεστιν τῷ σαββάτῳ ἀγαθοποιῆσαι ἢ κακοποιῆσαι, ψυχὴν σῶσαι ἢ ἀπολέσαι; [10] καὶ περιβλεψάμενος πάντας αὐτοὺς εἶπεν αὐτῷ· ἔκτεινον τὴν χεῖρά σου. ὁ δὲ ἐποίησεν καὶ ἀπεκατεστάθη ἡ χεὶρ αὐτοῦ. [11] αὐτοὶ δὲ ἐπλήσθησαν ἀνοίας καὶ διελάλουν πρὸς ἀλλήλους τί ἂν ποιήσαιεν τῷ Ἰησοῦ.

[6] On another Sabbath he entered the synagogue [*synagōgē*] and taught, and there was a man there whose right hand was withered. [7] The scribes and the Pharisees watched him to see whether he would cure on the Sabbath, so that they might find an accusation against him. [8] Even though he knew what they were thinking, he said to the man who had the withered hand, "Come and stand here." He got up and stood there. [9] Then Jesus said to them, "I ask you, is it lawful to do good or to do harm on the Sabbath, to save life or to destroy it?" [10] After looking around at all of them, he said to him, "Stretch out your hand." He did so, and his hand was restored. [11] But they were filled with fury and discussed with one another what they might do to Jesus.

Literature: As a general reference to commentaries, see Fitzmyer, Schürmann and Bovon, *Comm., ad loc.* Binder, *Temple Courts*, 155–56; Levine, *Ancient Synagogue*, 43–45; Runesson, *Origins*, 384–85, n. 466.

Comments: See the comments on Mark 3:1–6 (No. 46). Luke's version of what happened in the synagogue—whose specific location is unnamed—makes the situation clearer (another Sabbath, right hand, the opponents mentioned already in the beginning, the man immediately obeying Jesus) and gives a more Lucan picture of Jesus (teaching in the synagogue, knowing the opponents' thinking, putting an explicit question to the opponents, no expressions of Jesus' emotions). Jesus' question and his healing lead to lively discussions within the synagogue.

No. 56
Source: *Literary.* Luke 8:40–42, 49–56
Date: Ca. 80–90 c.e.

[40] Ἐν δὲ τῷ ὑποστρέφειν τὸν Ἰησοῦν ἀπεδέξατο αὐτὸν ὁ ὄχλος· ἦσαν γὰρ πάντες προσδοκῶντες αὐτόν. [41] καὶ ἰδοὺ ἦλθεν ἀνὴρ ᾧ ὄνομα Ἰάϊρος καὶ οὗτος ἄρχων τῆς συναγωγῆς ὑπῆρχεν, καὶ πεσὼν παρὰ τοὺς πόδας [τοῦ] Ἰησοῦ παρεκάλει αὐτὸν εἰσελθεῖν εἰς τὸν οἶκον αὐτοῦ. [42] ὅτι θυγάτηρ μονογενὴς ἦν αὐτῷ ὡς ἐτῶν δώδεκα καὶ αὐτὴ ἀπέθνῃσκεν.

[49] Ἔτι αὐτοῦ λαλοῦντος ἔρχεταί τις παρὰ τοῦ ἀρχισυναγώγου λέγων ὅτι τέθνηκεν ἡ θυγάτηρ σου· μηκέτι σκύλλε τὸν διδάσκαλον. [50] ὁ δὲ Ἰησοῦς ἀκούσας ἀπεκρίθη αὐτῷ· μὴ φοβοῦ, μόνον πίστευσον, καὶ σωθήσεται. [51] ἐλθὼν δὲ εἰς τὴν οἰκίαν οὐκ ἀφῆκεν εἰσελθεῖν τινα σὺν αὐτῷ εἰ μὴ Πέτρον καὶ Ἰωάννην καὶ Ἰάκωβον καὶ τὸν πατέρα τῆς παιδὸς καὶ τὴν μητέρα. [52] ἔκλαιον δὲ πάντες καὶ ἐκόπτοντο αὐτήν. ὁ δὲ εἶπεν· μὴ κλαίετε, οὐ γὰρ ἀπέθανεν ἀλλὰ καθεύδει. [53] καὶ κατεγέλων αὐτοῦ εἰδότες ὅτι ἀπέθανεν. [54] αὐτὸς δὲ κρατήσας τῆς χειρὸς αὐτῆς ἐφώνησεν λέγων· ἡ παῖς, ἔγειρε. [55] καὶ ἐπέστρεψεν τὸ πνεῦμα αὐτῆς καὶ ἀνέστη παραχρῆμα καὶ διέταξεν αὐτῇ δοθῆναι φαγεῖν. [56] καὶ ἐξέστησαν οἱ γονεῖς αὐτῆς· ὁ δὲ παρήγγειλεν αὐτοῖς μηδενὶ εἰπεῖν τὸ γεγονός.

[40] Now when Jesus returned, the crowd welcomed him, for they were all waiting for him. [41] Just then there came a man named Jairus, a leader of the synagogue [*archōn tēs synagogēs*]. He fell at Jesus' feet and begged him to come to his house. [42] for he had an only daughter, about twelve years old, who was dying.

[49] While he was still speaking, someone came from the leader's [*archisynagōgos*] house to say, "Your daughter is dead; do not trouble the teacher any longer." [50] When Jesus heard this, he replied, "Do not fear. Only believe, and she will be saved." [51] When he came to the house, he did not allow anyone to enter with him, except Peter, John, and James, and the child's father and mother. [52] They were all

weeping and wailing for her; but he said, "Do not weep; for she is not dead but sleeping." [53] And they laughed at him, knowing that she was dead. [54] But he took her by the hand and called out, "Child, get up!" [55] Her spirit returned, and she got up at once. Then he directed them to give her something to eat. [56] Her parents were astounded; but he ordered them to tell no one what had happened.

Literature: As a general reference to commentaries, see Fitzmyer, Schürmann and Bovon, *Comm., ad loc.* Binder, *Temple Courts,* 348–49; Levine, *Ancient Synagogue,* 43–45.

Comments: See the comments on Mark 5:22, 35–43 (No. 47). Luke has shortened the story, but not as much as Matthew (Matt 9:18–26). While Mark uses *archisynagōgos* four times, Luke first uses *archōn tēs synagōgēs* and then *archisynagōgos* once. Matthew prefers the term *archōn*, which he uses twice.

No. 57
Source: *Literary.* Luke 13:10–17
Date: Ca. 80–90 C.E.

[10] ῏Ην δὲ διδάσκων ἐν μιᾷ τῶν συναγωγῶν ἐν τοῖς σάββασιν. [11] καὶ ἰδοὺ γυνὴ πνεῦμα ἔχουσα ἀσθενείας ἔτη δεκαοκτὼ καὶ ἦν συγκύπτουσα καὶ μὴ δυναμένη ἀνακύψαι εἰς τὸ παντελές. [12] ἰδὼν δὲ αὐτὴν ὁ Ἰησοῦς προσεφώνησεν καὶ εἶπεν αὐτῇ· γύναι, ἀπολέλυσαι τῆς ἀσθενείας σου, [13] καὶ ἐπέθηκεν αὐτῇ τὰς χεῖρας· καὶ παραχρῆμα ἀνωρθώθη καὶ ἐδόξαζεν τὸν θεόν. [14] ἀποκριθεὶς δὲ ὁ ἀρχισυνάγωγος, ἀγανακτῶν ὅτι τῷ σαββάτῳ ἐθεράπευσεν ὁ Ἰησοῦς, ἔλεγεν τῷ ὄχλῳ ὅτι ἓξ ἡμέραι εἰσὶν ἐν αἷς δεῖ ἐργάζεσθαι· ἐν αὐταῖς οὖν ἐρχόμενοι θεραπεύεσθε καὶ μὴ τῇ ἡμέρᾳ τοῦ σαββάτου. [15] ἀπεκρίθη δὲ αὐτῷ ὁ κύριος καὶ εἶπεν· ὑποκριταί, ἕκαστος ὑμῶν τῷ σαββάτῳ οὐ λύει τὸν βοῦν αὐτοῦ ἢ τὸν ὄνον ἀπὸ τῆς φάτνης καὶ ἀπαγαγὼν ποτίζει; [16] ταύτην δὲ θυγατέρα Ἀβραὰμ οὖσαν, ἣν ἔδησεν ὁ σατανᾶς ἰδοὺ δέκα καὶ ὀκτὼ ἔτη, οὐκ ἔδει λυθῆναι ἀπὸ τοῦ δεσμοῦ τούτου τῇ ἡμέρᾳ τοῦ σαββάτου; [17] καὶ ταῦτα λέγοντος αὐτοῦ κατῃσχύνοντο πάντες οἱ ἀντικείμενοι αὐτῷ, καὶ πᾶς ὁ ὄχλος ἔχαιρεν ἐπὶ πᾶσιν τοῖς ἐνδόξοις τοῖς γινομένοις ὑπ' αὐτοῦ.

[10] Now he was teaching in one of the synagogues [*synagōgē*] on the Sabbath. [11] And just then there appeared a woman with a spirit that had crippled her for eighteen years. She was bent over and was quite unable to stand up straight. [12] When Jesus saw her, he called her over and said, "Woman, you are set free from your ailment." [13] When he laid his hands on her, immediately she stood up straight and began praising

God. [14] But the leader of the synagogue, indignant because Jesus had
cured on the Sabbath, kept saying to the crowd, "There are six days on
which work ought to be done; come on those days and be cured, and
not on the Sabbath day." [15] But the Lord answered him and said,
"You hypocrites! Does not each of you on the Sabbath untie his ox or
his donkey from the manger, and lead it away to give it water? [16] And
ought not this woman, a daughter of Abraham whom Satan bound for
eighteen long years, be set free from this bondage on the Sabbath day?"
[17] When he said this, all his opponents were put to shame; and the
entire crowd was rejoicing at all the wonderful things that he was doing.

Literature: As a general reference to commentaries, see Fitzmyer, Schürmann
and Bovon, *Comm., ad loc.* Binder, *Temple Courts*, 374; Levine, *Ancient Synagogue*,
43–45; Runesson, *Origins*, 379.

Comments: See the comment on Luke 4:16–30 (No. 33). This passage
constitutes the only instance where a first-century source specifically mentions
a woman as being present inside a synagogue of Palestine. Otherwise, the
teaching, healing, and discussions within the synagogue are typically combined
in this Lucan story where Jesus once again makes use of his "power." See the
comments on Luke 4:14–15 (No. 53). The use of *dei*, "it is nesessary," in v. 14
and v. 15, translated as "ought to," implies in Luke that what happens in the
synagogue is a part of God's plan of salvation-history. According to Luke, this
is the last time Jesus acts within a synagogue.

2.2.2   *Judaea*

No. 58
Source: *Literary.* Mark 12:38–39
Date: Ca. 70 C.E.

[38] Καὶ ἐν τῇ διδαχῇ αὐτοῦ ἔλεγεν· βλέπετε ἀπὸ τῶν γραμματέων
τῶν θελόντων ἐν στολαῖς περιπατεῖν καὶ ἀσπασμοὺς ἐν ταῖς ἀγοραῖς
[39] καὶ πρωτοκαθεδρίας ἐν ταῖς συναγωγαῖς καὶ πρωτοκλισίας ἐν
τοῖς δείπνοις.

[38] As he taught, he said, "Beware of the scribes, who like to walk
around in long robes, and to be greeted with respect in the marketplaces,
[39] and to have the best seats in the synagogues [*synagōgai*] and places
of honor at banquets!"

Literature: As a general reference to commentaries see Taylor, Pesch and
Evans, *Comm., ad loc.* Binder, *Temple Courts*, 97–98, 367.

Comments: Parallel texts in Matt 23:6–7 (No. 59), Luke 20:46 (No. 60), and Luke 11:43 (No. 69). In 12:38–40 Mark gives an example of loving oneself more than God and one's neighbour (12:28–34), followed by a postive illustration of love in 12:41–44. The scribes, the main opponents of Jesus in Mark, love to be seen and honoured in the synagogues.

The word *prōtokathedria* "first seat" is not attested before the Gospels. The singular form is used in Luke 11:43, the plural form in the other three passages. The word is translated by "first seat," "choice seat," "seat of honour," "best seat," "front seat." Probably there were seats or benches at the front of the synagogues, perhaps on a platform near an ark or niche containing the sacred scrolls. From this place the scribes could see people coming and going (cf. Jas 2:2–3). In *t. Meg.* 3.21 we read: "How did the elders sit in session? It was facing the people with their backs toward the sanctuary."

False prophets sought the first seats when Christians came together according to Herm. *Mand.* 11.12. Luke 20:46 is a near parallel to the Markan text with regard to context and wording (it contains some linguistic improvements). Matt 23:6–7 and Luke 11:43 are placed within longer diatribes against the Pharisees and the Scribes, with two examples in Luke (seats in synagogues and greetings in market places) and four in Matthew (the preceding as well as people calling them rabbi).

Walking in long robes, loving the best places at banquets, and chosing the first seats in synagogues may all be references to Sabbath customs. According to some scholars, "long robes" refers either to the ornate outer cloaks of the scribes and others, or to the festive garments that Jews wore for the celebration of the Sabbath.

No. 59
Source: *Literary.* Matt 23:6–7
Date: Ca. 80–90 C.E.

[6] φιλοῦσιν δὲ τὴν πρωτοκλισίαν ἐν τοῖς δείπνοις καὶ τὰς πρωτοκαθεδρίας ἐν ταῖς συναγωγαῖς [7] καὶ τοὺς ἀσπασμοὺς ἐν ταῖς ἀγοραῖς καὶ καλεῖσθαι ὑπὸ τῶν ἀνθρώπων ῥαββί.

[6] They love to have the place of honor at banquets and the best seats in the synagogues [*synagōgai*], [7] and to be greeted with respect in the marketplaces, and to have people call them rabbi.

Literature: As a general reference to commentaries, see Bonnard, Luz and Hagner, *Comm.*, *ad loc.* Binder, *Temple Courts*, 97–98, 367.

Comments: See the comments on Mark 12:38–39 (No. 58).

No. 60
Source: *Literary.* Luke 20:46
Date: Ca. 80–90 C.E.

[46] προσέχετε ἀπὸ τῶν γραμματέων τῶν θελόντων περιπατεῖν ἐν στολαῖς καὶ φιλούντων ἀσπασμοὺς ἐν ταῖς ἀγοραῖς καὶ πρωτοκαθεδρίας ἐν ταῖς συναγωγαῖς καὶ πρωτοκλισίας ἐν τοῖς δείπνοις

[46] Beware of the scribes, who like to walk around in long robes, and love to be greeted with respect in the marketplaces, and to have the best seats in the synagogues [*synagōgai*] and places of honor at banquets.

Literature: As a general reference to commentaries, see Fitzmyer, Schürmann and Bovon, *Comm., ad loc.* Binder, *Temple Courts*, 97–98, 367.

Comments: See the comment on Mark 12:38–39 (No. 58).

No. 61
Source: *Literary.* Josephus, *B.J.* 4.406–408
Date: *De bello Judaico* consists of seven books and was published in the late 70s.

[406] ἐκινεῖτο δὲ καὶ κατὰ τὰ ἄλλα τῆς Ἰουδαίας κλίματα τὸ τέως ἠρεμοῦν τὸ ληστρικόν, καθάπερ δὲ ἐν σώματι τοῦ κυριωτάτου φλεγμαίνοντος πάντα τὰ μέλη συνενόσει· [407] διὰ γοῦν τὴν ἐν τῇ μητροπόλει στάσιν καὶ ταραχὴν ἄδειαν ἔσχον οἱ κατὰ τὴν χώραν πονηροὶ τῶν ἁρπαγῶν καὶ τὰς οἰκείας ἕκαστος κώμας ἁρπάζοντες ἔπειτα εἰς τὴν ἐρημίαν ἀφίσταντο. [408] συναθροιζόμενοί τε καὶ συνομνύμενοι κατὰ λόχους στρατιᾶς μὲν ὀλιγώτεροι πλείους δὲ ληστηρίου προσέπιπτον ἱεροῖς καὶ πόλεσιν

[406] Throughout the other parts of Judaea, moreover, the predatory bands, hitherto quiescent, now began to bestir themselves. And as in the body when inflammation attacks the principal member all the members catch the infection, [407] so the sedition and disorder in the capital gave the scoundrels in the country free licence to plunder; and each gang after pillaging their own village made off into the wilderness. [408] Then joining forces and swearing mutual allegiance, they would proceed by companies—smaller than an army but larger than a mere band of robbers—to fall upon sanctuaries [*hiera*] and cities.[11]

---

[11] Translation adapted from Thackeray (LCL).

Literature: Levine, "Nature and Origin," 430, n. 14; Binder, *Temple Courts*, 125–26, 156; Bilde, "Synagoge," 25; Claußen, *Versammlung*, 135–36; Runesson, *Origins*, 462; See also Nos. 13, 14.

Comments: The description of events given in this passage refers to a situation during the early stages of the First Jewish Revolt (ca. 67/68 C.E.). Josephus refers to the plundering of *hiera* in the plural, clearly identifiable as Jewish structures (since some Jews are said to have asked the Romans for help; 410–411) in Judaea. Some scholars have interpreted the passage as referring to non-Jewish structures, translating *hiera* as "temples." For the reasons given, however, this is unlikely. In other passages Josephus could use the term *hieron* to refer to the synagogue (cf. *B. J.* 7.44–45, No. 190 [= No. T10]). See also *A.J.* 14.374; *B. J.* 1.277–278; 7.144: Nos. 13, 14); there is no reason to believe that this would not be the case here.

No. 62
Source: *Literary*. Josephus, *B. J.* 7.139–150
Date: *De bello Judaico* consists of seven books and was published in the late 70s.

[139] θαῦμα δ᾽ ἐν τοῖς μάλιστα παρεῖχεν ἡ τῶν φερομένων πηγμάτων κατασκευή· καὶ γὰρ διὰ μέγεθος ἦν δεῖσαι τῷ βεβαίῳ τῆς φορᾶς ἀπιστήσαντα, [140] τριώροφα γὰρ αὐτῶν πολλὰ καὶ τετρώροφα πεποίητο, καὶ τῇ πολυτελείᾳ τῇ περὶ τὴν κατασκευὴν ἦν ἡσθῆναι μετ᾽ ἐκπλήξεως. [141] καὶ γὰρ ὑφάσματα πολλοῖς διάχρυσα περιβέβλητο, καὶ χρυσὸς καὶ ἐλέφας οὐκ ἀποίητος πᾶσι περιεπεπήγει. [142] διὰ πολλῶν δὲ μιμημάτων ὁ πόλεμος ἄλλος εἰς ἄλλα μεμερισμένος ἐναργεστάτην ὄψιν αὐτοῦ παρεῖχεν· [143] ἦν γὰρ ὁρᾶν χώραν μὲν εὐδαίμονα δῃουμένην, ὅλας δὲ φάλαγγας κτεινομένας πολεμίων, καὶ τοὺς μὲν φεύγοντας τοὺς δ᾽ εἰς αἰχμαλωσίαν ἀγομένους, τείχη δ᾽ ὑπερβάλλοντα μεγέθει μηχαναῖς ἐρειπόμενα καὶ φρουρίων ἁλισκομένας ὀχυρότητας καὶ πόλεων πολυανθρώπους περιβόλους κατ᾽ ἄκρας ἐχομένους, [144] καὶ στρατιὰν ἔνδον τειχῶν εἰσχεομένην, καὶ πάντα φόνου πλήθοντα τόπον, καὶ τῶν ἀδυνάτων χεῖρας ἀνταίρειν ἱκεσίας, πῦρ τε ἐνιέμενον ἱεροῖς καὶ κατασκαφὰς οἴκων ἐπὶ τοῖς δεσπόταις, [145] καὶ μετὰ πολλὴν ἐρημίαν καὶ κατήφειαν ποταμοὺς ῥέοντας οὐκ ἐπὶ γῆν γεωργουμένην, οὐδὲ ποτὸν ἀνθρώποις ἢ βοσκήμασιν, ἀλλὰ διὰ τῆς ἐπιπανταχόθεν φλεγομένης· ταῦτα γὰρ Ἰουδαῖοι πεισομένους αὐτοὺς τῷ πολέμῳ παρέδοσαν. [146] ἡ τέχνη δὲ καὶ τῶν κατασκευασμάτων ἡ μεγαλουργία τοῖς οὐκ ἰδοῦσι γινόμενα τότ᾽ ἐδείκνυεν ὡς παροῦσι. [147] τέτακτο δ᾽ ἐφ᾽ ἑκάστῳ τῶν πηγμάτων ὁ τῆς ἁλισκομένης πόλεως στρατηγὸς ὃν τρόπον ἐλήφθη. [148] πολλαὶ δὲ καὶ νῆες εἵποντο. λάφυρα δὲ τὰ μὲν ἄλλα χύδην ἐφέρετο, διέπρεπε δὲ πάντων τὰ ἐγκαταληφθέντα

τῷ ἐν Ἰεροσολύμοις ἱερῷ, χρυσῆ τε τράπεζα τὴν ὁλκὴν πολυτάλαντος
καὶ λυχνία χρυσῆ μὲν ὁμοίως πεποιημένη, τὸ δ’ ἔργον ἐξήλλακτο τῆς
κατὰ τὴν ἡμετέραν χρῆσιν συνηθείας. [149] ὁ μὲν γὰρ μέσος ἦν κίων
ἐκ τῆς βάσεως πεπηγώς, λεπτοὶ δ’ ἀπ’ αὐτοῦ μεμήκυντο καυλίσκοι
τριαίνης σχήματι παραπλησίαν τὴν θέσιν ἔχοντες, λύχνον ἕκαστος
αὐτῶν ἐπ’ ἄκρον κεχαλκευμένος· ἑπτὰ δ’ ἦσαν οὗτοι τῆς παρὰ τοῖς
Ἰουδαίοις ἑβδομάδος τὴν τιμὴν ἐμφανίζοντες. [150] ὅ τε νόμος ὁ τῶν
Ἰουδαίων ἐπὶ τούτοις ἐφέρετο τῶν λαφύρων τελευταῖος.

[139] But nothing in the procession excited so much as the structure
of the moving stages; indeed, their massiveness afforded ground for
alarm and misgiving as to their stability, [140] many of them being
three or four stories high, while the magnificence of the fabric was a
source at once of delight and amazement. For many were enveloped in
tapestries interwoven with gold, and all had a framework of gold and
wrought ivory. [142] The war was shown by numerous representations,
in separate sections, affording a very vivid picture of its episodes. [143]
Here was to be seen a prosperous country devastated, there whole bat-
talions of the enemy slaughtered; here a party in flight, there others
led in captivity; walls of suppressing compass demolished by engines,
strong fortresses overpowered, cities with well-manned defences completely mastered [144] and an army pouring within the ramparts, an
area all deluged with blood, the hands of those incapable of resistance
raised in supplication, sanctuaries [hiera] set on fire, houses pulled down
over their owners’ heads, [145] and after general desolation and woe,
reverse flowing, not over a cultivated land, nor supplying drink to man
and beast, but across a country still on every side on flames. For to
such sufferings were the Jews destined when they plunged into the war;
[146] and the art and magnificent workmanship of these structures now
portrayed the incidents to those who had not witnessed them, as though
they were happening before their eyes. [147] On each of the stages
was stationed the general of one of the captured cities in the attitude
in which he was taken. [148] A number of ships also followed.

   The spoils in general were borne in promiscuous heaps; but conspicuous above all stood out those captured in the temple of Jerusalem. These
consisted of a golden temple, many talents in weight, and a lampstand,
likewise made of gold, but constructed on a different pattern from
those which we use in ordinary life. [149] Affixed to a pedestal was a
central shaft, from which there extended slender branches, arranged
trident-fashioned, a wrought lamp being attached to the extremity of

each branch; of these there were seven, indicating the honour paid to the number among the Jews. [150] After these, and the last of all the spoils, was carried a copy of the Jewish law.

Literature: Levine, "Nature and Origin," 430, n. 14; Binder, *Temple Courts*, 123–24, 155; Bilde, "Synagoge," 26; Runesson, *Origins*, 462; Claußen, *Versammlung*, 134–35.

Comments: The triumphal procession described in the passage was held in Rome shortly after the fall of Jerusalem in 70 c.e. Josephus' description of the triumphal procession mentions not only the display of spoils, but also artistic depictions of the disasters that had befallen the Jewish people. Of interest here is the depiction of *hiera* set on fire (144). The context makes clear that these buildings were Jewish. In addition to the plural used, which itself would prevent us from understanding this as a reference to the Jerusalem temple, the temple is explicitly dealt with later in the text. This passage is thus evidence that: a) Josephus used *hieron* to refer to synagogue buildings, and b) that the Romans destroyed many of these assembly places—or "sanctuaries" as Josephus describes them—during the First Jewish Revolt.

2.2.3   *General*

No. 63
Source: *Literary*. Susanna 28 (Old Greek)
Date: Ca. 150–100 b.c.e.

[28] οἱ δὲ παράνομοι ἄνδρες ἀπέστρεψαν ἀπειλοῦντες ἐν ἑαυτοῖς καὶ ἐνεδρεύοντες ἵνα θανατώσουσιν αὐτήν καὶ ἐλθόντες ἐπὶ τὴν συναγωγὴν τῆς πόλεως οὗ παρῳκοῦσαν καὶ συνήδρευσαν οἱ ὄντες ἐκεῖ πάντες οἱ υἱοὶ Ισραηλ.

[28] But the lawless men turned away, murmuring threats among themselves and plotting to put her [Susanna] to death. They came to the synagogue [*synagōgē*] of the city where they sojourned, and all the Israelites who were there assembled [*synedreuō*].[12]

Literature: Levine, "Nature and Origin," 441; Collins, *Daniel*, 431; Binder, *Temple Courts*, 93, n. 4, 446, n. 135; Runesson, *Origins*, 461, n. 204; Claußen, *Versammlung*, 268–69.

Comments: This passage may be the earliest evidence of the use of the term *synagōgē* to designate a building in which public assemblies took place. The nature of the assembly is of judicial character. The Theodotion version,

---

[12] Translation by John J. Collins, *Daniel*, 420.

which is later than the OG version and dependent upon it, places the trial
inside the house of Joakim, Susanna's husband.

No. 64
Source: *Literary. Bib. Ant.* 11.8
Date: *Liber antiquitatum biblicarum* probably originated sometime between 135
B.C.E. and 70 C.E.

[8] Conserva diem sabbati sanctificare eum. Sex diebus fac opera,
septima autem dies sabbatum Domini est. Non facies in eo omne opus,
tu et omnis operaio tua, nisi ut in ea laudes Dominum in ecclesia pres-
biterorum et glorifices Fortem in cathedra seniorum.

[8] Take care to sanctify the Sabbath day. Work for six days, but the
seventh day is the Sabbath of the Lord. You shall not do any work on
it, you and all your help, except to praise the LORD in the assembly
[*ecclesia*] of the elders and to glorify the Mighty One in the council
[*cathedra*] of older men.[13]

Literature: Binder, *Temple Courts*, 49–54, 413; Runesson, *Origins*, 345–46;
Claußen, *Versammlung*, 66; Levine, *Ancient Synagogue*, 166.

Comments: If *Liber antiquitatum* is dated before the turn of the era, this
passage constitutes, together with some Qumran texts, the oldest explicit
reference to the Sabbath as a day of assembly that included ritual worship.
Contrary to the sectarian writings, however, the present text combines Exod
20:8–11 and Ps 107:32 to describe a public setting in which worship takes
place. Such public assemblies are mentioned in Sir 24:23 (connecting Torah
to assemblies[*synagōgai*]) and *Pss. Sol.* 10:7 (mentioning the glorification of God
in assemblies [*synagōgai*]). Neither of these latter texts, however, state that such
activities took place on the Sabbath, although it is likely that they did.

No. 65
Source: *Literary.* Mark 13:9
Date: Ca. 70 C.E.

[9] Βλέπετε δὲ ὑμεῖς ἑαυτούς· παραδώσουσιν ὑμᾶς εἰς συνέδρια καὶ
εἰς συναγωγὰς δαρήσεσθε καὶ ἐπὶ ἡγεμόνων καὶ βασιλέων σταθήσεσθε
ἕνεκεν ἐμοῦ εἰς μαρτύριον αὐτοῖς.

---

[13] Translation adapted from Harrington, "Pseudo-Philo," in OT pseudepigrapha
vol 2.

[9] As for yourselves, beware; for they will hand you over to councils; and you will be beaten in synagogues [*synagōgai*]; and you will stand before governors and kings because of me, as a testimony to them.

Literature: As a general reference to commentaries see Taylor, Pesch and Evans. *Comm., ad loc.* Binder, *Temple Courts*, 445–49; Runesson, *Origins*, 190, n. 84, 376, Stegemann, *Synagoge und Obrigkeit*, 97–100.

Comments: Parallel texts in Matt 10:17–18 (No. 66) and Luke 21:12–13 (No. 71). Compare also Matt 23:34, Luke 11:49 and 12:11–12 (No. 70). Mark 13:9, as with Luke 21:12–13, is a part of Jesus' eschatological discourse. The introductory words, "As for yourselves, beware," mark the beginning of a second section (see v. 5 and vv. 21–23) with focus on the Christ-believers themselves. Verses 9–13 deal with persecution and mission. Luke changes the introduction to "But before all this occurs," so that the persecutions are regarded as preceding the destruction of Jerusalem and the temple. Such persecutions are attested in Acts 4:16–18; 8:1–3; 12:1–5; 1 Thess 2:14 and Gal 1:13.

Matthew has moved a part of the eschatological discourse to his mission discourse in chapter 10, and he has applied it more to his own situation than to the actual sending out of the twelve. Thus the Jesus-believing Jews in Matthew's day have been persecuted both by Jews and by Gentiles, "as a testimony to them and the Gentiles," 10:18. Such Christ-believers should beware "all men," 10:17.

The Markan text can be segmented in two different ways: (1) "They will hand you over" with two effects: "In councils and in synagogues you will be beaten" and "You will stand before governors and kings"; or (2) as the three clauses in the translation above. In both cases, the phrases "because of me" and "as a testimony to them" belong to all sentences. The first verb, "hand over" (*paradidōmi*) also means "betray" in v. 12, explicitly by family members.

There are reasons to take councils and synagogues as refering to Jewish authorities, and governors and kings to Gentile authorities—as in Matt 10:17–18. Jesus-believing Jews (and God-fearers) were for a long time related to local synagogues. According to Mark, local Jewish courts, which were often connected to the synagogues, had the power to discipline. The punishment "forty lashes less one" was carried out publically in the synagogues (2 Cor 11:24f) as a warning to other members. Stephen, Peter, James, and Paul are examples of Christ-believers persecuted before 70 C.E.

The words "because of me" or "because of my name" state the reason for the persecution and remind readers about Jesus, who was also handed over, beaten and killed under Jewish and Gentile authorities. The last phrase can be translated, "as a testimony against them," but the mission context and the clear rewording in Luke 21:13 suggest the above translation.

No. 66
Source: *Literary.* Matt 10:17–18
Date: Ca. 80–90 C.E.

[17] Προσέχετε δὲ ἀπὸ τῶν ἀνθρώπων· παραδώσουσιν γὰρ ὑμᾶς εἰς συνέδρια καὶ ἐν ταῖς συναγωγαῖς αὐτῶν μαστιγώσουσιν ὑμᾶς· [18] καὶ ἐπὶ ἡγεμόνας δὲ καὶ βασιλεῖς ἀχθήσεσθε ἕνεκεν ἐμοῦ εἰς μαρτύριον αὐτοῖς καὶ τοῖς ἔθνεσιν.

17 Beware of them, for they will hand you over to councils [*synedria*] and flog you in their synagogues [*synagōgai*]; 18 and you will be dragged before governors and kings because of me, as a testimony to them and the Gentiles.

Literature: As a general reference to commentaries, see Bonnard, Luz and Hagner, *Comm.*, *ad loc.* Binder, *Temple Courts*, 445–49; Runesson, *Origins*, 355–57; idem, "Re-Thinking."

Comments: See the comments on Mark 13:9 (No. 65). The rewording of Mark 13:9 makes the segmentation of the text clear. *Mastigoun*, translated "flog" above, means "to beat severely with a whip" (cf. *phragelloun*). It is a technical term for a type of punishment meted out in the synagogues. (Cf. No. 86.) Mark uses the more general term *derein*, "to strike or beat repeatedly."

No. 67
Source: *Literary.* Matt 23:1–3
Date: Ca. 80–90 C.E.

[1] Τότε ὁ Ἰησοῦς ἐλάλησεν τοῖς ὄχλοις καὶ τοῖς μαθηταῖς αὐτοῦ [2] λέγων· ἐπὶ τῆς Μωϋσέως καθέδρας ἐκάθισαν οἱ γραμματεῖς καὶ οἱ Φαρισαῖοι. [3] πάντα οὖν ὅσα ἐὰν εἴπωσιν ὑμῖν ποιήσατε καὶ τηρεῖτε, κατὰ δὲ τὰ ἔργα αὐτῶν μὴ ποιεῖτε· λέγουσιν γὰρ καὶ οὐ ποιοῦσιν.

[1] Then Jesus said to the crowds and to his disciples, [2] "The scribes and the Pharisees sit on Moses' seat; [3] therefore, do whatever they teach you and follow it; but do not do as they do, for they do not practice what they teach.

Literature: As a general reference to commentaries, see Bonnard, Luz and Hagner, *Comm.*, *ad loc.* Binder, *Temple Courts*, 300–302, 306; Claußen, *Versammlung*, 80, 121–22; Levine, *Synagogues*, 84–86, 100–101, 104, 323–27; Runesson, *Origins*, 222–23.

Comments: If Matt 23:2 is not read in a metaphorical way it is our earliest literary evidence of the "seat of Moses," a seat in synagogues for a leader in a congregation or for a teacher of the Mosaic Law. In the synagogue on Delos (room A, last century before our era; see No. 102) there are benches at the western wall with a carved marble chair in the middle, facing the east entrance and Jerusalem. There could be honorary seats in the early synagogues (see Nos. 58, 196) and according to *t. Sukkah* 4.6 the large synagogue in Alexandria had seventy-one cathedrae of gold for the seventy-one elders. Later on the seat of Moses was the special chair for the rabbis who expounded, applied and developed the Mosaic Torah, or according to some scholars the place where the Torah scroll was placed after the reading. Levine suggests an influence from non-Jewish temples, where you find seats for priests, and argues more generally that the cathedra probably was a piece of furniture in some synagogues on which an important person of the congregation sat.

No. 68
Source: *Literary.* Matt 23:34
Date: Ca. 80–90 c.e.

[34] Διὰ τοῦτο ἰδοὺ ἐγὼ ἀποστέλλω πρὸς ὑμᾶς προφήτας καὶ σοφοὺς καὶ γραμματεῖς· ἐξ αὐτῶν ἀποκτενεῖτε καὶ σταυρώσετε καὶ ἐξ αὐτῶν μαστιγώσετε ἐν ταῖς συναγωγαῖς ὑμῶν καὶ διώξετε ἀπὸ πόλεως εἰς πόλιν·

[34] Therefore I send you prophets, sages, and scribes, some of whom you will kill and crucify, and some you will flog in your synagogues [*synagōgē*] and pursue from town to town.

Literature: As a general reference to commentaries, see Bonnard, Luz and Hagner, *Comm.*, *ad loc.* Binder, *Temple Courts*, 445–49; Runesson, *Origins*, 355–57; Stegemann, *Synagoge und Obrigkeit*, 99–103.

Comments: The parallel text in Luke 11:49 does not refer to synagogues. See the comments on Mark 13:9 (No. 65) and Matt 10:17–18 (No. 66). Matt 23:34 functions as a final appendix to the long diatribe against the "Scribes and Pharisees" found in the preceding 33 verses. The introductory word can be translated as "accordingly" or "in keeping with this" (Hagner).

God's messengers—here sent by Jesus and called by such Jewish appellations as "prophets, sages, and scribes"—will be persecuted and killed, just as those righteous emissaries sent before them. The description reminds the reader of what Jesus suffered. On flogging in synagogues, see comments on Matt 10:17–18 (No. 66).

No. 69
Source: *Literary.* Luke 11:43
Date: Ca. 80–90 c.e.

[43] Οὐαὶ ὑμῖν τοῖς Φαρισαίοις, ὅτι ἀγαπᾶτε τὴν πρωτοκαθεδρίαν ἐν ταῖς συναγωγαῖς καὶ τοὺς ἀσπασμοὺς ἐν ταῖς ἀγοραῖς.

[43] Woe to you Pharisees! For you love to have the seat of honor in the synagogues [*synagōgai*] and to be greeted with respect in the marketplaces.

Literature: As a general reference to commentaries, see Fitzmyer, Schürmann and Bovon, *Comm., ad loc.* Binder, *Temple Courts*, 97–98, 367.

Comments: See comments on Mark 12:38–39 (No. 58).

No. 70
Source: *Literary.* Luke 12:11–12
Date: Ca. 80–90 C.E.

[11] Ὅταν δὲ εἰσφέρωσιν ὑμᾶς ἐπὶ τὰς συναγωγὰς καὶ τὰς ἀρχὰς καὶ τὰς ἐξουσίας, μὴ μεριμνήσητε πῶς ἢ τί ἀπολογήσησθε ἢ τί εἴπητε· [12] τὸ γὰρ ἅγιον πνεῦμα διδάξει ὑμᾶς ἐν αὐτῇ τῇ ὥρᾳ ἃ δεῖ εἰπεῖν.

[11] When they bring you before the synagogues [*synagōgai*], the rulers, and the authorities, do not worry about how you are to defend yourselves or what you are to say; [12] for the Holy Spirit will teach you at that very hour what you ought to say.

Literature: As a general reference to commentaries, see Fitzmyer, Schürmann and Bovon, *Comm., ad loc.* Binder, *Temple Courts*, 445–49; Runesson, *Origins*, 376; Stegemann, *Synagoge und Obrigkeit*, 40–90.

Comments: See the comments on Mark 13:9 (No. 65), Matt 10:17–18 (No. 66) and Luke 21:12–13 (No. 71). After some transitional statements in 11:53f and 12:1, Jesus exhorts his disciples to confess without fear (12:2–12). To be a Christ-believer in secret was not possible. When they had to defend themselves in the (Gentile) courts, the Holy Spirit would help them (12:11–12). According to Stegemann, Luke never describes synagogues as having forensic competence; nevertheless, punishments could be executed in synagogues. Luke 21:12 refers to inter-Jewish prosecutions before 70 C.E. when the Sanhedrin and its agents (like Saul) functioned as a Jewish court. The above passage clearly alludes to the situation of Luke's addressees, where "rulers and authorities" (*archai* and *exousiai*) referred to magistates and authorities in the Diaspora towns. Luke does not use technical terms in v. 11 for handing over somebody to a court.

No. 71
Source: *Literary.* Luke 21:12–13
Date: Ca. 80–90 C.E.

[12] Πρὸ δὲ τούτων πάντων ἐπιβαλοῦσιν ἐφ᾽ ὑμᾶς τὰς χεῖρας αὐτῶν καὶ διώξουσιν, παραδιδόντες εἰς τὰς συναγωγὰς καὶ φυλακάς, ἀπαγομένους ἐπὶ βασιλεῖς καὶ ἡγεμόνας ἕνεκεν τοῦ ὀνόματός μου· [13] ἀποβήσεται ὑμῖν εἰς μαρτύριον.

[12] But before all this occurs, they will arrest you and persecute you; they will hand you over to synagogues [*synagōgai*] and prisons, and you will be brought before kings and governors because of my name. [13] This will give you an opportunity to testify.

Literature: As a general reference to commentaries, see Fitzmyer, Schürmann and Bovon, *Comm., ad loc.* Binder, *Temple Courts*, 445–49; Runesson, *Origins*, 376; Stegemann, *Synagoge und Obrigkeit*, 80–90, 114–18.

Comments: See the comments on Mark 13:9 (No. 65) and Matt 10:17–18 (No. 66). Luke changes the introduction to "But before all this occurs" with the effect that the persecutions are regarded as preceding the destruction of Jerusalem and the temple. Luke uses "persecute/persecution" only about inner-Jewish activities, especially about persecutions of God's messengers in Israel and of the first Christ-believers in Jerusalem (Luke 11:49; 21:12; Acts 7:52; 8:1; 9:4–5; 13:50; 22:4, 7–8; 26:11, 14–15).

According to Luke, synagogues had no forensic competence; that existed only with the Sanhedrin in Jerusalem and its agents, such as Saul. See the comments on Luke 12:11–12 (No. 70). Here synagogues and prisons seem to have been put together as places of punishments.

No. 72
Source: *Literary.* Acts 15:21
Date: Ca. 90–110 c.e.

[21] Μωϋσῆς γὰρ ἐκ γενεῶν ἀρχαίων κατὰ πόλιν τοὺς κηρύσσοντας αὐτὸν ἔχει ἐν ταῖς συναγωγαῖς κατὰ πᾶν σάββατον ἀναγινωσκόμενος.

[21] For in every city, for generations past, Moses has had those who proclaim him, for he has been read aloud every Sabbath in the synagogues [*synagōgai*].

Literature: As a general reference to commentaries see Barrett, Fitzmyer and Jervell, *Comm., ad loc.* Binder, *Temple Courts*, 209–10; Levine, *Ancient Synagogue*, 506–10; Claußen, *Versammlung*, 152, 213–18; Runesson, *Origins*, 83–84, 213–23.

Comments: According to Philo and Josephus, a public reading (*anaginōskein*) of the Torah every Sabbath goes back to the time of Moses (see comments on Philo, *Mos.* 2.214–216, No. 166; cf. Josephus, *C.Ap.* 2.175). Luke here presents James as similarly believing that both this custom and the institution of the synagogue date back into distant antiquity. The word "proclaim" (*kēryssein*) seems to include not only reading but also expounding and teaching. See comments on No. 174.

No. 73
Source: *Literary.* Acts 22:19
Date: Ca. 90–110 C.E.

[19] κἀγὼ εἶπον· κύριε, αὐτοὶ ἐπίστανται ὅτι ἐγὼ ἤμην φυλακίζων καὶ δέρων κατὰ τὰς συναγωγὰς τοὺς πιστεύοντας ἐπὶ σέ.

[19] And I said, "Lord, they themselves know that in every synagogue [*synagōgai*] I imprisoned and beat those who believed in you."

Literature: As a general reference to commentaries see Barrett, Fitzmyer and Jervell, *Comm., ad loc.* Binder, *Temple Courts*, 445–49; Stegemann, *Synagoge und Obrigkeit*, 100–103.

Comments: In Acts 22:19–20 Paul is arguing with Jesus about Paul's actions against Jesus-believing Jews in Jerusalem and its vicinity. See comments on Acts 24:12 (No. 19) and Acts 26:9–11 (No. 20). Regarding the beating of people in synagogues, see comments on Mark 13:9 (No. 65) and its parallels.

No. 74
Source: *Literary.* John 16:1–4a
Date: Ca. 90–100 C.E.

[1] Ταῦτα λελάληκα ὑμῖν ἵνα μὴ σκανδαλισθῆτε. [2] ἀποσυναγώγους ποιήσουσιν ὑμᾶς· ἀλλ᾽ ἔρχεται ὥρα ἵνα πᾶς ὁ ἀποκτείνας ὑμᾶς δόξῃ λατρείαν προσφέρειν τῷ θεῷ. [3] καὶ ταῦτα ποιήσουσιν ὅτι οὐκ ἔγνωσαν τὸν πατέρα οὐδὲ ἐμέ. [4] ἀλλὰ ταῦτα λελάληκα ὑμῖν ἵνα ὅταν ἔλθῃ ἡ ὥρα αὐτῶν μνημονεύητε αὐτῶν ὅτι ἐγὼ εἶπον ὑμῖν.

[1] I have said these things to you to keep you from stumbling. [2] They will put you out of the synagogues [*aposynagōgos*]. Indeed, an hour is coming when those who kill you will think that by doing so they are offering worship to God. [3] And they will do this because they have not known the Father or me. [4] But I have said these things to you so that when their hour comes you may remember that I told you about them.

Literature: As a general reference to commentaries, see Brown, Moloney and Thyen, *Comm., ad loc.* Binder, *Temple Courts*, 75–78; Levine, *Ancient Synagogue*, 193; Runesson, *Origins*, 376; Stegemann, *Synagoge und Obrigkeit*, 139–42; Horst, *Birkat ha-minim*; Olsson, *In synagogues*, 217–18.

Comments: See the comments on John 9:22–23 (No. 16). Chapters 15–16 belong to the later stages of the Gospel's production and most scholars read 16:1–4a as reflecting the later situation of the Johannine Christ-believers.

For them, there was a real threat to the strong unity and the mutual love of the new fellowship. The most serious danger is described as "stumbling" (*skandalizesthai*)—that is, to fall away, to lose one's faith. Compare the use of this verb in John 6:60–71. The anaphoric *tauta*, "these things," refers back to 15:18–27 and its theme of unity, or the opposite of unity. The agents in this section are called "they" (= some Jews) and "the world" (15:18–19). "They" hate the Jesus-believing Jews in their synagogues because they do not know the One who has sent Jesus (15:21; 16:3). The context makes clear that the phrase "to offer *latreia* to God" refers to Jewish rather than Roman persecution of Jesus-believers: killing perceived apostates would be regarded as an act of piety in the service of religion.

Many scholars refer to texts about Jewish practices, such as *Num. Rab.* 21; *m. Sanh.* 9:6; Josephus, *A. J.* 20.200; *Mart. Poly.* 13:1 and Justin, *Dial.* 95:4; 133:6. For examples of the accusation that Jews attacked Jesus-believing Jews, see Acts 7:58–60; 26:9; Gal 1:13–14 and Josephus, *A. J.* 20.9.

No. 75
Source: *Literary.* John 18:19–21
Date: Ca. 90–100 C.E.

[19] Ὁ οὖν ἀρχιερεὺς ἠρώτησεν τὸν Ἰησοῦν περὶ τῶν μαθητῶν αὐτοῦ καὶ περὶ τῆς διδαχῆς αὐτοῦ. [20] ἀπεκρίθη αὐτῷ Ἰησοῦς· ἐγὼ παρρησίᾳ λελάληκα τῷ κόσμῳ, ἐγὼ πάντοτε ἐδίδαξα ἐν συναγωγῇ καὶ ἐν τῷ ἱερῷ, ὅπου πάντες οἱ Ἰουδαῖοι συνέρχονται, καὶ ἐν κρυπτῷ ἐλάλησα οὐδέν. [21] τί με ἐρωτᾷς; ἐρώτησον τοὺς ἀκηκοότας τί ἐλάλησα αὐτοῖς· ἴδε οὗτοι οἴδασιν ἃ εἶπον ἐγώ.

[19] Then the high priest questioned Jesus about his disciples and about his teaching. [20] Jesus answered, "I have spoken openly to the world; I have always taught in synagogues [*synagōgai*] and in the temple, where all the Jews come together. I have said nothing in secret. [21] Why do you ask me? Ask those who heard what I said to them; they know what I said."

Literature: As a general reference to commentaries, see Brown, Moloney and Thyen, *Comm., ad loc.* Binder, *Temple Courts*, 75–78; Runesson, *Origins*, 221, 226, 353; Lieu, "Temple and Synagogue"; Olsson, "In synagogues", 217–18.

Comments: See the comment on Luke 4:16–30 (No. 33). In many ways the temple courts in Jerusalem shared similar functions with the synagogues of the towns and villages (Binder). In the Gospel of John, a central part of Jesus' revelation of himself to the Jews occured in both the synagogues and the temple—places "where Jews come together" (6:59; 7:14, 18; 8:20; 10:23). As in the Johannine Passion Narrative as a whole, the focus is both on Jesus and his disciples. The phrase "they know what I said," v. 21, reminds the reader of the disciples who received the Paraclete: they too could witness about Jesus' teaching to subsequent generations in the same manner as Jesus did—openly in the synagogues.

No. 76
Source: *Literary. m. Ber.* 7:3
Date: Ca. 200 C.E.

אמר רבי עקיבה, מה מצינו בבית הכנסת? אחד מרובין ואחד מועטין אומרין
ברכו את ה׳; רבי ישמעאל אומר, ברכו את ה׳ המבורך.

Said R. Akiba, How do we find in the Synagogue [*bet ha-kneset*]? Whether there are many or whether there are few he says, *Bless ye the Eternal*; R. Ishmael says, *Bless ye the Eternal Who is to be blessed.*

Literature: Schürer, *HJP* 2.449; Fine, *This Holy Place*, 51, 181 n. 4; Zahavy, *Jewish Prayer*, 55–56.

Comments: The context for this discussion is not the synagogue but the meal, in particular, the question of how many individuals must be present for the recital of a blessing to be mandatory. The view that the number of participants does not matter, a blessing should always be said, is attributed to R. Akiva (ca. 50–ca. 135 C.E.) and supported by the argument that this is what is done in the synagogue (*bet ha-kneset*). As Zahavy notes, the language here is descriptive, not prescriptive, indicating that the rabbis took part in synagogue worship. It does not prove, however, that they held authority in the synagogues. One may also note that prayer is taken for granted as being part of synagogue liturgy, a fact for which there is meagre evidence in the first century and earlier sources.

No. 77
Source: *Literary. m. Ter.* 11:10
Date: Ca. 200 C.E.

מדליקין שמן שרפה בבתי כנסיות, ובבתי מדרשות, ובמבואות האפלין, ועל גבי
החולין ברשות כהן.

They may kindle oil of priest's due, that must be burnt, in the synagogues (*bate knesiot*) and in houses of study (*bate midrashot*), and in dark alleys, and for sick people by permission of a priest.

Literature: Schürer, *HJP* 2.446; Fine, *This Holy Place*, 185, n. 53; Levine, *Ancient Synagogue*, 359, n. 227.

Comments: This Mishnah is concerned with the topic of how to dispose of oil from the priest's due (*terumah*) that has become ritually impure (*tame'*) and therefore must be burnt. The reference to the use of such oil for lamps within synagogues shows: a) the existence of public synagogue buildings, and b) that, in addition to natural lighting from windows, or clerestory windows, artificial sources of light were also used on a regular basis. The reference to the rabbis' own institution, the house of learning (*bet ha-midrash*), suggests that this institution may have been housed in separate purpose-built edifices, perhaps similar in architectural design to the public synagogues (cf. Runesson, *Origins*, 223–34). Regarding the date of the saying, a later portion of the passage, not quoted here, refers to several second-century rabbis and their opinions on this matter: R. Judah, R. Jose, R. Meir, and R. Simon, who were all students of R. Akiva (R. Jose became the mentor of R. Judah ha-Nasi, who codified the Mishnah).

No. 78
Source: *Literary. m. Bik.* 1:4
Date: Ca. 200 C.E.

וכשהוא מתפלל בינו לבין עצמו, אומר אלהי אבות ישראל; וכשהוא בבית
הכנסת, אומר, אלהי אבותיכם.

And when he [the proselyte] prays privately, he says, *O God of the ancestors of Israel*; and when he is in the synagogue [*bet ha-kneset*], he says, *O God of your ancestors*; and if his mother were an Israelite, he may say, *O God of our ancestors*.

Literature: Schürer, *HJP* 3.1.176; Zahavy, *Jewish Prayer*, 56–57.

Comments: It is difficult to date this passage which focusses on the fixed wording of public and private prayers for proselytes. As has been attested elsewhere (No. 43), prayer was part of public synagogue ritual; here we find additional information that prayer was fixed in form. The rabbis had their own views on how such prayer should be said by proselytes. Blackman (*ad loc.*) notes that the Rambam (Rabbi Moshe ben Maimon, or Maimonides, 1135–1204) rules that no distinction should be made between Jews and proselytes: the latter become "spiritual descendents of Abraham" at the moment they convert.

No. 79
Source: *Literary. m. Pesah.* 4:4
Date: Ca. 200 C.E.

מקום שנהגו להדליק את הנר בלילי יום הכפורים מדליקין; מקום שנהגו
שלא להדליק אין מדליקין. ומדליקין בבתי כנסיות ובבתי מדרשות, ובמבואות
האפלים, ועל גבי החולים.

Where they are accustomed to kindle light on the night of the Day of Atonement they may light up; in any place where the custom is not to kindle they may not light up. But they may light up in the synagogues [*bate knesioth*], in the houses of study [*bate midrashoth*], in the dark alleys and for the sick.

Literature: Fine, *This Holy Place*, 85, 185, n. 53; Levine, *Ancient Synagogues*, 241.

Comments: The custom of introducing an eternal light (*ner tamid*) in synagogues, attested in late midrashim, established a close religious connection between the synagogue and the temple by applying to the former biblical commandments meant for the latter. In this early text, however, such symbolism is less likely; candles simply provided light (so Levine; see also above, No. 77). The above passage attests the rabbis' approval of some variation within local synagogue practices.

No. 80
Source: *Literary. m. Sukkah* 3:13
Date: Ca. 200 c.e.

יום טוב הראשון של חג שחל להיות בשבת כל העם מוליכין את לוליביהן לבית
הכנסת, למחרת משכימין ובאין, כל אחד ואחד מכיר את שלו ונוטלו, מפני
שאמרו חכמים, אין אדם יוצא ידי חובתו ביום טוב הראשון של חג בלולבו של
חבירו. ושאר ימות החג אדם יוצא ידי חובתו בלולבו של חבירו.

If the first Holyday day of the Festival of Tabernacles happened to fall on the Sabbath, all the people bring their *Lulavin* to the synagogue [*bet ha-kneset*]. On the morrow they come early, and every man discerns his own and takes it up, because the sages have said, No man can fulfil his obligation on the first Festival day of the Tabernacles with the *Lulav* of his fellow. But on the other days of the Festival of Tabernacles a man may fulfil his obligation with the *Lulav* of his fellow.

Literature: Zahavy, *Jewish Prayer*, 58; Fine, *This Holy Place*, 50–51; Levine, *Ancient Synagogue*, 486.

Comments: This passage, which regulates the use of ritual objects (the *lulav*) on Sukkoth, is noteworthy for its designation of the synagogue (*bet ha-kneset*) as the proper place to fulfill the mitzvah in question. While this does not demonstrate that the rabbis were leaders of Jewish communities, it does show that rabbinic authorities acknowledged the synagogue as a place where certain religious duties could and should be fulfilled (cf. Levine). Rabbinic recognition of the (religious) importance of the synagogue increases in the third and fourth centuries, as does their involvement in it, although the house of study (*bet ha-midrash*) was still the preferred institution for many of the sages (Levine, 486–87).

No. 81
Source: Literary. *m. Rosh Hash.* 3:7
Date: Ca. 200 C.E.

וכן, מי שהיה עובר אחורי בית הכנסת, או שהיה ביתו סמוך לבית הכנסת,
ושמע קול שופר או קול מגילה, אם כוון לבו יצא ואם לאו לא יצא. אף על
פי שזה שמע וזה שמע זה כוון לבו וזה לא כוון לבו.

And likewise, if one were passing behind a synagogue [*bet ha-kneset*],
and he heard the sound of the *shofar*, or the reading of the *Megillah*,
if he concentrated his mind on it, he has performed his duty, but if
not, he has not carried out his obligation. Though the former heard
and the latter heard, but one directed his mind and the other did not
direct his mind.

Literature: Zahavy, *Jewish Prayer*, 57; Fine, *This Holy Place*, 50–51, 181, n. 4.

Comments: The importance of inner devotion and intention is here related
to public rituals taking place in the synagogue (*bet ha-kneset*). The context makes
clear that the rituals mentioned took place inside a purpose-built edifice. For
the significance of intention within temple ritual, see, e.g., *m. Yoma* 8:9. In
both cases, participation in a ritual, as well as the ritual's efficacy, is defined
by a person's intentions. Cf. also *m. Ber.* 4:4–5; 5:1.

No. 82
Source: *Literary. m. Meg.* 3:1–3
Date: Ca. 200 C.E.

בני העיר שמכרו רחובה של עיר לוקחין בדמיו בית הכנסת; בית הכנסת לוקחין
תיבה; תיבה לוקחים מטפחות; מטפחות לוקחים ספרים; ספרים לוקחים תורה.
אבל אם מכרו תורה לא יקחו ספרים; ספרים לא יקחו מטפחות; מטפחות לא
יקחו תיבה; תיבה לא יקחו בית הכנסת; בית הכנסת לא יקחו את הרחוב. וכן
במותריהן. אין מוכרין את של רבים ליחיד מפני שמורידין אותו מקדושתו; דברי
רבי יהודה. אמרו לו, אם כן אף לא מעיר נדולה לעיר קטנה.

ג,ב אין מוכרין בית הכנסת אלא על תנאי, שאם ירצו, יחזירוהו. דברי רבי
מאיר. והחכמים אומרים, מוכרים אותו ממכר עולם חוץ מארבעה דברים, למרחץ,
ולבוסקי, ולטבילה, ולבית המים. רבי יהודה אומר, מוכרון אותו לשם חצר,
והלוקח, מה שירצה יעשה.

ג,ג ועוד אמר רבי יהודה, בית הכנסת שחרב אין מספידין בתוכו, ואין מפשילין
בתוכו חבלים, ואין פורשין לתוכו מצודות, ואין שוטחין על ננו פירות, ואין עושין
אותו קפנדריא. שנאמר, והשימותי את מקדשיכם, קדושתן אף כשהן שוממין עלו
בו עשבים, לא יתלוש מפני ענמת נפש.

[1] If the people of a town have sold its open space, they may purchase a *synagogue* [*bet ha-kneset*] with the proceeds thereof; a *synagogue*, they may purchase an *Ark*; an *Ark*, they may buy *mantles; mantles*, they may buy *Books; Books*, they may purchase a *Scroll of the Law*. But if they sold a *Scroll of the Law* they may not buy *Books; Books*, they must not buy *mantles; mantles*, they may not purchase an *Ark*; an *Ark*, they may not buy a *synagogue*; a *synagogue*, they may not purchase an open space. And likewise also with any surplus. They may not sell the property of a community to a private person for thereby they degrade its sanctity—this is the opinion of R. Judah. They said to him, if so, then not even from a large town to a small town.

[2] They may not sell a synagogue except on the condition that, when they may so desire, it will be returned. This is the view of R. Meir. But the Sages say, They may sell it in perpetuity save for four purposes: for a bath-house, or for a tannery, or for a ritual bath, or for a urinal. R. Judah says, They may sell it for a courtyard, and the purchaser may do whatever he desires.

[3] And moreover R. Judah said, If a synagogue be derelict, they may not deliver a funeral oration therein, nor may they twist ropes therein, nor may they spread out nets therein, nor spread out produce upon its roof, nor make of it a short-cut. As it is said, *And I will bring your sanctuaries into desolation*—their holiness remains even though they by desolate. If grasses sprang up therein, one may not pluck them up because of grief of soul.

Literature: Schürer, *HJP* 2.446; Zahavy, *Jewish Prayer*, 58–60; Levine, *Ancient Synagogue*, 200–203; Fine, *This Holy Place*, 38–40, 68, 91, 131–32. Haber, "Common Judaism, Common Synagogue?"

Comments: According to the rabbis, objects and places could be arranged in a hierarchy on the basis of their holiness. This notion is found in connection to the Jerusalem temple and the land of Israel: from the general concept of the land as holy, sanctity proceeds to higher levels. Thus one "ascends" to the city of Jerusalem, enters the temple courts, and finally faces toward the holy of holies, the summit of all sanctity.

In the above citation, the Torah scroll occupies the highest degree of sanctity, as is reflected in the regulations relating to the buying or selling things holy (cf. *m. Yad.* 3:5; 4:6.). At the bottom of the scale rested the city square (*rehov shel 'ir*), the place where public prayers were performed during fast days (Zahavy). Thus in the second century, the synagogue, defined as a purpose-built edifice, was regarded as holy by the rabbis, though not as holy as the Torah scrolls. Not even a synagogue taken out of use could properly be treated as any kind of building: its sanctity endured, a view attributed to the second century authority R. Judah (3:3).

Over time, the rabbis viewed the synagogue as increasingly holy. The underlying reasons for this evolution are still debated. Was it because of an increasing awareness that the temple would not be re-built and therefore the synagogue assumed the former's holiness? Or was it because of the placement of the Torah scrolls in special apses or niches in the main hall of the synagogue from about the fourth century onward?

On the other hand, it should not be overlooked that synagogues were already considered holy places by Jewish communities (particularly in the Diaspora) prior to the temple's destruction (e.g., Josephus, *B. J.* 285–292). The sanctity of Torah scrolls was also evident during the early period (e.g., *Letter of Aristeas*, 305–306). The link between sanctity and synagogue thus did not originate in the fourth century C.E., though it clearly became more pronounced then in rabbinic circles.

While a variety of influences may have been at work in this shift, primary importance should be attributed to the fact that synagogue holiness increased co-terminously with rabbinnic interest in the synagogue as the primary locus for maintaining Jewish identity at a time when Christianity (which likewise claimed the Jewish Scriptures as their own) became the official religion of the empire.

With the rise of rabbinic Judaism within Jewish communities, rabbinic understanding of the Torah as the most holy object of Judaism (absent the temple) became prevalent in the synagogues, transforming these buildings into increasingly sacred places. Such transformation can particularly be seen in the addition of special architectural features related to the Torah scrolls (niches and apses, etc.). The earlier Diaspora emphasis upon the sanctity of the synagogues, based more on local ideas about sanctity in relation to temples, may also have played a role in the reception of such perspectives outside the land of Israel. In the second century, however, this development had only begun, as the above passage reveals.

No. 83
Source: *Literary. m. Meg.* 3:4–4:10
Date: Ca. 200 C.E.

ג,ד ואש חדש אדר שחל להיות בשבת קורין בפרשת שקלים; חל להיות בתוך
השבת, מקדימין לשעבר ומפיקין לשבת אחרת. בשניה, זכור; בשלישית, פרה
אדומה; ברביעית, החודש הזה לכם; בחמישית, חוזרין לכסדרן. לכל מפסיקין,
בראשי חדשים, וחנוכה, ובפורים, בתעניות, ובעמדות, וביום הכפורים.

ג,ה בפסח קורין בפרשת מועדות של תורת כהנים; בעצרת, שבעה שבועות;
בראש השנה, בחדש השביעי באחד לחדש; ביום הכפורים, אחרי מות; ביום
טוב הראשון של חג, קורין בפרשת מועדות שבתורת כהנים; ובשאר כל ימות
החג, בקרבנות החג.

ג,ו בחנוכה, בנשיאים, בפורים, ויבא עמלק; בראשי חודשים, ובראשי חדשיכם;
במעמדות, במעשה בראשית; בתעניות, ברכות וקללות, אין מפסיקין בקללות,
אלא אחד קורא את כולן; בשני ובחמישי ובשבת במנחה קורין כסדרן, ואין
עולין להם מן החשבון. שנאמר, וידבר משה את מועדי ה' אל בני ישראל, מצותן
שיהו קורין כל אחד ואחד בזמנו.

מסכת מגילה פרק ד

ד,א הקורא את המגילה עומד, יושב; קראה אחד, קראוה שנים, יצאו. מקום
שנהגו לברך יברך, ושלא לברך לא יברך. בשני, ובחמישי, ובשבת במנחה
קורין שלשה; אין פוחתין ואין מוסיפין עליהן; ואין מפטירין בנביא. הפותח
והחותם בתורה מברך, לפניה ולאחריה.

ד,ב בראשי חדשים ובחולו של מועד קורין ארבעה, אין פוחתין מהן ואין מוסיפין
עליהן; ואין מפטירין בנביא. הפותח והחותם בתורה נברך לפניה ולאחריה. זה
הכלל, כל שיש בו מוסף, ואינו יום טוב, קורין ארבעה; ביום טוב, חמשה, ביום
הכפורים, ששה; בשבת, שבעה. אין פוחתין מהן אבל מוסיפין עליהן, ומפטירין
בנביא. הפותח והחותם בתורה, מברך לפניה ולאחריה.

ד,ג אין פורסין את שמע, ואין עוברין לפני התיבה, ואין נושאין את כפיהם,
ואין קורין בתורה, ואין מפטירין בנביא, ואין עושין מעמד ומושב, ואין אומרים
ברכת אבלים ותנחומי אבלים וברכת וחתנים, ואין מזמנים בשם פחות מעשרה.
ובקרקעות תשעה וכהן, ואדם, כיוצא בהן.

ד,ד הקורא בתורה לא יפחות משלשה פסוקים; לא יקרא למתורגמן יותר מפסוק
אחד, ובנביא שלשה; היו שלשתן שלש פרשיות קורין אחד אחד. מדלגין בנביא,
ואין מדלגין בתורה. עד כמה הוא מדלג? עד כדי שלא יפסוק התורגמן.

ד,ה המפטיר בנביא הוא פורס על שמע, והוא עובר לפני התיבה, והוא נושא
את כפיו; ואם היה קטן, אביו או רבו עוברין על ידו.

ד,ו קטן קורא בתורה ומתרגם, אבל אינו פורס על שמע, ואינו עובר לפני התיבה
ואינו נושא את כפיו. פוחח פורס את שמע ומתרגם, אבל אינו קורא בתורה ואינו
עובר לפני התיבה ואינו נושא את כפיו. סומא פורס את שמע ומתרגם. רבי
יהודה אומר, כל שלא ראה מאורות מימיו אינו פורס על שמע.

ד,ז כהן שיש בידיו מומין לא ישא את כפיו. רבי יהודה אומר, אף מי שהיו ידיו
צבועות אסטיס ופואה לא ישא את כפיו מפני שהעם מסתכלין בו.

ד,ח האומר, איני עובר לפני התיבה בצביעין, אף בלבנים לא יעביר. בסנדל
איני עובר, אף יחף לא יעביר. העושה תפלתו עגולה סכנה ואין בה מצוה.
נתנה על מצחו או על פס ידו, הרי זו דרך המינות. ציפן זהב ונתנה על נית
אונקלי שלו, הרי זו דרך החיצונים.

ד,ט האומר, יברכון טובים, הרי זו דרך המינות. על קן צפור יגיעו רחמיך,
ועל טוב יזכר שמך, מודים מודים, משתקין אותו, המכנה בעריות משתקין אותו.
האומר, מזרעך לא תתן להעביר למולך ומזרעך לא תתן לאעברא בארמיותא,
משתקין אותו בנזיפה.

ד,י מעשה ראובן נקרא ולא מתרגם, מעשה תמר נקרא ומיתרגם; מעשה עגל
ראשון נקרא ומיתרגם, והשני נקרא ולא מיתרגם; ברכת כהנים, מעשה דוד
ואמנון לא נקראין ולא מיתרגמין. אין מפטירין במרכבה; ורבי יהודה מתיר.
רבי אליעזר אומר, אין מפטירין בהודע את ירושלים.

[3.4] When the first day of the month of Adar falls on a Sabbath they
read the *section of Shekalim*; if it fall during the week, they read it earlier
on the preceding one and they interrupt to the next Sabbath. On the
second one, *Remember*; on the third one, *The Red Heifer*; on the fourth one,
This month shall be unto you; on the fifth one, they revert to the regular
order. For all of these they break off: on the first days of the months,
on the Festival of Dedication, and on Purim, on fast days, and a the
Lay Guards, and on the Day of Atonement.

[3.5] On the Passover they read from the portion *Festivals* in the *Law of
the Priests*; and on the Festival of Weeks, *Seven Weeks*; and on the New
Year, *In the seventh month on the first day of the month*; and on the Day of
Atonement, *After the death*; and on the first holyday day of the Festival
of Tabernacles, they read from the portion of the *Festivals* in the *law of
the priests*; and on all the other days of the Festival of Tabernacles they
read about the sacrifices at the Festival of Tabernacles.

[3.6] On the Festival of Dedication, *The Princes*; on Purim, *And then came
Amalek*; on the first days of the months, *And on the first days of your months*;
and at the *Lay Divisions*, from *They Story of the Creation*; on fast days, *The
Blessings and the Curses*—they must not interrupt in the reading of *The
Curses*, but one person only reads them all; and on Monday and on
Thursday and on the Sabbath at the *Afternoon Service* they read in the
regular order, but it is not taken into account. As it is said, *And Moses
declared the appointed seasons of the Eternal unto the children of Israel*—their prescribed law is that every one of them shall be read in its due season.

[4.1] He who reads the *Scroll* may stand or sit; if one read it, or if two
read it, they have fulfilled they duty. In a place where the custom is
to recite a Benediction one should recite it, but where it not customary to recite a Benediction he does not recite it. On Monday, and on
Thursday, and on Sabbath at the *Afternoon Service* three persons read;

they must not reduce the number nor add it; nor do they conclude with a reading from the Prophets. He that begins the reading from the *Law* and he that concludes it recites a Benediction, the one at the start and the other at the conclusion.

[4.2] On the first days of the months and on the *Intermediate Festival Days* four read; they must not reduce the number nor add to it; nor may they conclude with a reading from the Prophets. He that begins and he who concludes the reading from the *Law* recite a Benediction, one at the beginning and the other after it. This is the general principle: any day when there is *Additional Service* but is not a Holyday, four read; on a Holyday, five; on the Day of Atonement six; on the Sabbath, seven. They must not reduce the number but they may increases it, and they conclude with a reading from the Prophets. He who commences and he that concludes recites a Benediction, the one before it and the other at the completion.

[4.3] They may not recite the *Shema*, nor may anyone step before the *Ark*, nor may they lift up their hands, nor may the read the *Law* or the portion from the Prophets, nor may the observe the *funeral halts*, nor recite the *Mourner' Benediction* or the *Mourners' Consolation*, or the *Newly-Wed Benediction*, nor mention the Name of God in the *Grace After Meals* when less than ten are present. Also for lands, nine and a priest are required, and similarly for a person.

[4.4] He that reads (in) the *Law* may not read less than three verses; he may not read to the translator more than one verse at a time, or three in the case of the reading from the Prophets; but if these three form three separate paragraphs they must read them one by one. They may omit in the reading of the Prophet, but they may not omit in the *Law*. And how much may one leave out?—Only so much that the translator will not have time to make a pause.

[4.5] He that reads the concluding lesson from the Prophet also recites the *Shema*, and he steps before the *Ark*, and he lifts up his hands; but if he were a minor, his father or his teacher steps on his behalf.

[4.6] A minor may read (in) the *Law* and translate, but he may not recite the *Shema*, nor go before the *Ark*, nor raise his hands. One clothed in ragged garments may recite the *Shema* and translate, but he may not read (from) the *Law* or go before the *Ark* or lift up his hands. A blind person may recite the *Shema* and translate. R. Judah says, Anyone who has never in his lifetime seen the light may not recite the *Shema*.

[4.7] A priest whose hands have blemishes may not raise his hands. R. Judah says, Moreover one whose hands are stained with woad or madder may not lift up his hands because the people would gaze at him.

[4.8] If one declare, 'I will not step before the *Ark* in coloured raiment,' he may not go even in white garments. 'I will not go in sandals,' he may not step up even barefoot. He who makes his phylactery round is in danger for there is no fulfilment of the obligation therewith. If he set it upon his forehead or on the palm of his hand, then this is a practice of heresy. If one covered it with gold or placed it over his sleeve, then this is the practice of the separatists.

[4.9] If one say, 'The good shall bless Thee'—this is heretical practice. 'Over the nest of a bird do Thy mercies extend,' or, 'For the good may Thy Name be remembered.' or, 'We give thanks, we give thanks'—they must silence him. If one render in periphrasis the law about incest, they must silence him. If one say *And thou shalt not give any of thy seed to pass through to Molech* by *And thou shalt not give any of thy seed to a heathen woman to become pregnant*, they must silence him with a rebuke.

[4.10] The story of Reuben is read but not explained; the episode of Tamar is read and interpreted; the first story of the Calf is read and translated, and the second account is read but not interpreted; the Priestly Benediction and the narrative of David and that of Amnon are neither read nor translated. They may not conclude with the Chariot chapter as a reading from the Prophets; but R. Judah permits it. R. Eliezer says, They do not read the chapter *Cause Jerusalem to know* as the concluding reading from the Prophets.

Literature: Schürer, *HJP* 2.450–54; Fine, *This Holy Place*, 12, 36, 57; Levine, *Ancient Synagogue*, 150–51, 154, 168, 202, 209, 475, 526–27, 555–56.

Comments: These sections describe rabbinic views on Torah readings in synagogues on different occasions: what to read, when and how. To be sure, the word "synagogue" (*bet ha-kneset*) is not mentioned, but the contents and context make it clear that the rulings apply to the reading rituals of communal assemblies (note, e.g., the rule of the *minyan* in 4:3, as well as the mention of an ark throughout; for additional rulings, cf. *m. Ber.* 4:7; 5:4). Several reconstructions of early synagogue liturgy have taken these passages to be indicating actual practice, even in first-century synagogues. Apart from the obvious problem of anachronism in such reconstructions, one needs also to emphasise the fact that these rulings represent only the rabbinic view on how public synagogue worship should be constituted, not what actually transpired in local public assemblies. As noted above (No. 82), rabbinic authority in synagogues did not become reality until about the fourth century C.E. at the earliest. However, what eventually became mainstream synagogue liturgy originated to some degree in second-century rabbinic circles.

No. 84
Source: *Literary. m. Ned.* 5:5
Date: Ca. 200 C.E.

וְאֵיזֶהוּ דָבָר שֶׁל אוֹתָהּ הָעִיר? כְּגוֹן, הָרְחָבָה וְהַמֶּרְחָץ, וּבֵית הַכְּנֶסֶת, הַתֵּיבָה, וְהַסְּפָרִים.

And what sort of thing would belong to the town?—For example, the public square, and the bath-house, and the synagogue [*bet ha-kneset*], and the ark,[14] and the books.

Literature: Schürer, *HJP* 2.428, 446; Fine, *This Holy Place*, 183 n. 24; Zahavy, *Jewish Prayer*, 60–61; Levine, *Ancient Synagogue*, 42, 381, 448, 455–56; Runesson, *Origins*, 322.

Comments: The importance of this Mishnah goes beyond the rabbinic group, since its descriptive nature indicates a prevalent custom, namely, how things were arranged in Jewish society at this time. The public synagogue (*bet ha-kneset*), defined as a purpose-built edifice, belonged not to any one specific group or party, but to the local Jewish community, just as the town square and bathhouse. In the same way, the Torah scrolls and the ark (*ha-tevah*) belonged to the town. As Levine notes, synagogue officials were thus accountable before the local community, not any supra-local authority. Local authority in this regard may go back to the Hellenistic period (Runesson).

No. 85
Source: *Literary. m. Ned.* 9:2
Date: Ca. 200 C.E.

קוֹנָם לְבַיִת הַזֶּה שֶׁאֵינִי נִכְנָס, וְנַעֲשָׂה בֵית הַכְּנֶסֶת וְאָמַר, אִלּוּ הָיִיתִי יוֹדֵעַ שֶׁהוּא נַעֲשָׂה בֵית הַכְּנֶסֶת לֹא הָיִיתִי נוֹדֵר. רַבִּי אֱלִיעֶזֶר מַתִּיר, וַחֲכָמִים אוֹסְרִין.

Konam! that I do not enter this house!'—and it was made into a synagogue [*bet ha-kneset*] and he said, 'If I had known that it was going to be made into a synagogue [*bet ha-kneset*] I would not have made a vow. R. Eliezer permits it, but the Sages forbid it.

---

[14] Blackman's translation of *tevah* as "book-case," suggesting that such could be located not only in synagogues but also in libraries and houses of study, is here less likely. *Tevah* is the common word used for the ark in the Mishnah (later, picking up temple terminology, the rabbis referred to the ark as *'aron,*), and the association with the synagogue makes it clear that what is meant is the ark of the Torah.

Literature: Zahavy, *Jewish Prayer*, 61.

Comments: As Zahavy notes, the reference to the synagogue (*bet ha-kneset*) in this Mishnah is rhetorical, serving the purpose of supporting a ruling about how changing conditions may affect a vow. For our purposes, we may note that "synagogue" refers to a building. In addition, a synagogue building may not originally have been constructed to serve this purpose (it may have been a private house or a community building of some sort converted to synagogue use). Further, while R. Eliezer (late first to early second century CE, a disciple of R. Johanan ben Zakkai) is said to have held the synagogue in such a high regard that a vow should not prevent a person from entering the building and taking part in the activities there, the majority (the sages) ruled that the vow remains valid, and thus takes precedence over synagogue attendance.

No. 86
Source: *Literary. m. Mak.* 3:12
Date: Ca. 200 C.E.

כיצד מלקין אותו? כופת שתי ידיו על העמוד, הילך והילך, וחזן הכנסת אוחז
בבנדיו, אם נקרעו נקרעו, ואם נפרמו נפרמו, עד שהוא מגלה את לבו. והאבן
נתון מאחוריו, וחזן הכנסת עומד עליה, ורצועה של עגל בידו כפולה אחד
לשנים ושנים לארבעה ושני רצועות עולות ויורדות בה.

In what manner do they scourge him? They tie his two hands to a post, on either side, and the superintendent of the synagogue [*hazzan ha-kneset*] takes hold of his garments [at the neck and lays bare his body]—if they are rent they are rent, and if the seams are torn apart they are torn apart—so that he exposes his chest; and a stone is placed behind him on which the superintendent of the synagogue [*hazzan ha-kneset*] stands and a strap of calf [-hide] is in his hand, first folded into two and the two folded into four and [fastened] thereto are two strips [of ass-hide] which rise and fall.

Literature: Schürer, *HJP* 2.438; Levine, *Ancient Synagogue*, 143, 395–96, 435–42; Cf. Binder, *Temple Courts*, 448; Runesson, *Origins*, 370–77.

Comments: This Mishnah highlights the function of the synagogue as both a courtroom and a place where court decisions could be meted out. The regulations given here continue in *m. Mak.* 3:13–14. The attendant (*hazzan ha-kneset*) is instrumental in the implementation of the punishment (for this and other tasks of the *hazzan*, see Levine, *Ancient Synagogue*, 435–42). The synagogue as setting for Jewish legal proceedings is also evidenced in the New Testament (Mark 13:9; Matt 10:17, 23:24 cf. Josephus *Ant.* 16.168; Luke 12:11; 21:20; 2 Cor. 11:24. See Binder; Runesson, *Origins*, 375–77).

Tracing the court setting back in time from the first century, the trail leads us to the city-gates of ancient Israel (cf. Amos 5:10–15; Zech 8:16; Ruth 4:1–12; Isa 29:21). The overlap of this and other functions between the first-century public synagogue and the city-gate has led several scholars to argue that the latter was the matrix in which the former was born (e.g., Löw, "Synagogale Ritus"; Silber, *Origin*; Levine, *Ancient Synagogue*, 28–44; Binder, *Temple Courts*, 204–226; Runesson, *Origins*, especially ch. 4). Both rabbinic and non-rabbinic sources attest that judicial and administrative functions of the public synagogue were not affected by the first Jewish war and thus retained after 70 C.E. (Runesson, *Origins*, 377).

No. 87
Source: *Literary. m. Shebu.* 4:10
Date: Ca. 200 C.E.

עמד בבית הכנסת ואמר משביע אני עליכם שאם אתם יודעים לי עדות, שתבואו
ותעידוני הרי אלו פטורין, (עד שיהיה מתכוין להם).

If one stood in the synagogue [*bet ha-kneset*] and said, 'I adjure you, if you know of evidence on my behalf, that you come and bear witness for me', these are exempt (unless he particularly indicates which ones among them).

Literature: Zahavy, *Jewish Prayer*, 61; Levine, *Ancient Synagogue*, 409.

Comments: Levine discusses this text as an example of the synagogue serving as a place where individual needs could be met: a person is said here to be able to use the public setting of the synagogue (*bet ha-kneset*) to ask witnesses to step forward and testify in his or her favour. We are not told in which kind of assembly this might be done, but it makes sense to assume that it is the public building itself (or the public setting) that is important, not the specific nature of the gathering taking place.

No. 88
Source: *Literary. m. Neg.* 13:12
Date: Ca. 200 C.E.

נכנס לבית הכנסת עושים לו מחיצה גבוהה עשרה טפחים, על רוחב ארבע
אמות. נכנס ראשון, ויוצא אחרון.

If [a leper] enter a synagogue [*bet ha-kneset*], they make for him a partition ten *handbreadths* high by four *cubits* in width. He must enter [the] first and come out [the] last.

Literature: Zahavy, *Jewish Prayer*, 62; Levine, *Ancient Synagogue*, 341.

Comments: Contrary to the view of older studies, there is not widespread evidence in the early synagogues of partitions or balconies aimed at separating men and women. The passage quoted here indicates that partitions could sometimes be put up, but for the purpose of allowing people suffering from leprosy to take part in the public synagogue assemblies.

CHAPTER THREE

THE DIASPORA

3.1   *Identified Locations*

3.1.1   *Achaia*

3.1.1.1   *Aegina*

No. 89
Source: *Archaeological.*
Date: Late second century C.E.

Literature: Krauss, *Synagogale Altertümer*, 243; Sukenik, *Ancient Synagogues*, 44–45; Mazur, *Jewry in Greece*, 26–27, 29; Foerster, "Diaspora Synagogues," 166–67; Hachlili, *Diaspora*, 25, 30; White, *Social Origins*, 2.356–59; Levine, *Ancient Synagogue*, 268; Williams, *The Jews*, 41, 45.

Comments: Located close to the harbour and discovered in 1829, this structure measures 13.50 × 7.60 m, with an apse on the eastern side measuring 5.5 m in diameter. While the fourth-century building is safely classified as a synagogue, identification of the second-century structure underneath is problematic due to the limited nature of the remains. The similarity in plan and orientation between the two phases, however, argues for functional continuity. The later synagogue contained a mosaic floor with elaborate geometric designs and inscriptions; no such evidence exists for the earlier structure.

3.1.1.2   *Athens*

No. 90
Source: *Literary.* Acts 17:16–17
Date: Ca. 90–110 C.E.

[16] Ἐν δὲ ταῖς Ἀθήναις ἐκδεχομένου αὐτοὺς τοῦ Παύλου παρωξύνετο τὸ πνεῦμα αὐτοῦ ἐν αὐτῷ θεωροῦντος κατείδωλον οὖσαν τὴν πόλιν. [17] διελέγετο μὲν οὖν ἐν τῇ συναγωγῇ τοῖς Ἰουδαίοις καὶ τοῖς σεβομένοις καὶ ἐν τῇ ἀγορᾷ κατὰ πᾶσαν ἡμέραν πρὸς τοὺς παρατυγχάνοντας.

[16] While Paul was waiting for them in Athens, he was deeply distressed to see that the city was full of idols. [17] So he argued in the synagogue [*synagōgē*] with the Jews and the devout persons, and also in the marketplace every day with those who happened to be there.

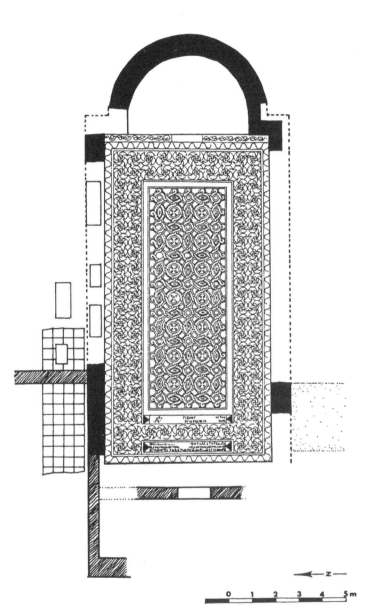

Figure 16. Plan of the Aegina synagogue. The plan of synagogue I was
identical to that of synagogue II, shown here.

Literature: As a general reference to commentaries see Barrett, Fitzmyer and Jervell, *Comm., ad loc.* Binder, *Temple Courts*, 295, 380–88; Levine, *Ancient Synagogue*, 109–11; Stegemann, *Synagoge und Obrigkeit*, 161–63; Wander, *Gottefürchtige*, 228–34; Levinskaya, *Book of Acts*, 51–125, 158–62; Koch, *God-fearers*, 80–82.

Comments: While Jakob Jervell and some others translate *dialegesthai* in Acts as "verkündigen" ("preach") rather than "argue, dispute, argument," the latter is to be preferred. See comments on Acts 24:12 (No. 19). The word was especially suitable to Paul's activity in the marketplace: the apostle here acts as Socrates some centuries before him.

Luke refers to three categories in Athens: Jews, God-fearers and Gentiles. Paul met the first two in the synagogue. Several times he mentions non-Jews, both men and women, who were related to the Jews in different ways. They took part in the synagogue assemblies without making the Jews unclean. Luke refers to them as "fearing God" (*phoboumenos ton theon*) or "worshipping God" (*sebomenos ton theon*, or *sebomenos* as noun or adjective). In Acts we encounter the following examples:

1. A Roman centurion in Caesarea named Cornelius, a pious and God-fearing man, who made many charitable gifts to the Jewish people and constantly prayed to God (10:1–2). He is presented as "a righteous man and one who fears God, of good reputation with the whole nation of the Jews" (10:22). Almsgiving and prayer were fundamental in Jewish piety (Matt 6:2–15). Since Cornelius was not a member of the Jewish community, Peter was astonished that Cornelius was qualified to receive the Holy Spirit (10:45). As a centurion he held an official position and had to participate in the official cult. However, according to Luke, in some way the God of Israel accepted him, since he feared God and worked righteousness (10:35). The Cornelius story is told twice in Acts 9–10, a sign of its great importance in the Lukan work.

2. God-fearers in the synagogue in Pisidian Antioch, addressed by Paul together with the Jews, when he was asked to preach to them (13:16), "those among you who fear God" (13:26). The problematic phrase in 13:43, *hoi sebomenoi proselytai*, probably means "devout proselytes" (Barrett).

3. Devoted women (*hai sebomenai gynaikes*) of high standing in Pisidian Antioch (13:50). Some Jews incited both them and some leading men of the city so that Paul and Barnabas were driven out of their borders. These Gentiles were in some ways recognized adherents of the synagogue, probably as God-fearers. A great number of God-fearers in Acts accept the message about Jesus as the Messiah, but here some of them reject it.

4. A woman at Philippi named Lydia, a dealer in purple from the city of Thyatira, who worshipped God (*sebomenē ton theon*), 16:14.

5. A large company of God-fearing Greeks (*tōn te sebomenōn Hellenōn plēthos poly*), some of them leading women, became Jesus-believers in the synagogue in Thessalonica (17:4). Because they are described as Greeks, it is very unlikely that they were proselytes. In the new situation in the synagogues where many God-fearers became Jesus-believers, it was important for the Jews to win the God-fearers to their side. The Jews' relations to the different forms of sympathizers were in many places of great importance for their social status.

6. Devout persons (*sebomenoi*) in the synagogue in Athens (17:17), in a Lucan context, probably people who were not Jews by birth or conversion. The historical setting of the first century and Luke's usage of *sebomenoi* make it reasonable to regard them as God-fearers.

7. Titus Justus, "one worshipping God" (*sebomenos ton theon*), who had a house adjacent to the synagogue in Corinth. He became Paul's host in Corinth when he had to leave the synagogue (18:7).

While Judaism was attractive to many Gentiles in antiquity (Josephus, *A.J.* 14:110), it is not easy to describe the relations between these sympathatic Gentiles and the Jews: there is still a lively debate about the God-fearers both in Luke and in other ancient sources.

Bernd Wander argues for different designations for the different relations: "Proselyten" ("Proselytes"), "Gottesfürchtigen" ("God-fearers"), "Sympathisanten" ("Sympathisers"), "Interessierten" ("Interested ones"), or "Nachahmern" ("Imitators"). Koch stresses the different aspects of social relationship and religious commitment in different places and at different times.

In Luke, God-fearers are separate from the proselytes. They visit the synagogues on the Sabbath, take part in Jewish prayers, practise some of the laws of the Torah, and make charitable gifts to the Jews. Many of them are women of high standing who can influence a local political situation.

Luke has his own interests in these God-fearers as the first Gentiles who hear Paul's message about God's salvation together with Jews. When he refers to "Jews and Greeks" in the synagogue, the latter is probably an allusion to God-fearers (18:4). Although Luke offers his picture of the God-fearers, this picture "has its equivalence in the social and religious world of Luke and his readers" (Koch). "The status enjoyed by many Diaspora communities may have been due, at least in part, to the presence and support of many pagan sympathizers" (Levine). On the God-fearers in the Bosporan Kingdom, see Nos. 123, 124, 126.

3.1.1.3 *Corinth*

No. 91
Source: *Literary.* Acts 18:4–8
Date: Ca. 90–110 C.E.

[4] διελέγετο δὲ ἐν τῇ συναγωγῇ κατὰ πᾶν σάββατον ἔπειθέν τε Ἰουδαίους καὶ Ἕλληνας. [5] Ὡς δὲ κατῆλθον ἀπὸ τῆς Μακεδονίας ὅ τε Σιλᾶς καὶ ὁ Τιμόθεος, συνείχετο τῷ λόγῳ ὁ Παῦλος διαμαρτυρόμενος τοῖς Ἰουδαίοις εἶναι τὸν χριστὸν Ἰησοῦν. [6] ἀντιτασσομένων δὲ αὐτῶν καὶ βλασφημούντων ἐκτιναξάμενος τὰ ἱμάτια εἶπεν πρὸς αὐτούς· τὸ αἷμα ὑμῶν ἐπὶ τὴν κεφαλὴν ὑμῶν· καθαρὸς ἐγὼ ἀπὸ τοῦ νῦν εἰς τὰ ἔθνη πορεύσομαι. [7] καὶ μεταβὰς ἐκεῖθεν εἰσῆλθεν εἰς οἰκίαν τινὸς ὀνόματι Τιτίου Ἰούστου σεβομένου τὸν θεόν, οὗ ἡ οἰκία ἦν συνομοροῦσα τῇ συναγωγῇ. [8] Κρίσπος δὲ ὁ ἀρχισυνάγωγος ἐπίστευσεν τῷ κυρίῳ σὺν

ὅλῳ τῷ οἴκῳ αὐτοῦ, καὶ πολλοὶ τῶν Κορινθίων ἀκούοντες ἐπίστευον καὶ ἐβαπτίζοντο.

[4] Every Sabbath he would argue in the synagogue [*synagōgē*] and would try to convince Jews and Greeks. [5] When Silas and Timothy arrived from Macedonia, Paul was occupied with proclaiming the word, testifying to the Jews that the Messiah was Jesus. [6] When they opposed and reviled him, in protest he shook the dust from his clothes and said to them, "Your blood be on your own heads! I am innocent. From now on I will go to the Gentiles." [7] Then he left the synagogue [*synagōgē*] and went to the house of a man named Titius Justus, a worshiper of God; his house was next door to the synagogue [*synagōgē*]. [8] Crispus, the official of the synagogue [*archisynagōgos*], became a believer in the Lord, together with all his household; and many of the Corinthians who heard Paul became believers and were baptized.

Literature: As a general reference to commentaries see Barrett, Fitzmyer and Jervell, *Comm., ad loc.* Binder, *Temple Courts*, 295–97; Levine, *Ancient Synagogue*, 108–9; Claußen, *Versammlung*, 261–62; Runesson, *Origins*, 219; Levinskaya, *Book of Acts*, 162–66.

Comments: As in Acts 17:16, Luke refers to three categories: Jews, Greeks, and Gentiles. Since the Greeks are in the synagogue, they are probably God-fearers. Titius Justus, who lived next door to the synagogue (v. 7), is also presented as a God-fearer. See comments on Acts 17:16–17 (No. 90). Paul disputed (*dialegesthai*; see comment on Acts 24:12, No. 19) with the congregation who gathered on the weekly Sabbath services in the synagogue. He proclaimed (*synechesthai*: "continue to apply oneself to") the word, and testified to the Jews that the Messiah was Jesus.

The apostle tried to convince them (imperfect tense in the Greek text) probably through references to the Scripture. The negative reactions from some Jews in this and other synagogue settings are described by such verbs as "oppose" (*antitassesthai*, "to oppose, to be hostile toward, to show hostility," 18:6), "revile" (*blasphēmein*, "to speak against persons or divine beings in such a way as to harm or injure his or her reputation," 18:6; 13:45), "contradict" (*antilegein*, "to speak against something or someone," 13:45), "stir up" (*epegeirein*, "to cause to begin and to intensify an activity," 14:2) followed by "poison their minds against" (*kakoun tēn psychēn kata*, "to turn someone against, to cause to dislike," 14:2) and "speak evil of" (*kakologein*, "to insult in a particularly strong and unjustified manner," 19:9) with "the Way" as the object. In 13:45 and 14:2 it is clear that Jews spoke evil about the apostle(s) or Jesus-believers to Gentiles or their representatives, and the situation is probably the same in 18:6 (cf. 13:50; 14:5, 19; 17:5–13; 18:12–17). Some (sometimes most) Jews in the synagogues distanced themselves from the Jesus-believing people.

Paul's departure from the synagogue to minister among the Gentiles does not mean that his mission to the Jews had finished. Crispus, the official of the synagogue (for the title see comments on Mark 5:22, 35–43, No. 47), among others, became a believer. Likewise, in the next town Paul at once turned to the Jews in the synagogue. Thus Acts 18:6 refers only to Corinth, not to a general policy. It should also be noted that Paul had already spoken to Greeks before he "went to the Gentiles." See comments on Acts 13:14–16, 42–49 (No. 174).

No. 92
Source: *Literary.* Acts 18:17
Date: Ca. 90–110 C.E.

[17] ἐπιλαβόμενοι δὲ πάντες Σωσθένην τὸν ἀρχισυνάγωγον ἔτυπτον ἔμπροσθεν τοῦ βήματος· καὶ οὐδὲν τούτων τῷ Γαλλίωνι ἔμελεν.

[17] Then all of them seized Sosthenes, the official of the synagogue [*archisynagōgos*], and beat him in front of the tribunal. But Gallio paid no attention to any of these things.

Literature: As a general reference to commentaries see Barrett, Fitzmyer and Jervell, *Comm., ad loc.*

Comments: See the comments on Acts 18:4–8 (No. 91). The reference to "all of them" is unclear: does it mean "all Jews" because Sosthenes had not succeeded in convincing Gallio? Or is the reference to "all Gentiles" because of their ill-will against the Jews? Or does it signify "both Jews and Gentiles" who seized Sosthenes, each for different reasons? The answer remains elusive.

3.1.1.4 *Delos*

No. 93
Source: *Literary.* Josephus, *A.J.* 14.213–16
Date: The decree quoted by Josephus is dated to the first century B.C.E.; *Antiquitates Judaicae* was published in 93/94 C.E.

[213] Ἰούλιος Γάιος υἱοσο στρατηγὸς ὕπατος Ῥωμαίων Παριανῶν ἄρχουσι βουλῇ δήμῳ χαίρειν. ἐνέτυχόν μοι οἱ Ἰουδαῖοι ἐν Δήλῳ καί τινες τῶν παροίκων Ἰουδαίων παρόντων καὶ τῶν ὑμετέρων πρέσβεων καὶ ἐνεφάνισαν, ὡς ὑμεῖς ψηφίσματι κωλύετε αὐτοὺς τοῖς πατρίοις ἔθεσι καὶ ἱεροῖς χρῆσθαι. [214] ἐμοὶ τοίνυν οὐκ ἀρέσκει κατὰ τῶν ἡμετέρων φίλων καὶ συμμάχων τοιαῦτα γίνεσθαι ψηφίσματα καὶ κωλύεσθαι αὐτοὺς ζῆν κατὰ τὰ αὐτῶν ἔθη καὶ χρήματα εἰς σύνδειπνα καὶ τὰ ἱερὰ εἰσφέρειν, τοῦτο ποιεῖν αὐτῶν μηδ' ἐν Ῥώμῃ κεκωλυμένων.

[215] καὶ γὰρ Γάιος Καῖσαρ ὁ ἡμέτερος στρατηγὸς [καὶ] ὕπατος
ἐν τῷ διατάγματι κωλύων θιάσους συνάγεσθαι κατὰ πόλιν μόνους
τούτους οὐκ ἐκώλυσεν οὔτε χρήματα συνεισφέρειν οὔτε σύνδειπνα
ποιεῖν. [216] ὁμοίως δὲ κἀγὼ τοὺς ἄλλους θιάσους κωλύων τούτοις
μόνοις ἐπιτρέπω κατὰ τὰ πάτρια ἔθη καὶ νόμιμα συνάγεσθαί τε καὶ
ἑστιᾶσθαι. καὶ ὑμᾶς οὖν καλῶς ἔχει, εἴ τι κατὰ τῶν ἡμετέρων φίλων
καὶ συμμάχων ψήφισμα ἐποιήσατε, τοῦτο ἀκυρῶσαι διὰ τὴν περὶ ἡμᾶς
αὐτῶν ἀρετὴν καὶ εὔνοιαν.

[213] Julius Gaius commander, consul of the Romans, to the magistrates, council and people of Parium, greeting. The Jews in Delos[1]
and some other Jews being dwellers there, some of your envoys also
being present, have appealed to me and declared that you by statute
prevent them from performing their native customs and sacred rituals. [214] Now it is not acceptable to me that such statutes should be
made against our friends and allies and that they are prevented to live
according to their customs, to collect money for common meals and
to perform sacred rituals: not even in Rome are they prohibited to do
this. [216] For in fact Gaius Caesar, our commander and consul,[2] by
edict forbade religious guilds to assemble in the city but, as a single
exception, he did not forbid these people to do so, or to collect money
or to have common meals. [216] Likewise do I prohibit other religious
guilds [*thiasoi*] exempting only these people whom I permit to assemble
and feast according to their native customs and laws. And if you have
made any statute against our friends and allies you will do well to revoke
them because of their good service and goodwill toward us.

Literature: McLean, "The Place of Cult," 192–95; Shanks, *Judaism in Stone*,
43–44; Binder, *Temple Courts*, 297–317; Levine, *Ancient Synagogue*, 100–105;
Runesson, *Origins*, 175, 185–87; Williams, *The Jews*, 12, 60–61; White, "Delos,"
White, *Social Origins*, 332–42; Eilers, *Jewish Privileges*, ch. 9.

Comments: This decree is fraught with difficulties. If understood as translated
here, the document provides evidence that a Jewish community existed on the
island of Delos at this time. It has been suggested that *en Dēlō* (on Delos) has

---

[1] Cf. Eilers, *Jewish Privileges*, ch. 9, who argues that *en Dēlō*, in Delos, should be
understood as referring to where the meeting was held, not where the Jews came from.
Thus, Eilers translates, "The Jews appealed to me in Delos, together with some of the
resident Jews, while some of your envoys were also present."
[2] Cf. the comment by Marcus, *LCL*, VII, p. 562, n. 2 and p. 563, n. b. These titles
are, as Marcus notes, strange applied to Caesar, and need to be emended.

a technical significance and indicates a special residency status of the group mentioned (White, 342, n. 93). This would explain the reference to "some other Jews being dwellers [*paroikoi*] there": not all Jews on the island would have had special residency status, and those who did not were also present at the meeting.[3]

However, if Eilers' translation is correct, "on Delos" refers to the place where the Jews met with the magistrate. In this case, the document with its rulings is not concerned with a Delian Jewish community at all, but with the city to which the edict is addressed, Parium, which was located on the coast of the Troad.[4] This interpretation would solve the question of why a Jewish community on Delos would be concerned with anti-Jewish legislation in such a far-away city as Parium: if we are dealing with a Jewish delegation from Parium that simply caught up with the magistrate on Delos and requested a meeting, no Delian Jews were involved. The words "some other Jews being dwellers there" would then refer to Jews in Parium who were not citizens, but who were also affected by the anti-Jewish legislation (so Eilers). If this is correct, *A.J.* 14.213–216 offers evidence of a synagogue community in Parium, not on Delos.

In any case, as is evident from several other sources, Jewish gatherings included—and were known by non-Jews to include—communal meals and the performance of sacred rites. For Jews, "sacred rites" in this context would most likely have referred to the ritual reading and expounding of Torah on Sabbaths (cf. Runesson, *Origins*, 193–96), but may have been understood by uninformed outsiders as referring to any rituals, including sacrifices, since this was the standard method of paying honours to the gods. Of interest in the present document is also the reference to Jewish synagogue gatherings being exempted by Gaius Caesar at a time when all other *thiasoi* were prohibited.

No. 94
Source: *Inscription. IJO* 1, Ach60 (*CIJ* 1.727; *ID* 2331)
Date: First to second century C.E.

Ζωσᾶς
Πάριος
Θεῷ
Ὑψίστῳ
εὐχήν.   5

---

[3] Marcus' translation (LCL), "some of the neighbouring Jews," should be rejected, as also noted by Eilers.

[4] The emendation suggested by Schürer, to read Paros instead Parium, referring to the island ca. 16 kilometres south of Delos, should be rejected as without foundation.

Zosas of Paros to God Most High, (in fulfillment of) a vow.

Literature: Plassart, "La synagogue juive," 205–6 (no. 4); Lifshitz, *DF*, 15 (no. 4); Krauss, *Synagogale Altertümer*, 244 (no. 97); Bruneau, *Recherches sur les cultes de Delos*, 484; Schürer, *HJP*, 3.1.70; White, "The Delos Synagogue Revisited," 139–40; idem, *Social Origins*, 2.338–39 (no. 3); Binder, *Temple Courts*, 303, n. 137; Levine, *Ancient Synagogue*, 109 (no. 1).

Comments: One of five inscriptions unearthed by Plassart in his 1912–13 excavations of the building he identified as a synagogue (*GD* 80), this monument is typical of votive offerings found in Gentile temples throughout this period: a petition is made by the devotee of a particular deity, often for the healing of an infirmity. Accompanying the supplication is the offering of a vow—usually the erection of a monument in the god's sanctuary once the prayer is answered.

Frequently, statuettes of healed body parts or other figures were mounted on such votives, and indeed, this inscription appears to have been the base for such a representation, as a mounting hole remains on its upper surface. It differs from most Gentile examples, however, in its reference to the "Most High God" (*theos hypsistos*), a common Jewish (or Samaritan) locution for the divine (cf. *JIGRE* 9, 27, 105, 126 [Nos. 143, 151, 154, 172]. The appearance of the title on this and most of the other inscriptions inside *GD* 80 contributed towards Plassart's identification of the building as a synagogue.

The name Zosas is not otherwise attested in Jewish inscriptions, though it appears on two other monuments, one from Delos and one from Paros.

No. 95
Source: *Inscription. IJO* 1, Ach61 (*CIJ* 1.730; *ID* 2332)
Date: First to second century C.E.

Ὑψίς-
τῳ εὐ-
χὴν Μ-
αρκία.

Marcia to the Most High (in fulfillment of) a vow.

Literature: Plassart, "La synagogue juive," 206 (no. 5); Lifshitz, *DF*, 16 (no. 7); Krauss, *Synagogale Altertümer*, 244 (no. 97); Bruneau, *Recherches sur les cultes de Delos*, 484; Schürer, *HJP*, 3.1.70; White, "The Delos Synagogue Revisited," 139–40; idem, *Social Origins*, 2.338–39 (no. 4); Binder, *Temple Courts*, 303, n. 137; Levine, *Ancient Synagogue*, 109 (no. 4); Brooten, *Women Leaders*, 157 (no. 2).

Comments: Similar in wording to the preceding entry, this votive differs primarily in its abbreviated reference to "the Most High" (*hypsistos*). Also noteworthy is the gender of the dedicator, whose name is attested in Jewish monuments from Rome (*JIWE* 2.128, 208, 233, 431, 490).

No. 96
Source: *Inscription. IJO* 1, Ach62 (*CIJ* 1.728; *ID* 2330)
Date: First century B.C.E.

Λαωδίκη Θεῶι
'Υψίστωι σωθεῖ-
σα ταῖς ὑφ' αὐτο-
ῦ θαραπήαις
εὐχήν.   5

Laodice, to God Most High, having been saved by his therapies, (in fulfillment of) a vow.

Literature: Plassart, "La synagogue juive," 205 (no. 3); Lifshitz, *DF*, 15 (no. 5); Krauss, *Synagogale Altertümer*, 244 (no. 97); Bruneau, *Recherches sur les cultes de Delos*, 484; Schürer, *HJP*, 3.1.70; White, "The Delos Synagogue Revisited," 139–40; idem, *Social Origins*, 2.338–39 (no. 2); Binder, *Temple Courts*, 303, n. 137; Levine, *Ancient Synagogue*, 109 (no. 2); Brooten, *Women Leaders*, 157 (no. 1).

Comments: The wording of this inscription is somewhat more elaborate than that of the other votives found in *GD* 80: it reveals more explicitly that Laodice's petition concerned the healing of a fairly severe infirmity. Moreover, it hints at the prescription of specific medical treatments, probably by the religious leaders themselves. Along with the preceding entry, it preserves an example of a woman offering a votive inside this edifice.

No. 97
Source: *Inscription. IJO* 1, Ach63 (*CIJ* 1.729; *ID* 2328)
Date: First century B.C.E.

Λυσίμαχος
ὑπὲρ ἑαυτοῦ
Θεῷ 'Υψίστῳ
χαριστήριον.

Lysimachus on behalf of himself to God Most High, a thank-offering.

Literature: Plassart, "La synagogue juive," 205 (no. 1); Lifshitz, *DF*, 15 (no. 6); Krauss, *Synagogale Altertümer*, 244 (no. 97); Bruneau, *Recherches sur les cultes de Delos*, 484; Schürer, *HJP*, 3.1.70; White, "The Delos Synagogue Revisited," 139–40; idem, *Social Origins*, 2.338–39 (no. 1); Binder, *Temple Courts*, 303, n. 137; Levine, *Ancient Synagogue*, 109 (no. 3).

Comments: While this votive differs in wording from the other examples found in *GD* 80, its use of the term *charistērion* ("thank-offering," a shortened

form of the word *eucharistērion*) parallels similar usages in both Gentile and
Jewish dedications (cf. *DF* 35, 70, 72). Because the upper surface of this
monument contains a sizable mounting hole encrusted with melted lead, it
is clear that the inscription served as the base of a statuette, as was common
with votives. The name Lysimachus is attested in a Jewish inscription from
Cyrenaica (*CJZ* 45b), as well as in an inscription unearthed on Delos in *GD*
79, a nearby insula (*IJO* 1, Ach65; see No. 99 below).

No. 98
Source: *Inscription. IJO* 1, Ach64 (*CIJ* 1.731; *ID* 2333)
Date: First to second century C.E.

......
(rosette) (rosette)
γενόμενος
ἐλεύθερος.

...having been set free

Literature: Plassart, "La synagogue juive," 205 (no. 6); Lifshitz, *DF*, 16 (no.
8); Krauss, *Synagogale Altertümer*, 244 (no. 97); Bruneau, *Recherches sur les cultes
de Delos*, 484; Schürer, *HJP*, 3.1.70; Binder, *Temple Courts*, 303, n. 137, 445,
n. 134; Levine, *Ancient Synagogue*, 109, n. 154.

Comments: While the wording of this inscription suggests that *GD* 80 served
as a place for manumission, as was common in synagogues of the Bosporus
Kingdom, its fragmentary state does not allow for firm conclusions on the
matter.

No. 99
Source: *Inscription. IJO* 1, Ach65 (*CIJ* 1.726; *ID* 2329)
Date: First century B.C.E.

Ἀγαθοκλῆς
καὶ Λυσίμα-
χος ἐπὶ
προσευχῇ.

Agathocles
and Lysimachus
for the prayer hall [*proseuchē*]

Literature: Plassart, "La synagogue juive," 205 (no. 1); Mazur, *Studies on
Jewry*, 21; Lifshitz, *DF*, 15 (no. 3); Krauss, *Synagogale Altertümer*, 244 (no. 97);

Goodenough, *JSGRP*, 2.72–74; Bruneau, *Recherches sur les cultes de Delos*, 484; Schürer, *HJP*, 3.1.70; White, "The Delos Synagogue Revisited," 139–40; idem, *Social Origins*, 2.338–39 (no. 5); McLean, "The Place of Cult," 192–94; Binder, *Temple Courts*, 303–4; Levine, *Ancient Synagogue*, 109.

Comments: Plassart discovered this monument not in *GD* 80, but in the southwest section of a nearby insula (*GD* 79, House IIA). He nevertheless linked it to the former structure because it shared the name Lysimachus with an inscription unearthed in *GD* 80 (*IJO*, Ach63 [No. 97]), and because of its use of the term *proseuchē*. Indeed, Plassart viewed this last as a reference to *GD* 80, which he had previously identified as a synagogue. Mazur, however, noted the absence of the definite article before *proseuchē* and so considered the word a variant of *euchē*, "vow." Yet because epigraphic attestations of such a usage are lacking, this seems unlikely. Moreover, the subsequent discovery of the next entry presented a local example of *proseuchē* referencing a building, despite the absence of an accompanying definite article. Thus Plassart's original rendering, reflected in the above translation, is to be preferred.

The name Agathocles is attested in Jewish inscriptions from Egypt (*JIGRE* 36 and 46) and Cyrenaica (*CJZ* 7a, 10).

No. 100
Source: *Inscription. IJO* 1, Ach66 (*SEG* 32.810)
Date: Between 250–175 B.C.E.

$$[?\ Οἱ\ ἐν\ Δήλῳ]$$
(wreath)

'Ισραηλῖται οἱ ἀπαρχόμενοι εἰς ἱερὸν ἅγιον 'Αρ-
γαρζεὶν ἐτίμησαν *vacat* Μένιππον 'Αρτεμιδώρου 'Ηρα-
κλειον αὐτὸν καὶ τοὺς ἐγγόνους αὐτοῦ κατασκευ-
άσαντα καὶ ἀναθένθα ἐκ τῶν ἰδίων ἐπὶ προσευχῇ τοῦ   5
θε[οῦ] ΤΟΝ[-]
ΟΛΟΝΚΑΙΤΟ[- - ᶜᵃ ⁶⁻⁸ - - καὶ ἐστεφάνωσαν] χρυσῷ στε[φά-]
νῳ καὶ [- - - - - - - - - - - - - - - - - - -]
ΚΑ - -
Τ - -   10

The Israelites [on Delos?] who make first-fruit offerings to the temple on holy Mt. Gerizim honour Menippus, son of Artemidorus, of Herakleion, both himself and his descendants, for constructing and dedicating from his own funds for the prayer hall [*proseuchē*] of God the…and the…, and crown him with a golden crown and…

Literature: Bruneau, "«Les Israélites de Délos»," 471–75 (no. 2); Kraabel, "New Evidence," 331–34; White, "The Delos Synagogue Revisited," 141–47;

idem, *Social Origins*, 2.341–42 (no. 71b); Pummer, "Inscriptions," 190–94; McLean, "The Place of Cult," 191–94; Binder, *Temple Courts*, 305, 472–74; Levine, *Ancient Synagogue*, 110–11; Llewelyn, *New Documents*, 148–51 (no. b); Schürer, *HJP*, 3.1.71.

Comments: In 1979, a team from the École Française d'Athènes discovered this and the following entry on the shoreline approximately 90 m north of *GD* 80. The upper part of the monument contains a beautifully carved wreath just above the inscription. The mention of Mt. Gerizim indicates that the Israelites referenced in the monument were not Jews, but Samaritans. Their central sanctuary was located on that mountain until destroyed by John Hyrcanus in 128 B.C.E. (Josephus, *A.J.* 13.254–56). The early date of this inscription (assigned on palaeographic grounds), as well as the reference to first-fruit offerings, argues that *hieron* should be rendered "temple," despite the lack of a preceding definite article.

Likewise, *proseuchē*, though not preceded by a definite article, clearly references a synagogue, as the construction of one or more of its parts or features is mentioned in ll. 4–5. While the exact nature of Menippus's donation to the building is unknown—it likely would have been mentioned in the lacunae in ll. 5–6—the bequest was clearly very generous: the golden crown awarded him was the most costly and highly prized of public bestowals. Also unclear is whether Menippus was a member of the Samaritan community or an outside benefactor. His hometown of Herakleion was probably the city of that name on the northern shore of Crete, where it served as the port of Knossos.

Bruneau initially offered the reconstruction of the first line ("on Delos") on the basis of similar wording in the next entry. White, however, points out that this designation of quasi-citizenship for foreign groups came into use only after the start of Athenian control over Delos in 166 B.C.E. Because the above monument predates this period, it was probably never part of the inscription.

Further excavation around the discovery site is needed to help clarify whether this dedication belonged to *GD* 80 or to a synagogue that has yet to be unearthed. In either case, it is clear that the Samaritan occupants viewed their local institution in concert with the ritual operations of their central cultic site on Mt. Gerizim.

No. 101
Source: *Inscription. IJO* 1, Ach67 (*SEG* 32.809)
Date: Between 150–50 B.C.E.

(wreath)
Οἱ ἐν Δήλῳ Ἰσραελεῖται οἱ ἀ-
παρχόμενοι εἰς ἱερὸν Ἀρχα-
ριζεὶν στεφανοῦσιν χρυσῷ
στεφάνῳ Σαραπίωνα Ἰάσο-
νος Κνώσιον εὐεργεσίας   5
ἕνεκεν τῆς εἰς ἑαυτούς.

The Israelites on Delos, who make first-fruit offerings to the temple on Mt. Gerizim crown with a golden crown Serapion, son of Jason, of Knossos for his benefactions toward them

Literature: Bruneau, "«Les Israélites de Délos»," 469–71 (no. 2); Kraabel, "New Evidence," 331–34; White, "The Delos Synagogue Revisited," 141–47; idem, *Social Origins*, 2.340–41 (no. 71a); Pummer, "Inscriptions," 190–94; McLean, "The Place of Cult," 191–94; Binder, *Temple Courts*, 305, 472–74; Levine, *Ancient Synagogue*, 110–11; Llewelyn, *New Documents*, 148–51 (no. a); Schürer, *HJP*, 3.1.71.

Comments: As with the preceding monument, this Samaritan dedication is adorned with an elaborate wreath above the inscription. While Serapion's benefactions to the community are left unspecified, they were no doubt extensive, as the reference to the golden crown indicates. Like Mennipus, Serapion was also native of Crete, if not necessarily a Samaritan. His name is attested in Jewish inscriptions from Cyrenaica (*CJZ* 53a, 53c, 72), but it was also commonly used among Gentiles.

On the circumstances of this inscription's discovery, the use of the phrase translated "on Delos," and the translation of the term *hieron*, please refer to the preceding entry.

No. 102
Source: *Archaeological.*
Date: Second century B.C.E.

Literature: Plassart, "La synagogue"; Mazur, *Studies*; Bruneau, *Recherches*, 465–504; idem, *Guide de Delos*; Sukenik, *Ancient Synagogues*, 37–40; Kraabel, "Diaspora Synagogue," 491–94; McLean, "Place of Cult," 192–95; Binder, *Temple Courts*, 297–317; Levine, *Ancient Synagogue*, 107–13; Runesson, *Origins*, 185–87; Williams, *The Jews*, 12, 60–61; White, "Delos Synagogue"; White, *Social Origins*, 2.332–42; Trümper, "Oldest Original Synagogue Building."

Comments: Located on the eastern shore of Delos, building 80 in the *Guide de Délos* (*GD* 80) was originally identified as a synagogue by Plassart during his 1912–13 excavations, partially on the basis of inscriptions found inside the building (*IJO* 1, Ach60–64 [Nos. 94–98]) and in a nearby insula (*GD* 79, *IJO* 1, Ach65 [No. 99]). Mazur later questioned this identification, arguing that the structure served as a Gentile cultic hall. Subsequent excavations, however, led Bruneau to reassert Plassart's original judgement, a view bolstered by the later discovery of two Samaritan inscriptions (*IJO* 1, Ach66–67 [Nos. 100–101]) 90 m north of *GD* 80, which raised the additional possibility that the synagogue was not Jewish, but Samaritan.

While this last question remains unresolved, most recent studies (Binder, Trümper) leave no doubt that the structure was originally constructed as a public building, not a domestic residence (White). The edifice may initially have been built as a cultic hall by a non-Jewish association, who used it until the Mithridatic raids in 88 B.C.E. when either Jews or Samaritans moved in

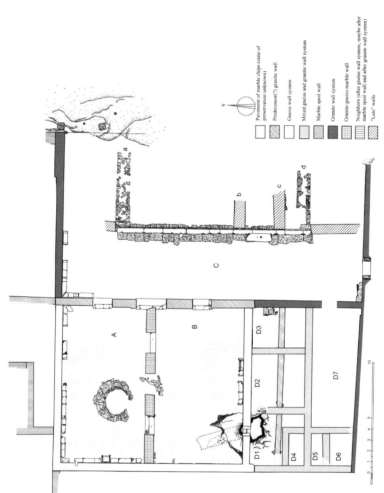

Figure 17. Plan of the Delos synagogue indicating different wall systems.

Figure 18. The so-called chair of Moses, located by the western wall of room A.

and soon transformed it into a synagogue. Alternatively, one of these two ethnic groups may have constructed the building as a synagogue from the very beginning (Trümper).

The date of the initial construction is uncertain, ranging from the third century B.C.E. to the beginning of the first century B.C.E. According to Trümper, the building went through five architectural phases and was abandoned in the second century C.E. Phase one involved the construction of a freestanding building measuring 16.80 × 14.40 m (hall A/B). Additional rooms may have existed to the south. The existing water reservoir may also have been constructed during this phase. The hall itself had three entrances facing east, possibly with a monumental entryway that included a colonnade.

In the second phase, several rooms were added to the south; these were used for storage and possibly as living quarters. The third phase, with a *terminus post quem* of 88 B.C.E., is distinguished through renovations in the main hall. Extensions to the east, in the form of a pi-shaped portico, were built during a fourth phase.

While the existing benches and the marble throne may have been present in some arrangement in the earlier phases of the building (though they probably were not manufactured for the synagogue), their present position belongs to the fifth phase when the main hall was divided into two sections (A and B). The dividing wall between areas A and B had three entrances, giving access to the more secluded inner room (B). This phase dates to after 69 B.C.E.

As noted above, many questions remain regarding this building. Their resolution will come only with further excavations around both *GD* 80 and the area of the beach where the Samaritan inscriptions were found. Regarding the so-called chair of Moses, see No. 67.

3.1.2   *Asia*

3.1.2.1   *Acmonia*

No. 103
Source: *Inscription. IJO* 2.168 (*CIJ* 2.766; *DF* 33; *MAMA* 6.264)
Date: Second half of the first century C.E.

τὸν κατασκευασθέντα οἶκον ὑπὸ
Ἰουλίας Σεουήρας Π. Τυρρώνιος Κλά-
δος ὁ διὰ βίου ἀρχισυνάγωγος καὶ
Λούκιος Λουκίου ἀχισυνάγωγος
καὶ Ποπίλιος Ζωτικὸς ἄρχων ἐπεσ-   5
κεύασαν ἐκ τε τῶν ἰδίων καὶ τῶν συνκατα-
καταθεμένων καὶ ἔγραψαν τοὺς τοίχους καὶ τὴν ὀροφὴν καὶ ἐποίησαν
τὴν τῶν θυρίδων ἀσφάλειαν καὶ τὸν
λυπὸν πάντα κόσμον. οὕστινας κα[ὶ]   10
ἡ συναγωγὴ ἐτείμησεν ὅπλῳ ἐπιχρύ-
σῳ διά τε τὴν ἐνάρετον αὐτῶν δ[ι]άθ[ε-]
σιν καὶ τὴν πρὸς τὴν συναγωγὴν εὐνοιάν
τε καὶ σπουδήν.

This building was erected by Julia Severa; P(ublius) Tyrronios Clados, ruler of the synagogue for life [*archisynagōgos dia biou*], and Lucius, son of Lucius, ruler of the synagogue [*archisynagōgos*], and Popilios Zoticos, ruler [*archōn*], restored it with their own funds and with money which had been contributed: they painted the walls and the ceiling, and they secured the windows and made all the rest of the ornamentation; and the congregation [*synagōgē*] honoured them with a golden shield on account of their virtuous disposition, goodwill and zeal for the congregation [*synagōgē*].

Literature: Reinach, "Chronique," 225–26 (no. 13); Ramsey, *Cities*, 1.2 (no. 559), 2.638–40, 647–51; idem, "Deux jours", 272; idem, "Nouvelles remarques," 270; Krauss, *Synagogale Altertümer*, 25; *IGRR* 4.655; Robert, "Inscriptions," 41; Schürer, *HJP*, 3.1.31; Brooten, *Women Leaders*, 144, 158; Trebilco, *Jewish Communities*, 58–60; White, *Social Origins*, 2.307–10 (no. 65); Fine, *Sacred Realm*, 51; Feldman, "Diaspora Synagogues," 582; Binder, *Temple Courts*, 145–47, 286–88, 349–51; Levine, *Ancient Synagogue*, 118–20; Williams, *The Jews*, 168; Claußen, *Versammlung*, 102–3, 140–41.

Comments: Julia Severa served as high priestess of the imperial cult in Acmonia during the reign of Nero (54–68 C.E.). Within this period, her name appears on the reverse of several imperial coins, along with that of her husband, Lucius Servenius Capito. Both served as archons of Acmonia from 59–63 C.E. Given Julia's prominence as a leader of a Gentile cult, it seems unlikely that she was anything more than a patron of the local Jewish community. Nevertheless, her erection of the synagogue was a major benefaction.

The above inscription probably dates some years later, when the building was in need of repair. The three men who were honoured each bear a different title, suggesting a high degree of institutionalization within the Acmonian synagogue. The title "synagogue ruler for life" (*archisynagōgos dia biou*), while possibly an honorific, more likely carried the sense of *emeritus*—that is, P. Tyrronios Clados (a Roman citizen) was probably the retired synagogue ruler. The distinction between the offices of the other two men—"synagogue ruler" (*archisynagōgos*) and "ruler" (*archōn*)—is unclear. One possibility is that the former presided over religious ritual (cf. Luke 13:14, No. 57; Acts 13:15, No. 174), while the latter tended to the community's legislative and judicial affairs.

3.1.2.2 *Ephesus*

No. 104
Source: *Literary.* Philo, *Legat.* 315
Date: Ca. 41–45 C.E.

[315] Γάιος Νορβανὸς Φλάκκος ἀνθύπατος Ἐφεσίων ἄρχουσι χαίρειν. Καῖσάρ μοι ἔγραψεν, Ἰουδαίους, οὗ ἂν ὦσιν, ἰδίῳ ἀρχαίῳ ἐθισμῷ νομίζειν συναγομένους χρήματα φέρειν, ἃ πέμπουσιν εἰς Ἱεροσόλυμα· τούτους οὐκ ἠθέλησε κωλύεσθαι τοῦτο ποιεῖν. ἔγραψα οὖν ὑμῖν, ἵν᾿ εἰδῆτε, ὡς ταῦτα οὕτως γίνεσθαι κελεύει.'

[315] 'Gaius Norbanus Flaccus the proconsul greets the magistrates of Ephesus. Caesar has written to me saying that it is a native traditional custom of the Jews, wherever they live, to meet [*synagō*] regularly and contribute money, which they send to Jerusalem. He does not wish them

to be prevented from doing this. I am therefore writing to you so that you may know that these are his instructions.'

Literature: Radice and Runia, *Bibliography 1937–1986*; Runia, *Bibliography 1987–1996*; Smallwood, *Legatio*, 309–10.

Comments: See No. 194.

No. 105
Source: *Literary.* Acts 18:19–21
Date: Ca. 90–110 C.E.

[19] κατήντησαν δὲ εἰς Ἔφεσον, κἀκείνους κατέλιπεν αὐτοῦ, αὐτὸς δὲ εἰσελθὼν εἰς τὴν συναγωγὴν διελέξατο τοῖς Ἰουδαίοις. [20] ἐρωτώντων δὲ αὐτῶν ἐπὶ πλείονα χρόνον μεῖναι οὐκ ἐπένευσεν, [21] ἀλλὰ ἀποταξάμενος καὶ εἰπών· πάλιν ἀνακάμψω πρὸς ὑμᾶς τοῦ θεοῦ θέλοντος, ἀνήχθη ἀπὸ τῆς Ἐφέσου

[19] When they reached Ephesus, he left them there, but first he himself went into the synagogue [*synagōgē*] and had a discussion with the Jews. [20] When they asked him to stay longer, he declined; [21] but on taking leave of them, he said, "I will return to you, if God wills." Then he set sail from Ephesus.

Literature: As a general reference to commentaries see Barrett, Fitzmyer and Jervell, *Comm., ad loc.* Binder, *Temple Courts*, 279–82; Claußen, *Versammlung*, 101; Levinskaya, *Book of Acts*, 143–48; Trebilco, *Ephesus*, 110, 140–43.

Comments: The formulations here and in 18:26 and 19:8 indicate that there was only one synagogue (or one main synagogue) in Ephesus, the capital of the province Asia.

No. 106
Source: *Literary.* Acts 18:24–26
Date: Ca. 90–110 C.E.

[24] Ἰουδαῖος δέ τις Ἀπολλῶς ὀνόματι, Ἀλεξανδρεὺς τῷ γένει, ἀνὴρ λόγιος, κατήντησεν εἰς Ἔφεσον, δυνατὸς ὢν ἐν ταῖς γραφαῖς. [25] οὗτος ἦν κατηχημένος τὴν ὁδὸν τοῦ κυρίου καὶ ζέων τῷ πνεύματι ἐλάλει καὶ ἐδίδασκεν ἀκριβῶς τὰ περὶ τοῦ Ἰησοῦ, ἐπιστάμενος μόνον τὸ βάπτισμα Ἰωάννου· [26] οὗτός τε ἤρξατο παρρησιάζεσθαι ἐν τῇ συναγωγῇ. ἀκούσαντες δὲ αὐτοῦ Πρίσκιλλα καὶ Ἀκύλας προσελάβοντο αὐτὸν καὶ ἀκριβέστερον αὐτῷ ἐξέθεντο τὴν ὁδὸν [τοῦ θεοῦ].

[24] Now there came to Ephesus a Jew named Apollos, a native of Alexandria. He was an eloquent man, well-versed in the scriptures. [25] He had been instructed in the Way of the Lord; and he spoke with burning enthusiasm and taught accurately the things concerning Jesus, though he knew only the baptism of John. [26] He began to speak boldly in the synagogue [*synagōgē*]; but when Priscilla and Aquila heard him, they took him aside and explained the Way of God to him more accurately.

Literature: As a general reference to commentaries see Barrett, Fitzmyer and Jervell, *Comm., ad loc.* Binder, *Temple Courts*, 279–82; Levine, *Ancient Synagogue*, 110–11; Claußen, *Versammlung*, 101; Runesson, *Origins*, 191–92; Levinskaya, *Book of Acts*, 143–48; Trebilco, *Ephesus*, 110–25.

Comments: This passage joins several others in Acts in depicting Diaspora synagogues as welcoming teachers from abroad (cf. Acts 13:14–48). When Apollos began to teach in the synagogue at Ephesus, the Scriptures were an important part of his teaching. Significantly, Luke presents women as also taking part in this synagogue meeting. Thus Priscilla is here mentioned before her husband, implying that she was a significant teacher and leader in her own right. The Way of the Lord/God is a reference to Isaiah 40:3, a key verse in the writings of the Essenes (1QS 8:12–16), among the followers of John the Baptist, and within the early Jesus movement. It is related to the subject of Paul's teaching in Acts 19:8, viz., the Kingdom of God, the central theme of Jesus' preaching.

No. 107
Source: *Literary.* Acts 19:8–9
Date: Ca. 90–110 C.E.

[8] Εἰσελθὼν δὲ εἰς τὴν συναγωγὴν ἐπαρρησιάζετο ἐπὶ μῆνας τρεῖς διαλεγόμενος καὶ πείθων [τὰ] περὶ τῆς βασιλείας τοῦ θεοῦ. [9] ὡς δέ τινες ἐσκληρύνοντο καὶ ἠπείθουν κακολογοῦντες τὴν ὁδὸν ἐνώπιον τοῦ πλήθους, ἀποστὰς ἀπ' αὐτῶν ἀφώρισεν τοὺς μαθητὰς καθ' ἡμέραν διαλεγόμενος ἐν τῇ σχολῇ Τυράννου.

[8] He entered the synagogue [*synagōgē*] and for three months spoke out boldly, and argued persuasively about the kingdom of God. [9] When some stubbornly refused to believe and spoke evil of the Way before the congregation, he left them, taking the disciples with him, and argued daily in the lecture hall of Tyrannus.

Literature: As a general reference to commentaries see Barrett, Fitzmyer and Jervell, *Comm., ad loc.* Binder, *Temple Courts*, 279–82; Claußen, *Versammlung*, 101; Levinskaya, *Book of Acts*, 143–48; Trebilco, *Ephesus*, 140–43.

Comments: About speaking evil of the Way before "the congregation" (*plēthos* "crowd, multitude"), see comments on Acts 18:4–8 (No. 91). The referent of *to plēthos* is not clear. It may refer to: (a) the Christ-believers in the synagogue, (b) the synagogue community as a whole, or (c) the general public of the city. Parallel passages in Acts argue for the last alternative. The departure from the synagogue results in the formation of a Christ-believing fellowship outside the synagogue. See comments on Acts 13:14–16, 42–49 (No. 174). When Luke talks about Jews and Greeks, v. 10, he seems to refer to Jews and God-fearers (14:1; 17:4; 18:4, 19:17; 20:21). See comments on Acts 17:16–17 (No. 90).

No. 108

Source: *Literary.* Josephus, *A.J.* 14.225–27.
Date: The decree quoted by Josephus was issued in 43 B.C.E.; *Antiquitates Judaicae* was published in 93/94 C.E.

[225] Ἐπὶ πρυτάνεως Ἀρτέμωνος μηνὸς Ληναιῶνος προτέρᾳ. Δολοβέλλας αὐτοκράτωρ Ἐφεσίων ἄρχουσι βουλῇ δήμῳ χαίρειν. [226] Ἀλέξανδρος Θεοδώρου πρεσβευτὴς Ὑρκανοῦ τοῦ Ἀλεξάνδρου υἱοῦ ἀρχιερέως καὶ ἐθνάρχου τῶν Ἰουδαίων ἐνεφάνισέν μοι περὶ τοῦ μὴ δύνασθαι στρατεύεσθαι τοὺς πολίτας αὐτοῦ διὰ τὸ μήτε ὅπλα βαστάζειν δύνασθαι μήτε ὁδοιπορεῖν ἐν ταῖς ἡμέραις τῶν σαββάτων, μήτε τροφῶν τῶν πατρίων καὶ συνήθων κατὰ τούτους εὐπορεῖν. [227] ἐγώ τε οὖν αὐτοῖς, καθὼς καὶ οἱ πρὸ ἐμοῦ ἡγεμόνες, δίδωμι τὴν ἀστρατείαν καὶ συγχωρῶ χρῆσθαι τοῖς πατρίοις ἐθισμοῖς ἱερῶν ἕνεκα καὶ ἁγίοις συναγομένοις, καθὼς αὐτοῖς νόμιμον, καὶ τῶν πρὸς τὰς θυσίας ἀφαιρεμάτων, ὑμᾶς τε βούλομαι ταῦτα γράψαι κατὰ πόλεις.

[225] In the presidency of Artemon, on the first day of the month of Lenaeon, Dollabella, imperator, to the magistrates, council and people of Ephesus, greeting. [226] Alexander, son of Theodoros, ambassador of Hyrcanus son of Alexander, the high priest and ethnarch of the Jews has informed me that his fellow-Jews cannot do military service because they cannot carry arms or march on the days of the Sabbath. Nor can they obtain the traditional foods to which they are accustomed. [227] I therefore, as the governors before me, grant them exemption from military service and permit them to follow their native customs and to assemble [*synagō*] for sacred and holy rituals in accordance with

their law and to make contributions to sacrifices. It is my will that you write this to the various cities.

Literature: Binder, *Temple Courts*, 276–78; Barclay, *Diaspora*, 417–23.

Comments: Cf. *A.J.* 16:167–68, 172–73. The sacrifices mentioned in *A.J.* 14.227 refer to the sacrifices performed in the Jerusalem temple to which the Jews contributed economically irrespective of where they lived (cf. *A.J.* 18.312–13; Philo, *Spec.* 1.76–78; *Legat.* 157, 216, 291, 312–13). On the collection of temple dues and the relation between Diaspora Jews and the land of Israel, see Barclay.

3.1.2.3 *Halicarnassus*

No. 109
Source: *Literary.* Josephus, *A.J.* 14.256–58.
Date: The decree quoted by Josephus dates to the first century B.C.E.; *Antiquitates Judaicae* was published in 93/94 C.E.

[256] Ψήφισμα Ἁλικαρνασέων. ἐπὶ ἱερέως Μέμνονος τοῦ' Ἀριστείδου, κατὰ δὲ ποίησιν Εὐωνύμου, ᾽Ανθεστηριῶνος ἔδοξε τῷ δήμῳ εἰσηγησαμένου Μάρκου ᾽Αλεξάνδρου. [257] ἐπεὶ [τὸ] πρὸς τὸ θεῖον εὐσεβές τε καὶ ὅσιον ἐν ἅπαντι καιρῷ διὰ σπουδῆς ἔχομεν κατακολουθοῦντες τῷ δήμῳ τῶν ῾Ρωμαίων πάντων ἀνθρώπων ὄντι εὐεργέτῃ καὶ οἷς περὶ τῆς ᾽Ιουδαίων φιλίας καὶ συμμαχίας πρὸς τὴν πόλιν ἔγραψεν, ὅπως συντελῶνται αὐτοῖς αἱ εἰς τὸν θεὸν ἱεροποιίαι καὶ ἑορταὶ αἱ εἰθισμέναι καὶ σύνοδοι, [258] δεδόχθαι καὶ ἡμῖν ᾽Ιουδαίων τοὺς βουλομένους ἄνδρας τε καὶ γυναῖκας τά τε σάββατα ἄγειν καὶ τὰ ἱερὰ συντελεῖν κατὰ τοὺς ᾽Ιουδαίων νόμους καὶ τὰς προσευχὰς ποιεῖσθαι πρὸς τῇ θαλάττῃ κατὰ τὸ πάτριον ἔθος. ἂν δέ τις κωλύσῃ ἢ ἄρχων ἢ ἰδιώτης, τῷδε τῷ ζημιώματι ὑπεύθυνος ἔστω καὶ ὀφειλέτω τῇ πόλει.

[256] Decree of the people of Halicarnassos. "In the priesthood of Memnon, son of Aristides by descent and of Euonymos by adoption, [...of the month of]⁵ Anthesterion, the people passed the following decree on the motion of Marcus Alexander. [257] Since we at all times have a deep regard to piety towards the divine and holiness, and since we aim to follow the example of the people of Rome, the benefactors of all mankind, who has written to our city concerning their friendship

⁵ As Marcus notes (LCL), the day of the month is lacking but must have been given in the original decree.

and alliance with the Jews, to the effect that their sacred rituals to God and their customary festivals and assemblies shall be carried on, [258] we have also decreed that the Jews, men and women alike, who so wish may keep the Sabbaths and perform their sacred rituals according to the Jewish laws, and may build prayer halls [*proseuchas poieisthai*] by the sea, in accordance with their native custom. And if anyone, be it an *archōn* or a private person, prevents them from doing so, he shall be liable to this fine[6] and owe it to the city.

Literature: Trebilco, *Jewish Communities*, 13; Binder, *Temple Courts*, 285–86; Bilde, "Synagoge," 22; Levine, *Ancient Synagogue*, 114, 330–34; Runesson, "Water and Worship," 119–23; Claußen, *Versammlung*, 219–21; Catto, "'Build Places of Prayer'?"

Comments: As in many other decrees listed by Josephus, the rights of the Jews—both men and women—to perform sacred rituals according to Jewish law and gather on Sabbaths and festivals are established (cf., e.g., No. 108). Of particular interest here is the mention of the right to *proseuchas poieisthai* near the sea. Most scholars have translated these words as referring to the building of prayer halls, i.e., synagogue institutions, near the sea. It is known from other sources that synagogues were often built near water (several papyri from Egypt mention this, and some excavated synagogue buildings, e.g., Ostia and Delos, are located near the sea. Cf. also Acts 16:13 [No. 185] and Philo, *Flaccus* 122–23 [No. 139]). Other scholars translate *proseuchas poieisthai* as "offer prayer"; the ruling would then allow Jews to pray by the sea, rather than erect buildings (Catto).

3.1.2.4 *Miletus*

No. 110
Source: *Literary.* Josephus *A.J.* 14.244–46.
Date: The letter quoted by Josephus dates to the first century B.C.E., no earlier than 46 B.C.E.; *Antiquitates Judaicae* was published in 93/94 C.E.

[244] Πόπλιος Σερουίλιος Ποπλίου υἱὸς Γάλβας ἀνθύπατος Μιλησίων ἄρχουσι βουλῇ δήμῳ χαίρειν. [245] Πρύτανις Ἑρμοῦ υἱὸς πολίτης ὑμέτερος προσελθών μοι ἐν Τράλλεσιν ἄγοντι τὴν ἀγόραιον ἐδήλου παρὰ τὴν ἡμετέραν γνώμην Ἰουδαίοις ὑμᾶς προσφέρεσθαι καὶ κωλύειν αὐτοὺς τά τε σάββατα ἄγειν καὶ τὰ ἱερὰ τὰ πάτρια τελεῖν καὶ τοὺς καρποὺς μεταχειρίζεσθαι, καθὼς ἔθος ἐστὶν αὐτοῖς, αὐτόν τε κατὰ τοὺς νόμους εὐθυνκέναι τὸ [δίκαιον] ψήφισμα. [246] βούλομαι οὖν

---

[6] Originally, the amount of money to be paid must have been mentioned here.

ὑμᾶς εἰδέναι, ὅτι διακούσας ἐγὼ λόγων ἐξ ἀντικαταστάσεως γενομένων ἐπέκρινα μὴ κωλύεσθαι 'Ιουδαίους τοῖς αὐτῶν ἔθεσι χρῆσθαι.

[244] "Publius Servilius Galba, son of Publius, proconsul, to the magistrates, council and people of Miletus, greeting. [245] Prytanis, son of Hermas and a citizen of yours, came to me when I was holding court at Tralles and informed me that contrary to our will, you assault the Jews and prevent them from keeping the Sabbaths, from performing their native rituals, and from managing the first-fruits according to their custom. He announced this decree in accordance with the law. [246] I therefore want you to know that having heard the arguments from both parties, I have judged that the Jews should not be prevented from following their customs.

Literature: Trebilco, *Jewish Communities*, 56; A. von Gerkan, "Eine Synaoge in Milet," *ZNW* 20 (1921); Sukenik, *Ancient Synagogues*, 40–42; A. Kraabel, "Archaeological and Epigraphic Evidence Since Sukenik," 488–89; Hachlili, *Ancient Jewish Art*, 51; Binder, *Temple Courts*, 276–79; Williams, *The Jews*, 115; Levinskaya, *Book of Acts*, 63–65, 148–49.

Comments: It is possible and even likely that the letter quoted by Josephus refers to Jewish communal assemblies and rituals on the Sabbath, but it cannot be proved from the text. If the Jews in Miletus had communal gatherings, such assemblies could have been held in separate buildings constructed for the purpose or they could have taken place in private homes. The identification of a synagogue building dating to the late third or early fourth century C.E. (van Gorken, Sukenik) cannot be maintained (Kraabel, Trebilco, Hachlili): Trebilco suggests that the edifice may well have been a Graeco-Roman temple.

3.1.2.5   *Parium*

See comment on Josephus, *A.J.* 14.213–16 (No. 93).

3.1.2.6   *Philadelphia*

No. 111
Source: *Literary.* Rev 3:7–13
Date: Ca. 90–95 C.E.

[7] Καὶ τῷ ἀγγέλῳ τῆς ἐν Φιλαδελφείᾳ ἐκκλησίας γράψον· Τάδε λέγει ὁ ἅγιος, ὁ ἀληθινός, ὁ ἔχων τὴν κλεῖν Δαυίδ, ὁ ἀνοίγων καὶ οὐδεὶς κλείσει καὶ κλείων καὶ οὐδεὶς ἀνοίγει· [8] οἶδά σου τὰ ἔργα, ἰδοὺ δέδωκα ἐνώπιόν σου θύραν ἠνεῳγμένην, ἣν οὐδεὶς δύναται κλεῖσαι αὐτήν, ὅτι μικρὰν ἔχεις δύναμιν καὶ ἐτήρησάς μου τὸν λόγον καὶ οὐκ ἠρνήσω τὸ ὄνομά μου. [9] ἰδοὺ διδῶ ἐκ τῆς συναγωγῆς τοῦ σατανᾶ τῶν λεγόντων ἑαυτοὺς 'Ιουδαίους εἶναι, καὶ οὐκ εἰσὶν ἀλλὰ ψεύδονται.

ἰδοὺ ποιήσω αὐτοὺς ἵνα ἥξουσιν καὶ προσκυνήσουσιν ἐνώπιον τῶν ποδῶν σου καὶ γνῶσιν ὅτι ἐγὼ ἠγάπησά σε. [10] ὅτι ἐτήρησας τὸν λόγον τῆς ὑπομονῆς μου, κἀγώ σε τηρήσω ἐκ τῆς ὥρας τοῦ πειρασμοῦ τῆς μελλούσης ἔρχεσθαι ἐπὶ τῆς οἰκουμένης ὅλης πειράσαι τοὺς κατοικοῦντας ἐπὶ τῆς γῆς. [11] ἔρχομαι ταχύ· κράτει ὃ ἔχεις, ἵνα μηδεὶς λάβῃ τὸν στέφανόν σου. [12] Ὁ νικῶν ποιήσω αὐτὸν στῦλον ἐν τῷ ναῷ τοῦ θεοῦ μου καὶ ἔξω οὐ μὴ ἐξέλθῃ ἔτι καὶ γράψω ἐπ' αὐτὸν τὸ ὄνομα τοῦ θεοῦ μου καὶ τὸ ὄνομα τῆς πόλεως τοῦ θεοῦ μου, τῆς καινῆς Ἰερουσαλὴμ ἡ καταβαίνουσα ἐκ τοῦ οὐρανοῦ ἀπὸ τοῦ θεοῦ μου, καὶ τὸ ὄνομά μου τὸ καινόν. [13] Ὁ ἔχων οὖς ἀκουσάτω τί τὸ πνεῦμα λέγει ταῖς ἐκκλησίαις.

[7] And to the angel of the church in Philadelphia write: These are the words of the holy one, the true one, who has the key of David, who opens and no one will shut, who shuts and no one opens: [8] "I know your works. Look, I have set before you an open door, which no one is able to shut. I know that you have but little power, and yet you have kept my word and have not denied my name. [9] I will make those of the synagogue [*synagōgē*] of Satan who say that they are Jews and are not, but are lying—I will make them come and bow down before your feet, and they will learn that I have loved you. [10] Because you have kept my word of patient endurance, I will keep you from the hour of trial that is coming on the whole world to test the inhabitants of the earth. [11] I am coming soon; hold fast to what you have, so that no one may seize your crown. [12] If you conquer, I will make you a pillar in the temple of my God; you will never go out of it. I will write on you the name of my God, and the name of the city of my God, the new Jerusalem that comes down from my God out of heaven, and my own new name. [13] Let anyone who has an ear listen to what the Spirit is saying to the churches."

Literature: As a general reference to commentaries see Bousset, Ford and Aune, *Comm., ad loc.* Stegemann, *Synagoge und Obrigkeit*, 142–44, 255–57. Olsson, "In synagogues," 207–8.

Comments: The "synagogue of Satan" is here defined as "those who say that they are Jews and are not, but are lying" (taking *tōn legontōn* as an apposition to *tēs synagōgēs* and not to *ek tēs synagōgēs*). Some of these Jews, though not all (taking *ek tēs synagōgēs* as a partitive genative), "will come and bow down" before the feet of the Jesus-believers in Philadelphia (including Jesus-believing Jews). According to the author, these last belong to the true Israel of the end time. Those who bow down thus finally realize that Jesus-believers are included within God's covenantal love. The formulation is reminiscent of Isa

60:14 where the Gentiles in the eschatological future bow down before the feet of Israel.

According to the author, the Jews in Philadelphia who did not accept Jesus as the Messiah were no longer "Jews"; they did not belong to the people of God. Within this polarized view, because this group no longer constituted the synagogue of the Lord, they had become the "synagogue of the Satan." See comment on Rev 2:8–11 (No. 115).

3.1.2.7 *Priene*

No. 112
Source: *Archaeological.*
Date: Second or third century C.E.

Literature: Wiegand and Schrader, *Priene*, 480–81; Sukenik, *Ancient Synagogues*, 42–43; Kraabel, "Diaspora Synagogue," 489–91; A. Kraabel, "Judaism in Western Asia Minor," 20–25; Foertser, "Diaspora Synagogue," 165–166; White, *Social Origins*, 2.325–32; Hachlili, *Ancient Jewish Art*, 56–58; Runesson, *Origins*, 175–76; Levine, *Ancient Synagogue*, 266–67.

Comments: The excavators, Wiegand and Schrader, wrongly identified this building as a fourth or fifth century *Hauskirche* (house church). Today there is a consensus that this building was originally a Hellenistic private house turned into a synagogue in the second or third century C.E.

The main hall has an irregular form: 10 m east to west, by 12.59–13.70 m north to south. Benches were situated along the northern wall, while two stylobates created aisles to the north and south of a central nave. A large marble ablution basin stood in the main hall of the building just to the right of a square niche (1.35 × 1.37 m, most likely for the Torah shrine) in the eastern wall, which was oriented toward Jerusalem. Several smaller rooms were located next to the main hall to the north and west.

The building contained three reliefs adorned with Jewish symbols, including the menorah, *lulav*, and *ethrog*, as well as a rare early depiction of two rolled Torah scrolls (see Foerster for illustrations).

3.1.2.8 *Sardis*

No. 113
Source: *Literary.* Josephus, *A.J.* 14.259–61
Date: The decree by the council and people of Sardis probably dates to the late second century B.C.E.[7]; *Antiquitates Judaicae* was published in 93/94 C.E.

[259] Ψήφισμα Σαρδιανῶν. ἔδοξε τῇ βουλῇ καὶ τῷ δήμῳ στρατηγῶν εἰσηγησαμένων. ἐπεὶ οἱ κατοικοῦντες ἡμῶν ἐν τῇ πόλει ἀπ᾽ ἀρχῆς

---

[7] For this date, see Binder, *Temple Courts*, 138–139.

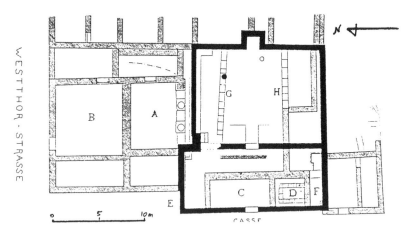

Figure 19. Plan of the Priene synagogue.

Ἰουδαῖοι πολῖται πολλὰ καὶ μεγάλα φιλάνθρωπα ἐσχηκότες διὰ παντὸς παρὰ τοῦ δήμου καὶ νῦν εἰσελθόντες ἐπὶ τὴν βουλὴν καὶ τὸν δῆμον παρεκάλεσαν, [260] ἀποκαθισταμένων αὐτοῖς τῶν νόμων καὶ τῆς ἐλευθερίας ὑπὸ τῆς συγκλήτου καὶ τοῦ δήμου τοῦ ʿΡωμαίων ἵνα κατὰ τὰ νομιζόμενα ἔθη συνάγωνται καὶ πολιτεύωνται καὶ διαδικάζωνται πρὸς αὑτούς, δοθῇ τε καὶ τόπος αὐτοῖς, εἰς ὃν συλλεγόμενοι μετὰ γυναικῶν καὶ τέκνων ἐπιτελοῦσιν τὰς πατρίους εὐχὰς καὶ θυσίας τῷ θεῷ· [261] δεδόχθαι τῇ βουλῇ καὶ τῷ δήμῳ συγκεχωρῆσθαι αὐτοῖς συνερχομένοις ἐν ταῖς ἀποδεδειγμέναις ἡμέραις πράσσειν τὰ κατὰ τοὺς αὑτῶν νόμους, ἀφορισθῆναι δ᾽ αὐτοῖς καὶ τόπον ὑπὸ τῶν στρατηγῶν εἰς οἰκοδομίαν καὶ οἴκησιν αὐτῶν, ὃν ἂν ὑπολάβωσιν πρὸς τοῦτ᾽ ἐπιτήδειον εἶναι, ὅπως τε τοῖς τῆς πόλεως ἀγορανόμοις ἐπιμελὲς ᾖ καὶ τὰ ἐκείνοις πρὸς τροφὴν ἐπιτήδεια ποιεῖν εἰσάγεσθαι.

[259] Decree of the people of Sardis. "On the motion of the magistrates, the council and people passed the following decree: Whereas the Jewish citizens[8] living in our city have continually received many and great privileges from the people, and have now come before the council and the people with the request that, [260] having their laws and freedom restored by the Roman Senate and people, they may, in accordance with their accepted customs, assemble [*synagō*] and have a communal life [*politeuō*] and settle suites among themselves, and that a

---

[8] On 'citizen', see Marcus comment (*LCL*), *ad loc.* Williams, *The Jews*, 57, has omitted the word.

place [*topos*] be given them in which they may gather with women and children and offer ancestral prayers and sacrifices [*euchai kai thysiai*] to God, [261] it has been decided by the council and people to permit them to come together on stated days in order to do the things which are in accordance with their laws, and also that a place be set aside for them by the magistrates to build and inhabit, such as they consider to be suitable for this purpose, and that the market-officials of the city shall be responsible for having suitable food for them brought in.

Literature: Sanders, *Judaism*, 133–34; Binder, *Temple Courts*, 135–40; Bilde, "Synagoge," 28–29; Runesson, *Origins*, 463–66; Leonhardt, "Opfer in der Jüdischen Synagoge on Sardes?" 189–203; Claußen, *Versammlung*, 243–46. Levine, *Ancient Synagogue*, 113–15, 139–40, 141, n. 33.

Comments: This document, which most likely predates No. 114, is rich on information relating to Jewish communal life in Asia Minor before the turn of the era. The "place" (*topos*) given to the Jewish community is clearly a public building designed for worship purposes, possibly even temple-like in appearance. Interestingly, women and children are mentioned as participants in the religious rituals. The words translated "prayers and sacrifices" have caused interpreters to wonder how precisely these liturgies were fashioned: did Jews sacrifice in their synagogues? If so, are we dealing then with a specific sacrifice, such as the Passover sacrifice attested in other sources as taking place elsewhere outside the Jerusalem temple (Sanders; cf. Martola, "House-Temples," and Bokser, *Origins*, 101–106; *t. Besa* [*Yom Tov*] 2:15)? Or should *topos* rather be translated "sanctuary" or "temple," indicating a Jewish sacrificial cult in Sardis, matching those evidenced in Egypt (cf. ch. 5 below)? Or, again, should we understand the reference to sacrifices (and prayers?) as a misunderstanding on the part of the non-Jewish author of the document, which Josephus reproduced? Does "sacrifices" refer to the money sent by Jews to the Jerusalem temple, attested in both Josephus and the NT? All of these interpretations are possible, and there is comparative material to support each view. It may be added that if sacrifices were offered, they may well have consisted of incense and vegetables rather than animals: this would depend on how far cult centralisation ideology had taken root throughout the Diaspora at this time. Torah reading rituals, which Philo and Josephus repeatedly declared to be the most prominent feature of synagogue worship in the first century, are not mentioned in the decree.

The reference to "stated days" most likely refers to Sabbath gatherings and festival assemblies. In addition to religious-liturgical functions, the decree confirms the right for the Jews to use their assembly building for court procedures. Finally, Jewish food laws were accommodated on an official level: the decree guarantees that the city market would provide kosher food.

No. 114
Source: *Literary.* Josephus, *A.J.* 14.235
Date: The decree by Lucius Antonius was issued in 49 B.C.E.; *Antiquitates Judaicae* was published in 93/94 C.E.

[235] Λούκιος ᾽Αντώνιος Μάρκου υἱὸς ἀντιταμίας καὶ ἀντιστράτηγος Σαρδιανῶν ἄρχουσι βουλῇ δήμῳ χαίρειν. ᾽Ιουδαῖοι πολῖται ἡμέτεροι προσελθόντες μοι ἐπέδειξαν αὐτοὺς σύνοδον ἔχειν ἰδίαν κατὰ τοὺς πατρίους νόμους ἀπ᾽ ἀρχῆς καὶ τόπον ἴδιον, ἐν ᾧ τά τε πράγματα καὶ τὰς πρὸς ἀλλήλους ἀντιλογίας κρίνουσιν, τοῦτό τε αἰτησαμένοις ἵν᾽ ἐξῇ ποιεῖν αὐτοῖς τηρῆσαι καὶ ἐπιτρέψαι ἔκρινα.

[235] Lucius Antonius, son of Marcus, proquaestor and propraetor, to the magistrates, council and people of Sardis, greeting. Jewish citizens of ours have come to me and pointed out that from earliest times, in accordance with their native laws, they have had a private association [*synodos*] and a place [*topos*] of their own, in which they decide their affairs and settle their disputes with one another. Upon their request that they be permitted to do these things, I have decided that they may be preserved and maintained.

Literature: Köster, "τόπος"; Binder, *Temple Courts*, 135–40; Bilde, "Synagoge," 28; Claußen, *Versammlung*, 243–46. Levine, *Ancient Synagogue*, 113–15, 139–40, 395.

Comments: The relationship between this decree and the above (No. 113) has been the object of scholarly discussion; most likely, the latter precedes the former (cf. Binder, 138–39). As in several other documents copied by Josephus, Jewish social and religious rights were confirmed. A limited degree of self-rule was granted the Jewish association (*synodos*), including the right to settle their own disputes (cf. Acts 18:14–16). This confirms allusions in other sources that one of the functions of the synagogue was that of a court. The use here of the word *topos*, "place," is technical, indicating a sanctuary or synagogue; the same term could refer to a temple (cf. No. T.1). The edifice referenced should not be confused with the monumental synagogue discovered in Sardis in 1962; that building was constructed at a much later date.

3.1.2.9 *Smyrna*

No. 115
Source: *Literary.* Rev 2:8–11
Date: Ca. 90–95 C.E.

[8] Καὶ τῷ ἀγγέλῳ τῆς ἐν Σμύρνῃ ἐκκλησίας γράψον· Τάδε λέγει ὁ πρῶτος καὶ ὁ ἔσχατος, ὃς ἐγένετο νεκρὸς καὶ ἔζησεν· [9] οἶδά σου τὴν

θλῖψιν καὶ τὴν πτωχείαν, ἀλλὰ πλούσιος εἶ, καὶ τὴν βλασφημίαν ἐκ τῶν λεγόντων Ἰουδαίους εἶναι ἑαυτοὺς καὶ οὐκ εἰσὶν ἀλλὰ συναγωγὴ τοῦ σατανᾶ. [10] μηδὲν φοβοῦ ἃ μέλλεις πάσχειν. ἰδοὺ μέλλει βάλλειν ὁ διάβολος ἐξ ὑμῶν εἰς φυλακὴν ἵνα πειρασθῆτε καὶ ἕξετε θλῖψιν ἡμερῶν δέκα. γίνου πιστὸς ἄχρι θανάτου, καὶ δώσω σοι τὸν στέφανον τῆς ζωῆς. [11] Ὁ ἔχων οὖς ἀκουσάτω τί τὸ πνεῦμα λέγει ταῖς ἐκκλησίαις. Ὁ νικῶν οὐ μὴ ἀδικηθῇ ἐκ τοῦ θανάτου τοῦ δευτέρου.

[8] And to the angel of the church in Smyrna write: These are the words of the first and the last, who was dead and came to life: [9] "I know your affliction and your poverty, even though you are rich. I know the slander on the part of those who say that they are Jews and are not, but are a synagogue [*synagōgē*] of Satan. [10] Do not fear what you are about to suffer. Beware, the devil is about to throw some of you into prison so that you may be tested, and for ten days you will have affliction. Be faithful until death, and I will give you the crown of life. [11] Let anyone who has an ear listen to what the Spirit is saying to the churches. Whoever conquers will not be harmed by the second death."

Literature: As a general reference to commentaries see Bousset, Ford and Aune, *Comm.*, *ad loc.* Stegemann, *Synagoge und Obrigkeit*, 142–44, 255–57. Olsson, "In synagogues," 206–7.

Comments: The referent of the term "the synagogue of Satan" in Rev 2:9 and 3:9 is not entirely clear. In the letters to Philadelphia and Smyrna, the term is defined as "those who say that they are Jews but are not" (3:9 adds "but are lying").

The phrase is used nowhere else in biblical or nonbiblical writings, but 1QH 2:22 alludes to "the assembly of Belial." Belial, an alternative name for Satan (cf. 2 Cor 6:15), literally means "destruction, uselessness." To the Qumran community, those Jews outside their group were thus viewed as being under the Belial's rule. Consequently, the term in Revelation probably refers to some, if not all members of the Jewish communities in Smyrna and Philadelphia.

These Jews have been described in different ways. One view holds that they were thoroughly assimilated Jews who were open to the worship of Zeus or involvement in Graeco-Oriental cults (Ford). Thus Rev 2:13 obliquely refers to the altar of Zeus at Pergamum as "the seat of Satan." It follows that the Jewish author of Revelation, like the covenanters at Qumran, regarded those who did not exercise his less tolerant form of Jewish adherence as an "assembly of Satan."

A second interpretation maintains that the Jews referenced were those who had betrayed the Jesus-believers to the Roman authorities. Thus verse 10 refers to believers who would be thrown into prison, a situation attested also in Acts (see comments to Acts 18:4–8, No. 91). In this view, the requirement for non-exempt groups to worship the emperor led some Jews to denounce the Jesus-believing Jews as outsiders to the Romans (Stegemann).

A final opinion holds that the "synagogue of Satan" consisted of Jews not accepting Jesus as the Messiah, people whom the author no longer regarded as members of the people of God: despite claiming to be the assembly of the Lord (Num 16:3; 31:16), as non-believers they constituted an assembly of Satan. Such dualism, like that seen at Qumran, posited a clear division between the forces of good and evil; in this case, only Christ-believers (whether Jew or Gentile) were viewed as the true inheritors of Judaism. And so, Revelation 12 depicts the covenant people as a renewed Israel that included both Jews and Greeks. Likewise, the New Jerusalem has the names of both the twelve tribes and the twelve apostles inscribed on its gates and foundations (Rev 21).

From a Roman point of view, the conflict in Smyrna and Philadelphia was very much an inner-Jewish affair. The situation for Jesus-believing Jews (and Greeks) was critical in the 90s, and many of them may have hoped to avoid the civic obligations of emperor worship by maintaining their connections to the Jewish communities. This may have become difficult when some Jews not believing in Jesus claimed that only *they* were Jews, but not the Jesus-believers. Thus some elements of the above views might be combined. See also the comment on Rev 3:7–13 (No. 111).

3.1.2.10   *Synnada*

No. 116
Source: *Inscription. IJO* 2.214 (*CIJ* 2.759, *MAMA* 4.90)
Date: First to second century C.E.

ἀ]ρχισυν[αγωγος
'Ιου]λίου 'ΑΡ[
]ΩΣ ἐκ τ[ῶν ?

...ruler of the synagogue [*archisynagōgos*]...[Jul]ius AR...OS from the...

Literature: Horsley, *New Documents*, 4.217; Trebilco, *Jewish Communities*, 216 n. 53.

Comments: This very fragmentary inscription seems to attest the presence of a synagogue in Synnada, as can be inferred from the probable mention of a synagogue ruler (*archisynagōgos*). On the presence of this title in other inscriptions, see Nos. 26, 103, 145 and 177.

3.1.2.11   *Thyatira*

No. 117
Source: *Inscription. IJO* 2.146 (*CIJ* 2.752)
Date: Early second century C.E.

Φάβιος Ζώσιμος κατασκευάσας σοπὸν ἔθετο ἐπὶ τόπου καθαροῦ, ὄντος
πρὸ τῆς πόλεως, πρὸς τῷ σαμβαθείῳ, ἐν τῷ χαλδαίου περι-
βόλωι, παρὰ τὴν δημοσίαν ὁδόν, ἑαυτῶι ἐφ’ ᾧ τεθῇ, καὶ τῆι
γλυκυτάτηι αὐτοῦ
γυναικὶ Αὐρηλίᾳ Ποντιανῆι...

Fabius Zosimos, who built the sarcophagus, put it on a pure place before
the city, close to the *sambatheion* in the Chaldean quarter alongside the
public road, for himself, in order to be placed in it, and for his very
sweet wife Aurelia Pontiane...

Literature: *CIG* 3509; *IGRR* 4.1281; Krauss, *Synagogale Altertümer*, 25–26, 231
(no. 61); *CPJ* 3, 46–51; van der Horst, *Ancient Jewish Epitaphs*, 150–51; Schürer,
HJP 3.1.19; Safrai, *Jewish People*, 151; Trebilco, *Jewish Communities*, 198, n. 65,
245–46, n. 79; Levine, *Ancient Synagogue*, 115, n. 180; Edwards, *Religion*, 133;
Williams, *The Jews*, 175.

Comments: The above excerpt is taken from the first two lines of a longer
inscription. The term *sambatheion*, mentioned incidentally, is most likely to be
understood as identical with *sabbateion*, meaning synagogue (cf. Josephus, *A.J.*
16.164, No. 120). However, some scholars have understood the reference to
be to a sanctuary of the Chaldean Sibyl Sambethe.

3.1.2.12   *General*

No. 118
Source: *Literary.* Philo, *Legat.* 311
Date: Ca. 41–45 C.E.

[311] τεκμηρίοις δὲ ἀφθόνοις πιστώσασθαι δυνάμενος τὸ βούλημα τοῦ
Σεβαστοῦ προπάππου σου δυσὶν ἀρκεσθήσομαι. τὸ μὲν γὰρ πρῶτον
ἐπέστειλε τοῖς ἐπιτρόποις τῶν κατὰ τὴν Ἀσίαν ἐπικρατειῶν, πυθόμενος
ὀλιγωρεῖσθαι τὰς ἱερὰς ἀπαρχάς, ἵνα ἐπιτρέπωσι τοῖς Ἰουδαίοις μόνοις
εἰς τὰ συναγώγια συνέρχεσθαι·

[311] I could demonstrate the intentions of Augustus, your great grandfather, by countless proofs, but I will content myself with two. First,
when he discovered that the sacred "first-fruits" were being neglected,
he instructed the governors of the provinces in Asia to grant to the
Jews alone the right of meeting in the synagogues (*synagōgia*).

Literature: Radice and Runia, *Bibliography 1937–1986*; Runia, *Bibliography 1987–1996*; Smallwood, *Legatio*, 308–9.

Comments: See No. 194.

No. 119

Source: *Literary.* Josephus, *A.J.* 16:42–43
Date: Nicolas of Damascus' speech before Marcus Agrippa is dated to 14 B.C.E.; *Antiquitates Judaicae* was published in 93/94 C.E.

[42] τὸ γὰρ θεῖον, εἰ χαίρει τιμώμενον, χαίρει τοῖς ἐπιτρέπουσι τιμᾶν, ἐθῶν τε τῶν ἡμετέρων ἀπάνθρωπον μὲν οὐδέν ἐστιν, εὐσεβῆ δὲ πάντα καὶ τῇ συνήθει δικαιοσύνῃ συγκαθωσιωμένα. [43] καὶ οὔτε ἀποκρυπτόμεθα τὰ παραγγέλματα, οἷς χρώμεθα πρὸς τὸν βίον ὑπομνήμασιν τῆς εὐσεβείας καὶ τῶν ἀνθρωπίνων ἐπιτηδευμάτων, τήν τε ἑβδόμην τῶν ἡμερῶν ἀνίεμεν τῇ μαθήσει τῶν ἡμετέρων ἐθῶν καὶ νόμου, μελέτην ὥσπερ ἄλλου τινὸς καὶ τούτων ἀξιοῦντες εἶναι δι' ὧν οὐχ ἁμαρτησόμεθα.

[42] None of our customs are inhuman, but all of them are pious and devoted to the preservation of justice. [43] Nor do we conceal the precepts with which we guide our life in religion and in human relations; we set aside every seventh day to the study of our customs and law, for we think it necessary to occupy ourselves, as with any other study, so with these through which we can avoid sinning.

Literature: Binder, *Temple Courts*, 399–404; Runesson, *Origins*, 191, n. 91, 213–32; Levine, *Ancient Synagogue*, 146–58.

Comments: Josephus is here quoting a speech reportedly held by Nicolas of Damascus before Marcus Agrippa (ca. 64/63 B.C.E.–12 B.C.E.), then visiting Ionia, on behalf of the Jews there. While no word for "synagogue" appears in this passage, the public reading or studying of Torah every seventh day clearly refers to what was practiced in synagogue institutions, as shown by several other sources (cf. Runesson, 191, n. 91 and Introduction above, n. 14). The passage indicates that when Jews experienced difficult social and political situations in the cities in which they lived, they could refer to the weekly study of Torah as something appropriate in the eyes of the Roman rulers. To be seen as good citizens, rid of troublemakers, was vital for the Jews in order to be able to preserve Jewish identity in a political system that would not automatically allow for Jewish religious customs and rituals. Reading law publicly appealed to Roman authorities, and thus the institution in which law was read, the synagogue, could be, and was, used rhetorically to drive home the point that the Jews were an orderly people worthy of protection.

No. 120
Source: *Literary.* Josephus, *A.J.* 16:162–65
Date: Augustus' decree dates to 2–3 C.E. *Antiquitates Judaicae* was published in 93/94 C.E.

[162] "Καῖσαρ Σεβαστὸς ἀρχιερεὺς δημαρχικῆς ἐξουσίας λέγει. ἐπειδὴ τὸ ἔθνος τὸ τῶν Ἰουδαίων εὐχάριστον εὑρέθη οὐ μόνον ἐν τῷ ἐνεστῶτι καιρῷ ἀλλὰ καὶ ἐν τῷ προγεγενημένῳ καὶ μάλιστα ἐπὶ τοῦ ἐμοῦ πατρὸς αὐτοκράτορος Καίσαρος πρὸς τὸν δῆμον τὸν Ῥωμαίων ὅ τε ἀρχιερεὺς αὐτῶν Ὑρκανός, [163] ἔδοξέ μοι καὶ τῷ ἐμῷ συμβουλίῳ μετὰ ὀρκωμοσίας γνώμῃ δήμου Ῥωμαίων τοὺς Ἰουδαίους χρῆσθαι τοῖς ἰδίοις θεσμοῖς κατὰ τὸν πάτριον αὐτῶν νόμον, καθὼς ἐχρῶντο ἐπὶ Ὑρκανοῦ ἀρχιερέως θεοῦ ὑψίστου, τά τε ἱερὰ εἶναι ἐν ἀσυλίᾳ καὶ ἀναπέμπεσθαι εἰς Ἱεροσόλυμα καὶ ἀποδίδοσθαι τοῖς ἀποδοχεῦσιν Ἱεροσολύμων, ἐγγύας τε μὴ ὁμολογεῖν αὐτοὺς ἐν σάββασιν ἢ τῇ πρὸ αὐτῆς παρασκευῇ ἀπὸ ὥρας ἐνάτης. [164] ἐὰν δέ τις φωραθῇ κλέπτων τὰς ἱερὰς βίβλους αὐτῶν ἢ τὰ ἱερὰ χρήματα ἔκ τε σαββατείου ἔκ τε ἀνδρῶνος, εἶναι αὐτὸν ἱερόσυλον καὶ τὸν βίον αὐτοῦ ἐνεχθῆναι εἰς τὸ δημόσιον τῶν Ῥωμαίων. [165] τό τε ψήφισμα τὸ δοθέν μοι ὑπ᾽ αὐτῶν ὑπὲρ τῆς ἐμῆς εὐσεβείας ἧς ἔχω πρὸς πάντας ἀνθρώπους καὶ ὑπὲρ Γαΐου Μαρκίου Κηνσωρίνου καὶ τοῦτο τὸ διάταγμα κελεύω ἀνατεθῆναι ἐν ἐπισημοτάτῳ τόπῳ τῷ γενηθέντι μοι ὑπὸ τοῦ κοινοῦ τῆς Ἀσίας ἐν Ἀγκύρῃ. ἐὰν δέ τις παραβῇ τι τῶν προειρημένων, δώσει δίκην οὐ μετρίαν." ἐστηλογραφήθη ἐν τῷ Καίσαρος ναῷ.

[162] "Caesar Augustus, Pontifex Maximus with tribunician power, decrees: since the Jewish nation has been found well disposed to the Roman people not only at the present time but also in the past, especially in the time of my father the emperor Caesar, as has their high priest Hyrcanus, [163] it has been decided by me and my council under oath, with the consent of the Roman people, that the Jews may follow their own customs in accordance with their ancestral law, just as they followed them in the time of Hyrcanus, high priest of God the Most High, and that their sacred monies shall be inviolable and may be sent to Jerusalem and delivered to the treasurers in Jerusalem, and that they need not give bond (to appear in court) on the Sabbath or on the day of preparation for it after the ninth hour. [164] If anyone is caught stealing their holy books or holy monies from a synagogue [*sabbateion*]

or a banqueting hall [*andrōn*],[9] he shall be regarded as sacrilegious, and his property shall be confiscated to the public treasury of the Romans. [165] The decree which was given to me by them concerning the piety which I show to all mankind, and on behalf of Gaius Marcius Censorinus, I order that it and the present edict be set up in the most conspicuous part [of the temple] assigned to me by the federation of Asia in Ancyra. If anyone transgresses any of the above ordinances he shall suffer severe punishment." This was inscribed on a monument in the temple of Caesar.

Literature: Binder, *Temple Courts*, 147–49; Bilde, "Synagoge," 27–28; Claußen, *Versammlung*, 141–42; Levine, *Ancient Synagogue*, 115.

Comments: Augustus confirms the same rights of the Jews as we have seen in several other document in relation to synagogues (for a list of decrees given in Josephus, see Runesson, *Origins*, 468, n. 226); the use of the term *sabbateion* here, a term obviously emphasising Sabbath gatherings (cf. *A.J.* 14.256–58; Philo, *Mos.* 2.214–16 [No. 166]), should thus be understood to refer to a synagogue. The term was rarely used in the period covered in this catalogue (but cf. Levine, 115, n. 180). That we are dealing with public buildings, understood as sacred and inviolable by the emperor, is clear from the safekeeping of holy books and monies there, as well as the use of the word sacrilegious (*hierosylos*, i.e., temple-robber) to denote a person caught stealing from these institutions. Synagogues, then, functioned as treasuries, as did Graeco-Roman temples, and copies of Torah scrolls owned by the community were kept there. As to the treasury, money was almost certainly kept both for local purposes and for sending to the Jerusalem temple (cf. Philo, *Legat.* 315 [No. 194]; Christ-believers are said to have gathered and sent money to the Jerusalem congregation: 1 Cor 16:1–4; Rom 15:25–27).

3.1.3 *The Bosporan Kingdom*

3.1.3.1 *Gorgippia*

Additional Comment: In addition to the below inscriptions, two other manumission inscriptions from Gorgippia, *IJO*, BS22/*CIRB* 1126/*CIJ* 690a, *IJO* 1, BS23/*CIRB* 1124/*CIJ* 690b, are badly damaged and the word *proseuchē* is not visible. Therefore, we have chosen not to include them in the catalogue.

---

[9] Following the Greek, *pace* Marcus and Wikgren, LCL, who conjecture ἀαρώνος, "ark (of the law)". Dining halls were common in the buildings of voluntary associations, or *collegia* (cf. "ἀνδρών" in the supplement to LSJ), and are attested in relation to several synagogues, e.g., the synagogues at Ostia (No. 179) and Stobi (No. 187), as well as the Theodotos synagogue in Jerusalem (No. 26). Communal meals are also attested for Qumran Essenes, the Theraputae, and for Christ-believers.

However, it is likely that, originally, these inscriptions included references to such a building in which the manumission took place, not the least since several other manumission inscriptions from the Bosporan Kingdom show that the *proseuchai* served as legitimising symbols at such ceremonies. On manumissions performed in *proseuchai* and the nature of these buildings, see Binder, *Temple Courts*, 439–45.

No. 121
Source: *Inscription.* *IJO* 1, BS20 (*CIJ* 1.690, *CIRB* 1123)
Date: October/November 41 c.e.

Θεῶι Ὑψίστωι παντο-
κράτορι εὐλογητῷ· βα-
σιλεύοντος βασιλέ-
ως [[[Μιθρ]ιδάτου]] φιλο-
ΓΕΡΜΑΚΟΥ καὶ φιλοπάτ-   5
ριδος· ἔτους ηλτ´ μη-
νὸς Δείου· Πόθος Στ-
ράβωνος ἀνέθηκεν<ἐν?>
τῇ προσευχῇι κατ᾽ εὐχὴ-
ν θ[ρ]επτὴν ἑαυτοῦ ᾗ ὄνο-   10
μα Χρύσα, ἐφ᾽ ᾧ ᾗ ἀνέπα-
φος καὶ ἀνεπηρέαστος
ἀπὸ παντὸς κληρον[όμ]-
ου ὑπὸ Δία, Γῆν, Ἥλιο[ν.]

To God Most High, almighty and blessed, in the reign of King [[Mith-ridates]], friend of [the emperor?] and friend of his homeland, in the year 338, in the month of Deios: Pothos, son of Strabo, dedicated in the prayer hall [*proseuchē*] according to a vow, his homebred slave, named Chrysa, so that she will remain free from seizure and unmolested by all his heirs, by Zeus, Gaia, Helios.

Literature: *IPE* 2.400; *SEG* 16.439, 19.503; Schürer, "Die Juden im bosporanischen Reiche," 204–6; idem, *HJP* 2.440 n. 61, 3.1.37; Krauss, *Synagogale Altertümer*, 240 (no. 84); Goodenough, "The Bosporus Inscriptions," 222–24; Lifshitz, *Prolegomenon*, 67; Horsley, *New Documents*, 1.27; Levinskya, *The Book of Acts*, 108–9, 222, 239–40 (no. 3.II.7); Williams, *The Jews*, no. V.53; Gibson, *Jewish Manumission Inscriptions*, 99–100, 107, 109–19, 121–22, 132, 166; Binder, *Temple Courts*, 274–75; Levine, *Ancient Synagogue*, 122.

Comments: The coupling of a Jewish invocation to "God Most High" with a concluding oath to the Gentile gods Zeus, Gaia and Helios led early commentators to question the Jewish provenance of this inscription. Goodenough, however, convincingly argued that the final formula was not evidence of religious syncretism, but simply a legal requirement peculiar to the Bosporus region, Gorgippia in particular (cf. *IJO* 1, BS22/*CIJ* 690a/*CIRB* 1126).

The above inscription, which dates to the reign of Mithradates I (39–41 c.e.), records Pothos's manumission of his slave Chrysa in the prayer hall (*proseuchē*), a venue that parallels Gentile release ceremonies in local temples.

These latter are well-attested at the temple of Pythian Apollo at Delphi, where over a thousand manumission inscriptions have been recovered. Within such ceremonies, a fictitious sale of the slave to the god would take place in the precincts, with the priests serving as witnesses. Following the rite, most of the sale price would be refunded to the former owner, and a stone recording the transaction set up within the temple confines. A human guarantor, listed on the stone, would act as the god's agent, insuring that potential claimants not harass the former slave.

The Jewish manumission inscriptions, attested only in the Bosporus Kingdom, reveal a similar proceeding. While the fictitious sale was dispensed with, the ceremony took place within the analogous religious sanctuary, the *proseuchē*. There, the slave was dedicated to the Deity, presumably in the presence of synagogue functionaries, and a stone was set up within the precincts. When guarantors are mentioned, they consist of the Jewish congregation.

Aside from the concluding formula, the above monument typifies this genre.

No. 122

Source: *Inscription. IJO* 1, BS24 (*CIRB* 1127)
Date: First to second century c.e.

[- - - - - - - - - - - - - - - - -]
[- - - - - - - - - -]++ ἦ ὄνο[μα]
[.]+++νώμη, ἐ{α}φ’ ᾧ τε ἦ ἀ[νέ-]
παφος καὶ ἀνεπηρεάστος ἀ[πό]
τε ἐμοῦ καὶ παντός μο[υ]   5
κληρονόμου προσμέ[νου-]
σα τῇ προσευχ[ῇ.]

...whose name is...*nōmē*, so that she will remain free from seizure from me and all my heirs, remaining true to the prayer hall [*proseuchē*].

Literature: Schürer, *HJP* 3.1.37; Levinskya, *The Book of Acts*, 241–42 (no. 3.II.9); Gibson, *Jewish Manumission Inscriptions*, 114 n. 16, 118, 133 n. 17, 147, 170.

Comments: This fragmentary inscription, like the preceding example, attests the release of a female slave inside a *proseuchē*. In this case, however, the release comes with the condition that the newly freed slave maintain an allegiance to the local Jewish sanctuary. For further discussion of this condition, see No. 124.

3.1.3.2   *Olbia*

No. 123
Source: *Inscription. IJO* 1, BS1 (*CIJ* 1.682)
Date: Late second to early third century c.e.

[- - - - - - - - - - οἱ]
περὶ Σ[άτυρον Ἀρτεμιδώ-]
ρου τὸ β′ Πουρθαῖ[ος β′?]
Ἀχιλλεὺς Δημητ[ρίου]
Διονυσιόδωρος Ἔρ[ωτος]   5
Ζώβεις Ζώβει ἄρχ[οντες]
τὴν προσευχὴν ἐ[πε-]
σκεύασαν τῇ ἑαυ[τῶν]
προνοίᾳ στεγάσα[ντες]
ἀπὸ τοῦ θε<μελί>ου μέχρι   10
[- - - - - - - - - - - - - - - -]

…the rulers [*archontes*] surrounding S[atyrus, son of Artemido]rus (chief ruler) for the second time: Pourthaius [II?], Achilles, son of Demetrius, Dionysiodorus, son of Eros, Zobeis, son of Zobeis, repaired the prayer hall [*proseuchē*] from their own forethought, covering it with a roof, from the foundation up to…

Literature: *CIG* 2.2079; *SEG* 3.590; *IPE* 1.98; Krauss, *Synagogale Altertümer*, 240–41 (no. 85); Schürer, *HJP* 2.440 n. 61, 3.1.38; Lifshitz, *DF*, no. 11; idem, *Prolegomenon*, 64; Levinskya, *The Book of Acts*, 114 n. 39, 219–22; Gibson, *Jewish Manumission Inscriptions*, 24 n. 44.

Comments: Unlike rulers (*archontes*) referenced in most synagogue inscriptions, those mentioned in the above monument were not Jewish, but Gentile: other Olbian inscriptions clearly attest each as a city official (Pourthaius, *IPE* 1.83; Achilles, *IPE* 1.80, 86; Dionysiodorus, *IPE* 1.132; Zobeis, *IPE* 1.105; Satyrus, reconstructed above from *IPE* 1.142). Moreover, the above inscription reflects the structure of the Olbian council, which consisted of five magistrates, one of whom served as the presiding officer. This monument thus records an instance where a Gentile city council contributed to the repair of a synagogue.

Unfortunately, lack of chronological indicators at Olbia make the firm dating of all inscriptions from this city problematic. The proposed date range is based upon an increase in building activity at Olbia during this period.

3.1.3.3 *Panticapaeum*

No. 124
Source: *Inscription. IJO* 1, BS5 (*CIJ* 1.683, *CIRB* 70)
Date: January/February, 81 c.e.

βασιλεύοντος βασιλέως Τιβερίου Ἰουλίου Ῥησκουπόριδος φιλοκαίσαρος καὶ φιλορωμαίου εὐσε-
βοῦς· ἔτους ζοτ΄, μηνὸς Περει[τί-]
ου ιβ΄· Χρήστη γυνὴ πρότε-   5
ρον Δρούσου ἀφείημι ἐπὶ τῆς π[ρο-]
συεχῆς θρεπτόν μου Ἡρακλᾶν
ἐλευθερὸν καθάπαξ κατὰ εὐχή[ν]
μου <ἀ>νεπίληπτον καὶ ἀπαρενό-
χλητον ἀπὸ π<α>ντὸς κληρονόμο[υ]   10
[τ]ρέπεσ<θ>αι αὐτὸν ὅπου ἂν βού-
λη[τ]αι ἀνεπικωλύτως καθὼς ηὐ-
ξάμην χωρὶς ἰς τ[ὴ]ν προσευχὴν θωπείας τε καὶ προσκαρτε-
ρήσεως· συνεπινευσάντων δὲ   15
καὶ τῶν κληρ<ο>νόμων μου Ἡρα-
κλείδου καὶ Ἑλικωνιάδος
συνεπ[ιτ]ροπευούσης δὲ καὶ τῆς
συναγωγῆς τῶν Ἰουδαίων.

In the reign of King Tiberius Julius Rhescuporis, friend of Caesar and friend of the Romans, pious, in the year 377, the twelfth of the month of Peritios, I Chreste, former wife of Drusus, release in the prayer hall [*proseuchē*], my home-bred slave Heraclas, free, once and for all, according to my vow, inviolable and undisturbed by all my heirs, and who may go wherever he desires, unhindered, as I have vowed, except that he show deference and devotion toward the prayer hall [*proseuchē*]; both with the consent of my heirs Heracleides and Heliconias and with the joint guardianship of the congregation [*synagōgē*] of the Jews.

Literature: *CIG* 2.2114bb; *IPE* 2.52; Schürer, "Die Juden im bosporanischen Reiche," 201–3; idem, *HJP* 3.1.36–37; Krauss, *Synagogale Altertümer*, 239–40 (no. 82); Goodenough, "The Bosporus Inscriptions," 221–2; Lifshitz, *Prolegomenon*, 64; Levinskya, *The Book of Acts*, 222, 231–32 (no. 3.II.1); Williams, *The Jews*, no. II.14; Gibson, *Jewish Manumission Inscriptions*, 1, 28 n. 65, 100, 124, 126, 128–40, 143, 149–50, 160; Overman, "Jews, Slaves and the Synagogue," 143–57; Binder, *Temple Courts*, 443 n. 126; Levine, *Ancient Synagogue*, 123 n. 219.

Comments: Of the manumission inscriptions unearthed at the temple of Pythian Apollo at Delphi, about a quarter contain a so-called *paramonē* clause, requiring the released slave to "abide with" his or her former owner, usually until the latter's death, rendering unspecified services.

Several of the Jewish manumission inscriptions from the Bosporus Kingdom, including the above example, appear to contain an adapted version of this clause. The primary difference is that, rather than specifying a continuing relationship between the former slave and master, the Bosporus inscriptions usually stipulate that the freed slave show "deference and devotion" (*thōpias kai proskarterēsōs*, ll. 14–15 above) towards the prayer hall.

Scholars are divided over the specific meaning of this ambiguous phrase. Was the nature of the relationship between the parties economic (i.e., the former slave became a servant of the synagogue), religious (he or she essentially became a "God-fearer"), or a combination of the two? A definitive answer remains elusive.

Whatever the case, it is clear the manumitted slave was required to attend the prayer hall (for reasons either of service or worship) and to be appropriately reverent within it. Because the latter stipulation would have been unnecessary for a Jew, it is most likely that the slaves released under these terms were Gentiles.

For more general information about manumission practices, see No. 121 above.

No. 125
Source: *Inscription. IJO* 1, BS6 (*CIJ* 1.684, *CIRB* 73)
Date: Late first to early second century C.E. (?)

[βασιλεύοντος βασιλέως - - -]
[- - - φιλοκαίσαρος καὶ φιλο-]
[ρωμαίου, εὐσεβοῦς ἔτους . . .]
[μηνὸς] Ἀρτ[εμ]ι[σίου - - - - -]
[ἀφ]ίημι τοὺς ἔ[μοὺς θρεπτοὺς ἐν τῇ]   5
[π]ροσευχῇ κα[τ' εὐχὴν ἐλευθέρους]
[καθάπαξ?], σώμα[τα ἀνδρεῖα? - -]
[- - - -] καὶ Ἑρμᾶν[ἀνεπιλήπτους]
[καὶ ἀπα]ρανοχλήτο[υς ἀπὸ τ' ἐμοῦ]
[καὶ παν]τὸς κληρονόμ[ου - - - - ἐπὶ]   10
[παραμ]ονῇ μέχρι τῆς ζωῆ[ς μου - -]
[- - - - -] εὐάρεστοι τῇ μ[ητρί μου?]
[- - - - -]ιτάδι καὶ πάντα ὥσ[περ?...]
[- - - - -] καὶ τελευτήσαντός μου
[- - - - -]ε ποιήσουσιν πα[ντα..]   15
[μετὰ δὲ τὴν] τελευτὴν εἶν[αι αὐτοῖς]
[τρέπεσθαι ἀν]επικωλύτως ἄν[ευ]

[πάσης ἀμφισ]βηστήσεος κα[θὼς ηὐξά-]
[μην ? ὅπου ἄ]ν γῆς βούλονται χ[ωρὶς]
[εἰς τὴν] προσευχὴν θωπείας τε καὶ προσ-   20
[καρτ]ερήσεος· συν[ε]πιτροπε[υούσης]
[δὲ] καὶ τῆς συναγωγῆς τῶν
vacat Ἰουδαίων. vacat

[In the reign of King...friend of Caesar and friend of the Romans, pious, in the year...in the month] of Artemisios I...release [my home-bred slaves in the] prayer hall [*proseuchē*] [according to a vow, once and for all],..., [male?] bodies...and Hermas, [inviolable and] undisturbed [by me and] all my heirs...on condition that they continue in my service until the end of my life...well-pleasing to [my mother?]...and everything [as?]...and when I die...they will do everything...[and after my] death, it will be permitted them to go to anywhere on earth they wish, unhindered and without any question, as [I have vowed?], except with regards to the prayer hall [*proseuchē*], to which they shall owe deference and devotion and be under the joint guardianship of the congregation [*synagōgē*] of the Jews.

Literature: *CIG* 2.2114b; *IPE* 2.53; Schürer, "Die Juden im bosporanischen Reiche," 203; idem, *HJP* 3.1.37; Lifshitz, *Prolegomenon*, 66; Levinskya, *The Book of Acts*, 234–36 (no. 3.II.4); Gibson, *Jewish Manumission Inscriptions*, 104 n. 17, 127–35, 146–47, 162; Overman, "Jews, Slaves and the Synagogue," 143–57; Binder, *Temple Courts*, 443 n. 126.

Comments: Although this inscription has been poorly preserved, much of it can be restored on the basis of a comparison with the previous entry. A key difference is that this stone contains the more widely attested *paramonē* clause (ll. 11–12) in addition to the adapted version more typical of Jewish manumission inscriptions from the Bosporus (ll. 20–21). Thus, the released slaves were expected to continue in the service of their former master (and perhaps his mother) throughout the remainder of his life, as well as to show deference and devotion to the prayer hall.

For more on this last condition, see the comments in the preceding entry. On manumission practices in general, see No. 121.

No. 126
Source: *Inscription. IJO* 1, BS7 (*CIJ* 1.683a, *CIRB* 71)
Date: First century C.E.

[- - ^{c.10} - - -]+ A++[- ^{c.6} -]κα-
κου ἀφίημι ἐπὶ τῆς προσευ-

χῆς Ἐλπία\<ν> [ἐμ]α[υ]τῆς θρεπτ[ὸν]
ὅπως ἐστὶν ἀπαρενόχλητος
καὶ ἀνεπίληπτος ἀπὸ παντὸς   5
κληρονόμου χωρὶς τοῦ προσ-
καρτερεῖν τῇ προσευχῇ· ἐπι-
τροπευούσης τῆς συναγω-
γῆς τῶν Ἰουδαίων καὶ θεὸν
σέβῶν. *vacat*   10

...I, [*unnamed woman*], release in the prayer hall [*proseuchē*] Elpias, my home-bred slave, so that he will be undisturbed and inviolable by all my heirs, except that he show devotion towards the prayer hall [*proseuchē*] under the guardianship of the congregation [*synagōgē*] of the Jews, and reveres God.

Literature: Schürer, *HJP* 3.1.37, 166; Lifshitz, "Notes," 95–96; idem, *Prolegome-non*, 65–66; Bellen, "Die Aussage," 171–76; Tribilco, *Jewish Communities*, 155–56; Levinskaya, *The Book of Acts*, 74–76, 232–34 (no. 3.II.2); idem, Review, 517–20; Gibson, *Jewish Manumission Inscriptions*, 28 n. 5, 117–18, 126, 128–35, 139–44, 156, 161; Overman, "Jews, Slaves and the Synagogue," 143–57; Binder, *Temple Courts*, 385–86, 441, 444; Levine, *Ancient Synagogue*, 123–24.

Comments: There is an ongoing debate among scholars over the correct transcription and translation of this inscription. The basis of the dispute is twofold.

First of all, the name of the released slave was incorrectly carved on the stone, leaving the gender unclear. The text must therefore be emended to read either the male Elpias (*Elpia\<ν>*) or the female Elpis (*Elpi\<d>a*).

Secondly, the final phrase *theon sebōn* ("reveres God") is grammatically awkward if read as a requirement of the release, since one condition had already been stated earlier in lines 6–7.

Bellen and Lifshitz, therefore, argued that the released slave was female, allowing them to emend the final phrase to read *theo{n}sebōn*, "God-fearers." As a result of this proposal, the above inscription has often been cited as evidence for Gentile God-fearers existing alongside the Jewish congregation in the synagogue (cf. Acts 13:16, 26, 50 [No. 174]; 16:14 [No. 185]; 17:4 [No. 186]; 17:17 [No. 90]; 18:7 [No. 91]; Josephus *A.J.* 14.110, 20.195).

More recently, Levinskaya has argued convincingly against this interpretation, contending that the awkwardness of the final phrase can be attributed to the grammatically loose Greek of the Bosporus Kingdom. Moreover, she points out that, when a release is conditional, most other Jewish manumission inscriptions make two requirements: for the freed slave to show devotion toward the prayer hall (*proskarterēsis*) *and* to express deference towards it (*thōpeia*). In her view, the phrase *theon sebōn* would correspond to the second of the usual conditions. Finally, Levinskaya notes that the word *theosebōn* does not appear in any other inscriptions from the Bosporus, making the proposed emendation questionable.

While the use of Bellen and Lifshitz's reading as evidence for the existence of God-fearers is therefore problematic, it should nevertheless be recognized that the release requirements prescribed in this and similar Bosporus inscriptions would be necessary only if the freed slaves were Gentile. Because these conditions contained a religious component, such newly released Gentiles could legitimately be classed as God-fearers.

For more information on manumission practices and release conditions, see Nos. 121 and 124.

No. 127
Source: *Inscription. IJO* 1, BS9 (*CIJ* 1.683b, *CIRB* 72)
Date: First to second century c.e.

[- - - - - - - - - συνεπι-]
[τροπευούσ]ης δὲ κα[ὶ]
[τῆς συναγω]γῆς τῶν
['Ιουδα]ίων. *vacat*

...and also [under joint guardianship of the congregation of the Jews].

Literature: Schürer, *HJP* 3.1.37, 166; Lifshitz, *DF*, 96 (no. 7); idem, *Prolegomenon*, 66; Bellen, "Die Aussage," 172–75; Levinskya, *The Book of Acts*, 234 (no. 3.II.3); Gibson, *Jewish Manumission Inscriptions*, 124, 161.

Comments: This very fragmentary inscription is almost totally reconstructed from the final lines of several other Bosporus manumission inscriptions (*IJO* 1, BS5, BS6, BS18 [Nos. 124, 125, and 129]).

For more information on manumission practices and release conditions, see Nos. 121 and 124.

3.1.3.4 *Phanagoria*

No. 128
Source: *Inscription. IJO* 1, BS17 (*CIJ* 1.691, *CIRB* 985)
Date: May/June 17 c.e.

[β]ασιλεύοντος [βα-]
[σ]ιλέως 'Ασπούργο[υ]
[φ]ιλορω{ι}μαίου· ἔτους
γιτ΄ μηνὸς Δαισίου ζ΄·
[Φ]όδακος Πόθωνος [ἀ-]   5
[ν]ατίθησι τὸν ἑαυτοῦ

[θρ]επ[τὸ]ν Διονύσιον
[τ]ὸν καὶ Λογ[γ]ίωνα ἐ-
π[ὶ τῆς προσευχῆς] ἀπολ-
[- - - - - - - - - - - -]ΟΛΗ   10
[- - - - - - - - - - - - - -]ΑΣ
[- - - - - - - - -]ΤΗ[- -]
[- - - - - - - - - - - - - - -]
[- - - - - - - - - - - - - - -]
[- - - - - - - - - - - - -]ΑΝ   15
[- - ^{c.5} - -]Ο[- ^{c.4} -]ΥΣ[.]
[- - - - - - - - - - - -] τῆς θω-
πεί[ας ἕνεκα ? καί] προσ-
καρ[τερ]ήνσεως.

In the reign of King Aspourgus, friend of the Romans, in the year 313, the seventh day of the month of Daisios, Phodacus, son of Pothon, dedicated his home-bred slave, Dionysius, and Longiona (?) in [the prayer hall [*proseuchē*]],...deference and devotion.

Literature: *IPE* 2.364; Schürer, *HJP* 3.1.37–38; Krauss, *Synagogale Altertümer*, 240 (no. 83); Lifshitz, *Prolegomenon*, 69; Danshin, "Jewish Community," 137–38; Levinskya, *The Book of Acts*, 236–37 (no. 3.II.5); Gibson, *Jewish Manumission Inscriptions*, 28 n. 65, 129, 164; Binder, *Temple Courts*, 442–43 n. 125; Levine, *Ancient Synagogue*, 123.

Comments: Presently, this monument is the earliest of the dated manumission inscriptions from the Bosporus Kingdom. Though it is poorly preserved, some of the lacunae can be restored in comparison with similar examples, especially the following entry.

For more information on manumission practices and release conditions, see Nos. 121 and 124.

No. 129
Source: *Inscription. IJO* 1, BS18
Date: March/April 52 c.e.

[β]ασιλέον[τος] βα-
σιλέως Κότυος·
ἔτους <η>μτ′ μηνὸς
Ξανδικοῦ α′· Ψυχα-
ρίων, Σόγος, Ἄνος   5
[ο]ἱ τούτο<υ> υειοὶ. Καρ-
σανδανος καὶ Καρ-

αγος καὶ Μετρό-^{vacat}
τειμος ἄφετοι τῇ
προσευχῇ ἀνεπίλ<η>-   10
πτοι, ἀνεπικόλυ-
τοι, χωρὶς εἰς τὴν
προ<σ>ευχὴν προσκαρ-
τερήσεως καὶ θωπία-
ς, καὶ ἔσταν ἄφετ[ο-]   15
[ι]· συνεπιτροπερύσ-
ης τῆς συναγω[γῆ-]
[ς] τῶν Ἰουδαί-
ων.

In the reign of King Cotys, in the year 348 on the first of the month of Xandikos: Psycharion and his sons Sogos and Anos (state that) Karsandanos and Karagos and Metrotimus were released in the prayer hall [*proseuchē*], inviolable and unhindered except that they show devotion and deference toward the prayer hall [*proseuchē*], under the joint guardianship of the congregation [*synagōgē*] of the Jews.

Literature: Danshin, "Jewish Community," 133–50; *SEG* 43.510; Levinskya, *The Book of Acts*, 237–38 (no. 3.II.6); Williams, *The Jews*, no. I.106; Gibson, *Jewish Manumission Inscriptions*, 98, 124–34, 172; Binder, *Temple Courts*, 442–44.

Comments: Recovered in 1989, this monument is the most recent addition to the collection of manumission inscriptions from the Bosporus Kingdom. It records the release of three male slaves in the Jewish *proseuchē* at Phanagoria during the reign of Cotys I (45–62 C.E.) and follows a formula similar to that used in manumission inscriptions from Panticapaeum, though the wording is more compressed (cf. Nos. 124 and 125).

For more information on manumission practices and release conditions, see Nos. 121 and 124.

3.1.4   *Cyprus*

3.1.4.1   *Salamis*

No. 130
Source: *Literary.* Acts 13:5
Date: Ca. 90–110 C.E.

[5] καὶ γενόμενοι ἐν Σαλαμῖνι κατήγγελλον τὸν λόγον τοῦ θεοῦ ἐν ταῖς συναγωγαῖς τῶν Ἰουδαίων. εἶχον δὲ καὶ Ἰωάννην ὑπηρέτην.

[5] When they arrived at Salamis, they proclaimed the word of God in the synagogues [*synagōgai*] of the Jews. And they had John also to assist them.

Literature: As a general reference to commentaries see Barrett, Fitzmyer and Jervell, *Comm., ad loc.* Binder, *Temple Courts*, 269–70; Stegemann, *Synagoge und Obrigkeit*, 124, 158–59; Williams, *The Jews*, 45.

Comments: Barnabas, who was from Cyprus, along with Saul and John Mark (Acts 12:12, 25), are said here to have first gone into the synagogues of Salamis seeking an audience for their message. This became a regular practice for Paul on his missionary journeys (9:20–25; 13:14–49; 14:1–3; 17:1–9, 10–14; 18:1–8; 19:9–10). In Acts, to proclaim (*katanggellein*, "to announce, to speak out about") the word of God was the same as proclaiming the Gospel, the good news about Jesus as Messiah. Very little is known about the Jewish community on Cyprus, but according to Luke there existed more than one synagogue in Salamis, the most important city on the island at this time.

3.1.5   *Cyrenaica*

3.1.5.1   *Berenice*

No. 131
Source: *Inscription. CJZ 70 (CIG 3.5362)*
Date: 8–6 B.C.E.?

Λ[.]γ´ Φ[αμ]ένωθ ε´ ἐπὶ ἀρχόντων Ἀρίμμα τοῦ
[. . . . . .]ος Δωρίωνος τοῦ Πτολεμαίου
Ζελαιου τοῦ [Γ]ναίου Ἀρίστωνος τοῦ Ἀραξα-
[..]ντος Σαρα[πί]ωνος τοῦ Ἀνδρομάχου Νικία
τ[οῦ . . . .]Α[.]ΣΑ[. . . .] τοῦ Σίμωνος ἐπεὶ   5
[Δέκ]μος Ο[ὐαλέριος Γ]αῖο[υ Διον]ύσιος ΠΡΗΠΟΤΗΣ
[. . . . .] ΩΓΗΣ ἀνὴρ καλὸς καὶ ἀγαθὸς ὢν δια-
τελε[ι λόγῳ καὶ ἔργῳ καὶ αἱρ]έσει καὶ ποιῶν ἀγαθὸν
[ὅτι] ἂ[ν] δ[ύναται καὶ κοι]νῇ καὶ ἰδίαι ἑκάστωι τῶν
π[ο]λιτ[ῶν] καὶ δ[ὴ καὶ] ἐκονίασεν τοῦ ἀνφιθεάτρου   10
τ[ὸ ἔδ]αφος καὶ τοὺ[ς] τοίχους ἐζωγράφησεν
ἔ[δοξε τοῖς ἄ]ρχουσι καὶ τῶι πολιτεύματι
τ[ῶν] ἐν Βερνικινδι Ἰουδαίων καταγράψαι αὐτὸν εἰς
τὸ τῶν τ[. . . . . .] ΕΥΕΙΣΥΔΙΟΥ καὶ εἶεν ἀλειτούρ-
γητο[ν πά]σης [λε]ιτουρ[γί]ας [ὁ]μοίως δὲ καὶ στε-   15
φα[νοῦν α]ὐτὸν καθ᾽ ἑκάστην συνοδον καὶ νουμη-
νίαν στε[φ]άνωι [ἐλ]αίνωι καὶ λημνίσκωι ὀνομαστί

τὸ [δ]ὲ ψήφισμα τόδε ἀναγράψαντες οἱ ἄρχον[τες]
[εἰ]ς στήλην λίθου Παρίου θέτωσαν εἰς τὸν ἐ[πι-]
[σημ]ότατον [τόπ]ον τοῦ ἀμφιθεάτρου *vacat*   20
vacat λευκαὶ πᾶσαι *vacat*
vacat
Δέκμος Οὐαλέριος Γαΐου Διονύσιος
τὸ ἔ[δ]α[φ]ος ἐκονίασεν καὶ τὸ ἀμφι-
θέατρον καὶ ἐζωγράφησεν τοῖς
ἰδίοις δαπανήμασιν ἐπίδομα   25
vacat τῶι πολιτεύματι *vacat*

In the year...3, on the 5th of Phamenoth, during the offices of Arim-
mas, son of..., Dorion, son of Ptolemaios, Zelaios, son of Gnaius,
Ariston, son of Araxa..., Serapion, son of Andromachos, Nikias, son
of..., N., son of Simon. Whereas Decimus Valerius Dionysius, son of
Gaius..., who continues to be a noble and good man in word and deed
and by nature, doing whatever good he can, both publicly and privately,
to each of the citizens; and especially in that he plastered the floor of
the amphitheatre [*amphitheatron*] and decorated its walls: therefore the
rulers [*archontes*] and the community [*politeuma*] of the Jews in Berenice
and its vicinity have resolved to record him in the...of the...and that
(in the future) he be excused from all public works; and likewise that at
each regular assembly [*synodos*] and each new moon he also be crowned
by name with an olive crown and a woollen band. When they have
inscribed this vote on a stele of Parian stone, the rulers [*archontes*] are to
erect it in the most prominent place in the amphitheatre [*amphitheatron*].
All (stones) white. Decimus Valerius Dionysius, son of Gaius, plastered
the floor and the amphitheatre [*amphitheatron*] and decorated it at his
own expense as a gift to the community [*politeuma*].

Literature: Roux and Roux, "Un décret," 292–93; Reynolds, "Inscriptions,"
245–47; Lüderitz, *CJZ*, 148–51; Binder, *Temple Courts*, 140–45, 257–58; Levine,
Ancient Synagogue, 96–100; Applebaum, *Jews and Greeks*, 160–61; Horsley, *New
Documents*, 4.202–9; White, *Social Origins*, 2.296–98; Runesson, *Origins*, 172, 190;
Claußen, *Versammlung*, 130; Lüderitz, "What is the Politeuma?" 211.

Comments: The term *amphitheatron*, used in this and the following inscription, literally means "having seats for spectators all around." Beginning in the
first century of the Common Era, the word typically referred to an elliptical
structure housing gladitorial contests and other spectacles (e.g., Josephus, *A.J.*
15.268–71, 17.194). While such structures existed during the prior century—the
earliest surviving example from Pompeii dates to 80 B.C.E.—these were then

known as *spectaculae* (e.g., *CIL* 10.852). Moreover, the floors of these buildings were not plastered, as was the case in this edifice (ll. 10–11). Thus the building referenced in these two inscriptions likely resembled a Greek *bouleterion* or council hall, which typically had seating on three or four sides.

Because the earliest extant synagogue remains featured similar seating arrangements, it is probable that the term *amphitheatron* was an early word for the synagogue in Berenice. This is further suggested by the reference to regular assemblies (*synodos*, l. 16), which were presumably the Sabbath gatherings of the local Jewish community. In addition, the community also met in the building for observances of the New Moon (ll. 16–17; cf. Neh 8:2, Jdt 8:6, Gal 4:20) and the Feast of the Tabernacles (*CJZ* 71, ll. 1–2 [No. 132]).

The inscription records a resolution honouring a certain Decimus Valerius Dionysius for plastering the floor and decorating the walls of the *amphitheatron*. Although he bears the name of a Roman citizen, Decimus was clearly a member of the Jewish community (though perhaps a convert), as the resolution excuses him from funding any future community projects—a benefit that would have been meaningless to an outsider (cf. the following inscription where this perquisite is omitted).

We should also note that the term *zōgrapheō* (l. 11, literally, "painted from life") means more than a whitewashing: it denoted the creation of an elaborate decoration, including the depiction of living figures. If the Jews of Berenice adhered to the Second Commandment as strictly as many other Jewish communities of this period, however, it is more likely that these were limited to floral and geometric designs.

Following Greek custom, the congregation voted on the resolution by dropping either a white (yea) or black (nay) stone in a ballot box. In this instance, the resolution passed unanimously, resulting in the erection of the stone, Decimus's release from future public works, and his ritual crowning thereafter at each assembly.

Although Lüderitz argues that the term *politeuma* (translated "community" above) referred only to the leaders of the Jewish community ("What is the Politeuma?" 215–19), this seems unlikely since the rulers (*archontes*) and the *politeuma* are mentioned separately as approving the resolution (l. 12). Moreover, the word elsewhere refers to semi-autonomous ethnic communities (e.g., *SEG* 2.872, 8.573)—which is exactly how Strabo described the legal classification of the Jewish community in Cyrenaica (quoted in Josephus, *A.J.* 14.115–18).

In connection with this, we note that the ruling body of the community numbered seven. The following two inscriptions reveal that its ranks increased over time, perhaps due to an expansion of the Jewish community in Berenice.

White suggests that, based upon the reading...*ōgēs* in line 7, the word [*syna*]*ōgēs* be reconstructed in the lacuna (*op. cit.* 297, n. 35). Although the reading is uncertain, if the suggestion is adopted, the term would likely be a reference to the Jewish congregation, rather than to its synagogue building (cf. *CJZ* 72, l. 3 [No. 133]).

No. 132
Source: *Inscription. CJZ* 71 *(CIG* 3.5361, *SEG* 16.931)
Date: 24 October, 24 c.e.

[ἔ]τους νε΄ Φαῶφ κε΄ ἐπὶ συλλόγου τῆς σκηνο-
πηγίας ἐπὶ ἀρχόντων Κλεάνδρου τοῦ
Στρατονίκου Εὐφράνορος τοῦ Ἀρίστωνος
Σωσιγένους τοῦ Σωσίππου Ἀνδρομάχου
τοῦ Ἀνδρομάχου Μάρκου Λαιλίου Ὀνασί-
ωνος τοῦ Ἀπολλωνίου Φιλωνίδου τοῦ Ἀγή-   5
μονος Αὐτοκλέους τοῦ Ζήνωνος Σωνί-
κου τοῦ Θεοδότου Ἰωσήπου τοῦ Στράτωνος
vacat
ἐπεὶ Μᾶρκος Τίττιος Σέξτου υἱὸς Αἰμιλίαι
ἀνὴρ καλὸς καὶ ἀγαθὸς παραγενηθεὶς εἰς   10
τὴν ἐπαρχείαν ἐπὶ δημοσίων πραγμάτων τήν
τε προστατίαν αὐτῶν ἐποιήσατο φιλανθρω΄-
πως καὶ καλῶς ἔν τε τῆι ἀναστροφῆι ἡσύχιον
ἦθος ἐνδικνύμενος ἀεὶ διατελῶν τυγχάνει
οὐ μόνον δὲ ἐν τούτοις ἀβαρῆ ἑαυτὸν παρέσ-   15
χηται ἀλλὰ καὶ τοῖς κατ᾽ ἰδίαν ἐντυγχάνουσι
τῶν πολιτῶν *vacat* ἔτι δὲ καὶ τοῖς ἐκ τοῦ πολιτεύ-
ματος ἡμῶν Ἰουδαίοις καὶ κοινῆι καὶ κατ᾽ ἰδίαν
εὔχρηστον προσστασίαν ποιούμενος οὐ δια-
λείπει τῆς ἰδίας καλοκἀγαθίας ἄξια πράσσων   20
ὧν χάριν ἔδοχε τοῖς ἄρχηουσι καὶ τῶι πολιτεύματι τῶν ἐν Βερενίκηι Ἰουδαίων ἐπαινέσαι τε αὐτὸν καὶ στεφανοῦν ὀνομαστὶ καθ᾽ ἑκάστην.
σύνοδον καὶ νουμηνίαν στεφάνωι ἐλαίνωι καὶ
λημνίσκωι τοὺς δὲ ἄρχοντας ἀναγράψαι τὸ   25
ψήφισμα εἰς στήλην λίθου Παρίου καὶ θεῖναι εἰς
τὸν ἐπισημότατον τόπον τοῦ ἀμφιθεάτρου
vacat Λευ *vacat* καὶ *vacat* πᾶ *vacat* σαι *vacat*

In the year 55, on the 25th of Phaoph, during the assembly of the Feast
of the Tabernacles, during the offices of Cleandros, son of Stratonicos,
Euphranor, son of Ariston, Sosigenes, son of Sosippos, Andromachos,
son of Andromachos, Marcus Laelius Onasion, son of Apollonios,
Philonides, son of Hagemon, Autocles, son of Zenon, Sonicos, son of
Theodotos, and Josepos, son of Straton. With regard to Marcus Tit-

tius, son of Sextus, (from the tribe of) Aemilia, a noble and good man: whereas he has assumed the office of prefect over public affairs, he has exercised kind and just leadership and has always displayed a peaceful demeanor in his daily affairs; whereas he has not been burdensome to the citizens who petition him privately; whereas he has exercised helpful leadership with regard to the Jews of our community [*politeuma*], both publicly and privately; and whereas he has not himself ceased to act worthily with his own noble kindness: therefore, it seemed well to the rulers [*archontes*] and to the community [*politeuma*] of the Jews in Berenice both to honour him and to crown him by name at each regular assembly [*synodos*] and each new moon with an olive crown and woollen band, and that the rulers [*archontes*] should inscribe the vote on a stele of Parian stone and place it in the most prominent place in the amphitheatre [*amphitheatron*]. All (stones) white.

Literature: Roux and Roux, "Un décret," 283–85, 294–96; Reynolds, "Inscriptions," 244–45; Lüderitz, *CJZ*, 151–55; Binder, *Temple Courts*, 258–60; Levine, *Ancient Synagogue*, 100–102; Applebaum, *Jews and Greeks*, 161–63; Claußen, *Versammlung*, 130; Lüderitz, "What is the Politeuma?" 211–14; White, *Social Origins*, 298, n. 39.

Comments: Although Lüderitz has suggested that this inscription originated during the Cyrenaican era and thus dates to 43 B.C.E. ("What is the Politeuma?" 212, n. 74), the presence of a Roman citizen among the Jewish rulers (M. Laelius Onasion, ll. 5–6) argues that the monument was erected instead during the Actium era. This leads to the year 24 C.E. given above, reflecting the position adopted by a majority of scholars.

As with the previous entry, the inscription records a resolution honouring a benefactor of the Jewish community. In contrast, however, Marcus Tittius was probably not a member of the community, but simply a local Roman prefect who treated them kindly. That the resolution was adopted at an assembly held during Sukkoth (the Feast of the Tabernacles) not only highlights the observance of a Jewish festival in this remote part of the Diaspora (cf. Philo, *Flacc.* 116–24; No. 139), but also demonstrates that, within the Jewish communities of this period, official business could be combined with religious commemorations (cf. Josephus, *Vita* 294–95; No. 43).

In the three decades since the erection of the earlier inscription, we see that the number of rulers (*archontes*) has increased from seven to nine. While none of the names repeat, Euphranor may have been the son, and Andromachos the brother or nephew of previously named rulers (Ariston [*CJZ* 70, l. 3; No. 131] and Serapion [*CJZ* 70, l. 4; No. 131], respectively).

On the voting procedure, as well as the use of the terms *amphitheatron* and *politeuma*, see the previous entry.

No. 133
Source: *Inscription. CJZ* 72 *(SEG* 17.823)
Date: 3 December, 55 c.e.

(ἔτους) β΄ Νέρωνος Κλαυδίου Καίσαρος Δρούσου
Γερμανικοῦ Αὐτοκράτορος χοϊάχι ϛ΄ *vacat*
ἐφάνη τῇ συναγωγῇ τῶν ἐν Βερνεικίδι
Ἰουδαίων τοὺς ἐπιδιδόντες εἰς ἐπισκευ-
ὴν τῆς συναγωγῆς ἀναγράψαι αὐτοὺς εἰστή-
λην λίθου Παρίου *vacat*   5

Ζηνίων Ζωίλου ἄρχων (δρ.) ι΄
Εἰσίδωρος Δωσειθέου ἄρχων (δρ.) ι΄
Δωσείθεος᾽ Ἀμμωνίου ἄρχων (δρ.) ι΄
Πρᾶτις Ἰωναθᾶ ἄρχων (δρ.) ι΄   10
Καρνήδας Κορνηλίου ἄρχων (δρ.) ι΄
Ἡρακλείδης Ἡρακλίδιου ἄρχων (δρ.) ι΄
Θαλίαρχος Δωσιθέου ἄρχων (δρ.) ι΄
Σωσίβος Ἰάσονος ἄρχων (δρ.) ι΄
Πρατομήδης Σωκράτου ἄρχων (δρ.) ι΄   15
Ἀντίγον(ο)ς Στράτωνος ἄρχων (δρ.) ι΄
Καρτισθένης᾽ Ἀρχία ἱερεύς (δρ.) ι΄
Λυσανίας Λυσανία (δρ.) κε΄
Ζηνόδωρος Θευφίλου (δρ.) κη΄
Μαριω[ν......]υος (δρ.) κε΄   20
[Stone broken]

Column 2

[5 lines blank]
Ἀλέξανδρος
Εὐφράνορος (δρ.) ε΄
vacat
Εἰσιδώρα
Σεραπωνος (δρ.) ε΄   5
Ζωσίμη Τερ-
πολίω (δρ.) ε΄
Πόλων
Δωσιθέου (δρ.) ε΄
vacat

In the second year of the emperor Nero Claudius Caesar Drusus Germanicus, on the 6th of Choiach. It was resolved by the congregation [*synagōgē*] of the Jews in Berenice and its vicinity that the names of those who donated to the repairs of the synagogue [*synagōgē*] be inscribed on a stele of Parian stone.

Column One

Zenion, son of Zoilos, ruler [*archōn*], 10 drachmae
Isidoros, son of Dositheos, ruler [*archōn*], 10 drachmae
Dositheos, son of Ammonius, ruler [*archōn*], 10 drachmae
Pratis, son of Jonathan, ruler [*archōn*], 10 drachmae
Carnedas, son of Cornelius, ruler [*archōn*], 10 drachmae
Heracleides, son of Heracleides, ruler [*archōn*], 10 drachmae
Thaliarchos, son of Dositheos, ruler [*archōn*], 10 drachmae
Sosibios, son of Jason, ruler [*archōn*], 10 drachmae
Pratomedes, son of Socrates, ruler [*archōn*], 10 drachmae
Antigonos, son of Straton, ruler [*archōn*], 10 drachmae
Cartisthenes, son of Archias, priest, 10 drachmae
Lysanias, son of Lysanias, 25 drachmae
Zenodoros, son of Theuphilos, 28 drachmae
Marion (?), [son of ?], 25 drachmae
[Stone broken]

Column Two

Alexander, son of Euphranor, 5 drachmae
Isidora, daughter of Serapion, 5 drachmae
Zosime, daughter of Terpolius, 5 drachmae
Polon, son of Dositheos, 5 drachmae

Literature: Reynolds, "Inscriptions," 242–44; Lüderitz, *CJZ*, 155–59; Lifshitz, *DF*, 82 (no. 100); Binder, *Temple Courts*, 109–10, 260–62; Levine, *Ancient Synagogue*, 102–4; Applebaum, *Jews and Greeks*, 163–67; White, *Social Origins*, 2.298–300; Oster, "Supposed Anachronism," 187–88; Claußen, *Versammlung*, 130; Runesson, *Origins*, 219.

Comments: The latest of the three synagogue inscriptions from Berenice, this monument contains several notable features. The most striking is the sudden disappearance of the terms *politeuma* and *amphitheatron* in reference to the Jewish community and its civic center. In lieu of these, the word *synagōgē* appears now for the first time, referring to the congregation in line 3 and the building in line 5.

Although the term *synagōgē* often referred to the synagogue building during the first century C.E., this usage was rare outside of Syro-Palestine, where the term *proseuchē* was most often employed. Presently, this monument represents the earliest such example in a Diaspora inscription. Its appearance in a relatively remote locale, however, suggests that this usage was gaining currency outside of Palestine in the second half of this century.

Why the sudden shift in terminology? A reasonable hypothesis is when the term *amphitheatron* was increasingly used to refer to a stadium housing gladiatorial contests (as it was during the first century C.E.), the Jewish community abandoned the word in favour of one being used in the homeland. This last consideration may also have led to the replacement of the word *politeuma*, since we have no evidence that the legal status of Jews in Cyrenaica was at all diminished during this time.

As in the previous examples, the inscription records a resolution honouring benefactors of the congregation, in this case for the repair of the synagogue. Because the rulers were among the patrons, they are not listed separately as issuing the decree. Their names do, however, appear at the head of the list of donors, and they now number ten.

In addition, a priest is recorded immediately afterwards as contributing an identical sum of ten drachmae. Because the subsequent donors are then loosely ranked according to the amount of their gift, it would seem that the priest was counted among the ruling body—or at least given a place of honour with them. Also noteworthy among the donors are two women, Isidora and Zosime, who each contributed five drachmae.

Although none of the rulers in this inscription match the names mentioned in the earlier monuments, Alexander may have been the son and Isidora the daughter (or granddaughter) of previous rulers (Euphranor [*CJZ* 71, l. 3; No. 132] and Serapion [*CJZ* 70, l. 4; No. 132], respectively). Likewise, Antigonos may have been the brother or nephew of a previous ruler (Josepos [*CJZ* 71, l. 8; No. 131]).

Since the lower half of the stone was broken, the total amount given for the repairs is unknown. The preserved donations, however, add up to 208 drachmae, a fairly sizeable sum. Thus the renovations to the building were rather extensive, though their precise nature is not made clear.

3.1.5.2   *Cyrene*

No. 134
Source: *ASAA* 39/40, no. 116
Date: End of the first century B.C.E.

[- - -]ου καὶ Δέκμος Σα-
[- - -]ου Σωσ[ά]νδρου
[- - -]ου τοῦ Τειμάρχο[υ]
[- - -]ς καὶ Λεωνίδης· Τι-

[- - -]ην συναγω-   5
[γήν - - -]

...and Decimus Sa-...of Sosandros...of Teimarchos...and Leonides,
Ti-...(the) synagogue (or congregation) [*synagōgē*]...

Literature: Applebaum, *Jews and Greeks*, 193–94; Binder, *Temple Courts*, 256–57;
Claußen, *Versammlung*, 234, n. 79.

Comments: This fragment is preserved from the upper part of a stele whose
top was inscribed with a leaf and plant-tendril motif. Although its Jewish provenance is uncertain, Applebaum notes that the form of the stele resembles the
two earlier inscriptions from Berenice (*CJZ* 70–71; Nos. 131 and 132).

More compelling in this regard, however, is the presence of the partially
restored term *synagōgē*, which may have referenced a local Jewish congregation
or its civic center, as in the previous example from Berenice. Nevertheless, the
highly fragmentary condition of the monument prevents the drawing of any
firm conclusions.

3.1.6   *Egypt*

Additional comment on Literature: Since a vast majority of synagogue
sources come from Egypt, it may be convenient here to refer generally to
important literature dealing with this area and which reoccurs in the individual
entries: Borgen, *Philo*; Borgen, *Education*; Griffiths, *Egypt*; Culpepper, *Johannine
School*, 197–214; Dion, *Synagogues et temples*; Hengel, *Proseuche und Synagoge*; Horst,
Flaccus; Kasher, *Synagogues*; Perrot, *Lecture*, Smallwood, *Legatio*; Sterling, *School*,
148–64; Yonge, *Works of Philo*. There are excellant bibliographies to Philo:
Radice and Runia, *Bibliography 1937–1986*; Runia, *Bibliography 1987–1996*.
These volumes are followed up year by year in *The Studia Philonica Annual*.

3.1.6.1   *Alexandria*

No. 135
Source: *Literary.* 3 Macc 2:28
Date: First half of the first century B.C.E.

[28] Μηδένα τῶν μὴ θυόντων εἰς τὰ ἱερὰ αὐτῶν εἰσιέναι πάντας δὲ
τοὺς Ιουδαίους εἰς λαογραφίαν καὶ οἰκετικὴν διάθεσιν ἀχθῆναι τοὺς
δὲ ἀντιλέγοντας βίᾳ φερομένους τοῦ ζῆν μεταστῆσαι

[28] None of those who do not sacrifice shall enter their sanctuaries
[*hiera*], and all Jews shall be subjected to a registration involving poll
tax and to the status of slaves. Those who object to this are to be taken
by force and put to death.

Literature: Dion, "Synagogues et temples," 48–49; Binder, *Temple Courts*, 43–46, 128–29, 249; Levine, *Ancient Synagogue*, 128, 165; Runesson, *Origins*, 434; Claußen, *Versammlung*, 57, 91, 132.

Comments: The narrative setting for this passage is the persecution of the Jews in Egypt by Ptolemy IV Philopater (221–203 B.C.E.). Binder and Levine identify these *hiera* as synagogues on the assumption that the cult centralisation was effective and recognised in the Diaspora at this time. Runesson reads the evidence as indicating the presence of Jewish temples, basing this conclusion on an identification of these *hiera* with the *proseuchai* found in earlier and contemporary Egyptian sources (see Runesson, *Origins*, 429–36 for a discussion of *proseuchē* as a temple term in this early period).

No. 136
Source: *Literary.* 3 Macc 3:29
Date: First half of the first century B.C.E.

[29] πᾶς δὲ τόπος οὗ ἐὰν φωραθῇ τὸ σύνολον σκεπαζόμενος Ιουδαῖος ἄβατος καὶ πυριφλεγὴς γινέσθω καὶ πάσῃ θνητῇ φύσει καθ᾽ ἅπαν ἄχρηστος φανήσεται εἰς τὸν ἀεὶ χρόνον

[29] Every place [*topos*] detected sheltering a Jew is to be made unapproachable and burned with fire, and shall become useless for all time to any mortal creature.

Literature: Binder, *Temple Courts*, 135–40, 249; Claußen, *Versammlung*, 58, 91.

Comments: See No. 135. The term used here, *topos*, could be used for both temples and synagogues. It is not likely that *topos* refers to homes in this context (cf. Nos. 113, 114, 157, 187, T1).

No. 137
Source: *Literary.* 3 Macc 4:17–18
Date: First half of the first century B.C.E.

[17] μετὰ δὲ τὸ προειρημένον τοῦ χρόνου διάστημα προσηνέγκαντο οἱ γραμματεῖς τῷ βασιλεῖ μηκέτι ἰσχύειν τὴν τῶν Ιουδαίων ἀπογραφὴν ποιεῖσθαι διὰ τὴν ἀμέτρητον αὐτῶν πληθὺν [18] καίπερ ὄντων ἔτι κατὰ τὴν χώραν τῶν πλειόνων τῶν μὲν κατὰ τὰς οἰκίας ἔτι συνεστηκότων τῶν δὲ καὶ κατὰ τόπον ὡς ἀδυνάτου καθεστῶτος πᾶσιν τοῖς ἐπ᾽ Αἴγυπτον στρατηγοῖς

[17] But after the previously mentioned interval of time the scribes declared to the king that they were no longer able to take the census

of the Jews because of their immense number, [18] though most of them were still in the country, some still residing in their homes, and some at the place [*topos*]; the task was impossible for all the generals in Egypt.

Literature: Binder, *Temple Courts*, 135–40, 249; Claußen, *Versammlung*, 58, 91.

Comments: See Nos. 135, 136. Note the distinction between "homes" [*oikos*] and "the place" [*topos*] in v. 18, the latter referring either to synagogue (so Binder) or temple (so Runesson).

No. 138
Source: *Literary.* Philo, *Flacc.* 41–53
Date: Ca. 40–41 c.e.

[41] ὅπερ συναισθόμενος ὁ ὄχλος–οὐχ ὁ καθεστὼς καὶ δημοτικός, ἀλλ᾽ ὁ πάντα θορύβου καὶ ταραχῆς εἰωθὼς ἀναπιμπλάναι διὰ φιλοπραγμοσύνην καὶ ζῆλον ἀβιώτου βίου καὶ τὴν ἐξ ἔθους ἀργίαν καὶ σχολήν, πρᾶγμα ἐπίβουλον–συρρυέντες εἰς τὸ θέατρον ἐξ ἑωθινοῦ Φλάκκον ἤδη τιμῶν ἀθλίων ἐωνημένοι, ἃς ὁ δοξομανὴς καὶ παλίμπρατος ἐλάμβανεν οὐ καθ᾽ αὑτοῦ μόνον ἀλλὰ καὶ τῆς κοινῆς ἀσφαλείας, ἀνεβόησαν ἀφ᾽ ἑνὸς συνθήματος εἰκόνας ἐν ταῖς προσευχαῖς ἀνατιθέναι, καινότατον καὶ μὴ δέπω πραχθὲν εἰσηγούμενοι παρανόμημα. καὶ τοῦτ᾽ εἰδότες ὀξύτατοι γὰρ τὴν μοχθηρίαν εἰσί κατασοφίζονται τὸ Καίσαρος ὄνομα [42] προκάλυμμα ποιησάμενοι, ᾧ προσάπτειν τι τῶν ἐπαιτίων οὐ θεμιτόν. [43] τί οὖν ὁ τῆς χώρας ἐπίτροπος; ἐπιστάμενος, ὅτι καὶ ἡ πόλις οἰκήτορας ἔχει διττούς, ἡμᾶς τε καὶ τούτους, καὶ πᾶσα Αἴγυπτος, καὶ ὅτι οὐκ ἀποδέουσι μυριάδων ἑκατὸν οἱ τὴν ᾿Αλεξάνδρειαν καὶ τὴν χώραν ᾿Ιουδαῖοι κατοικοῦντες ἀπὸ τοῦ πρὸς Λιβύην καταβαθμοῦ μέχρι τῶν ὁρίων Αἰθιοπίας, καὶ ὡς ἡ πεῖρα κατὰ πάντων ἐστὶ καὶ ὡς οὐ λυσιτελὲς ἔθη πάτρια κινεῖν, ἀμελήσας ἁπάντων ἐπιτρέπει ποιήσασθαι τὴν ἀνάθεσιν, μυρία καὶ πάντα προνοητικὰ δυνάμενος ἢ ὡς ἄρχων κελεύειν ἢ συμβουλεύειν ὡς φίλος. [44] ὁ δὲ συνεχειρούργει γὰρ ἕκαστα τῶν ἁμαρτανομένων καὶ ἀπὸ μείζονος ἐξουσίας ἀναρριπίζειν καινοτέραις ἀεὶ κακῶν προσθήκαις τὴν στάσιν ἠξίου καὶ τό γ᾽ ἐφ᾽ αὑτὸν ἧκον μέρος ἅπασαν ὀλίγου δεῖν φάναι τὴν οἰκουμένην ἐμφυλίων πολέμων ἐπλήρωσεν. [45] οὐ γὰρ ἦν ἄδηλον, ὅτι ἡ περὶ τὴν κατάλυσιν τῶν προσευχῶν φήμη λαβοῦσα τὴν ἀρχὴν ἀπὸ τῆς ᾿Αλεξανδρείας διαδοθήσεται μὲν εὐθὺς εἰς τοὺς ἐν Αἰγύπτῳ νομούς, δραμεῖται δ᾽ ἀπὸ μὲν Αἰγύπτου πρὸς ἀνατολὰς καὶ ἔθνη τὰ ἑῷα, ἀπὸ δὲ τῆς ὑποταινίου καὶ Μαρείας, αἳ Λιβύης εἰσὶν ἀρχαί, πρὸς δυσμὰς καὶ

ἔθνη τὰ ἑσπέρια· Ἰουδαίους γὰρ χώρα μία διὰ πολυανθρωπίαν οὐ χωρεῖ. [46] ἧς αἰτίας ἕνεκα τὰς πλείστας καὶ εὐδαιμονεστάτας τῶν ἐν Εὐρώπῃ καὶ Ἀσίᾳ κατά τε νήσους καὶ ἠπείρους ἐκνέμονται μητρόπολιν μὲν τὴν ἱερόπολιν ἡγούμενοι, καθ' ἣν ἵδρυται ὁ τοῦ ὑψίστου θεοῦ νεὼς ἅγιος, ἃς δ' ἔλαχον ἐκ πατέρων καὶ πάππων καὶ προπάππων καὶ τῶν ἔτι ἄνω προγόνων οἰκεῖν ἕκαστοι πατρίδας νομίζοντες, ἐν αἷς ἐγεννήθησαν καὶ ἐτράφησαν· εἰς ἐνίας δὲ καὶ κτιζομένας εὐθὺς ἦλθον ἀποικίαν στειλάμενοι, τοῖς κτίσταις χαριζόμενοι. [47] καὶ δέος ἦν, μὴ οἱ πανταχοῦ τὴν ἀφορμὴν ἐκεῖθεν λαβόντες ἐπηρεάζωσι τοῖς πολίταις αὐτῶν Ἰουδαίοις εἰς τὰς προσευχὰς καὶ τὰ πάτρια νεωτερίζοντες. [48] οἱ δέ–οὐ γὰρ ἔμελλον ἄχρι παντὸς ἡσυχάζειν καίτοι πεφυκότες εὖ πρὸς εἰρήνην, οὐ μόνον ὅτι παρὰ πᾶσιν ἀνθρώποις οἱ περὶ τῶν ἐθῶν ἀγῶνες καὶ τοὺς περὶ ψυχῆς κινδύνους ὑπερβάλλουσιν, ἀλλ᾽ ὅτι καὶ μόνοι τῶν ὑφ᾽ ἥλιον ἅμα ταῖς προσευχαῖς ἀπεστεροῦντο τὴν εἰς τοὺς εὐεργέτας εὐσέβειαν, ὃ μυρίων θανάτων ἐτετίμητο ἄν–οὐκ ἔχοντες ἱεροὺς περιβόλους, οἷς ἐνδιαθήσονται τὸ εὐχάριστον, καὶ τοῖς ἐναντιουμένοις εἶπον ἄν· [49] "λελήθατε ἑαυτοὺς οὐ προστιθέντες τοῖς κυρίοις τιμήν, ἀλλ᾽ ἀφαιρούμενοι, οὐκ εἰδότες ὡς τοῖς πανταχόθι τῆς οἰκουμένης Ἰουδαίοις ὁρμητήρια τῆς εἰς τὸν Σεβαστὸν οἶκον ὁσιότητός εἰσιν αἱ προσευχαὶ ἐπιδήλως, ὧν ἡμῖν ἀναιρεθεισῶν τίς ἕτερος ἀπολείπεται τόπος ἢ τρόπος τιμῆς; [50] εἰ μὲν γὰρ ἐφιέντων τῶν ἐθῶν ὀλιγωροῦμεν, τῆς ἀνωτάτω τιμωρίας δίκαιοι τυγχάνειν ἐσμὲν μὴ παρέχοντες ἀρτίους καὶ πλήρεις τὰς ἀμοιβάς. εἰ δ' οὐκ ἐξὸν τοῖς ἰδίοις ὑποστέλλομεν νομίμοις, ἃ καὶ τῷ Σεβαστῷ φίλον βεβαιοῦν, τί μικρὸν ἢ μέγα πλημμελοῦμεν οὐκ οἶδα· πλὴν εἰ μὴ ψέγειν τις ἐθελήσειε τὸ μὴ γνώμῃ ἑκουσίῳ παρανομεῖν τὰς ἐκδιαιτήσεις τῶν ἐθῶν οὐ φυλαξαμένους, αἵ, κἂν ἀφ᾽ ἑτέρων ἄρξωνται, τελευτῶσι πολλάκις εἰς τοὺς αἰτίους." [51] ἀλλ' ὁ μὲν Φλάκκος τά τε λεκτέα ἡσυχάζων καὶ τὰ ἡσυχαστέα λέγων οὕτως εἰς ἡμᾶς ἐξημάρτανεν. ἐκεῖνοι δ', οἷς ἐχαρίζετο, τίνα γνώμην εἶχον; ἆρά γε τὴν τῶν τιμῶν ἐθελόντων; εἶτα σπάνις ἦν ἱερῶν κατὰ τὴν πόλιν, ἧς τὰ πλεῖστα καὶ ἀναγκαιότατα μέρη τετεμένισται, πρὸς ἀνά- θεσιν ὧν ἐβούλοντο; [52] τὴν μὲν οὖν τῶν φιλαπεχθημόνων καὶ μετὰ τέχνης ἐπιβουλευόντων ὁρμὴν ἔφαμεν, δι᾽ ἣν οἱ μὲν ἐπηρεάζοντεςοὐ δόξουσιν ἀδικεῖν, τοῖς δ᾽ ἐπηρεαζομένοις οὐκ ἀσφαλὲς ἐναντιοῦσθαι. οὐ γάρ ἐστιν, ὦ γενναῖοι, τιμὴ καταλύειν νόμους, ἔθη πάτρια κινεῖν, ἐπηρεάζειν τοῖς συνοικοῦσι, διδάσκειν καὶ τοὺς ἐν ταῖς ἄλλαις πόλεσιν ὁμοφροσύνης ἀλογεῖν. [53] Ἐπειδὴ τοίνυν ἡ κατὰ τῶν νόμων πεῖρα εὐοδεῖν ἔδοξεν αὐτῷ τὰς προσευχὰς ἁρπάσαντι καὶ μηδὲ τοὔνομα ὑπολιπομένῳ, πάλιν ἐφ᾽ ἕτερον ἐτρέπετο, τὴν τῆς ἡμετέρας πολιτείας ἀναίρεσιν, ἵν᾽ ἀποκοπέντων οἷς μόνοις ἐφώρμει ὁ ἡμέτερος βίος ἐθῶν τε πατρίων καὶ μετουσίας πολιτικῶν δικαίων τὰς ἐσχάτας ὑπομένωμεν συμφορὰς οὐδενὸς ἐπειλημμένοι πείσματος εἰς ἀσφάλειαν.

(41) The crowd perceived this—I do not refer to the peaceful and decent inhabitants but to the rabble that is always intent on creating confusion and turmoil, interfering and in pursuit of a life not worth living, habitually idle and lazy and always causing trouble. They flocked into the theatre first thing in the morning, knowing that they already had Flaccus in their pocket for less than a penny, which this man in his lust for fame, this good-for-nothing, had accepted to the injury not only of himself but also of the public safety. They shouted, as if with one mouth, that statues should be erected in the prayer halls [*proseuchai*], thus proposing an entirely novel and unprecedented violation of the law. [42] And they knew this, for they are very acute in their wickedness, and they cunningly used the name of Caesar as a smokescreen, a name to which it is unlawful to attribute any blameworthy action. [43] What then did the governor of the country do? He knew that the city, as the rest of Egypt, has two kinds of inhabitants, us and them, and that there are no less than one million Jews living in Alexandria and the rest of the country, from the steep slope that separates us from Libya to the boundaries of Ethiopia. He also knew that the attack was directed against us all and that it would not yield anything good if they tried to disrupt our ancestral customs. Yet, in disregard of all this, he permitted them to erect the statues, even though there were innumerable considerations, all of cautionary character, which he could have put forward either as an order from the ruler or as advice from a friend. [44] He, however, co-operated with them in each and every one of their misdeeds and therefore thought fit to use his position of superior power to kindle the sedition by adding newer forms of evil and, as far as it was in his power, one may almost say that he filled the whole world with civil wars. [45] For it was more than clear that the rumor of the destruction of the prayer halls [*proseuchai*] that started in Alexandria would spread immediately to the districts of Egypt and speed from Egypt eastwards to the oriental nations, and from the coastal strip and Mareia, which are the borders of Libya, westwards to the nations living there. For there is not one country that can contain all the Jews, so numerous are they. [46] It is for this reason that they settle in most of the wealthiest countries of Europe and Asia, both their islands and the mainland. However, it is the holy city where the

sacred temple [*naos*] of the Most High God stands, that they regard
as their mother city, but the regions they obtained from their fathers,
grandfathers, greatgrandfathers, and even more remote ancestors, to live
in, (they regard) as their fatherland where they were born and brought
up. There are also some regions where they came to as immigrants
at the very moment of their foundation, much to the pleasure of the
founders. [47] There was reason to fear that people all over the world
would take their cue from there and treat their Jewish fellow-citizens
outrageously by taking violent measures against their prayer halls [*proseuchai*] and their ancestral customs. [48] The Jews, however, were not
going to remain quiet at all costs—even though they are by nature a
peaceful people—not only since, as is the case with all humankind, the
struggle to maintain one's own traditions overrules the dangers to one's
own life, but also since they were the only people under the sun who
by being deprived of their prayer halls [*proseuchai*] would at the same
time be deprived of their means of showing their piety towards their
benefactors, which is something they would have regarded as worth
dying for many thousands of deaths. They no longer would have sacred
precincts [*hieros peribolos*] in which they could declare their thankful-
ness, and they might have said to their opponents: [49] "It apparently
escaped your notice that in this way you did not pay homage to our
masters but actually deprived them of it! You do not realize that for
the Jews all over the world it is their prayer halls [*proseuchai*] that clearly
form the basis for their piety towards the imperial family. If these are
destroyed, what other place or method is left to us for paying this homage? [50] For if we neglect it when our ancestral customs permit us to
do it, we deservedly receive the severest punishment for not giving the
proper and full return for the benefits we received. But if we refuse
because it is not permitted by our own laws, which Augustus himself
was pleased to confirm, I do not know what kind of offence, small or
great, we have committed, unless someone would want to take us to
task for committing a transgression, albeit involuntarily, by not guarding
against deviations from our ancestral customs, which, even if they are
started by others, often end up affecting those who are not responsible
for them." [51] But by leaving unsaid what he should have said and
by saying what he should have left unsaid, Flaccus sinned against us in
that way. But what motives had those whose favor he was seeking? Did
they really want to honor the Emperor? Were temples [*hiera*] scarce in
the city? Have not the greatest and most important parts of the city
been consecrated to gods, ready for the erection of any statues they

wished? [52] On the contrary, what we have been talking about is the aggressive deed of persons who love to make enemies and are plotters who seek to injure us so craftily that it would seem that our attackers were not acting unjustly, whereas for us, the attacked, it was not safe to oppose them. For, gentlemen, abrogating the laws and disrupting the ancestral customs of a people, outraging fellow-citizens and teaching the inhabitants of other cities to disregard unanimity, all that cannot be seen as a matter of honoring the Emperor)." [53] His attack on our laws by means of a seizure of our prayer halls [*proseuchai*], of which he had even the names removed, seemed to be succesful to him. For that reason he proceeded to another project, namely, the destruction of our political organization. His purpose in that enterprise was that, if the only things to which our life was anchored were cut away, that is, our ancestral customs and our participation in political rights, we might be exposed to the worst misfortunes without having any rope left to which we could cling to for safety.

Literature: Horst, *Flaccus*, 132–55 (the comments below on the passages from *Flacc.* depend very much on Horst's commentary); Schürer, *HJP*, 443; Binder, *Temple Courts*, 132, 249–52; Runesson, *Origins*, 450–51; Levine, *Ancient Synagogue*, 83–84.

Comments: Philo's works *In Flaccum* and *Legatio ad Gaium* have often been described as historical treatises. Nevertheless, they have a clear apologetic purpose: Philo wanted to defend Jewish interests in the serious conflict between Greeks and Jews in Alexandria in 38–41 C.E. *In Flaccum* has variously been characterized as "first and foremost a plea for belief in divine justice, a theodicy," as a "Trostschrift" (consolation literature), and as "a mixture of historiography, pastoral theology, apologetics and theodicy." *Legatio ad Gaium* offers a Jewish perspective of what happened in Alexandria during the years in question; it also contains an account of the Jewish embassy to the Roman emperor Gaius Caligula, led by Philo himself (Mary Smallwood has made an excellent translation of *Legat.* with introduction and commentary [1961], and Pieter van der Horst has done the same for *Flacc.* [2003]).

In the late summer of 38 C.E., Greeks in Alexandria began to erect statues of the emperor in the synagogues, in this way depriving the Jews of their meeting places. After that the prefect Flaccus issued a decree that essentially made Jews illegal aliens in the city. Jewish houses and shops were plundered, synagogues were destroyed, and Jews were not only tortured and killed, but forced to live in the overcrowded Jewish section of the city. This has been called the first pogrom in Jewish history. *Flacc.* focusses on the events of 38–39 C.E., while *Legat.* expounds upon a longer period, ca. 38–41 C.E.

In *Flacc.*, Philo places responsibility for the pogrom squarely upon the shoulders of Flaccus (prefect 32–39 C.E.), while in *Legat.* Philo connects the disturbances in the city with Caligula's self-deification, manifested in his desire to have statues of him erected not only in synagogues, but in the Jerusalem temple. The latter is not historically accurate, since Caligula's demands for divine honours came after the pogrom.

In Flaccum is structured as a kind of diptych, the first part about Flaccus' persecution of the Jews (§§1–96), the second about the punishment and death of Flaccus (§§97–191). In §§41–44 Philo recounts the beginning of the pogrom, in §§45–53 the consequences for Jews all over the world, and in §§54–96 Flaccus' decree.

§41 *perceived this.* That Flaccus did not interfere with the humiliation of the Jews....*the theatre.* A large multi-purpose communal institution in Alexandria, probably in the neighbourhood of the Jewish section of the town (see comment on No. 140, §132)....*statues should be erected in the synagogues.* See comment to No. 164, §152 *the synagogues*; cf. Nos. 135, 153 and Runesson, *Origins*, 429–436, 446–454....*an entirely novel and unprecedented violation of the law.* See comment on No. 164, §152.

§42 ...*used the name of Caesar.* They argued that the emperor wanted to be worshipped by these statues. §43 *one million Jews.* The figure is exaggerated, but many Jews lived in Egypt. Modern estimates for Alexandria range from 50,000 to 200,000 Jews, about 10% of the population. If there were 100,000 Jews, there were probably also many synagogues (see also comment to No. 140, §132)....*our ancestral customs.* A very common phrase in Philo and Josephus, referring to Jewish unwritten laws inherited from the parents generation by generation (see Philo, *Spec.* 4.149–150).

§44 *he co-operated with them.* Here Philo makes Flaccus responsible for the statues in the synagogues; in *Legat.* 346 he makes Gaius responsible.

§45 *the rumour of the destruction of the synagogues.* We do not know about any consequences of the Alexandrian action in 38 C.E. for synagogues in other parts of the Diaspora....*so numerous are they.* The great number of Jews outside the Holy Land is attested by many ancient sources (see, e.g., Philo, *Legat.* 214, 281–282 and *Mos.* 2.232).

§46 *their mother city...their fatherland.* Philo often makes Jerusalem and its temple the only centre for Jews from all over the world; at the same time, he emphasises that Jews were in some ways "citizens" of their adopted countries, often with an organisation of their own. Note the phrase "Jewish fellow-citizens" in §47. Loyalty to the Jerusalem temple was also combined with loyalty to the synagogues....*the Most High God.* This phrase is often used for Israel's God in Graeco-Judaeo literature, but it can also refer to non-Jewish deities, mostly to Zeus.

§47 *taking violent measures against.* The original meaning of the Greek word was "to make innovations," but used as a euphemism, it could be translated, "to take violent measures against." Philo uses both it and its derivatives very often in describing attacks on the Jewish religion, especially in *Legat.* In No. 141 and No. 164 it is translated with "innovation" and "made changes" (see comment on No. 164, §152).

§48 *their means of showing their piety towards their benefactors.* See comment on No. 164, §152. *sacred precincts.* Clearly marked temple or synagogue spaces are regarded as holy. The same phrase appears in a synagogue inscription from Alexandria (see No. 143).

§49 *place or method...for paying this homage.* Runesson (*Origins*, 446–54) interprets this passage as a reference to Jewish temple buildings, which by this time had incorporated synagogue rituals such as the public reading of Torah.

§53 *even the names.* We do not know of any names of the Alexandrian synagogues. Acts 6:9 gives a name of one or more synagogues in Jerusalem (see comment to No. 18); also, the later Jewish catacombs in Rome attest several synagogue names....*the destruction of our political organization.* The second phase of Flaccus' actions against the Jews according to Philo. By making the Jews illegal aliens in Alexandria, he deprived them of their political rights. The word *politeia* has been translated in many ways: "political organization," "polity," "Gemeinschaft," "cité." Smallwood ("Jews," 225) gives the following definition: "A recognized, formally constituted corporation of aliens enjoying the right of domicile in a foreign city and forming a separate, semi-autonomous civic body, a city within the city; it had its own constitution and administered its internal affairs as an ethnic unit through officials distinct from and independent of those of the host city." See also Nos. 131, 132.

No. 139
Source: *Literary.* Philo, *Flacc.* 121–24
Date: Ca. 40–41 C.E.

[121] ὡς δ' ἤσθοντο τὴν ἀπαγωγὴν καὶ τὸν Φλάκκον ἐντὸς ἀρκύων ἤδη γεγενημένον, προτείνοντες τὰς χεῖρας εἰς οὐρανὸν ὕμνουν καὶ παιᾶνας ἐξῆρχον εἰς τὸν ἔφορον θεὸν τῶν ἀνθρωπίνων πραγμάτων, "οὐκ ἐφηδόμεθα", λέγοντες "ὦ δέσποτα, τιμωρίαις ἐχθροῦ, δεδιδαγμένοι πρὸς τῶν ἱερῶν νόμων ἀνθρωποπαθεῖν· ἀλλὰ σοὶ δικαίως εὐχαριστοῦμεν οἶκτον καὶ ἔλεον ἡμῶν λαβόντι καὶ τὰς συνεχεῖς καὶ ἐπαλλήλους κακώσεις ἐπικουφίσαντι." [122] πάννυχοι δὲ διατελέσαντες ἐν ὕμνοις καὶ ᾠδαῖς καὶ ἅμα τῇ ἕῳ διὰ πυλῶν ἐκχυθέντες ἐπὶ τοὺς πλησίον αἰγιαλοὺς ἀφικνοῦνται–τὰς γὰρ προσευχὰς ἀφῄρηντοκἀν τῷ καθαρωτάτῳ στάντες ἀνεβόησαν ὁμοθυμαδόν· [123] "γῆν καὶ θάλατταν, ἀέρα τε καὶ οὐρανόν, τὰ μέρη τοῦ παντὸς καὶ σύμπαντα τὸν κόσμον, ὦ μέγιστε βασιλεῦ θνητῶν καὶ ἀθανάτων, παρακαλέσοντες εἰς εὐχαριστίαν τὴν σὴν ἥκομεν, οἷς μόνοις ἐνδιαιτώμεθα, τῶν ἄλλων ὅσα δημιουργεῖται πρὸς ἀνθρώπων ἐληλαμένοι καὶ στερόμενοι πόλεως καὶ τῶν ἐν πόλει δημοσίων καὶ ἰδιωτικῶν περιβόλων, ἀπόλιδες καὶ ἀνέστιοι μόνοι τῶν ὑφ' ἥλιον ἐξ ἐπιβουλῆς ἄρχοντος γενόμενοι. [124] χρηστὰς ὑπογράφεις ἡμῖν ἐλπίδας καὶ περὶ τῆς τῶν λειπομένων ἐπανορθώσεως, ἤδη ταῖς ἡμετέραις λιταῖς ἀρξάμενος συνεπινεύειν, εἴ γε τὸν κοινὸν ἐχθρὸν τοῦ ἔθνους καὶ τῶν ἐπ' αὐτῷ συμφορῶν ὑφηγητὴν καὶ διδάσκαλον μέγα πνέοντα καὶ οἰηθέντα διὰ ταῦτα εὐδοκιμήσειν

ἐξαίφνης καθεῖλες, οὐ πορρωτάτω γενόμενον, ἵν' αἰσθόμενοι δι' ἀκοῆς
οἱ κακῶς πεπονθότες ἀμβλύτερον ἡσθῶσιν, ἀλλ' ἐγγὺς οὑτωσί, μόνον
οὐκ ἐν ὄψει τῶν ἠδικημένων, πρὸς τρανοτέραν φαντασίαν τῆς ἐν βραχεῖ
καὶ παρ' ἐλπίδας ἐπεξόδου.

[121] When they heard that Flaccus had been arrested and was already
ensnared within the hunter's nets, they stretched out their arms to
heaven and began to sing hymns and songs to God who oversees all
human affairs. They said, "O Lord, we are not delighted at the punishment of our enemy, for we have learned from our holy laws that
we should sympathize with our fellow humans. But it is right to give
thanks to you for having taken pity and compassion on us and for having relieved our constant and incessant oppression." [122] When they
had spent all night singing hymns and other songs, at daybreak they
poured out through the gates and made their way to the nearby parts
of the beach, for they had been deprived of their prayer halls [*proseuchai*]. And there, standing in the purest possible place they cried out
with one accord: [123] "O almighty King of mortals and immortals,
we have come here to call on earth and sea, on air and heaven, which
are the parts of the universe, and on the universe as a whole, to offer
thanks to you. In these alone we can dwell, expelled as we are from all
human-made buildings, deprived of the city and the public and private
areas within its walls, the only people under the sun to become cityless
and homeless because of the malice of their governor. [124] But you
make us realize that we may be confident that what is still in need of
restoration will indeed be restored, because you have already begun
to answer our prayers. After all, you have suddenly brought down the
common enemy of our nation, who was the instigator of our misfortunes, who thought so highly of himself and expected that these things
would bring him fame. And when you did so, you did not wait until
he was already far away so that those who had suffered badly under
him would only have learned about it by hearsay and hence have less
satisfaction, no, you did so right here, so close by that it was almost
before the very eyes of those whom he had wronged. Thus you gave
them a clearer picture of your swift and unexpected intervention."

Literature: Radice and Runia, *Bibliography 1937–1986*; Runia, *Bibliography
1987–1996*; Horst, *Flaccus*, 200–207. Binder, *Temple Courts*, 391–99; 408–9;
Runesson, "Water and Worship," 119–26; Haber, "Common Judaism, Common Synagogue?"

Comments: For a general introduction, see the introductory comment to No. 138. In autumn of 39 C.E., the Roman emperor Caligula sent troops to Alexandria and arrested Flaccus during the feast of Sukkoth (see *Flacc.* 104–118). He was executed in the spring of 39 C.E. In §§119–124 the Jews thank God for this sudden intervention. §§121–122 have been taken as a witness to hymns and songs in the Egyptian synagogues. Deprived of the synagogues they had to use the beach.

§122 *the purest possible place.* Ritual purifications were clearly connected with synagogues.

§123 *cityless and homeless.* Short expressions for the new situation of the Jews after Flaccus' decree and its consequences (see comment to No. 138, §53).

No. 140
Source: *Literary.* Philo, *Legat.* 132–39
Date: Ca. 41–45 C.E.

[132] Τοῦ δὲ ἐπιτρόπου τῆς χώρας, ὃς μόνος ἐδύνατο βουληθεὶς ὥρᾳ μιᾷ τὴν ὀχλοκρατίαν καθελεῖν, προσποιουμένου ἅ τε ἑώρα μὴ ὁρᾶν καὶ ὧν ἤκουε μὴ ἐπακούειν, ἀλλ᾽ ἀνέδην ἐφιέντος πολεμοποιεῖν καὶ τὴν εἰρήνην συγχέοντος, ἔτι μᾶλλον ἐξοτρυνόμενοι πρὸς ἀναισχύντους καὶ θρασυτέρας ὥρμησαν ἐπιβουλὰς καὶ συνταξάμενοι στίφη ὀλυανθρωπότατα τὰς προσευχάς—πολλαὶ δέ εἰσι καθ᾽ ἕκαστον τμῆμα τῆς πόλεως—τὰς μὲν ἐδενδροτόμησαν τὰς δὲ αὐτοῖς θεμελίοις κατέσκαψαν, εἰς ἃς δὲ καὶ πῦρ ἐμβαλόντες ἐνέπρησαν, ὑπὸ λύττης καὶ μανίας ἔκφρονος ἀλογήσαντες καὶ τῶν πλησίον οἰκιῶν· πυρὸς γάρ, ὁπότε λάβοιτο ὕλης, οὐδὲν ὠκύτερον. [133] καὶ σιωπῶ τὰς συγκαθαιρεθείσας καὶ συμπρησθείσας τῶν αὐτοκρατόρων τιμὰς ἀσπίδων καὶ στεφάνων ἐπιχρύσων καὶ στηλῶν καὶ ἐπιγραφῶν, δι᾽ ἃ καὶ τῶν ἄλλων ὤφειλον ἀνέχειν· ἀλλ᾽ ἐθάρρουν ἅτε τὴν ἐκ Γαΐου τίσιν οὐ δεδιότες, ὃν εὖ ἠπίσταντο μῖσος ἄλεκτον ἔχοντα πρὸς Ἰουδαίους, ὡς ὑπονοεῖν, ὅτι οὐδεὶς οὐδὲν αὐτῷ χαρίζοιτο μεῖζον ἢ πάσας κακῶν ἰδέας ἐπιφέρων τῷ ἔθνει. [134] βουλόμενοι δὲ καινοτέραις κολακείαις ὑπελθόντες αὐτὸν ἀνυπευθύνοις χρῆσθαι κατὰ τὸ παντελὲς ταῖς εἰς ἡμᾶς ἐπηρείαις τί ποιοῦσι; προσευχὰς ὅσας μὴ ἐδυνήθησαν ἐμπρήσεσι καὶ κατασκαφαῖς ἀφανίσαι διὰ τὸ πολλοὺς καὶ ἀθρόους πλησίον οἰκεῖν Ἰουδαίους ἕτερον τρόπον ἐλυμήναντο μετὰ τῆς τῶν νόμων καὶ ἐθῶν ἀνατροπῆς· εἰκόνας γὰρ ἐν ἁπάσαις μὲν ἱδρύοντο Γαΐου, ἐν δὲ τῇ μεγίστῃ καὶ περισημοτάτῃ καὶ ἀνδριάντα χαλκοῦν ἐποχούμενον τεθρίππῳ. [135] καὶ τοσοῦτον ἦν τὸ τάχος καὶ τὸ σύντονον τῆς σπουδῆς, ὥστε οὐκ ἔχοντες ἐν ἑτοίμῳ καινὸν τέθριππον ἐκ τοῦ γυμνασίου παλαιότατον <ἐκόμιζον> ἰοῦ γέμον, ἠκρωτηριασμένον ὦτα καὶ οὐρὰς καὶ βάσεις καὶ ἕτερα οὐκ ὀλίγα, ὡς δέ φασί τινες καὶ ὑπὲρ γυναικὸς ἀνατεθὲν τῆς ἀρχαίας Κλεοπάτρας,

ἥτις ἦν προμάμμη τῆς τελευταίας. [136] ἡλίκην μὲν οὖν καθ᾽ αὐτὸ
τοῦτο τοῖς ἀναθεῖσιν ἐπέφερε κατηγορίαν, παντί τῳ δῆλον. τί γάρ, εἰ
[καὶ] καινὸν γυναικός; τί δέ, εἰ παλαιὸν ἀνδρός; τί δέ, εἰ συνόλως
ἐπιφημισθὲν ἑτέρῳ; τοὺς τοιοῦτον ἀνατιθέντας ὑπὲρ αὐτοκράτορος οὐκ
εἰκὸς ἦν εὐλαβηθῆναι, μή τις γένηται μήνυσις τῷ πάντα σεμνοποιοῦντι
τὰ καθ᾽ αὐτὸν διαφε-ρόντως; [137] οἱ δέ γε ἐκ πολλοῦ τοῦ περιόντος
ἤλπιζον ἐπαινεθήσεσθαι καὶ μειζόνων καὶ λαμπροτέρων ἀπολαύσειν
ἀγαθῶν ἕνεκα τοῦ καινὰ τεμένη προσαναθεῖναι Γαΐῳ τὰς προσευχάς,
οὐχ ἕνεκα τιμῆς τῆς εἰς ἐκεῖνον, ἀλλ᾽ ὑπὲρ τοῦ πάντα τρόπον
ἐμφορεῖσθαι τῶν ἐπὶ τῷ ἔθνει κακοπραγιῶν. [138] ἐναργεῖς δὲ πίστεις
λαβεῖν ἔστι· πρῶτον μὲν ἀπὸ τῶν βασιλέων· δέκα που σχεδὸν ἢ καὶ
πλειόνων ἐν τριακοσίοις ἔτεσιν ἑξῆς γενομένων, ἀνάθεσιν εἰκόνων ἢ
ἀνδριάντων ἐν προσευχαῖς οὐδεμίαν ἐποιήσαντο, καίτοι γε οἰκείων
ὄντων καὶ συγγενῶν, οὓς θεοὺς καὶ ἐνόμιζον καὶ ἔγραφον καὶ ἐκάλουν.
[139] τί δὲ οὐκ ἔμελλον ἀνθρώπους γε ὄντας οἱ κύνας καὶ λύκους καὶ
λέοντας καὶ κροκοδείλους καὶ ἄλλα πλείονα θηρία καὶ ἔνυδρα καὶ
χερσαῖα καὶ πτηνὰ θεοπλαστοῦντες, ὑπὲρ ὧν βωμοὶ καὶ ἱερὰ καὶ ναοὶ
καὶ τεμένη κατὰ πᾶσαν Αἴγυπτον ἵδρυνται;

[132] The prefect of the country, who could have put an end to this mob-rule single-handed in an hour had he chosen to, pretended not to see and hear what he did see and hear, but allowed the Greeks to make war without restraint and so shattered the peace of the city. They consequently became still more excited and rushed headlong into outrageous plots of even greater audacity. Assembling enormous hordes together, they attacked the prayer halls [*proseuchai*], of which there are many in each section of the city. Some they smashed, some they rased to the ground, and others they set on fire and burned, giving no thought even to the adjacent houses in their madness and frenzied insanity. For nothing is swifter than fire when it gets plenty of fuel. [133] I say nothing about the simultaneous destruction and burning of the objects set up in honour of the Emperors—gilded shields and crowns, monuments, and inscriptions—which should have made the Greeks keep their hands off everything else also. But they derived confidence from the fact that they had no punishment to fear from Gaius, who, as they well knew, felt an indescribable hatred for the Jews; they therefore supposed that no-one could give him greater pleasure than by inflicting every type of suffering on their race. [134] Then they decided to subject us to insults for which there was absolutely no risk of being brought to book, because they were at the same time currying favour with him by novel flattery.

So what did they do? The prayer halls [*proseuchai*] which they could not destroy either by fire or by demolition, because large numbers of Jews lived crowded together close by, they outraged in a different way, which involved the overthrow of our Laws and customs. They placed portraits of Gaius in all of them, and in the largest and most famous they also placed a bronze statue riding in a four-horse chariot. [135] So great was their haste and the intensity of their enthusiasm that, since they had no new four-horse chariot available, they took a very old one out of the gymnasium. It was very rusty, and the ears, tails, hooves, and a good many other parts were broken off. According to some people, it had been dedicated in honour of a woman, the earlier Cleopatra, great-grandmother of the last one. [136] It is clear to everyone what a serious charge this action in itself brought against the dedicators. What if it had been a recent dedication in honour of a woman? What if it had been an old one in honour of a man? What if it had been absolutely anything which had been dedicated to someone else? Surely the people who made a dedication of this kind in the Emperor's honour should have been on their guard lest information about it reached the ears of one who took everything concerning himself very seriously? [137] But these people entertained extravagant hopes of being praised and of enjoying even greater and more conspicuous rewards for having dedicated the prayer halls [*proseuchai*] to Gaius as new precincts, although they had done this not for his honour but in order to take their fill in every way of the sufferings of the Jewish race. [138] There are clear proofs of this. The first is taken from the kings. There were about ten, or even more, kings in succession in three hundred years, and yet the Alexandrians did not dedicate a single portrait or statue of them in the prayer halls [*proseuchai*], although the kings whom they regarded, described, and spoke of as gods were of the same race and species as themselves. [139] When they deify dogs, wolves, lions, crocodiles, and many other animals of the land, the sea, and the air, and establish altars, temples, shrines, and sacred precincts to them throughout the whole of Egypt, what reason was there against so treating those who were at least human beings?

Literature: Radice and Runia, *Bibliography 1937–1986*; Runia, *Bibliography 1987–1996*, andespecially Smallwood, *Legatio*, 219–26 (the following comments are very much depending on Smallwood's commentary); Schürer, *HJP*, 443; Binder, *Temple Courts* 249–51; Runesson, *Origins*, 450–52; Levine, *Ancient Synagogue*, 83–85.

Comments: For a general introduction, see the introductory comment to No. 138. After a presentation of Gaius' attitude toward the Jews (§§114–119) and the anti-Jewish riots in Alexandria (§§120–131), Philo treats the attack on the synagogues in Alexandria (§§132–137), underscoring the previous immunity of the synagogues from attack (§§138–140).

§132 *The prefect of the country.* The governor of Egypt, A. Avillius Flaccus, who had the official title *praefectus Alexandreae et Aegypti....many in each section of the city.* The city was divided in five sections named after the first letters of the Greek alphabet. Two of them were called Jewish quarters "because the majority of the inhabitants are Jews," *Flacc.* 55. The section Delta, situated on the harbourless coastline in the north-eastern area of the city, seems to have been the principle Jewish quarter. Similar Jewish quarters existed also in other Egyptian cities; they were not ghettos but ethnic neighbourhoods, created by the Jews themselves.

§133 *the objects set up in honour of the Emperors.* According to Philo the Jews had no temple-precincts in which they could express gratitude to benefactors. Therefore they showed their loyalty by dedicating a synagogue (or a part thereof) on their behalf, or by displaying honorific inscriptions and emblems in the synagogues, as noted here. Portraits of emperors—Gaius Caligula is mentioned in §134—transformed the synagogues into shrines of the imperial cult (§137, § 346), and thus could never be accepted by Jews (see the comment to No. 164, §152)....*an indescribable hatred for the Jews.* See also *Legat.* 115. Gaius' anti-semitism seems to have been antedated by Philo to the summer of 38 C.E. This enabled him to make Gaius responsible for the riots in Alexandria....*race* A frequent word in Philo for the Jewish people, in Greek *ethnos.*

§134 *large numbers of Jews lived crowded together close by.* See the comment to §132....*the largest and most famous.* This synagogue is also described in rabbinic sources, "a huge basilica, one collonade within the other" (*t. Sukkah* 4.6; *b. Sukkah* 51b; *y. Sukkah* V.1). According to the passage from the Jerusalem Talmud, the synagogue was destroyed during Trajan's reign (98–117 C.E.).

No. 141
Source: *Literary.* Philo, *Legat.* 165
Date: Ca. 41–45 C.E.

[165] εἶτα καὶ τὴν περὶ τὰς προσευχὰς νεωτεροποιίαν ἀπὸ καθαροῦ τοῦ συνει-δότος καὶ τῆς εἰς αὐτὸν ἀκραιφνοῦς τιμῆς ᾤετο γεγενῆσθαι.

[165] Then he thought that the innovation in connection with the prayer halls [*proseuchai*] had sprung from a clear conscience and genuine respect for him.

Literature: Smallwood, *Legatio,* 246.

Comments: For a general introduction, see the introductory comment to No. 138. *Legat.* 162–165 describes the attitude of the Alexandrian Greeks to the deification of Gaius. §165 *the innovation*. See comments to No. 138, §47 and No. 164, §152.

No. 142
Source: *Literary.* Philo, *Legat.* 191–92
Date: Ca. 41–45 C.E.

[191] ἐξέσται δὲ προσελθεῖν ἢ διᾶραι τὸ στόμα περὶ προσευχῶν τῷ λυμεῶνι τοῦ πανιέρου; δῆλον γὰρ ὡς οὐ φροντιεῖ τῶν ἀφανεστέρων καὶ τιμῆς ἐλάττονος ἠξιωμένων ὁ τὸν περισημότατον καὶ ἐπιφανέστατον νεών, εἰς ὃν ἀνατολαὶ καὶ δύσεις ἀποβλέπουσιν ἡλίου τρόπον πανταχόσε λάμποντα, καθυβρίζων. [192] εἰ δὲ καὶ γένοιτό τις ἄδεια προσόδου, τί χρὴ προσδοκᾶν ἢ θάνατον ἀπαραίτητον; ἀλλ᾽ ἔστω, τεθνηξόμεθα· ζωὴ γάρ τίς ἐστιν ὁ ὑπὲρ φυλακῆς νόμων εὐκλεέστατος θάνατος.

[191] Shall we be allowed to approach the desecrator of the holiest place or to open our mouths on the subject of the prayer halls [*proseuchai*] to him? It is obvious that a man who insults the famous and glorious temple [*naos*], which shines everywhere like the sun and receives the admiration of East and West, will pay no attention to less conspicuous [192] and less deeply revered places. Even if we were free to approach him, what have we to expect but death against which there can be no appeal? Well, let that be; we shall die anyhow. A glorious death met in the defence of the Law is a kind of life.

Literature: Smallwood, *Legatio*, 257.

Comments: For a general introduction, see the introductory comment to No. 138. *Legat.* 184–196 gives an account of Gaius' order for the desecration of the temple in Jerusalem.
   §191 *the desecrator of the holiest place...the prayer halls*. References to Gaius' attempt to make the Jerusalem temple and the synagogues shrines to himself by filling them with his images and statues. See §346 (No. 165).

No. 143
Source: *Inscription.* *JIGRE* 9 (*CIJ* 2.1433)
Date: Second century B.C.E. (?)

[- - -] | [- -θε]ῶι ὑψίστωι | [- - τ]ὸν ἱερὸν | [περίβολον (?) καὶ] τὴν προσ|[ευχὴν καὶ τὰ συγ]κύροντα.

...to God Most High...the sacred [precinct] [*hieros peribolos*] and the prayer hall [*proseuchē*] and the appurtenances...

Literature: Binder, *Temple Courts*, 131–32; Dion, "Synagogues et temples," 60; Kasher, "Synagogues," 215–16; Levine, *Ancient Synagogue*, 86; Runesson, *Origins*, 454; Fine, *This Holy Place*, 28; Lifshitz, *DF*, 76 (no. 87); Horsley, *New Documents*, 3.121; Schürer, *HJP*, 2.425–26; Frasier, *Ptolemaic Alexandria*, 1.284.

Comments: The Jewish provenance of this inscription is established by the reference to "God Most High" (*theos hypsistos*) and the partially restored term *proseuchē*. Although "sacred precinct" (*hieros peribolos*) is also partially reconstructed, the rendering is based upon close parallels to contemporary Egyptian temples (*OGIS* 52, 65, 92, 182; *SB* 4206). Moreover, Philo makes use of this term when speaking of the synagogues (*Flacc.* 48; No. 138). Taken together, these references suggest that synagogues in Egypt were typically set inside bounded sacred areas, possibly delineated by walls or fences.

No. 144
Source: *Inscription. JIGRE* 13 (*CIJ* 2.1432)
Date: 37 B.C.E. (?)

[ὑπὲρ] βας[ιλίσ|ση]ς καὶ β[ασι|λ]έως θεῶι [με]|γάλωι ἐ[πηκό]|ωι (?), ᾿Αλυπ[ος τὴν] || προσε[υχὴν] | ἐπόει [?*vacat*] | (ἔτους) ιε΄ Με[χείρ..]

On behalf of the queen and the king, to the great God who hears prayer (?), Alypus built the prayer hall [*proseuchē*] in the fifteenth year, Mecheir...

Literature: Binder, *Temple Courts*, 248–49; Levine, *Ancient Synagogue*, 87; Horsley, "A New *Corpus Inscriptionum Iudaicarum*," 98; Schürer, *HJP*, 3.1.49; Dion, "Synagogues et temples," 55; Horsley, *New Documents*, 3.121; Lifshitz, *DF*, 76 (no. 86).

Comments: Discovered in the Gabbary section of Alexandria (SW of the western harbour), this inscription is one of three existing examples of Egyptian synagogue benefactions made solely by individuals (cf. *JIGRE* 28, 126; Nos. 152, 172). The name Alypus is attested elsewhere in Jewish inscriptions (*CIJ* 1.502), and it is likely that he was one of the wealthy Jewish aristocracy living in Alexandria around the turn of the era (Josephus, *A.J.* 18.159–160). The mention of God as one "who hears prayer," while a reconstruction, may be an allusion to 2 Chron 6:40 and 7:15 (**LXX**). The tentative dating presumes that the synagogue was built during the reigns of Cleopatra VII and Ptolemy XIV, a view consistent with the inscription's letter forms.

No. 145
Source: *Inscription. JIGRE* 18
Date: 3 C.E.

[- - ᾿Α]θὺρ ιη΄ ἐπὶ τῆς π[- -]
[- -]ς τῶν ἀπὸ τῆς τ[- -]
[- -]ων ἀρχισυναγω[- -]
[- - ἀρ]χιπροστάτης διο[- -]
[- - ἐπειδὴ Β]ρασίδας Ἡρακλε[ίδου - -]   5
[- -]γλ΄ (ἔτους) Καίσαρος [- -]
[- -] ἐν ἅπασι ἀναστ[- -]
[- -]ς καὶ ὑγιῶς ἐπ[- -]
[- -] τὴν δαπάνην π[- -]
[- -]ομηνιακὰς ἡμέ[ρας - -]   10
[- - ἐ]πισκευὰς ἀκολ[- -]
[- -]ου λόγῳ ἐπὶ το[- -]
[- -]οδεξάμενον ι[- -]
[- -] στεφάνῳ ἐπ[- -]
[- -]λοις δυσί[- -]   15

...Hathyr 18, in the...of those from the...ruler(s) of the synagogue
[*archisynagōgos (-oi)*]...presiding officer [*archiprostatēs*]...since Brasidas,
son of Heracleides...33rd year of Caesar in all...and soundly...the
expense...days...repair...by word in...crown...with two...

Literature: Binder, *Temple Courts*, 353–55; Krauss, *Synagogale Altertümer*, 163;
Fraser, "᾿Αρχιπροστάτης," 162–63; idem, "A Correction," 290.

Comments: While the Jewishness of this inscription has sometimes been
questioned, the use of *archisynagōgos* argues strongly in favour of it: outside of its
appearance in a few Gentile inscriptions from the Aegean, the term is otherwise
exclusively a Jewish title (e.g., Mark 5:22; Luke 13:14; Acts 13:15; *CIJ* 2.1404;
Nos. 47, 57, 174, and 26). It typically denotes an individual who oversees the
spiritual and (in some instances) temporal well-being of the synagogue community. The title *archiprostatēs*, a *hapax legomenon*, is more problematic. Because
the office of *prostatēs* is mentioned in at least one other synagogue inscription
from Egypt (*JIGRE* 24; No. 159), *archiprostatēs* likely refers to a similar leadership office, albeit in a synagogue with a higher degree of institutionalization.
How this office was distinguished from that of the *archisynagōgos* is unclear. One
possibility is that the former was in charge of judicial and legislative matters,
while the latter maintained oversight of religious ritual. Although the badly preserved state of the inscription makes a specific interpretation difficult, it clearly
references a repair, probably of the synagogue itself. Like a similar inscription

from Berenice (*CJZ* 70; No. 131), this monument would have honoured the individual(s) who provided the underwriting for the project.

No. 146
Source: *Inscription. JIGRE* 20 (*CIJ* 2.1447)
Date: First century B.C.E. to first century C.E.

Ἀρτέμων| Νίκωνος πρ(οστάτης)| τὸ ια΄ (ἔτος) τῇ| συναγωγῇ |
[..]ντηκηι.

Artemon, son of Nikon, being president (*prostatēs*) for the eleventh year, to the association [*synagōgē*] …

Literature: Binder, *Temple Courts*, 248, n. 44; Levine, *Ancient Synagogue*, 83, n. 8, 87, n. 41; Horsley, *New Documents*, 4.255; Kasher, *The Jews*, 111–14; Lifshitz, *DF*, 80 (no. 98).

Comments: The Jewish provenance of this inscription has been questioned on two counts. First of all, the usual term for synagogues in Egypt, *proseuchē*, is absent. And while the word *synagōgē* is certainly present, there are no clear cases in the epigraphic record where this term references an Egyptian synagogue. Secondly, the inscribed monument forms the base of a statue (itself missing) and so would clash with Philo's credible account that Egyptian Jews strictly prohibited graven images within their synagogues (*Legat.* 138–39; No. 140). Thus, a majority of researchers view this monument as belonging to a Gentile association. That is the position adopted in the above translation.

3.1.6.2   *Alexandrou-Nesos*

No. 147
Source: *Papyrus Text. CPJ* 1.129
Date: May 11, 218 B.C.E.

[Βασιλεῖ Πτολεμαίωι χαίρειν τῶ]ν ἐν τῆι Ἀλεξάνδρου νήσωι. ἀδικοῦ-
μαι ὑπὸ

[Δωροθέου Ἰουδαίου κατοικοῦντος τὴν [[α]ὐτὴν]] κώμην. τοῦ γὰρ ε
(ἔτους), ὡς αἱ πρόσοδοι, Φαμενὼ[θ]

[ὁ Δωρόθεος μου σὺν] τῆι συνερίθωι μου, προσνοήσας ἱμάτιόν
μου

[ἄξιον (δραχμὰς)   ]αὐτὸ ὤιχετο ἔχων. αἰσθομένης δέ μου
κατε[

τὸ ἱμ]άτιον ἐν τῆι προσευχῆι τῶν Ἰουδαίων ἐπιλα-   5

[   ]ωπους. ἐπιπαραγίνετα[ι] δὲ Λήζελμις (ἑκατοντάρουρος)

[το ἱμά]τιον Νικομάχωι τῶι νακόρωι ἕως κρίσεως

[   ] δέομαι οὖν σου, βασιλεῦ,
      προστάξαι Διοφάνει

[τῶι στρατηγῶι γράψαι   τῶι ἐπι]στάτει ἀποστεῖλαι τὸν
      Δωρόθεον καὶ Νι-

[κόμαχον   ἱμ]άτιον ἐπ’ αὐτὸν καί, ἐὰν ἦι ἃ γράφω 10
      ἀληθῆ,

[ἐπαναγκάσαι αὐτὸν ἀποδοῦναι μοι τὸ ἱμ]άτιον ἢ τὴν τιμήν, περὶ δὲ
      τῆς ῥαιδιουργίας

[τούτου γὰρ γενομένου, ἔσομα[ι]
      διὰ σέ, βασιλε[ῦ],

[τοῦ δικαίου τετευχυῖα].   εὐτ[ύ]χει.

To King Ptolemy, greeting from…who lives in Alexandrou Nesos. I have been wronged by Dorotheos, (a Jew who lives in the) same village. In the 5th year, according to the financial calendar, on Phamenoth …(as I was talking to) my co-worker, my mantle (which is worth… drachmae) caught Dorotheos' eye, and he took it. When I saw him, (he fled) to the Jewish prayer hall [*proseuchē*] (holding) the mantle, (while I called for help). Lezelmis, a holder of 100 arourai, came up to help (and gave) the mantle to Nikomachos the (prayer hall) warden to keep till the case was tried. Therefore I beg you, my king, to command Diophanes the magistrate (to write to the) chief of police telling him to order Dorotheos and Nikomachos to hand over the mantle to him, and, if what I write is true (to make him give me the) mantle or its value; as for the injury…If this happens, I shall have received justice through you, my king. Farewell.

Literature: Binder, *Temple Courts*, 238–40, 368–70, 437; Levine, *Ancient Synagogue*, 83 n. 10, 86; Runesson, *Origins*, 174 n. 15; Kasher, *The Jews*, 147; Dion, "Synagogues et temples," 65–74.

Comments: This letter, addressed to King Ptolemy IV (221–204 B.C.E.), records the account of an alleged robbery of the petitioner's mantle. In it, the victim (an unnamed woman) ran after Dorotheos, who fled with the mantle into the nearby synagogue. A wealthy landholder, Lezelmis, intervened in the affair, handing over the mantle to the synagogue attendant until the matter could be officially resolved. The description suggests that the synagogue in this village served as a place of asylum, a right bestowed upon at least some Egyptian synagogues (cf. *JIGRE* 125; No. 171). The title of the synagogue attendant, *nakoros* (Doric for *neōkoros*), is attested only here of synagogue functionaries. More literally translated "temple keeper," the term elsewhere references levitical temple functionaries (Philo, *Spec.* 1.156; Josephus, *B.J.* 1.153).

3.1.6.3 *Arsinoë-Crocodilopolis*

No. 148
Source: *Papyrus Text. CPJ* 1.134
Date: Late second century B.C.E.

Col. II

[βο(ρρᾶ) ἐχο(μένης) Ἑρμι]όνηι Ἀπολλωνίδου ἱερᾶς παρα(δείσου),

(ὧν) ὑποδο(χείου) (τέταρτον), περιστε(ρῶνος) ἐρή(μου) λ′β′,   15

χέ(ρσου) εή. γεί(τονες) νό(του) Δημητρίου Θρα(κὸς) χέ(ρσος), βο(ρρᾶ)

προσευ(χή), λι(βὸς) περίστασις πό(λεως), ἀπη(λιώτου) Ἀργα(ίτιδος)
      διῶρυ(ξ).

βο(ρρᾶ) [ἐ]χ[ο(μένης)] προσευχῆς Ἰουδαίων διὰ Π̣ε̣ρ̣τ̣όλλου

διὰ μι(σθωτοῦ) Πετεσούχου τοῦ Μαρρήους

ἱερᾶς παρα(δείσου) γ (ἥμισυ) (τέταρτον) ιˊϛˊ, [σ]τεφά(νοις) καὶ λαχά(νοις) 20

α (ἥμισυ).

γεί(τονες) νό(του) Ἑρμιόνης τῆς Ἀπολλωνίδου, βο(ρρᾶ) καὶ λι(βὸς)

περίστασις τῆς πό(λεως), ἀπα(λιώτου) Ἀργα(ίτιδος) διῶρυ(ξ).

βο(ρρᾶ) ἐχο(μένη) [ε]ἰσβαί(νουσα) λι(βὸς) παρὰ τὴν πό(λιν) σχοι(νίου)
      δ (ἥμισυ)

Σαραπίων ὁ παρὰ τῆς βα(σιλίσσης) ἱερὰ α, (ὧν) οἰκιῶν   25

ἐρή(μων) (ἥμισυ), ἐρή(μου) (ἥμισυ). [[. . . . .]] ιη.

Col. III

β... [...] . α . [

γεί(τονες) νό(του) προσευχῆς Ἰουδαίων, βο(ρρᾶ) [καὶ λι(βὸς) περίστα(σις)
πόλεως,

ἀπη(λιώτου) Ἀργαίτιδος διῶρυ(ξ).   30

ἕως περιστάσεως πό(λεως) βο(ρρᾶ). [

Col. II

Situated to the north, a sacred garden the property of Hermione daughter of Apollonides (5 13/32 arourai). Of these a quarter (of an aroura) is occupied by a storehouse, 1/32 by an empty dovecote, and $5^1/_8$ are waste land. Neighbours: to the south, waste land belonging to Demetrios the Thracian; to the north, a prayer hall [*proseuchē*]; to the west the city boundary; to the east the canal of Argaitis. Situated to the north, a Jewish prayer hall [*proseuchē*] represented by Pertollos, and a sacred garden cultivated by a tenant, Petesouchos son of Marres, of 3 13/16 arourai and 1½ arourai planted with flowers and vegetables. Neighbours: to the south Hermione daughter of Apollonides; to the north and west the city boundary; to the east the canal of Argaitis. Situated to the north, and narrowing to the west outside the city for 4½ schoinia, Sarapion, who holds from the Queen 1 aroura of sacred land, of which half is occupied by empty houses, and half is unoccupied.

Col. III

...Neighbours: to the south the Jewish prayer hall [*proseuchē*]; to the north and west the city boundary; to the east the canal of Argaitis. Northwards as far as the city boundary...

Literature: Binder, *Temple Courts*, 236–38; Levine, *Ancient Synagogue*, 83 n. 10, 81; Runesson, *Origins*, 432–33; Fine, *This Holy Place*, 26; Kasher, *The Jews*, 138–39.

Comments: This land survey locates the synagogue just southeast of the city boundaries and west of the Argaitis canal. Built on sacred land, the synagogue was surrounded by a sizeable estate, equal to about 10,427 square metres or just over 2½ acres. The adjoining sacred garden, leased by the congregation to Petesouchos, measured 4,102 square metres or about one acre. That the synagogue was built outside the city limits and near a canal suggests a concern for ritual purity (cf. *Ep. Arist.* 305–6). The synagogue described here is likely identical to the one attested in a dedicatory inscription from the third century B.C.E. (*JIGRE* 117; No. 150).

No. 149
Source: *Papyrus Text. CPJ* 2.432
Date: 113 C.E.

Col. III, ll. 57–61

ἀρχόντων Ἰ[ου]δαίων προσευχῆς Θηβαίων μηνιαίω(ν) (δρ.) ρκη·

Παχὼν (δρ.) ρκ[η], Παῦνι (δρ.) ρκη, Ἐπεὶφ (δρ.) ρκη, Μεσορὴ (δρ.) ρκη,

ιζ (ἔτους) Θὼθ (δρ.) ρκη, Φαῶφι (δρ.) ρκη (γίνονται) (δρ.) ψ[ξη].

εὐχείου ὁμοίως Παχὼν (δρ.) ρκη, Παῦνι (δρ.) ρκη, Ἐπεὶφ (δρ.) ρκη,   60
Μεσο(ρὴ) (δρ.) [ρκη],

ιζ (ἔτους) Θὼθ (δρ.) ρκ[η], Φαῶφι (δρ.) ρκη (γίγονται) (δρ.) ψξη.

From the rulers [*archontēs*] of the prayer hall [*proseuchē*] of the Thebian Jews, 128 drachmae monthly: Pachon, 128 drachmae; Payni, 128 drachmae; Epeiph, 128 drachmae; Mesore, 128 drachmae; 17th year, Thoth, 128 drachmae; Phaophi, 128 drachmae. Total: 768 drachmae.

From the prayer hall [*eucheion*] similarly, 128 drachmae monthly: Pachon, 128 drachmae; Payni 128 drachmae; Epeiph 128, drachmae; Mesore 128, drachmae; 17th year, Thoth, 128 drachmae; Phaophi, 128 drachmae. Total: 768 drachmae.

Literature: Binder, *Temple Courts*, 238 n. 24; Levine, *Ancient Synagogue*, 83 n. 10, 87–88; Runesson, *Origins*, 433, 452; Kasher, *The Jews*, 143–44.

Comments: Two synagogues are mentioned in this water assessment, one belonging to Thebian Jews (called a *proseuchē*) and the other (called a *eucheion*), to an unspecified subgroup. Notably, each building is taxed almost twice the monthly amount charged to a nearby bath house. The high fees imply elevated water usage—and thus present possible evidence for the observance of ritual ablutions in or near these structures.

No. 150
Source: *Inscription. JIGRE* 117 (*CPJ* 3.1532a)
Date: 246–221 B.C.E.

ὑπὲρ βασιλέως |Πτολεμαίου τοῦ| Πτολεμαιου καὶ | βασιλίσσης |
Βερενίκης τῆς || γυναικὸς καὶ |ἀδελφῆς καὶ τῶν |τέκνων οἱ ἐν
Κροκ[ο]|δίλων πόλει Ἰου[δαῖ]|οι τὴν προ[σ]ε[υχ]ή[ν] || κ[αι - - -]

On behalf of King Ptolemy, son of Ptolemy, and Queen Berenice
his wife, and his sister, and their children, the Jews of Crocodilopolis
dedicated the prayer hall [*proseuchē*] and...

Literature: Binder, *Temple Courts*, 112–13; Levine, *Ancient Synagogue*, 83, n. 7,
87, n. 39; Runesson, *Origins*, 172, 430, 432, 451–52; Lifshitz, *DF*, 80–81 (no.
99); Dion, "Synagogues et temples," 55; Horsley, *New Documents*, 3.121; Horsley,
"A New *Corpus Inscriptionum Iudaicarum*," 94; Kasher, *The Jews*, 110 n. 7, 138,
202 n. 50; Schürer, *HJP*, 3.1.52; Williams, *The Jews*, 90, 119.

Comments: One of the oldest of all synagogue inscriptions, this dedication
likely belonged to the synagogue mentioned in an early land survey of this city
(*CPJ* 1.134; No. 148). Ptolemy III Euergetes and Berenice II, who were married
in 246 B.C.E., are also mentioned in a nearly identical synagogue inscription
from Schedia (*JIGRE* 22; No. 158)—as is Ptolemy's sister Berenice. While
the wording closely follows that of non-Jewish temple dedications (e.g., *OGIS*
64, 65, 91, 92; *SB* 429, 1436, 1567, 1570, 4206), this monument is typical of
other synagogue dedications in Egypt: all were careful not to ascribe divinity to
the Ptolemaic rulers. Instead, the buildings were dedicated "on behalf of" the
royal families, with "God Most High" either explicitly or implicitly being
the primary recipient of the benefaction. For a discussion of *proseuchē* as a
Jewish temple term, see Runesson, *Origins*, 429–36.

3.1.6.4 *Athribis*

No. 151
Source: *Inscription. JIGRE* 27 (*CIJ* 2.1443)
Date: Second to first century B.C.E.

ὑπὲρ βασιλέως Πτολεμαίου | καὶ βασιλίσσης Κλεοπάτρας, |
Πτολεμαῖος Ἐπικύδου, |ὁ ἐπιστάτης τῶν φυλακιτῶν, |καὶ οἱ ἐν
Ἀθρίβει Ἰουδαῖοι, ||τὴν προσευχὴν |θεῶι ὑψίστωι.

On behalf of King Ptolemy and Queen Cleopatra, Ptolemy, son of
Epikydes, the chief of police, and the Jews of Athribis dedicated the
prayer hall [*proseuchē*] to God Most High.

Literature: Binder, *Temple Courts*, 243–44, 384–85; Levine, *Ancient Synagogue*, 83, n. 7, 87, n. 39; Runesson, *Origins*, 432–34; Lifshitz, *DF*, 79 (no. 95); Krauss, *Synagogale Altertümer*, 264, 349; Dion, "Synagogues et temples," 55–56; Schürer, *HJP*, 3.1.49; Horsley, *New Documents*, 4.201; Kasher, *The Jews*, 116–18.

Comments: Most of the scholarly discussion of this inscription has revolved around the question of Ptolemy Epikydes' ethnicity, with some researchers maintaining that he was Jewish and others, a Gentile. Those adopting the latter view argue that the office of police chief—which was the second highest police official in an Egyptian nome—was too lofty a position for a Jew. Others rightly point out that Jews were not excluded from such offices, and so the possibility should not be so easily dismissed. If, on the other hand, Ptolemy was indeed a Gentile, then the question arises as to whether he was a benefactor or an early example of a "God-fearer." These latter were Gentile sympathizers who participated in some Jewish customs and rituals without fully converting (cf. Josephus, *A.J.* 14.110; Acts 13:16, 26, 50 [No. 174]; 16:14 [No. 185]; 17:4 [No. 186], 17:17 [No. 90]; 18:17 [No. 91]). In fact, there are no decisive arguments in this debate, and all three possibilities remain live options.

No. 152
Source: *Inscription. JIGRE* 28 (*CIJ* 2.1444)
Date: Second to first century B.C.E.

ὑπὲρ βασιλέως Πτολεμαίου | καὶ βασιλίσσης Κλεοπάτρας | καὶ τῶν τέκνων | Ἑρμίας καὶ Φιλοτέρα ἡ γυνὴ | καὶ τὰ παιδία τήνδε ἐξέδραν || τῆι προσευχῆ<ι>.

On behalf of King Ptolemy and Queen Cleopatra and their children, Hermias and his wife Philotera and their children donated this exedra to the prayer hall [*proseuchē*].

Literature: Binder, *Temple Courts*, 243–44; Levine, *Ancient Synagogue*, 83, n. 7, 87, n. 40; Runesson, *Origins*, 443–44, 450–51; Lifshitz, *DF*, 79–80 (no. 96); Krauss, *Synagogale Altertümer*, 349; Dion, "Synagogues et temples," 55; Schürer, *HJP*, 3.1.49; Horsley, *New Documents*, 4.201; Kasher, *The Jews*, 115–17.

Comments: This inscription is of interest not only because it is one of the few examples from Egypt of a private synagogue dedication (cf. *JIGRE* 13, 126; Nos. 144, 172), but because the donation is of an exedra, an ancillary room off the main hall. This term has a wide array of meanings, ranging from a chamber where priests stored sacred articles (Ezek 42:13, LXX) to a judgment hall (Josephus, *A.J.* 8.134) to a classroom for philosophical discussions (Strabo, *Geog.* 18.1.8). All three functions are attested for Second Temple synagogues (see Binder, *Temple Courts*, 399–404, 430–35, 445–49), so this room may have served any or all of these purposes in this particular case. Given Philo's stress upon the philosophical debates that took place in the Egyptian synagogues (*Legat.* 156; No. 182), perhaps this would have been the most

likely (or frequent) function of the Athribis exedra. The addition of the room
is interpreted by Runesson as spatial evidence of a development of Jewish
temple buildings to accommodate synagogue actitivies such as the reading
and expounding of Torah.

3.1.6.5   *Leontopolis*

No. 153 (cf. T5, 7)
Source: *Literary.* Josephus, *A.J.* 13.65–68
Date: *Antiquitates Judaicae* was published in 93/94 C.E.; the letter of Onias IV
(which may not have been written by Onias but by someone else devoted to
the temple of Leontopolis), reproduced by Josephus, is dated to the second
century B.C.E.

[65] ῎πολλὰς καὶ μεγάλας ὑμῖν χρείας τετελεκὼς ἐν τοῖς κατὰ πόλεμον
ἔργοις μετὰ τῆς τοῦ θεοῦ βοηθείας, καὶ γενόμενος ἔν τε τῇ κοίλῃ Συρίᾳ
καὶ Φοινίκῃ, καὶ εἰς Λεόντων δὲ πόλιν τοῦ Ἡλιοπολίτου σὺν τοῖς
Ἰουδαίοις καὶ εἰς ἄλλους τόπους ἀφικόμενος τοῦ ἔθνους, [66] καὶ
πλείστους εὑρὼν παρὰ τὸ καθῆκον ἔχοντας ἱερὰ καὶ διὰ τοῦτο δύσνους
ἀλλήλοις, ὃ καὶ Αἰγυπτίοις συμβέβηκεν διὰ τὸ πλῆθος τῶν ἱερῶν καὶ
τὸ περὶ τὰς θρησκείας οὐχ ὁμόδοξον, ἐπιτηδειότατον εὑρὼν τόπον ἐν
τῷ προσαγορευομένῳ τῆς ἀγρίας Βουβάστεως ὀχυρώματι βρύοντα
ποικίλης ὕλης καὶ τῶνἱερῶν ζῴων μεστόν, [67] δέομαι συγχωρῆσαί μοι
τὸ ἀδέσποτον ἀνακαθάραντι ἱερὸν καὶ συμπεπτωκὸς οἰκοδομῆσαι ναὸν
τῷ μεγίστῳ θεῷ καθ᾽ ὁμοίωσιν τοῦ ἐν Ἱεροσολύμοις αὐτοῖς μέτροις ὑπὲρ
σοῦ καὶ τῆς σῆς γυναικὸς καὶ τῶν τέκνων, ἵν᾽ ἔχωσιν οἱ τὴν Αἴγυπτον
κατοικοῦντες Ἰουδαῖοι εἰς αὐτὸ συνιόντες κατὰ τὴν πρὸς ἀλλήλους
ὁμόνοιαν, [68] ταῖς σαῖς ἐξυπηρετεῖν χρείαις· καὶ γὰρ Ἡσαΐας ὁ
προφήτης τοῦτο προεῖπεν· ἔσται θυσιαστήριον ἐν Αἰγύπτῳ κυρίῳ τῷ
θεῷ· καὶ πολλὰ δὲ προεφήτευσεν ἄλλα τοιαῦτα διὰ τὸν τόπον.

[65] "Many and great are the services which I have rendered you in
the course of the war, with the help of God, when I was in Coele-Syria
and Phoenicia. When I came with the Jews to Leontopolis in the nome
of Heliopolis and to other places where our nation is settled, [66] I
found that most of them have temples [*hiera*], contrary to what is proper,
and that for this reason they are ill-disposed toward one another, as is
also the case with the Egyptians because of their temples [*hiera*] and
their varying opinions about the forms of worship. Now I have found
a most suitable place in the fortress called after Bubastis-of-the-Fields,
which abounds in various kinds of trees and is full of sacred animals.
[67] Therefore, I beg you to give me permission to cleanse the temple,
which belongs to no one and is in ruins, and to build a temple [*naos*]

to the Most High God in the likeness of that in Jerusalem and with the
same dimensions, on behalf of you and your wife and your children,
so that the Jews who live in Egypt may be able to come together in
mututal harmony and serve your interests; [68] for this is what the
prophet Isaiah foretold: 'there shall be an altar [*thysiastērion*] in Egypt
to the Lord God,' and many other similar things did he prophesy
regarding this place."

Literature: Dion, "Synagogues et temples," 55; Delcor, "Le Temple d'Onias,"
192–93; Binder, *Temple Courts*, 234–36; Bilde, "Synagoge," 26; Runesson, *Origins*,
412–14; Levine, *Ancient Synagogue*, 84–85.

Comments: Scholars differ in their interpretation of the *hiera* mentioned
in v. 66. Binder sees these institutions as sacred precincts without sacrificial
cults, i.e., as synagogues; Runesson understands these as a reference to Jewish
temples in Egypt, which the temple of Onias IV was meant to replace. On
the temple at Leontopolis and the question of other Jewish temples in Egypt,
see below, No. T5.

No. 154
Source: *Inscription. JIGRE* 105
Date: Mid-second B.C.E. to mid-second C.E.

[- - -] | [- - τὴν] προσε[υχὴν - -] | [- - θε]ῶι ὑψίσ[τωι - -]

…the prayer hall [*proseuchē*]…to God Most High…

Literature: Binder, *Temple Courts*, 245, n. 39; Levine, *Ancient Synagogue*, 83,
n. 9; Runesson, *Origins*, 434.

Comments: The fragmentary nature of this inscription makes it difficult to
draw any firm conclusions. Given parallels with other synagogue dedications
from Egypt (cf. *JIGRE* 27; No. 151), it is more likely that *proseuchē* here means
prayer hall rather than *prayer*. In this case, it could be a dedication of one of
the Leontopolis synagogues attested by Josephus (*A.J.* 13.65–68; No. 153). On
the other hand, it may be a reference to the rival temple of the Jewish priest
Onias IV, which was located in this region.

3.1.6.6 *Naucratis*

No. 155
Source: *Inscription. JIGRE* 26
Date: 30 B.C.E. to 14 C.E.

[- - ᾽Α]μμωνίου συναγωγὸς | [- - σ]υνόδῳ Σαμβαθικῇ | [(ἔτους)..
Καί]σαρος, Φαμενὼθ ζ΄.

...son of Ammonios, leader [*synagōgos*] ...to the Symbathic Association, in the year of Caesar, Phamenoth 7.

Literature: Krauss, *Synagogale Altertümer*, 26; Williams, *The Jews*, 176.

Comments: Though not a synagogue inscription, this monument is notable because of the term rendered *Symbathic Association* in the above translation: it may derive its origin from the Jewish custom of Sabbath observance. If so, its usage here presents epigraphic evidence of the attractiveness to Gentiles of certain Jewish observances (cf. Josephus, *C. Ap.* 2.124; Philo, *Mos.* 2.20).

3.1.6.7 *Nitriai*

No. 156
Source: *Inscription. JIGRE* 25 (*CIJ* 2.1442)
Date: 140–116 B.C.E.

ὑπὲρ βασιλέως Πτολεμαίου | καὶ βασιλίσσης Κλεοπάτρας | τῆς ἀδελφῆς καὶ βασιλίσσης | Κλεοπάτρας τῆς γυναικὸς | Εὐεργετῶν, οἱ ἐν Νιτρίαις || Ἰουδαῖοι τὴν προσευχὴν | καὶ τὰ συνκύροντα.

On behalf of King Ptolemy and Queen Cleopatra his sister and Queen Cleopatra his wife, benefactors, the Jews of Nitriai dedicated the prayer hall [*proseuchē*] and the appurtenances.

Literature: Binder, *Temple Courts*, 244–45; Levine, *Ancient Synagogue*, 83, n. 7, 87, n. 39; Runesson, *Origins*, 432–33, 451; Lifshitz, *DF*, 79 (no. 94); Dion, "Synagogues et temples," 55, 57, 60; Schürer, *HJP*, 3.1.49; Horsley, *New Documents*, 4.201; Kasher, *The Jews*, 57, 114–16, 213; Williams, *The Jews*, 28.

Comments: The term translated *benefactors* (*euergetōn*, l. 5) is a standard royal honorific in Egyptian dedications from the Graeco-Roman period. Notably, this example does not include the fuller phrase, *divine benefactors* (*theōn euergetōn*), normally found in contemporaneous dedications of non-Jewish temples (e.g., *OGIS* 64–65). This omission clearly reflects the Jewish adherence to the First Commandment. The term *appurtenances* (*synkyronta* l. 7; cf. *JIGRE* 9; No. 143), also frequently found in non-Jewish temple dedications (e.g., *OGIS* 52, 92, 182), could be a reference to architectural features such as pylons or exedras (cf. *JIGRE* 24, 28; Nos. 159, 152). Alternatively, it could refer to furniture or sacred vessels.

3.1.6.8 *Ptolemais*

No. 157
Source: *Literary.* 3 Macc. 7:18–20
Date: First half of the first century B.C.E.

[18] ἐκεῖ ἐποίησαν πότον σωτήριον τοῦ βασιλέως χορηγήσαντος αὐτοῖς εὐψύχως τὰ πρὸς τὴν ἄφιξιν πάντα ἑκάστῳ ἕως εἰς τὴν ἰδίαν οἰκίαν [19] καταχθέντες δὲ μετ' εἰρήνης ἐν ταῖς πρεπούσαις ἐξομολογήσεσιν ὡσαύτως κἀκεῖ ἔστησαν καὶ ταύτας ἄγειν τὰς ἡμέρας ἐπὶ τὸν τῆς παροικίας αὐτῶν χρόνον εὐφροσύνους [20] ἃς καὶ ἀνιερώσαντες ἐν στήλῃ κατὰ τὸν τῆς συμποσίας τόπον προσευχῆς καθιδρύσαντες ἀνέλυσαν ἀσινεῖς, ἐλεύθεροι, ὑπερχαρεῖς, διά τε γῆς καὶ θαλάσσης καὶ ποταμοῦ ἀνασῳζόμενοι τῇ τοῦ βασιλέως ἐπιταγῇ, ἕκαστος εἰς τὴν ἰδίαν

[18] There they celebrated their deliverance, for the king had generously provided all things to them for their journey until all of them arrived at their own houses. [19] And when they had all landed in peace with appropriate thanksgiving, there too in like manner they decided to observe these days as a joyous festival during the time of their stay. [20] Then, after inscribing them as holy on a pillar and dedicating a prayer hall [topos proseuchēs] at the site of the festival, they departed unharmed, free, and overjoyed, since at the king's command they had all of them been brought safely by land and sea and river to their own homes.

Literature: Williams, *The Jews*, 84; Binder, *Temple Courts*, 245–46; Runesson, *Origins*, 434–35; Levine, *Ancient Synagogue*, 86, n. 34.

Comments: The narrative setting is the liberation of the Jews from the persecutions of Ptolemy IV Philopater (see also Nos. 135–137). Scholars differ in their interpretation of the character of the institution mentioned. While Binder understands *topos proseuchēs* as referring to a synagogue, Runesson maintains that it alludes to a memorial shrine of modest proportions where Jewish passers-by could offer prayers and sacrifices (probably incense and/or vegetables). While noting that the text holds the institution in question as sacred in nature, most scholars discount the historicity of the events narrated within 3 Maccabees, including those in the above passage.

3.1.6.9 *Schedia*

No. 158
Source: *Inscription. JIGRE* 22 (*CIJ* 2.1440)
Date: 246–221 B.C.E.

ὑπὲρ βασιλέως | Πτολεμαίου καὶ | βασιλίσσης | Βερενίκης ἀδελ|φῆς καὶ γυναικὸς καὶ || τῶν τέκνων | τὴν προσευχὴν | οἱ Ἰουδαῖοι.

On behalf of King Ptolemy and Queen Berenice, his sister, and his wife, and their children, the Jews dedicated the prayer hall [*proseuchē*].

Literature: Binder, *Temple Courts*, 240–41; Levine, *Ancient Synagogue*, 83; Runesson, *Origins*, 172, 430, 432, 451; Lifshitz, *DF*, 78 (no. 92); Krauss, *Synagogale Altertümer*, 263; Dion, "Synagogues et temples," 55, 57, 60; Schürer, *HJP*, 3.1.46, 87; Horsley, *New Documents*, 3.121–22; Kasher, *The Jews*, 107, 110, 189, 258.

Comments: This monument is one of the oldest of all synagogue dedications. For further exposition, please refer to the above comments on the similarly worded inscription from Arsinoë-Crocodilopolis (*JIGRE* 117; No. 150).

3.1.6.10 *Xenephyris*

No. 159
Source: *Inscription. JIGRE* 24 (*CIJ* 2.1441)
Date: 140–116 B.C.E.

ὑπὲρ βασιλέως Πτολεμαίου | καὶ βασιλίσσης Κλεοπάτρας τῆς | ἀδελφῆς καὶ βασιλίσσης Κλε|οπάτρας τῆς γυναικός, οἱ ἀπὸ | Ξενεφύρεος ᾿Ιουδαῖοι τὸν || πυλῶνα τῆς προσευχῆς, | προστάντων Θεοδώρου | καὶ ᾿Αχιλλίωνος.

On behalf of King Ptolemy and Queen Cleopatra his sister and Queen Cleopatra his wife, the Jews of Xenephyris dedicated the pylon of the prayer hall [*proseuchē*] during the presidencies of Theodorus and Achillion.

Literature: Binder, *Temple Courts*, 242–43, 353; Levine, *Ancient Synagogue*, 83, n. 7, 87, n. 39; Runesson, *Origins*, 174, 432–33; Fine, *This Holy Place*, 26; Lifshitz, *DF*, 78–79 (no. 93); Krauss, *Synagogale Altertümer*, 264; Dion, "Synagogues et temples," 55, 62, 65; Schürer, *HJP*, 3.1.49; Horsley, *New Documents*, 4.201; Kasher, *The Jews*, 111–14; Williams, *The Jews*, 38.

Comments: This dedication is not of the synagogue itself, but of an attached pylon. In an Egyptian context, this term typically referenced a gate-house built at the entryway of a sacred precinct (cf. *JIGRE* 9 [No. 143], *OGIS* 677). Thus, the synagogue at Xenephyris was most likely set in the centre of a walled-in sacred area that was accessed through the pylon. On the term translated *presidencies* (*prostantōn*, l. 7), see No. 145.

3.1.6.11 *General References and Uncertain Locations*

No. 160
Source: *Literary.* Philo, *Contempl.* 30–33
Date: Ca. 30–45 C.E.

[30] τὰς μὲν οὖν ἓξ ἡμέρας χωρὶς ἕκαστοι μονούμενοι παρ᾿ ἑαυτοῖς ἐν τοῖς λεχθεῖσι μοναστηρίοις φιλοσοφοῦσι, τὴν αὔλειον οὐχ

ὑπερβαίνοντες, ἀλλ᾽ οὐδὲ ἐξ ἀπόπτου θεωροῦντες· ταῖς δὲ ἑβδόμαις
συνέρχονται καθάπερ εἰς κοινὸν σύλλογον καὶ καθ᾽ ἡλικίαν ἑξῆς
καθέζονται μετὰ τοῦ πρέποντος σχήματος, εἴσω τὰς χεῖρας ἔχοντες,
τὴν μὲν δεξιὰν μεταξὺ στέρνου καὶ γενείου, τὴν δὲ εὐώνυμον
ὑπεσταλμένην παρὰ τῇ λαγόνι. [31] παρελθὼν δὲ ὁ πρεσβύτατος καὶ
τῶν δογμάτων ἐμπειρότατος διαλέγεται, καθεστῶτι μὲν τῷ βλέμματι,
καθεστώσῃ δὲ τῇ φωνῇ, μετὰ λογισμοῦ καὶ φρονήσεως, οὐ δεινότητα
λόγων ὥσπερ οἱ ῥήτορες ἢ οἱ νῦν σοφισταὶ παρεπιδεικνύμενος, ἀλλὰ
τὴν ἐν τοῖς νοήμασι διηρευνηκὼς καὶ διερμηνεύων ἀκρίβειαν, ἥτις οὐκ
ἄκροις ὠσὶν ἐφιζάνει, ἀλλὰ δι᾽ ἀκοῆς ἐπὶ ψυχὴν ἔρχεται καὶ βεβαίως
ἐπιμένει. Καθ᾽ ἡσυχίαν δὲ οἱ ἄλλοι πάντες ἀκροῶνται, τὸν ἔπαινον
νεύμασιν ὄψεως ἢ κεφαλῆς παραδηλοῦντες αὐτὸ μόνον. [32] τὸ δὲ
κοινὸν τοῦτο σεμνεῖον, εἰς ὃ ταῖς ἑβδόμαις συνέρχονται, διπλοῦς ἐστι
περίβολος, ὁ μὲν εἰς ἀνδρῶνα, ὁ δὲ εἰς γυναικωνῖτιν ἀποκριθείς· καὶ
γὰρ καὶ γυναῖκες ἐξ ἔθους συνακροῶνται τὸν αὐτὸν ζῆλον καὶ τὴν
αὐτὴν προαίρεσιν ἔχουσαι. [33] ὁ δὲ μεταξὺ τῶν οἴκων τοῖχος τὸ μὲν
ἐξ ἐδάφους ἐπὶ τρεῖς ἢ τέσσαρας πήχεις εἰς τὸ ἄνω συνῳκοδόμηται
θωρακίου τρόπον, τὸ δὲ ἄχρι τέγους ἀνάγειον ἀχανὲς ἀνεῖται, δυοῖν
ἕνεκα, τοῦ τε τὴν πρέπουσαν αἰδῶ τῇ γυναικείᾳ φύσει διατηρεῖσθαι
καὶ τοῦ τὴν ἀντίληψιν ἔχειν εὐμαρῆ καθεζομένας ἐν ἐπηκόῳ, μηδενὸς
τὴν τοῦ διαλεγομένου φωνὴν ἐμποδίζοντος.

[30] For six days they seek wisdom by themselves in solitude in the
closets mentioned above, never passing the outside door of the house
or even getting a distant view of it. But every seventh day they meet
together as for a general assembly and sit in order according to their
age in the proper attitude, with their hands inside the robe, the right
hand between the breast and the chin and the left withdrawn along
the flank. [31] Then the senior among them who also has the fullest
knowledge of the doctrines which they profess comes forward and
with visage and voice alike quiet and composed gives a well-reasoned
and wise discourse. He does not make an exhibition of clever rhetoric
like the orators or sophists of to-day but follows careful examination
by careful expression of the exact meaning of the thoughts, and this
does not lodge just outside the ears of the audience but passes through
the hearing into the soul and there stays securely. All the others sit still
and listen showing their approval merely by their looks or nods. [32]
This common sanctuary [*semneion*] in which they meet every seventh
day is a double enclosure, one portion set apart for the use of the men,

the other for the women. For women too regularly make part of the audience with the same ardour and the same sense of their calling. [33] The wall between the two chambers rises up from the ground to three or four cubits built in the form of a breast work, while the space above up to the roof is left open. This arrangement serves two purposes; the modesty becoming to the female sex is preserved, while the women sitting within ear-shot can easily follow what is said since there is nothing to obstruct the voice of the speaker.

Literature: Radice and Runia, *Bibliography 1937–1986*; Runia, *Bibliography 1987–1996*; Levine, *Ancient Synagogues*, 141, 146, 475–77; Culpepper, *Schools*, 202–3; Borgen, *Philo*, 158–59; Schürer, *HJP*, 448; Binder, *Temple Courts*, 149–51, 468–71; Runesson, *Origins*, 455–58; Claußen, *Versammlung*, 142–44.

Comments: Most of *De vita contemplativa* approvingly describes a Jewish religious group called the Therapeutae. While the authenticity of the text was formerly debated, the work is now regarded as genuine. Likewise, because Philo presents such an idealized picture of the community, some have questioned the historicity of the Therapeutae. Nevertheless, there is now a general agreement that this group did indeed exist. Other scholars have noted similar descriptions of the Essenes in Philo. While there are parallels between the passages dealing with the gathering places of the two groups (clearly called *synagōgai* in the case of the Essenes), the above quotation can only serve as an indirect witness to the synagogue. It is a part of Philo's description of the sect's activities on the seventh day—activities that the Therapeutae (and Philo) considered a complete festival of perfect holiness (*paneortos* and *panhieros*).

§30 *seek wisdom.* As Philo is writing for Greek readers, he uses general Greek terms in describing the activities of the Therapeutae in the synagogue and elsewhere: here and in §28 and §34 the verb *philosophein* "pursue knowledge, discuss, investigate, study," in §26, and in §28, the noun *philosophia*, describing "the celebrated doctrines of the holy philosophy" and "their ancestral philosophy." The last passage makes it clear that it was a study of "the holy scriptures" (cf. Nos. 40, 166, 168, and the presentation of philosophical studies in *Agr.* 14–15)....*meet together as for a general assembly.* The Greek word for "assembly," *syllogos*, means a meeting for a specific purpose, whether for deliberations, consultations, etc. There is some kind of mutual activity.

§31 *the senior.* In Greek *presbytatos*, the superlative form of *presbys* "old." It is not said that he must be most skilled in the Holy Scriptures, but rather in their principles or doctrines (*dogmata*). The word is especially used of philosophical doctrines....*comes forward.* The senior leaves his seat and goes to a place for reading (?) and teaching. Note that Philo says nothing about a public reading of the Scriptures here or in §75 and §79....*gives a well-reasoned and wise discourse.* In Greek, "discourses...with argument and wisdom." Philo uses here and in §33 §79 the word *dialegesthai*, "to discuss a question with another, to elicit conclusions by discussions, discourse." The lecture ends in discussions or in a question and answer session (cf. §30 and No. 167). "With argument and wisdom" means "with the power of reasoning and with practical wisdom."...*follows careful examination by careful expression*. Philo uses two related verbs, both in form and meaning: "having carefully interpreted and interpreting." *Diereunan* means "carefully examine, search, investigate," *diermeneuein*, "expound, interpret." This intensive activity of interpretation is further emphasized by the phrase "the exact meaning." Yonge translates: "investigating with great pains, and explaining with minute accuracy the precise meaning."...*the thoughts*. The thoughts must, according to the context, in some way be related to the content of passages in the Holy Scriptures. In §25 Philo mentions the laws, the divine oracles of the prophets, the hymns and psalms and the other things (*ta alla*). The interpretation of the Scriptures is followed by a teaching on virtues, founded on self-control, §24.

§32 *sanctuary*. The uncommon Greek word *semneion*, used three times in *Contempl*. (the other two referring to a room in private house, §25 and §89), means "holy place/house, shrine."

No. 161
Source: *Literary.* Philo, *Deus* 8–9
Date: Ca. 30–45 C.E.

[8] καὶ γὰρ εὔηθες εἰς μὲν τὰ ἱερὰ μὴ ἐξεῖναι βαδίζειν, ὃς ἂν μὴ πρότερον λουσάμενος φαιδρύνηται τὸ σῶμα, εὔχεσθαι δὲ καὶ θύειν ἐπιχειρεῖν ἔτι κεκηλιδωμένῃ καὶ πεφυρμένῃ διανοίᾳ. καίτοι τὰ μὲν ἱερὰ λίθων καὶ ξύλων ἀψύχου τῆς ὕλης πεποίηται, καθ' αὐτὸ δὲ καὶ τὸ σῶμα ἄψυχον· ἀλλ' ὅμως ὂν ἄψυχον ἀψύχων οὐ προσάψεται μὴ περιρραντηρίοις καὶ καθαρσίοις ἁγνευτικοῖς χρησάμενον, ὑπομενεῖ δέ τις τῷ θεῷ προσελθεῖν ἀκάθαρτος ὢν ψυχὴν τὴν ἑαυτοῦ τῷ καθαρωτάτῳ, καὶ ταῦτα μὴ μέλλων μετανοήσειν; [9] ὁ μὲν γὰρ πρὸς τῷ μηδὲν ἐπεξεργάσασθαι κακὸν καὶ τὰ παλαιὰ ἐκνίψασθαι δικαιώσας γεγηθὼς προσίτω, ὁ δ' ἄνευ τούτων δυσκάθαρτος ὢν ἀφιστάσθω· λήσεται γὰρ οὐδέποτε τὸν τὰ ἐν μυχοῖς τῆς διανοίας ὁρῶντα καὶ τοῖς ἀδύτοις αὐτῆς ἐμπεριπατοῦντα.

[8] For it is absurd that a man should be forbidden to enter the temples [*hiera*] save after bathing and cleansing his body, and yet should attempt to pray [*euchomai*] and sacrifice [*thuō*] with a heart still soiled and spotted. The temples [*hiera*] are made of stones and timber, that is of soulless matter, and soulless too is the body in itself. And can it be that while it is forbidden to this soulless body to touch the soulless stones, except it have first been subjected to lustral and purificatory consecration, a man will not shrink from approaching with his soul impure the absolute purity of God and that too when there is no thought of repentance in

his heart? [9] He who is resolved not only to commit no further sin, but also to wash away the past, may approach with gladness: let him who lacks this resolve keep far away, since hardly shall he be purified. For he shall never escape the eye of Him who sees into the recesses of the mind and treads its inmost shrine.

Literature: Radice and Runia, *Bibliography 1937–1986*; Runia, *Bibliography 1987–1996*; Binder, *Temple Courts*, 122–30, 395–7, 407–9; Claußen, *Versamm-lung*, 132–38; Runesson, *Origins*, 446–54; Runesson, "Water and Worship," 119–29.

Comments: Philo's *Quod Deus ist immutabiblis*, one of his many commentaries on Genesis, is a continuous explanation of Gen 6:2–12. The first part of the commentary focusses on "and they bore children unto them [God's angels]." Men have to bear children unto God, like Abraham and his disciple and successor Hannah. Giving God gratitude and honour, they have to purify themselves from sin, washing off all things that can stain their life in words, appearance, or actions. §§8–9 present an argument for that. While this could be a general argument, the context and some formulations show that Philo was thinking of Jewish practices.

§8 *the temples.* This would seem to imply that there were Jewish temples in Egypt in Philo's time, though Binder interprets *hiera* as referring to synagogues. . . . *bathing and cleansing his body.* Ablutions and purifying ceremonies of holiness. Going into a synagogue also required purifications. . . . *prayer and sacrifices.* Here possibly offerings of vegetables and incense combined with the recitation of prayers; these are typical temple activities. See No. 169.

No. 162
Source: *Literary.* Philo, *Hypoth.* 7.11–14
Date: Ca. 30–45 c.e.

[7.11] ἆρ' οὐ πρὸς ἀσκήσεως μόνον αὐτοῖς τοῦτο ἐγκρατείας ἐστίν, ὡς ἐξ ἴσου καὶ δρᾶν τι πονοῦντας καὶ ἀνέχειν ἰσχύειν ἀπὸ τῶν ἔργων, εἰ δέ οὐ δῆτα. ἀλλα' καὶ προς ἔργου μεγάλου καὶ θαυμαστοῦ τινος ᾠήθη δεῖν ὁ νομοθέτης αὐτοὺς μὴ τἆλλα μόνον ἱκανοὺς εἶναι δρᾶν καὶ μὴ δρᾶν ὡσαύτως, ἀλλ' ἔτι καὶ τῶν πατρίων νόμων καὶ ἐθῶν ἐμπείρως ἔχειν. [7.12] τί οὖν ἐποίησε ταῖς ἑβδόμαις ταύταις ἡμέραις αὐτοὺς εἰς ταὐτὸν ἠξίου συνάγεσθαι καὶ καθεζομένους μετ' ἀλλήλων σὺν αἰδοῖ καὶ κόσμῳ τῶν νόμων ἀκροᾶσθαι τοῦ μηδένα ἀγνοῆσαι χάριν. [7.13] καὶ δῆτα συνέρχονται μὲν αἰεὶ καὶ συνεδρεύουσι μετ' ἀλλήλων. οἱ μὲν πολλοὶ σιωπῇ, πλὴν εἴ τι προσεπευφημῆσαι τοῖς ἀναγινωσκομένοις νομίζεται. τῶν ἱερέων δέ τις ὁ παρὼν ἢ τῶν γερόντων εἷς ἀναγινώσκει τοὺς ἱεροὺς νόμους αὐτοῖς και' καθ' ἕκαστον ἐξηγεῖται μέχρι σχεδὸν

δείλης ὀψίας. κἀκ τοῦδε ἀπολύονται τῶν τε νόμων τῶν ἱερῶν ἐμπείρως
ἕξοντες καὶ πολὺ δὴ προς εὐσέβειαν ἐπιδεδωκότε. [7.14] ἀρά σοι δοκεῖ
ταῦτα ἀργούντων εἶναι καὶ οὐ παντὸς ἔργου μᾶλλον ἀναγκαῖα αὐτοῖς
τοι γαρ οὖν οὐκ ἐπὶ θεσμῳδοὺς ἔρχονται περὶ τῶν πρακτέων καὶ μὴ
διερωτῶντες οἰδὲ καθ᾽ ἑαυτοὺς ὑπ᾽ ἀγνοίας τῶν νόμων ῥαδιουργοῦσιν,
ἀλλ᾽ ὅντινα αὐτῶν κιν εἷς καὶ περὶ τῶν πατρίων διαπυνθάνῃ, προχείρως
ἔχει καὶ ῥαδίως εἰπεῖν. καὶ ἀνὴρ γυναικὶ καὶ παισὶ πατὴρ καὶ δούλοις
δεσπότης ἱκανὸς εἶναι δοκεῖ τοὺς νόμους παραδιδόναι.

[7.11] Is not this merely a case of practising self-control so that they
should be capable of abstaining from toil if necessary no less than of
toilsome activity? No, it was a great and marvellous achievement, which
the lawgiver had in view. He considered that they should not only be
capable of both action and inaction in other matters but also should
have expert knowledge of their ancestral laws and customs. [7.12] What
then did he do? He required them to assemble [*synagō*] in the same
place on these seventh days, and sitting together in a respectful and
orderly manner hear the laws read so that none should be ignorant of
them. [7.13] And indeed they do always assemble and sit together, most
of them in silence except when it is the practice to add something to
signify approval of what is read. But some priest who is present or one
of the elders reads the holy laws to them and expounds them point by
point till about the late afternoon, when they depart having gained both
expert knowledge of the holy laws and considerable advance in piety.
[7.14] Do you think that this marks them as idlers or that any work is
equally vital to them? And so they do not resort to persons learned in
the law with questions as to what they should do or not do, nor yet by
keeping independent transgress in ignorance of the law, but any one of
them whom you attack with inquiries about their ancestral institutions
can answer you readily and easily. The husband seems competent to
transmit knowledge of the laws to his wife, the father to his children,
the master to his slaves.

Literature: Binder, *Temple Courts*, 402–8; Levine, *Ancient Synagogues*, 135–42,
145–47, Runesson, *Origins*, 80–82; Claußen, *Versammlung*, 213–18.

Comments: In the eighth book of his *Preparatio*, Eusebius gives us an extract
(6.1–9, 7.1–20) from a book by Philo entitled "Hypothetica." In it, the author
defends the Jews to the Greeks, as he does in another extract (11.1–18) from
the "Apology for the Jews." These fragments probably come from one and the
same work, now generally called *Hypothetica* (or *Apologia pro Judaeis*). The last

section of the first extract (7.10–20) concerns the observation of the Sabbath. Tacitus, *Hist.* 5.4, and Seneca, according to Augustine (*Civ. Dei*, 6.11), accuse the Jews of being idle, not working on the seventh day. There are some similarities to Philo's description of the Therapeutae in this passage.

§7.11 *have expert knowledge of.* The Greek verbal phrase has the nuance of learning something by personal experience. Every man (no women are mentioned in this passage) has to accumulate enough knowledge to answer all who pose questions about their beliefs.

§7.14. *their ancestral laws and customs.* These words refer to the Mosaic law and later Jewish oral traditions (see comment on No. 138, §43). In what follows, Philo speaks only about the (holy) laws (plural also in §7.14) being read and expounded; in 7:14 this includes also "their ancestral institutions" (*ta patria*, "the ancestral things").

§7.12 *sitting together.* Or "sitting down with one another." §7.13 uses another verb for the same action, *synedreuein met' allelon* "sit in council with one another, deliberate with one another." ... *hear the laws read.* The reading of Torah, mentioned three times in this passage, was the central activity in the development of the Jewish synagogues (Runesson, *Origins*). If present, one of the priests or elders reads and expounds upon the texts, though anyone could contribute something to the discussion.

§7.13 *expounds them point by point.* Or "interprets each of them separately." Philo uses here the common word *exēgeisthai*, "expound, interpret." ... *Having gained ... considerable advance in piety.* The activity in the synagogue has a double purpose: to gain knowledge of the Jewish laws and customs and to advance in piety, *eusebeia*, the queen of all virtues (see comment on No. 166, §2.216).

§7.14 *persons learned in the law.* The Greek text contains a general word for "one who delivers oracular precepts, one who delivers ordinances."

No. 163
Source: *Literary.* Philo, *Legat.* 148
Date: Ca. 41–45 C.E.

[148] τοῦτον οὖν τὸν τοσοῦτον εὐεργέτην ἐν τρισὶ καὶ τεσσαράκοντα ἐνιαυτοῖς, οὓς ἐπεκράτησεν Αἰγύπτου, παρεκαλύψαντο, μηδὲν ἐν προσευχαῖς ὑπὲρ αὐτοῦ, μὴ ἄγαλμα, μὴ ξόανον, μὴ γραφὴν ἱδρυσάμενοι.

[148] During the forty-three years of this wonderful benefactor's rule over Egypt, the Alexandrians neglected him and did not make a single dedication on his behalf in the prayer halls [*proseuchai*]—neither a statue, nor a wooden image nor a painting.

Literature: Smallwood, *Legatio*, 229.

Comments: For a general introduction, see the introductory comment to No. 138. *Legat.* 143–153 contains a eulogy on Augustus (31 B.C.E.–14 C.E.), "this wonderful benefactor." Philo goes on to highlight Augustus' favourable treatment of the Jews (§§154–158).

§148 *a single dedication on his behalf.* See comment to No. 164, §152.

No. 164
Source: *Literary.* Philo, *Legat.* 152–53
Date: Ca. 41–45 C.E.

[152] ἔχοντες οὖν τοιαύτας ἀφορμὰς καὶ τοὺς πανταχοῦ πάντας ὁμογνώμονας οὔτε περὶ τὰς προσευχὰς ἐνεωτέρισαν καὶ καθ᾽ ἕκαστον <τὸ> νόμιμον ἐφύλαξαν· ἢ τινα σεβασμὸν παρέλιπον τῶν ὀφειλομένων Καίσαρι; καὶ τίς ἂν εὖ φρονῶν εἴποι; διὰ τί οὖν ἐστέρησαν; ἐγὼ φράσω μηδὲν ὑποστειλάμενος. [153] ᾔδεσαν αὐτοῦ τὴν ἐπιμέλειαν καὶ ὅτι τοσαύτην ποιεῖται τῆς βεβαιώσεως τῶν παρ" ἑκάστοις πατρίων, ὅσην καὶ τῶν: Ῥωμαϊκῶν, καὶ ὅτι δέχεται τὰς τιμὰς οὐκ ἐπὶ καθαιρέσει τῶν παρ᾽ ἐνίοις νομίμων τυφοπλαστῶν ἑαυτόν, ἀλλὰ τῷ μεγέθει τῆς τοσαύτης ἡγεμονίας ἑπόμενος, ἢ διὰ τῶν τοιούτων πέφυκε σεμνοποιεῖσθαι.

[152] So although the Greeks had these powerful incentives, and knew that all the nations of the world felt as they did, they nevertheless made no changes in regard to the prayer halls [*proseuchai*], but maintained our Law in every particular. Does this mean that they were omitting any mark of reverence due to Caesar? Who in his senses would say that? Why, then, did they deprive him of this honour? I will explain fully. [153] They knew that he was very careful and cared as much for the preservation of the customs of the various nations as for the preservation of Roman ones, and that he received honours not for doing away with the practices of a particular people as an act of self-deception, but in accordance with the dignity of his great empire which was bound to win respect for itself by these means.

Literature: Smallwood, *Legatio*, 232–33.

Comments: For a general introduction, see the introductory comment to No. 138. For the context, see the comments on No. 163.

§152 *no changes in regard to the synagogues.* On the verb used by Philo, see the comment to No. 138, §47. Several times Philo declares that statues or other images of the emperor had never before been placed in a synagogue. He especially mentions the attitude of Augustus and the situation during his time. Thus what happened in 38 C.E. in Alexandria was something "entirely novel" (*Flacc.* 41 [dot] [No. 138], *Legat.* 148 [No. 163]). The Jewish Law forbid the worship of graven images (Exod 20:4). By erecting statues of Gaius in the synagogues, the Alexandrians tried to force the Jews to partake in worship of the emperor. While Jews could honour and pray for emperors and high officials in the synagogues (*Flacc.* 48, *Legat.* 133 [No. 140]), they could not worship them. It is not likely that Gaius himself ordered this innovation, as Philo states in *Legat.* 346 (No. 165).

No. 165
Source: *Literary.* Philo, *Legat.* 346
Date: Ca. 41–45 c.e.

[346] τοσαύτη μὲν οὖν τις ἡ περὶ τὸ ἦθος ἦν ἀνωμαλία πρὸς ἅπαντας, διαφερόντως δὲ πρὸς τὸ Ἰουδαίων γένος, ᾧ χαλεπῶς ἀπεχθανόμενος τὰς μὲν ἐν ταῖς ἄλλαις πόλεσι προσευχὰς ἀπὸ τῶν κατ' Ἀλεξάνδρειαν ἀρξάμενος σφετερίζεται, καταπλήσας εἰκόνων καὶ ἀνδριάντων τῆς ἰδίας μορφῆς—ὁ γὰρ ἑτέρων ἀνατιθέντων ἐφεὶς αὐτὸς ἱδρύετο δυνάμει—, τὸν δὲ ἐν τῇ ἱεροπόλει νεών, ὃς λοιπὸς ἦν ἄψαυστος ἀσυλίας ἠξιωμένος τῆς πάσης, μεθηρμόζετο καὶ μετεσχημάτιζεν εἰς οἰκεῖον ἱερόν, ἵνα Διὸς Ἐπιφανοῦς Νέου χρηματίζῃ Γαΐου.

[346] Such was the inconsistency of his behaviour towards everyone. But it was particularly marked towards the Jewish race. Because of his bitter hatred for it he appropriated the prayer halls [*proseuchai*] in every city, starting with those in Alexandria, and filled them with images and statues of himself. (For in allowing others to make dedications, he was virtually setting up the statues himself.) Then he proceeded to adapt and alter the temple [*naos*] in the Holy City, which still remained unmolested and was regarded as completely inviolable, into a shrine of his own, to be called that of "Gaius, the New Zeus made Manifest."

Literature: Smallwood, *Legatio*, 314–16.

Comments: For a general introduction, see the introductory comment to No. 138. In *Legat.* 339–348, Philo focusses on the character of Gaius, emphasizing the inconsistency of all his actions.

§346 *the Jewish race.* See the comment to No. 140, §133.... *he appropriated the synagogues...with images and statues of himself.* See comment to No. 140, §133 and No. 164, §152.... *in every city.* See the comment to No. 138, §45.... *into the shrine of his own.* By ordering the erection of a statue of himself in the Jerusalem temple, Gaius tried to make it a temple of the imperial cult (§§184–196 and §§337–338).... *Gaius, the New Zeus made Manifest.* An identification of Gaius with Jupiter is mentioned by Philo only in this passage but is attested in other ancient sources. The words "made Manifest" translate the adjective *epiphanēs*, a divine epithet, Epiphanes, often used by the Seleucid kings and later by the Roman emperors.

No. 166
Source: *Literary.* Philo, *Mos.* 2.214–16
Date: Ca. 30–45 C.E.

[214] συλλαβόντες ἄγουσιν αὐτὸν ἐπὶ τὸν ἄρχοντα, ᾧ συνήδρευον μὲν οἱ ἱερεῖς, παρειστήκει δὲ σύμπασα ἡ πληθὺς πρὸς ἀκρόασιν. [215] ἔθος γὰρ ἦν, ἀεὶ μὲν κατὰ τὸ παρεῖκον, προηγουμένως δὲ ταῖς ἑβδόμαις, ὡς ἐδήλωσα καὶ πρόσθεν, φιλοσοφεῖν, τοῦ μὲν ἡγεμόνος ὑφηγουμένου καὶ διδάσκοντος ἅ τε χρὴ πράττειν καὶ λέγειν, τῶν δ' εἰς καλοκἀγαθίαν ἐπιδιδόντων καὶ βελτιουμένων τά τε ἤθη καὶ τὸν βίον. [216] ἀφ' οὗ καὶ εἰσέτι νῦν φιλοσοφοῦσι ταῖς ἑβδόμαις Ἰουδαῖοι τὴν πάτριον φιλοσοφίαν τὸν χρόνον ἐκεῖνον ἀναθέντες ἐπιστήμῃ καὶ θεωρίᾳ τῶν περὶ φύσιν· τὰ γὰρ κατὰ πόλεις προσευκτήρια τί ἕτερόν ἐστιν ἢ διδασκαλεῖα φρονήσεως καὶ ἀνδρείας καὶ σωφροσύνης καὶ δικαιοσύνης εὐσεβείας τε καὶ ὁσιότητος καὶ συμπάσης ἀρετῆς, ᾗ κατανοεῖται καὶ κατορθοῦται τά τε ἀνθρώπεια καὶ θεῖα;

[214] Accordingly they arrested him, and took him before the ruler beside whom the priests were seated, while the whole multitude stood around to listen; [215] for it was customary on every day when opportunity offered, and pre-eminently on the seventh day, as I have explained above, to pursue the study of wisdom with the ruler [*hēgemōn*] expounding and instructing the people what they should say and do, while they received edification and betterment in moral principles and conduct. [216] Even now this practice is retained, and the Jews every seventh day occupy themselves with the philosophy of their fathers, dedicating that time to the acquiring of knowledge and the study of the truths of nature. For what are our places of prayer [*proseuktēria*] throughout the cities but schools [*didaskaleia*]of prudence and courage and temperance and justice and also of piety, holiness and every virtue by which duties to God and men are discerned and rightly performed?

Literature: Radice and Runia, *Bibliography 1937–1986*; Runia, *Bibliography 1987–1996*; Borgen, *Philo*, 74, 100, 171; Borgen, "Education", 65–67, 79–70; Culpepper, *Schools*, 211–12, Runia, *Creation*, 297–98; Schürer, *HJP*, 425, 427; Sterling, "School", 154–55; Binder, *Temple Courts*, 133–35, 434–35; Levine, *Ancient Synagogues*, 144–47; Claußen, *Versammlung*, 130–31.

Comments: Some of Philo's writings can be classified as ancient biography, among them *De vita Mosis*. This work seems to have been written for Gentile readers, probably those living outside both Alexandria and Egypt. It follows a chronological order but has many thematic digressions. In Philo's eyes, Moses was unique, "the god and king of the entire nation" (1.158), with extraordinary knowledge obtained from an ascetic life. In the second book Moses is presented as king (1–8), lawgiver (66–180), high priest (187–287) and prophet (288ff.).

§§209ff. tell about Moses and "the sacred seventh day," with all its pre-eminent beauty. On this day all should abstain from every kind of work and "meet in a solemn assembly" devoted to "the study of philosophy." This is the only purpose of this Jewish festival. Once a certain man disregarded these commandments and went through camp picking up sticks. Some pious persons saw it and wanted to kill him, but reflection caused them "to restrain the fierceness of their anger." The result is given in the quotation above.

§§214–215 present a court scene where both the civil and religious laws of the Torah were applied. "The all-great Moses" (§211) was the leader (*ho archōn*), while the priests sat as assessors (the verb *synedreuein*; see comment to No. 162) and the people stood around them.

§215 *to pursue the study of wisdom.* The activity in Moses' time is here described by the Greek word *philosophein*. Even in Philo's day the Jews are said to have been studying their ancestral philosophy (*philosophousi tēn patrion philosophian*). Philo's implicit claim is that the Sabbath activities in the synagogue have their roots in the time of Moses (cf. Acts 15:21 and "the ancestral philosophy" in *Legat.* 156, *Contempl.* 2 and *Somn.* 2.127, as well as "the ancestral laws" in *Prob.* 82; see also comment to No. 160, §30)…. *expounding and instructing.* As the leader (*ho hēgemōn*) of the people, Moses taught them his own laws. The first verb, *hyphēgeisthai*, means "show the way to, instruct in, pick up and develop (a subject)." The second is the common verb *didaskein*, "teach," often used about Jesus' activity in the synagogues.

§216 *places of prayer.* In Greek *proseuktērion*, "place of prayer,"used in reference to synagogues by Philo only here…. *Schools.* The common word for philosophical schools in Philo's time, *didaskaleion*, "teaching-place, school." See also "in every city thousands of schools" in *Spec.* 2.62 (No. 168) and "the schools of the holy laws" in *Dec.* 40 (No. 198)…. *prudence and courage and temperance and justice and also of piety, holiness and every virtue.* Philo wants to say to the Greeks that the philosophical study of the Jewish laws has a very practical purpose: "moral principles and conduct" in §215, and virtues in §216. The first four virtues in this list are the Greek cardinal virtues, often listed by Philo (*Agr.* 18, *Spec.* 2.62, and *QG* 1.13; 1.99). Piety, *eusebeia*, and holiness, *hosiotes*, both of them related to God, are the specific Jewish virtues, mentioned first in the list in *Spec.* 4.135 and *Prob.* 83. Both are described as queens among the virtues (*Dec.* 119). Piety is the source of all virtues (*Dec.* 52), the highest and greatest of them all (*Abr.* 60).

No. 167
Source: *Literary.* Philo, *Somn.* 2.123–28
Date: Ca. 40–45 C.E.

[123] χθὲς δ' οὐ πρῴην ἄνδρα τινὰ οἶδα τῶν ἡγεμονικῶν, ὅς, ἐπειδὴ τὴν προστασίαν καὶ ἐπιμέλειαν εἶχεν Αἰγύπτου, τὰ πάτρια κινεῖν ἡμῶν διενοήθη καὶ διαφερόντως τὸν ἁγιώτατον καὶ φρικωδέστατον περὶ τῆς ἑβδόμης ὑπάρχοντα νόμον καταλύειν καὶ ὑπηρετεῖν ἠνάγκαζεν αὐτῷ καὶ τὰ ἄλλα ποιεῖν παρὰ τὸ καθεστὼς ἔθος, νομίζων ἀρχὴν ἔσεσθαι καὶ τῆς περὶ τὰ ἄλλα ἐκδιαιτήσεως καὶ τῆς τῶν ὅλων παραβάσεως, εἰ τὸ ἐπὶ τῇ ἑβδόμῃ πάτριον ἀνελεῖν δυνηθείη. [124] καὶ μήθ' οὓς ἐβιάζετο ὁρῶν εἴκοντας τοῖς ἐπιτάγμασι μήτε τὴν ἄλλην πληθὺν ἠρεμοῦσαν, ἀλλὰ βαρέως καὶ τραχέως φέρουσαν τὸ πρᾶγμα καὶ ὡς ἐπ' ἀνδραποδισμῷ καὶ πορθήσει καὶ κατασκαφῇ πατρίδος πενθοῦντάς τε καὶ κατηφοῦντας, ἠξίου λόγῳ διδάσκειν παρανομεῖν, φάσκων· [125] εἰ πολεμίων ἔφοδος αἰφνίδιον γένοιτο ἢ κατακλυσμοῦ φορὰ τοῦ ποταμοῦ ταῖς πλημμύραις παραρρήξαντος τὸ χῶμα ἢ ῥιπὴ πυρὸς ἢ κεραυνία φλὸξ ἢ λιμὸς ἢ λοιμὸς ἢ σεισμὸς ἢ ὅσα ἄλλα κακὰ χειροποίητα καὶ θεήλατα, μεθ' ἡσυχίας πάσης οἴκοι διατρίψετε; [126] ἢ μετὰ τοῦ συνήθους σχήματος προελεύσεσθε, τὴν μὲν δεξιὰν εἴσω χεῖρα συναγαγόντες, τὴν δὲ ἑτέραν ὑπὸ τῆς ἀμπεχόνης παρὰ ταῖς λαγόσι πήξαντες, ἵνα μηδ' ἄκοντές τι τῶν εἰς τὸ σωθῆναι παράσχησθε; [127] καὶ καθεδεῖσθε ἐν τοῖς συναγωγίοις ὑμῶν, τὸν εἰωθότα θίασον ἀγείροντες καὶ ἀσφαλῶς τὰς ἱερὰς βίβλους ἀναγινώσκοντες κἂν εἴ τι μὴ τρανὲς εἴη διαπτύσσοντες καὶ τῇ πατρίῳ φιλοσοφίᾳ διὰ μακρηγορίας ἐνευκαιροῦντές τε καὶ ἐνσχολάζοντες; [128] ἀλλὰ γὰρ ἀποσεισάμενοι πάντα ταῦτα πρὸς τὴν ἑαυτῶν καὶ γονέων καὶ τέκνων καὶ τῶν ἄλλων οἰκειοτάτων καὶ φιλτάτων σωμάτων, εἰ δὲ δεῖ τἀληθὲς εἰπεῖν, καὶ κτημάτων καὶ χρημάτων, ὡς μηδὲ ταῦτα ἀφανισθείη, βοήθειαν ἀποδύσεσθε.

[123] Not long ago I knew one of the ruling class, who when he had Egypt in his charge and under his authority, purposed to disturb our ancestral customs and especially to do away with the law of the Seventh Day which we regard with most reverence and awe. He tried to compel men to do service to him on it and perform other actions, which contravene our established custom, thinking that if he could destroy the ancestral rule of the Sabbath it would lead the way to irregularity in all other matters, and a general backsliding. [124] And when he saw that those on whom he was exercising pressure were not submitting to his orders, and that the rest of the population instead of taking

the matter calmly were intensely indignant and shewed themselves as mournful and disconsolate as they would were their native city being sacked and razed, and its citizens being sold into captivity, he thought good to try to argue them into breaking the law. [125] "Suppose," he said, "there was a sudden inroad of the enemy or an inundation caused by the river rising and breaking through the dam, or a blazing conflagration or a thunderbolt or famine, or plague or earthquake, or any other trouble either of human or divine agency, will you stay at home perfectly quiet? [126] Or will you appear in public in your usual guise, with your right hand tucked inside and the left held close to the flank under the cloak lest you should even unconsciously do anything that might help to save you? [127] And will you sit in your conventicles [*synagōgiai*] and assemble your regular company and read in security your holy books, expounding any obscure point and in leisurely comfort discussing at length your ancestral philosophy? [128] No, you will throw all these off and gird yourselves up for the assistance of yourselves, your parents and your children, and the other persons who are nearest and dearest to you, and indeed also your chattels and wealth to save them too from annihilation."

Literature: Levine, *Ancient Synagogues*, 135–42; Schürer, *HJP*, 440; Binder, *Temple Courts*, 118–21, 402–3; Claußen, *Versammlung*, 147–48; Borgen, *Philo*, 80–101.

Comments: The second book of *De Somniis* comments on enigmatic dreams, which require a skilled interpreter to be explained. It begins with the two dreams of Joseph when he was a boy (5–154). The sun, the moon and the stars of the second dream (Gen 37:9–11) lead Philo to speak about impious men who attempt to change nature and do what is impossible to do. As examples he tells about Xerxes who shot his arrows at the sun, the Germans who tried to repel the tide with armed forces, and a tyrannous ruler in Alexandria who wanted to abrogate the Sabbath law (the quotation above).

§123 *one of the ruling class.* Flaccus, or according to one scholar, Philo's nephew Tiberius Julius Alexander.... *our ancestral customs.* In Greek *ta patria*, which has the same meaning as "your ancestral philosophy" in §127 (see comments to No. 162, §7.11 and No. 166, § 215).... *with most reverence and awe.* See Nos. 160, 162, 166, 168.

§126 The Therapeutae are described in the same way in No. 160, §30.

§127 *conventicles.* Philo uses the word *synagōgion* "meeting house."... *company.* The ordinary word for association, religious guild, confraternity in Greek. It is a very common organizational form in the Graeco-Roman world (in Latin, *collegium*).... *read in security your holy books.* See comment to No. 162, §7.12.... *expounding any obscure point.* Or "disclosing whatever is not quite clear."

Philo uses the verb *diaptyssein* "open and spread out, unfold, disclose." The Jews unfold the obscure passages or phrases of what has been read through various discussions.... *discussing at length.* Or "passing your time in long-winded discussions (*makregoriai*)." The passage may refer to a type of question and answer session held in the synagogues (see comment to No. 160, §31).

No. 168
Source: *Literary.* Philo, *Spec.* 2.61–64
Date: Ca. 30–45 c.e.

[61] προστάξας μέντοι μὴ διαπονεῖν τοῖς σώμασι κατὰ τὰς ἑβδόμας ἐφῆκε τὰς ἀμείνους πράξεις ἐπιτελεῖν· αὗται δ᾽ εἰσὶν αἱ διὰ λόγων καὶ δογμάτων τῶν κατ᾽ ἀρετήν· προτρέπει γὰρ φιλοσοφεῖν τότε βελτιοῦντας τὴν ψυχὴν καὶ τὸν ἡγεμόνα νοῦν. [62] ἀναπέπταται γοῦν ταῖς ἑβδόμαις μυρία κατὰ πᾶσαν πόλιν διδασκαλεῖα φρονήσεως καὶ σωφροσύνης καὶ ἀνδρείας καὶ δικαιοσύνης καὶ τῶν ἄλλων ἀρετῶν, ἐν οἷς οἱ μὲν ἐν κόσμῳ καθέζονται σὺν ἡσυχίᾳ τὰ ὦτα ἀνωρθιακότες μετὰ προσοχῆς πάσης ἕνεκα τοῦ διψῆν λόγων ποτίμων, ἀναστὰς δέ τις τῶν ἐμπειροτάτων ὑφηγεῖται τὰ ἄριστα καὶ συνοίσοντα, οἷς ἅπας ὁ βίος ἐπιδώσει πρὸς τὸ βέλτιον. [63] ἔστι δ᾽ ὡς ἔπος εἰπεῖν τῶν κατὰ μέρος ἀμυθήτων λόγων καὶ δογμάτων δύο τὰ ἀνωτάτω κεφάλαια, τό τε πρὸς θεὸν δι᾽εὐσεβείας καὶ ὁσιότητος καὶ τὸ πρὸς ἀνθρώπους διὰ φιλανθρωπίας καὶ δικαιοσύνης· ὧν ἑκάτερον εἰς πολυσχιδεῖς ἰδέας καὶ πάσας ἐπαινετὰς τέμνεται. [64] ἐξ ὧν δῆλόν ἐστιν, ὅτι Μωυσῆς οὐδένα καιρὸν ἀπράκτους ἐᾷ τοὺς χρωμένους αὐτοῦ ταῖς ἱεραῖς ὑφηγήσεσιν· ἀλλ᾽ ἐπειδὴ συνέστημεν ἐκ ψυχῆς καὶ σώματος, ἀπένειμε καὶ τῷ σώματι τὰ οἰκεῖα ἔργα καὶ τῇ ψυχῇ τὰ ἐπιβάλλοντα καὶ ἐφεδρεύειν τὰ ἕτερα τοῖς ἑτέροις ἐσπούδασεν, ἵνα πονοῦντος μὲν τοῦ σώματος ἡ ψυχὴ διαναπαύηται, ἀναπαύλῃ δὲ χρωμένου διαπονῇ, καὶ οἱ ἄριστοι τῶν βίων, ὅ τε θεωρητικὸς καὶ ὁ πρακτικός, ἀμείβωσιν ἀντιπαραχωροῦντες ἀλλήλοις, ὁ μὲν πρακτικὸς λαχὼν ἑξάδα κατὰ τὴν τοῦ σώματος ὑπηρεσίαν, ὁ δὲ θεωρητικὸς ἑβδομάδα πρὸς ἐπιστήμην καὶ τελειότητα διανοίας.

[61] Further, when He forbids bodily labour on the seventh day, He permits the exercise of the higher activities, namely, those employed in the study of the principles of virtue's lore. For the law bids us take the time for studying philosophy and thereby improve the soul and the dominant mind. [62] So each seventh day there stand wide open in every city thousands of schools [*didaskaleia*] of good sense, temperance, courage, justice and the other virtues in which the scholars sit in order

quietly with ears alert and with full attention, so much do they thirst for the draught which the teacher's words supply, while one of special experience rises and sets forth what is the best and sure to be profitable and will make the whole of life grow to something better. [63] But among the vast number of particular truths and principles there studied, there stand out practically high above the others two main heads: one of duty to God as shewn by piety and holiness, one of duty to men as shewn by humanity and justice, each of them splitting up into multiform branches, all highly laudable. [64] These things shew clearly that Moses does not allow any of those who use his sacred instruction to remain inactive at any season. But since we consist of body and soul, he assigned to the body its proper tasks and similarly to the soul what falls to its share, and his earnest desire was, that the two should be waiting to relieve each other. Thus while the body is working, the soul enjoys a respite, but when the body takes its rest, the soul resumes its work, and thus the best forms of life, the theoretical and the practical, take their turn in replacing each other. The practical life has six as its number allotted for ministering to the body. The theoretical has seven for knowledge and perfection of the mind.

Literature: Borgen, *Philo*, 100–101, 171; Sterling, "School", 154–55; Levine, *Ancient Synagogues*, 144–45; Binder, *Temple Courts*, 133–35, 434–35; Claußen, *Versammlung*, 130–31.

Comments: The second book of *De specialibus legibus* covers laws that can be related to the Third, Fourth and Fifth Commandments of the Decalogue. §§56–70 deal with the holy seventh day (cf. Nos. 162, 166).

§61 *the study of the principles of virtue's lore.* A description of the Jewish study of philosophy on the seventh day (see comment on No. 166, §215).... *the law bids.* The Greek text has only *protrepei*, which means "He impels."... *in every city thousands of schools.* See comment on No. 166, §216. Yonge translates the phrase as "innumerable lessons," but the general meaning of *didaskaleion* is "teaching-place, school." Menge-Gütling translates it as "Schule, Schulzimmer, Klasse." *good sense, temperance, courage, justice.* The four cardinal virtues in the Graeco-Roman society. On lists of virtues in Philo, see comment on No. 166, §216. *scholars.* The Greek text has only "they," perhaps a reference to the common people.... *the draught which the teacher's words supply.* In Greek *logoi potimoi* "drinkable words."... *one of special experience.* One of those who by experience are most learned (see comment to No. 162, §7.11).... *rises.* See comment on No. 160, §31.... *sets forth.* In Greek *hypēgeitai.* See comment on No. 166, §215.... *piety and holiness.* See comment on No. 166, §216.... *his sacred instruction.* Or "his holy guidelines." The noun is related to the verb "sets forth" above.... *for knowledge and perfection of the mind.* A double purpose of the teaching in the synagogues (see comment to No. 150, §216; cf. improving of the soul and the mind in §61).

No. 169
Source: *Literary.* Philo, *Spec.* 3.169–71
Date: Ca. 30–45 c.e.

[169] Ἀγοραὶ καὶ βουλευτήρια καὶ δικαστήρια καὶ θίασοι καὶ σύλλογοι πολυανθρώπων ὁμίλων καὶ ὁ ἐν ὑπαίθρῳ βίος διὰ λόγων καὶ πράξεων κατὰ πολέμους καὶ κατ᾽ εἰρήνην ἀνδράσιν ἐφαρμόζουσι, θηλείαις δὲ οἰκουρία καὶ ἡ ἔνδον μονή, παρθένοις μὲν εἴσω κλισιάδων τὴν μέσαυλον ὅρον πεποιημέναις, τελείαις δὲ ἤδη γυναιξὶ τὴν αὔλειον. [170] διττὸν γὰρ πόλεων εἶδος, μειζόνων καὶ βραχυτέρων· αἱ μὲν οὖν μείζους ἄστη καλοῦνται, οἰκίαι δ᾽ αἱ βραχύτεραι. τὴν δ᾽ ἑκατέρων προστασίαν διειλήχασιν ἄνδρες μὲν τῶν μειζόνων, ἧς ὄνομα πολιτεία, γυναῖκες δὲ τῶν βραχυτέρων, ἧς ὄνομα οἰκονομία. [171] μηδὲν οὖν ἔξω τῶν κατὰ τὴν οἰκονομίαν πολυπραγμονείτω γυνὴ ζητοῦσα μοναυλίαν μηδ᾽ οἷα νομὰς κατὰ τὰς ὁδοὺς ἐν ὄψεσιν ἀνδρῶν ἑτέρων ἐξεταζέσθω, πλὴν εἰς ἱερὸν ὁπότε δέοι βαδίζειν, φροντίδα ποιουμένη καὶ τότε μὴ πληθυούσης ἀγορᾶς, ἀλλ᾽ ἐπανεληλυθότων οἴκαδε τῶν πλείστων, ἐλευθέρας τρόπον καὶ τῷ ὄντι ἀστῆς ἐν ἠρεμίᾳ θυσίας ἐπιτελοῦσα καὶ εὐχὰς εἰς ἀποτροπὴν κακῶν καὶ μετουσίαν ἀγαθῶν.

[169] Market-places and council-halls and law-courts and gatherings and meetings where a large number of people are assembled, and open-air life with full scope for discussion and action—all these are suitable to men both in war and peace. The women are best suited to the indoor life which never strays from the house, within which the middle door is taken by the maidens as their boundary, and the outer door by those who have reached full womanhood. [170] Organized communities are of two sorts, the greater which we call cities and the smaller which we call households. Both of these have their governors; the government of the greater is assigned to men under the name of statesmanship, that of the lesser, known as household management, to women. [171] A woman, then, should not be a busybody, meddling with matters outside her household concerns, but should seek a life of seclusion. She should not shew herself off like a vagrant in the streets before the eyes of other men, except when she has to go to the temple [*hieron*], and even then she should take pains to go, not when the market is full, but when most people have gone home, and so like a free-born lady worthy of the name, with everything quiet around

her, make her oblations [*thysias*] and offer her prayers to avert the evil and gain the good.

Literature: Horst, *Flaccus*, 179–80; Binder, *Temple Courts*, 122–30, 407–9; Claußen, *Versammlung*, 132–38.

Comments: The third book of *De specialibus legibus* covers laws that can be related to the Sixth and Seventh Commandments. When Philo comes to the commandment of not murdering, he discusses different cases. §§169ff. deals with assaults that do not cause death. The case in Deut 25:11 makes him reflect on the modesty demanded of women.

§171 *except when she has to go to the temple*. See comment to No. 161, §8.... make her oblations and offer her prayers. See comment to No. 161, §8.

No. 170
Source: *Papyrus Text. CPJ* 1.138
Date: Second half of the first century B.C.E.

].—ἐπὶ τῆς γ[ε]γηθείσης σψγαγωγῆς εν τῆι προσευχῆι

Δημητ]ρίωι τῶν [(προώτων)] φίλων καὶ θ[υ(ρωρῶν)] (?) καὶ εἰσαγγελέων καὶ ἀρχυπηρε(τῶν)

]-Κάμακος [...]..[......]ξ[......].[..γραμ]ματεὺς

..].....[   ]κυον εἰς τὴν σ[ύνοδον

.]ου σὺν τοῖ[ς.]....[.......].ρασιος καὶ συλλελόχισται   5

]ρκως το ε.[.].αλλ εμ[....]υ ἐν τοῖς ἐρχο.[.].....ντας

.]με δικαι .[..]......[......]ειν ἐφ' ᾦτε ἐτεάς [.]ς

σ]υνόδου[   ].φ[.]..[...]καιροις

.]ωι κατ' ἔτο[ς.]ει επτ.[.......]ιου γ.ιλι...ωι με[.]ε

.]ινων ε.[.]σου   κ[οινοῦ(?)...ταφι]αστῶν ἐκ τῆς   10

..]τε ατε[.].πον[.........]φαλλισμων κα [2–5 letters]

].ο τοῦ ἐσομένου και[νοῦ.....οὑ]δ ' [[ι]] ἐν αὑλῶ[ι 2–6 letters]

..]μαι Ευδ[..] . ι[...........]τοῦ συνταφιά[στου]

..]σεται [ο]ῖς προσ[ήκει.......γ]ραμματεῖ ἀκολ[ούθως]

.]εἰς ἱερο.[..].απ[...........]ια τοῦ δελ.[15

το]ῖς λει[του]ρ[γ............]συνόδου τοῦ[

...].......[...............].θησεται ξ[

]αθες[

...At the assembly [synagōgē] that took place in the prayer hall [pro-seuchē]

To Demetrios of the first friends and the door-keepers (?) [thyrōros] and the ushers [eisangeloi] and the chief attendants [archypēretai]
...of Kamax...scribe [grammateus]...
...to the association
...with...and has been incorporated
...on the condition that
...association [synodos]...the times
...every year
...the corporation of...taphiastai
...future new
...the syntaphiastes
...whom it concerns...to the scribe [grammateus] according
...the association [synodos]

Literature: Binder, *Temple Courts*, 370, 447–48; Levine, *Ancient Synagogue*, 83 n. 10, 87 n. 44; Runesson, *Origins*, 172, 174, 452; Kasher, *The Jews*, 138–39.

Comments: This badly preserved papyrus attests the meeting of a burial association inside an Egyptian synagogue. While the poor state of the document makes interpretation problematic, the mention of several officers such as the scribe, the chief attendants, the ushers, and (possibly) the door-keepers indicates that the group was highly structured and well-organized.

No. 171
Source: *Inscription. JIGRE* 125 (*CIJ* 2.1449)
Date: 145–116 B.C.E. (original); 47–31 B.C.E. (replacement)

Βασιλίσσης καὶ βασι|λέως προσταξάντων | ἀντὶ τῆς
προανακει|μένης περὶ τῆς ἀναθέσε|ως τῆς προσευχῆς πλα||κὸς ἡ

ὑπογεγραμμένη| ἐπιγραφήτω. [*vacat*] | βασιλεὺς Πτολεμαῖος
Εὐ|εργέτης τὴν προσευχὴν ἄσυλον. | *Regina et* | | *rex iusser(un)t.*

On the orders of the Queen and King, in place of the previous tablet concerning the dedication of the prayer hall [*proseuchē*], let the following be written: King Ptolemy Euergetes proclaimed the prayer hall [*proseuchē*] inviolate. The Queen and King issued the order.

Literature: Binder, *Temple Courts*, 239–40, 436–39; Levine, *Ancient Synagogue*, 83 n. 7, 84 n. 15, 85–86, 87, n. 39; Runesson, *Origins*, 432–33, 451; Fraser, *Ptolemaic Alexandria*, 1.283–84; Fine, *This Holy Place*, 26; Griffiths, *Egypt*, 12; Krauss, *Synagogale Altertümer*, 264–67; Dion, "Synagogues et temples," 55, 57–59; Schürer, *HJP*, 3.1.47; Horsley, *New Documents*, 4.201; Kasher, *The Jews*, 110–11.

Comments: This inscription, erected during the reigns of Cleopatra VII and either Ptolemy XIV (47–44 B.C.E.) or Ptolemy XV (44–31 B.C.E.), was a replacement for an earlier proclamation probably issued by Ptolemy VIII Euergetes II (145–116 B.C.E.). It indicates that this synagogue enjoyed the same right of asylum granted many non-Jewish temples in Egypt (cf. *OGIS* 761). Literary references hint that this privilege was extended to other synagogues in that country, at least during the Hellenistic period (*CPJ* 1.129 [Nos. 135–37]; 3 Macc 3:27–29; 4:17–18 [No. 147]). Its bestowal further highlights the sacred nature of the synagogues in Egypt. The appearance of Latin in the last two lines of this inscription may indicate the presence of a nearby Roman camp.

No. 172
Source: *Inscription. JIGRE* 126
Date: First to early second century C.E.

Παποῦς οἰκο|δόμηση τὴν |προσευχὴν |ὑπὲρ αὐτοῦ| καὶ τῆς
<γ>υν| |αικὸς καὶ τ|ῶν τέκνων· | (ἔτους) δ' Φαρμοῦθι <ζ>'.

Papous erected the prayer hall [*proseuchē*] on behalf of himself and his wife and children. In the 4th year, Pharmouthi 7.

Literature: Binder, *Temple Courts*, 377; Levine, *Ancient Synagogue*, 83, n. 7, 87, n. 40; Hengel, "Proseuche und Synagoge," 159 n. 6; Noy, "A Jewish Place of Prayer," 118–22.

Comments: One of three extant examples of a private synagogue dedication in Egypt (cf. *JIGRE* 13, 28 [Nos. 144, 152]), this inscription dates later than the other two, as can be determined not only from the letter forms, but from the absence of the standard dedication to the Ptolemaic royal family.

3.1.7   *Galatia*

3.1.7.1   *Iconium*

No. 173
Source: *Literary.* Acts 14:1–7
Date: Ca. 90–110 C.E.

[1] Ἐγένετο δὲ ἐν Ἰκονίῳ κατὰ τὸ αὐτὸ εἰσελθεῖν αὐτοὺς εἰς τὴν συναγωγὴν τῶν Ἰουδαίων καὶ λαλῆσαι οὕτως ὥστε πιστεῦσαι Ἰουδαίων τε καὶ Ἑλλήνων πολὺ πλῆθος. [2] οἱ δὲ ἀπειθήσαντες Ἰουδαῖοι ἐπήγειραν καὶ ἐκάκωσαν τὰς ψυχὰς τῶν ἐθνῶν κατὰ τῶν ἀδελφῶν. [3] ἱκανὸν μὲν οὖν χρόνον διέτριψαν παρρησιαζόμενοι ἐπὶ τῷ κυρίῳ τῷ μαρτυροῦντι [ἐπὶ] τῷ λόγῳ τῆς χάριτος αὐτοῦ, διδόντι σημεῖα καὶ τέρατα γίνεσθαι διὰ τῶν χειρῶν αὐτῶν. [4] ἐσχίσθη δὲ τὸ πλῆθος τῆς πόλεως, καὶ οἱ μὲν ἦσαν σὺν τοῖς Ἰουδαίοις, οἱ δὲ σὺν τοῖς ἀποστόλοις. [5] ὡς δὲ ἐγένετο ὁρμὴ τῶν ἐθνῶν τε καὶ Ἰουδαίων σὺν τοῖς ἄρχουσιν αὐτῶν ὑβρίσαι καὶ λιθοβολῆσαι αὐτούς, [6] συνιδόντες κατέφυγον εἰς τὰς πόλεις τῆς Λυκαονίας Λύστραν καὶ Δέρβην καὶ τὴν περίχωρον, [7] κἀκεῖ εὐαγγελιζόμενοι ἦσαν.

[1] The same thing occurred in Iconium, where Paul and Barnabas went into the Jewish synagogue [*synagōgē*] and spoke in such a way that a great number of both Jews and Greeks became believers. [2] But the unbelieving Jews stirred up the Gentiles and poisoned their minds against the brothers. [3] So they remained for a long time, speaking boldly for the Lord, who testified to the word of his grace by granting signs and wonders to be done through them. [4] But the residents of the city were divided; some sided with the Jews, and some with the apostles. [5] And when an attempt was made by both Gentiles and Jews, with their rulers, to mistreat them and to stone them, [6] the apostles learned of it and fled to Lystra and Derbe, cities of Lycaonia, and to the surrounding country; [7] and there they continued proclaiming the good news.

Literature: As a general reference to commentaries see Barrett, Fitzmyer and Jervell, *Comm., ad loc.* Binder, *Temple Courts*, 271; Levine, *Ancient Synagogue*, 108–11; Levinskaya, *Book of Acts*, 150–52; Stegemann, *Synagoge und Obrigkeit*, 124–25, 158–59.

Comments: In spite of what happened in Pisidian Antioch (Acts 13:14–52), Paul and Barnabas went to "the synagogue of the Jews" when they came to Iconium. The same phrase appears in Acts 13:3; 17:1, 10 (see comments on Acts 13:5, No. 30). The words at the beginning of v. 1 (*kata to auto* "according

the same") probably mean "according their custom" (17:2) and not "together."
The word "spoke" (*lalein* "speak") recalls Paul's sermon at the synagogue
service in Pisidian Antioch (13:17–41) and also the general terms in Acts
13:5, "proclaim the word of God" and Acts 14:7, "proclaim the good news"
(*euanggelizein* "tell the good news").

There are many categories in this short passage. In the synagogue there
were Jews and Greeks, these last probably God-fearers or sympathizers (see
comment to No. 90). Some of each group became Jesus-believers while others did not. Outside the synagogue there were the Gentiles, called also the
residents (in Greek *plēthos* "crowd") of the city. Also mentioned were the rulers
of both the Jews and the Gentiles.

What happened in Iconium is in many ways a recurrent pattern in Acts:
proclamation of the Gospel to Jews and God-fearers in the synagogues,
divisions in the synagogues between those who believe and those who do
not, the latter stirring up the Gentiles against the Jesus-believers so that the
rulers and people of the city are divided, some siding with those who reject
the messege, others with the believers. Then follows the mistreatment of the
believers by some groups, including the rulers, and the flight of the apostle(s)
(see the comment on No. 174). On the negative treatment of Jesus-believers,
see comment on No. 92.

3.1.7.2   *Pisidian Antioch*

No. 174
Source: *Literary*. Acts 13:14–16, 42–48
Date: Ca. 90–110 c.e.

[14] Αὐτοὶ δὲ διελθόντες ἀπὸ τῆς Πέργης παρεγένοντο εἰς Ἀντιόχειαν
τὴν Πισιδίαν, καὶ [εἰσ] ελθόντες εἰς τὴν συναγωγὴν τῇ ἡμέρᾳ τῶν
σαββάτων ἐκάθισαν. [15] μετὰ δὲ τὴν ἀνάγνωσιν τοῦ νόμου καὶ τῶν
προφητῶν ἀπέστειλαν οἱ ἀρχισυνάγωγοι πρὸς αὐτοὺς λέγοντες· ἄνδρες
ἀδελφοί, εἴ τίς ἐστιν ἐν ὑμῖν λόγος παρακλήσεως πρὸς τὸν λαόν, λέγετε.
[16] Ἀναστὰς δὲ Παῦλος καὶ κατασείσας τῇ χειρὶ εἶπεν· ἄνδρες
Ἰσραηλῖται καὶ οἱ φοβούμενοι τὸν θεόν, ἀκούσατε.

[42] Ἐξιόντων δὲ αὐτῶν παρεκάλουν εἰς τὸ μεταξὺ σάββατον
λαληθῆναι αὐτοῖς τὰ ῥήματα ταῦτα. [43] λυθείσης δὲ τῆς συναγωγῆς
ἠκολούθησαν πολλοὶ τῶν Ἰουδαίων καὶ τῶν σεβομένων προσηλύτων τῷ
Παύλῳ καὶ τῷ Βαρναβᾷ, οἵτινες προσλαλοῦντες αὐτοῖς ἔπειθον αὐτοὺς
προσμένειν τῇ χάριτι τοῦ θεοῦ. [44] Τῷ δὲ ἐρχομένῳ σαββάτῳ σχεδὸν
πᾶσα ἡ πόλις συνήχθη ἀκοῦσαι τὸν λόγον τοῦ κυρίου. [45] ἰδόντες δὲ
οἱ Ἰουδαῖοι τοὺς ὄχλους ἐπλήσθησαν ζήλου καὶ ἀντέλεγον τοῖς ὑπὸ
Παύλου λαλουμένοις βλασφημοῦντες. [46] παρρησιασάμενοί τε ὁ
Παῦλος καὶ ὁ Βαρναβᾶς εἶπαν· ὑμῖν ἦν ἀναγκαῖον πρῶτον λαληθῆναι

τὸν λόγον τοῦ θεοῦ· ἐπειδὴ ἀπωθεῖσθε αὐτὸν καὶ οὐκ ἀξίους κρίνετε
ἑαυτοὺς τῆς αἰωνίου ζωῆς, ἰδοὺ στρεφόμεθα εἰς τὰ ἔθνη. [47] οὕτως
γὰρ ἐντέταλται ἡμῖν ὁ κύριος· τέθεικά σε εἰς φῶς ἐθνῶν τοῦ εἶναί
σε εἰς σωτηρίαν ἕως ἐσχάτου τῆς γῆς. [48] Ἀκούοντα δὲ τὰ ἔθνη
ἔχαιρον καὶ ἐδόξαζον τὸν λόγον τοῦ κυρίου καὶ ἐπίστευσαν ὅσοι ἦσαν
τεταγμένοι εἰς ζωὴν αἰώνιον·

[14] But they went on from Perga and came to Antioch in Pisidia. And
on the Sabbath day they went into the synagogue [*synagōgē*] and sat
down. [15] After the reading of the law and the prophets, the officials
of the synagogue [*archisynagōgoi*] sent them a message, saying, "Brothers, if you have any word of exhortation for the people, give it." [16]
So Paul stood up and with a gesture began to speak: "You Israelites,
and others who fear God, listen.

[42] As Paul and Barnabas were going out, the people urged them
to speak about these things again the next Sabbath. [43] When the
meeting of the synagogue [*synagōgē*] broke up, many Jews and devout
converts to Judaism followed Paul and Barnabas, who spoke to them
and urged them to continue in the grace of God. [44] The next Sabbath almost the whole city gathered to hear the word of the Lord. [45]
But when the Jews saw the crowds, they were filled with jealousy; and
blaspheming, they contradicted what was spoken by Paul. [46] Then
both Paul and Barnabas spoke out boldly, saying, "It was necessary that
the word of God should be spoken first to you. Since you reject it and
judge yourselves to be unworthy of eternal life, we are now turning to
the Gentiles. [47] For so the Lord has commanded us, saying, 'I have
set you to be a light for the Gentiles, so that you may bring salvation
to the ends of the earth.'" [48] When the Gentiles heard this, they
were glad and praised the word of the Lord; and as many as had been
destined for eternal life became believers.

Literature: As a general reference to commentaries see Barrett, Fitzmyer and
Jervell, *Comm., ad loc.* Binder, *Temple Courts,* 271–72; Levine, *Ancient Synagogue,*
108–11, 135–47, 393–402; Claußen, *Versammlung,* 74–75, 216, 261; Runesson,
Origins, 214–15, 219–21; Stegemann, *Synagoge und Obrigkeit,* 124–34; Barclay,
Jews, 245; Levinskaya, *Book of Acts,* 129–30, 150.

Comments: Paul and Barnabas came to Antioch of Pisidia in the late 40s
or early 50s, and Luke wrote about their visit in the 80s. Acts 13 is an important source on the Sabbath-morning liturgy in the first century C.E. (see also
comments on No. 33), for it presents the basic outline of a service (or major

portion thereof). There is the reading of the Scripture, both a section from the Torah and the Prophets (v. 15; cf v. 27). Then there is a sermon, according to Luke a "word of exhortation" (*paraklēsis*, "exhortation, encouragement"; the same phrase is used about the Letter to the Hebrews, Heb 13:2). What is told in vv. 17–41, however, is not a hortatory speech, but a sermon in Lucan style (cf. Acts 2, 7). Paul speaks about God's promises to his people Israel and their fulfilment through Jesus, a savior to Israel and a light for the Gentiles (v. 47), as attested by several passages from the Scripture (vv. 22, 33, 34, 35 and 41), all of them from the Prophets and the Psalms as quoted from the Septuagint.

There are both Jews and God-fearers in the synagogue (v. 16, 26) and also proselytes (v. 43). There is more than one official of the synagogue (*archisynagōgoi*; see the comments on No. 47), and they send word (by an attendant?) inviting the two "brothers" (fellow Jews) to speak if they wanted to. Were Paul and Barnabas sitting at special seats, as coming from abroad or as teachers (cf. Jas 2:2–4, No. 196)?

Paul stood when preaching (v. 16) as opposed to Jesus, who sat (Luke 4:20). Does not Luke care about such details? Was there at this time no general fixed order of standing or sitting? Or was there one custom in Palestine and another in the Diaspora? Philo states that the preacher stood while expounding the Scriptures (*Spec.* 2.62, No. 168). Diaspora synagogues may well have been influenced by Greek customs.

What happened after the sermon has a programmatic character for the ensuing missionary reports (cf. Acts 18:5–7 and 28:23–28). It is related to people of different categories in the synagogue meetings who heard the good news about Jesus, the savior of Israel. The situation is not quite clear, but already in the synagogue Jews and Greeks listened to the message about Jesus as the Messiah, with some of them reacting positively, others negatively. When Paul and Barnabas left the synagogue, some asked them to come back next Sabbath. The synagogue gathering (in Greek *synagōgē*) broke up and many literally followed Paul and Barnabas so they could continue their teaching.

Many more Jews and Greeks wanted to hear them next Sabbath meeting. In this situation some Jews were filled with zeal for God or Torah (*zēlos* means "zeal, ernest concern" or "jealousy, envy") and tried to stop the apostasy, like Phinehas in Num 25 or Saul himself at the beginning of Acts. Even devout women of high standing and leading men of the city helped these zealous Jews (v. 50). On the mistreatment of Jesus-believers, see comment on No. 92. With reference to the Scripture—mission to the Gentiles is a part of the promises to Israel—Paul left the synagogue and spoke the word of God to the Gentiles. The exodus from the synagogue became in Luke's eyes a historical legitimation of new communities outside the synagogue (Stegemann).

3.1.8 *Hungary*

3.1.8.1 *Osijek (Mursa)*

No. 175
Source: *Inscription. IJO* 1, Pan5 (*CIJ* 1.678a)
Date: 198–210 C.E.

[pro salute im]p(eratorum)
[L(ucii) Sept(imii) Severi Pe]rtinacis,
[et M(arci) Aur(elii) Antonini] Aug(ustorum)
[[et P(ublii) Sep(timii) Getae nob(ilissimi) Cae(saris)]]
[et Iuliae Aug(ustae) matris cast]rorum   5
[- - - - - ?Secu]ndus
[- - - - - pro]seucham
[- - - - - vetu]state
[collapsam a so]lo
[restituit].   10

[For the health of the] Emperors [L(ucius) Sept(imius) Severus Pe]rtinax, [and M(arcus) Aur(elius) Antoninus], the Augusti [[and P(ublius) Sep(timius) Geta, the most noble Cae(sar)]] [and Julia Aug(usta), mother of the] camps, [?Secu]ndus [restored from the foundations] the prayer hall [*proseucha*], which had [collapsed] from old age.

Literature: Pinterović, "Mursa," 28–29; idem, "Synagogue," 61–74; idem, *Mursa*, 63–65; Radan, "Comments," 266–67; Selem, *Religions Orientales*, 258–61; Scheiber, *Jewish Inscriptions*, 51–55 (no. 8); Schürer, *HJP*, 3.1.73; Trebilco, *Jewish Communities*, 260 n. 38.

Comments: While the above inscription is quite fragmentary, much of it can be reconstructed from its partial references to the Emperor Septimius Severus (146–211 C.E.), his wife Julia Domna, and his sons Aurelius Antoninus (Caracalla) and Septimius Geta. The name of the last was erased following his murder by Caracalla in 211 C.E.

The monument appears to record the restoration of a prayer-hall (called in Latin a *proseucha*; cf. No. 183) that had suffered major damage. If so, the structure referenced has yet to be discovered.

3.1.9 *Italy*

3.1.9.1 *Ostia*

No. 176
Source: *Inscription. JIWE* 1.13
Date: Second half of the second century C.E. (original); second half of the third century C.E. (reinscribed lines 6–7).

pro salute Aug(usti/ustorum).
οἰκοδόμησεν κὲ αἰπο[ί-]
ησεν ἐκ τῶν αὐτοῦ δο-
μάτων καὶ τὴν κειβωτὸν
ἀνέθηκεν νόμῳ ἁγίῳ   5
[[Μίνδις Φαῦστος με-]]
[[[τὰ τῶν ἰ]]][[διῶ]][[[ν]]].

For the health of the Emperor(s). [[Mindi(u)s Faustus]] [[[with his household]]] built and produced (it) from his own gifts and erected the ark for the holy law.

Literature: Squarciapino, "La Sinagoga di Ostia," 315; idem, "Plotius Fortunatus," 183–84; Guarducci, *Epigrafia greca,* 15–17 (fig. 5); *SEG* 45.916; Meiggs, *Roman Ostia,* 587–88; Kraabel, "The Diaspora Synagogue," 497–500; Schürer, *HJP* 3.1.82; Horsley, *New Documents,* 4.112 (no. 25); White *Social Origins,* 2.392–94 (no. 84); idem, "Synagogue and Society," 39–41; Binder, *Temple Courts,* 326–31; Runesson, "The Synagogue at Ancient Ostia," 85–88; Levine, *The Ancient Synagogue,* 276; Claußen, *Versammlung,* 197–99.

Comments: Recovered in the vestibule of the Ostia synagogue, this discarded inscription was used as part of the flooring in that building's final renovations in the fourth century C.E. The stone dates two centuries earlier, when it recorded the dedication of an unnamed appurtenance of the synagogue. The mention of an ark's erection in line three suggests that this bequest was a wooden pedestal upon which the holy shrine was set.

The original gift apparently needed to be replaced a century later, since the initial donor's name was scratched out and "Mindi(u)s Faustus" inscribed over it in letter-forms dating to that period. The construction of an *aedicula* in the fourth-century renovations would have made such a replacement obsolete, leading to the stone's removal to secondary use.

The word *doma,* "gift," (ll. 3–4) is rare outside of the LXX, where it appears fifty-four times, often describing sacred gifts (e.g., Num 18:11, 29; Deut 12:11, LXX). Accordingly, the term exists elsewhere in the epigraphic record only in several fourth-century inscriptions from the synagogue at Sardis (nos. 20–22 in Kroll, "The Greek Inscriptions").

No. 177
Source: *Inscription. JIWE* 1.14
Date: First to second century C.E.

Plotio Fortunato
archisyn(agogo) fec(erunt) Plotius
Ampliatus Secundinus
Secunda p(a?)t(ri?) n(ostro?) et Ofilia Basilia coiugi b(ene) m(erenti).

For Plotius Fortunatus, ruler of the synagogue [*archisynagogo*]. Plotius
Ampliatus, Secundinus and Secunda built it (for our father?), and Ofilia
Basilia for her well-deserving husband.

Literature: Squarciapino, "Plotius Fortunatus," 187–91; Schürer, *HJP* 3.1.82;
Horsley, *New Documents*, 4.214 (no. 12), 5.148 (no. 113); Rajak & Noy, "*Archisynagogoi*"; Binder, *Temple Courts*, 335; Runesson, "The Synagogue at Ancient
Ostia," 91–92; idem, "Oldest Original Synagogue," 427–28; White "Reading
the Ostia Synagogue," 451 n. 74; Levine, *The Ancient Synagogue*, 278.

Comments: This monument was found south of Ostia in the region of Piana-
bella-Procoio, where an ancient necropolis once rested. Given the proximity of
the find to the city, it is likely that Plotius Fortunatus served as the *archisynagōgos*
of the synagogue at Ostia during the first or second centuries C.E.

For additional information about the nature of this office, see No. 179,
below.

No. 178
Source: *Inscription. JIWE* 1.18 (*CIJ* 1.533)
Date: Second century C.E. (?)

[synagoga/universitas/collegium?] *Iudeorum*
[in col(onia) Ost(iensi) commor]antium qui compara
[verunt ex conlat?]ione locum C(aio) Iulio Iusto
[gerusiarche ad m]unimentum struendum
[donavit, rogantib?]us Livio Dionysio patre et   5
[.........]no gerusiarche et Antonio
[.....dia] biu anno ipsorum, consent(iente) ge[r-
us(ia). C(aius) Iulius Iu]stus gerusiarches fecit sib[i]
[et coniugi] suae lib(ertis) lib(ertabusque) posterisque eorum.
[in fro]nte p(edes) XVIII, in agro p(edes) XVII.   10

[The congregation/community/association?] of the Jews living [in the
colony of Ostia?], who received the plot [from a contribution, gave?]
it to Gaius Julius Justus [ruler of the council (*gerusiarch*)] to erect a

monument. [On the motion?] of Livius Dionysius the father [*pater*] and...NUS the ruler of the council [*gerusiarch*] and Antonius...[for] life, in their year, with the consent of the council [*gerusia*]. [Gaius Julius Ju]stus, ruler of the council [*gerusiarch*], built it for himself and his wife, and his freedmen and freedwomen and their descendants. Eighteen feet wide, seventeen feet deep.

Literature: Ghislanzoni, *Notizie degli scavi* (1906), 410–15; Squarciapino, "Plotius Fortunatus," 186; Meiggs, *Roman Ostia*, 389; Kraabel, "The Diaspora Synagogue," 499 n. 77; Schürer, *HJP* 3.1.82; Kant, "Jewish Inscriptions," 693–95; White, *Social Origins*, 2.394–97 (no. 85); idem, "Synagogue and Society," 42–48; Runesson, "The Synagogue at Ancient Ostia," 88–89; Levine, *The Ancient Synagogue*, 278.

Comments: This monument was discovered at Castel Porziano near the sixteenth milestone of the road to Lavinium, an area long associated with Ostian burials. Though much of the stone's left side is missing and needs to be reconstructed, the general contours of the inscription are clear: it records the resolution of a Jewish community or association that bestowed a memorial plot upon one of its leaders, Gaius Julius Justus.

The inscription is particularly notable for its reference to the ruling body of the Jewish group, the *gerusia* ("council," ll. 7–8), as well as the delineation of its officers. These last included the *pater* ("father," l. 5), the *gerusiarch* ("ruler of the council," ll. 4, 6, 8), and a third official whose title has been lost, but who apparently held his position *dia biu*, "for life" (l. 7; cf. No. 103, l. 3). Such an organizational scheme mirrored that of the Graeco-Roman *collegia*—incorporated associations tied to specific trades, religions or ethnic groups. The precise relationship of this leadership council to the wider Jewish community at Ostia—as well as to the organization of the synagogue there—remains unclear.

No. 179
Source: Source: *Archaeological*.
Date: Second half of the first century C.E.

Literature: Floriani Squarciapino, "Second campagna di Scavao"; eadem, "Ebrei"; eadem, "Synagogue at Ostia"; eadem, "Most Ancient Synagogue"; Zevi, "La sinagoga di Ostia"; Pavolini, "Via Severiana"; Zappa, "Nuovi bolli laterizi"; Kraabel, "The Diaspora Synagogue," 497–500; Foerster, "Diaspora Synagogue," 169–70; Rutgers, "Synagogue Archaeology," 67–94; White "Synagogue and Society"; idem, "Reading the Ostia Synagogue"; Hachlili, *Diaspora*, 68–69; Binder, *Temple Courts*, 322–36; Runesson, "Synagogue at Ancient Ostia"; idem, "Water and Worship"; idem, "Monumental Synagogue"; idem, "Oldest Original Synagogue Building"; idem, *Origins*, 187–89;

Mitternacht, "Current Views"; 533–56; Brandt, "Jews and Christians"; Levine, *Ancient Synagogue*, 273–78.

Comments: One of the most important Diaspora buildings due to its early date and use over several centuries, this synagogue was located south of the city walls, outside the *porta marina*, on the shore. The edifice was discovered by coincidence in the 1960s during the construction of a highway between Rome and the Fiumicino Airport. Excavations were carried out in two consecutive seasons in 1961 and 1962 under the direction of Maria Floriani Squarciapino (1917–2003). Important information and results from the excavations were published in several preliminary reports from the first and second seasons, and further analysis was provided in specialised studies on specific aspects relating to the building and its surroundings (e.g., Zappa, Pavolini). Unfortunately, a final report was never published; this, together with the fact that most publications were in Italian, left the field open for a host of various misunderstandings and misrepresentations of the findings.

In the late 1990s, the Synagogue Project at Lund University, led by Birger Olsson, undertook comprehensive investigations of the building and its surroundings. The results were published in several studies, those dealing directly with the synagogue by Runesson. Subsequently, Olof Brandt at the Swedish Institute in Rome has contributed further analysis of the building (2004). Simultaneously with the Lund project and independently from it, Binder had studied the site, publishing his results in 1999. While Binder's and Runesson's work led to similar conclusions, White's analysis, which was published in 1997, provided radically different results, leading to a debate between him and Runesson (published in *HTR* and *JSJ*). Since then, White has begun renewed investigations at the site, a project that will extend over several years. This project, entitled *The Ostia Synagogue Area Masonry Analysis Project,* is a welcome contribution to the study of this synagogue; it will without doubt yield significant new information and provide material for further discussion. Until publications from this project begin to appear, including such new information,[10] the following reconstruction is considered by the authors to be the most probable.

The original, monumental edifice was constructed as a public building in the second half of the first century and functioned as a synagogue already at this time. The main hall (D; 15 × 12 m) was entered via a four-column construction in area C; the columns were of white marble, measuring 4.65–4.75 m. Benches for sitting lined three of the walls, including the north-western slightly curved wall, where a podium similar to the one found in the later building and connected to the benches may have stood. Southeast of area C was an entry hall (B) into which the main door of the building led (w. 3.80 m). Immediately to the left after entering via this door was a *triclinium* (area

---

[10] White has noted in personal communication with Runesson in 2006 that such publications will be forthcoming soon. White is currently renumbering the areas of the building; however, at present, until the new system has been published, it is best to use the system previously adopted by most scholars in order to facilitate discussion.

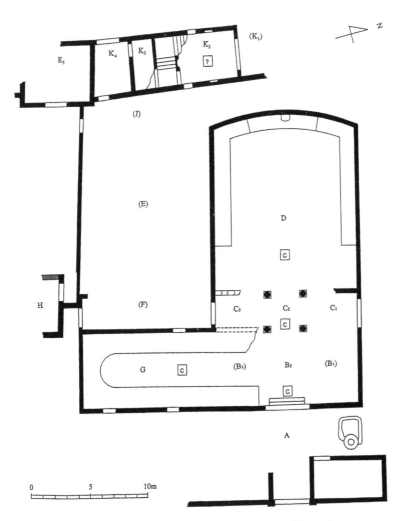

Figure 20. Plan of the Ostia synagogue, Phase 1

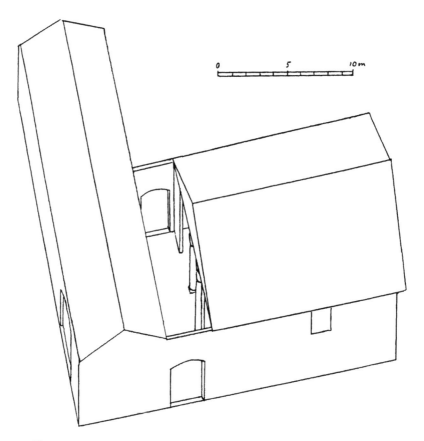

Figure 21. Reconstruction of the first phase of the Ostia synagogue

G) containing a large bench (depth 1.83 m). Outside the main entrance (area A) stood a well with a shallow basin attached to it.

Adjacent to the synagogue building to the west was a private two-story house (K). While building K was not integral to the architecture of the synagogue, it is reasonable to assume some sort of social connection; perhaps this was a dwelling place for officials of the synagogue (cf. Nos. 177, 178). If so, it is possible that Plotius Fortunatus, the *archisynagōgos* (No. 177), lived here for a period of time.

A first major renovation of the edifice took place in the early second century, perhaps during the reign of Hadrian. Changes to the original structure mainly concerned areas G and B. The bench in G was removed, the room divided into two sections, and mosaic floors replaced earlier cocciopesto floors. While the main entrance was kept intact, area B was divided into smaller rooms, of which the northern one contained a large shallow basin. At the

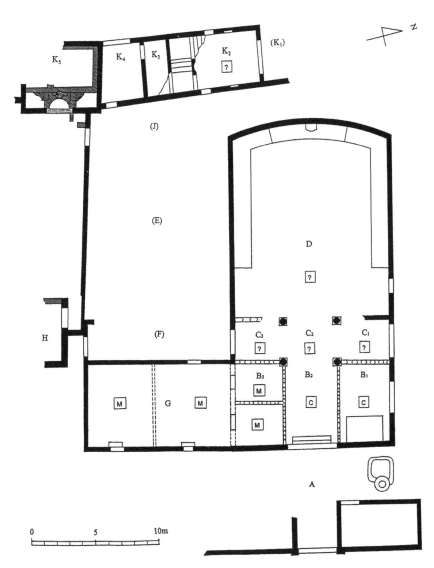

Figure 22. Plan of the Ostia synagogue, phase 2

same time, a nymphaeum was introduced in the southern part of building K (K₅). Further major renovations and changes to the building were carried out in the fourth century.

3.1.9.2 *Rome*

No. 180
Source: *Literary*. Josephus, *A.J.* 14.213–15
Date: The decree quoted by Josephus is dated to the first century B.C.E.; *Antiquitates Judaicae* was published in 93/94 C.E.

[213] Ἰούλιος Γάιος υἱοσο στρατηγὸς ὕπατος Ῥωμαίων Παριανῶν ἄρχουσι βουλῇ δήμῳ χαίρειν. ἐνέτυχόν μοι οἱ Ἰουδαῖοι ἐν Δήλῳ καί τινες τῶν παροίκων Ἰουδαίων παρόντων καὶ τῶν ὑμετέρων πρέσβεων καὶ ἐνεφάνισαν, ὡς ὑμεῖς ψηφίσματι κωλύετε αὐτοὺς τοῖς πατρίοις ἔθεσι καὶ ἱεροῖς χρῆσθαι. [214] ἐμοὶ τοίνυν οὐκ ἀρέσκει κατὰ τῶν ἡμετέρων φίλων καὶ συμμάχων τοιαῦτα γίνεσθαι ψηφίσματα καὶ κωλύεσθαι αὐτοὺς ζῆν κατὰ τὰ αὐτῶν ἔθη καὶ χρήματα εἰς σύνδειπνα καὶ τὰ ἱερὰ εἰσφέρειν, τοῦτο ποιεῖν αὐτῶν μηδ᾽ ἐν Ῥώμῃ κεκωλυμένων. [215] καὶ γὰρ Γάιος Καῖσαρ ὁ ἡμέτερος στρατηγὸς [καὶ] ὕπατος ἐν τῷ διατάγματι κωλύων θιάσους συνάγεσθαι κατὰ πόλιν μόνους τούτους οὐκ ἐκώλυσεν οὔτε χρήματα συνεισφέρειν οὔτε σύνδειπνα ποιεῖν.

[213] Julius Gaius commander, consul of the Romans, to the magistrates, council and people of Parium, greeting. The Jews in Delos[11] and some other Jews being dwellers there, some of your envoys also being present, have appealed to me and declared that you by statute prevent them from performing their native customs and sacred rituals. [214] Now it is not acceptable to me that such statutes should be made against our friends and allies and that they are prevented to live according to their customs, to collect money for common meals and to perform sacred rituals: not even in Rome are they prohibited to do this. [215] For in fact Gaius Caesar, our commander and consul,[12] by edict forbade religious guilds [*thiasoi*] to assemble in the city but, as a

---

[11] Cf. Eilers, *Jewish Privileges*, ch. 9, who argues that the idiom should be understood as referring to where the meeting was held, not where the Jews came from. Thus, Eilers translates, "The Jews appealed to me in Delos, together with some of the resident Jews, while some of your envoys were also present."

[12] Cf. the comment by Marcus, LCL, VII, p. 562, n. 2 and p. 563, n. b. These titles are, as Marcus notes, strange applied to Caesar, and need to be emended.

single exception, he did not forbid these people to do so, or to collect money or to have common meals.

Literature: See above, No. 93.

Comments: The full document is discussed above, No. 93. While the edict is concerned with the situation in Delos, or Parium, the position of the Jewish community in Rome is used as a comparative example and serves as a basis for how other Jewish communities should be treated. The document thus provides evidence for synagogues in Rome in the first century B.C.E. Although the synagogue is given special treatment, the category in which it is listed and compared to other institutions is the *thiasoi*, the religious guilds.

No. 181

Source: Literary. Juvenal, *Satire* 3.278–300
Date: *Satires* were written ca. 110–130 C.E.

[278] "Ebrius ac petulans, qui nullum forte cecidit, dat poenas, noctem patitur lugentis amicum [280] Pelidae, cubat in faciem, mox deinde supinus; [ergo non aliter poterit dormire: quibusdam] somnum rixa facit. Sed quamvis improbus annis atque mero fervens, cavet hunc, quem coccina laena vitari iubet et comitum longissimus ordo, [285] multum praeterea flammarum et aenea lampas; me, quem luna solet deducere vel breve lumen candelae, cuius dispenso et tempero filum, contemnit. Miserae cognosce prohoemia rixae, si rixa est, ubi tu pulsas, ego vapulo tantum. [290] Stat contra starique iubet: parere necesse est; nam quid agas, cum te furiosus cogat et idem fortior? "unde venis?", exclamat, "cuius aceto, cuius conche tumes? quis tecum sectile porrum sutor et elixi vervecis labra comedit? [295] nil mihi respondes? aut dic aut accipe calcem. Ede ubi consistas; in qua te quaero proseucha?" dicere si temptes aliquid tacitusve recedas, tantumdem est: feriunt pariter, vadimonia deinde irati faciunt. Libertas pauperis haec est [300] pulsatus rogat et pugnis concisus adorat ut liceat paucis cum dentibus inde reverti.

[278] "Your drunken bully who has by chance not slain his man passes a night of torture like that of Achilles when he bemoaned his friend, [280] lying now upon his face, and now upon his back; he will get no rest in any other way, since some men can only sleep after a brawl. Yet however reckless the fellow may be, however hot with wine and young blood, he gives a wide berth to one whose scarlet cloak and long retinue of attendants, [285] with torches and brass lamps in their hands, bid

him keep his distance. But to me, who am wont to be escorted home by
the moon, or by the scant light of a candle whose wick I husband with
due care, he pays no respect. Hear how the wretched fray begins—if
fray it can be called when you do all the thrashing and I get all the
blows! [290] The fellow stands up against me, and bids me halt; obey
I must. What else can you do when attacked by a madman stronger
than yourself? "Where are you from?" shouts he; "whose vinegar,
whose beans have blown you out? With what cobbler have you been
munching cut leeks and boiled wether's chaps? [295]—What, sirrah,
no answer? Speak out, or take that upon your shins! Say, where is your
stand? In what prayer hall [*proseucha*] shall I find you?" Whether you
venture to say anything, or make off silently, it's all one: he will thrash
you just the same, and then, in a rage, take bail from you. Such is the
liberty of the poor man: [300] having been pounded and cuffed into
a jelly, he begs and prays to be allowed to return home with a few
teeth in his head![13]

Literature: Stern, *GLAJJ* II. no. 297; Binder, *Temple Courts*, 115, n. 62; Levine,
Ancient Synagogue, 105–7.

Comments: Juvenal's use of the term *proseucha* (cf. the Greek *proseuchē*) for
synagogues in Rome provides a parallel to Philo's use of *proseuchē* for synagogues
in the same city (*Legat.* 155–61; No. 182). Stern notes the connection between
a stand for begging ("where is your stand?") and synagogues, and refers to
Cleomedes for comparative material (see below, No. 208).

No. 182
Source: *Literary.* Philo, *Legat.* 155–61
Date: Ca. 41–45 c.e.

[155] πῶς οὖν ἀπεδέχετο; τὴν πέραν τοῦ Τιβέρεως ποταμοῦ μεγάλην
τῆς Ῥώμης ἀποτομήν [ἣν] οὐκ ἠγνόει κατεχομένην καὶ οἰκουμένην πρὸς
Ἰουδαίων· Ῥωμαῖοι δὲ ἦσαν οἱ πλείους ἀπελευθερωθέντες· αἰχμάλωτοι
γὰρ ἀχθέντες εἰς Ἰταλίαν ὑπὸ τῶν κτησαμένων ἠλευθερώθησαν,
οὐδὲν τῶν πατρίων παραχαράξαι βιασθέντες. [156] ἠπίστατο οὖν καὶ
προσευχὰς ἔχοντας καὶ συνιόντας εἰς αὐτάς, καὶ μάλιστα ταῖς ἱεραῖς
ἑβδόμαις, ὅτε δημοσίᾳ τὴν πάτριον παιδεύονται φιλοσοφίαν. ἠπίστατο
καὶ χρήματα συνάγοντας ἀπὸ τῶν ἀπαρχῶν ἱερὰ καὶ πέμποντας εἰς
Ἱεροσόλυμα διὰ τῶν τὰς θυσίας ἀναξόντων. [157] Ἀλλ' ὅμως οὔτε

---

[13] Adapted from Ramsay (LCL).

ἐξῴκισε τῆς Ῥώμης ἐκείνους οὔτε τὴν Ῥωμαϊκὴν αὐτῶν ἀφείλετο
πολιτείαν, ὅτι καὶ τῆς Ἰουδαϊκῆς ἐφρόντιζον, οὔτε ἐνεωτέρισεν εἰς τὰς
προσευχὰς οὔτε ἐκώλυσε συνάγεσθαι πρὸς τὰς τῶν νόμων ὑφηγήσεις οὔτε
ἠναντιώθη τοῖς ἀπαρχομένοις, ἀλλ' οὕτως ὡσίωτο περὶ τὰ ἡμέτερα, ὥστε
μόνον οὐ πανοίκιος ἀναθημάτων πολυτελείαις τὸ ἱερὸν ἡμῶν ἐκόσμησε,
προστάξας καὶ διαιωνίους ἀνάγεσθαι θυσίας ἐντελεχεῖς ὁλοκαύτους
καθ' ἑκάστην ἡμέραν ἐκ τῶν ἰδίων προσόδων ἀπαρχὴν τῷ ὑψίστῳ θεῷ,
αἳ καὶ μέχρι νῦν ἐπιτελοῦνται καὶ εἰς ἅπαν ἐπιτελεσθήσονται, μήνυμα
τρόπων ὄντως αὐτοκρατορικῶν. [158] οὐ μὴν ἀλλὰ κἀν ταῖς μηνιαίοις
τῆς πατρίδος διανομαῖς, ἀργύριον ἢ σῖτον ἐν μέρει παντὸς τοῦ δήμου
λαμβάνοντος, οὐδέποτε τοὺς Ἰουδαίους ἠλάττωσε τῆς χάριτος, ἀλλ' εἰ
καὶ συνέβη τῆς ἱερᾶς ἑβδόμης ἐνεστώσης γενέσθαι τὴν διανομήν, ὅτε
οὔτε λαμβάνειν οὔτε διδόναι ἢ συνόλως τι πράττειν τῶν κατὰ βίον καὶ
μάλιστα τὸν ποριστὴν ἐφεῖται, προσετέτακτο τοῖς διανέμουσι ταμιεύειν
τοῖς Ἰουδαίοις εἰς τὴν ὑστεραίαν τὴν κοινὴν φιλανθρωπίαν. [159]
Τοιγαροῦν οἱ πανταχοῦ πάντες, εἰ καὶ φύσει διέκειντο πρὸς Ἰουδαίους
οὐκ εὐμενῶς, εὐλαβῶς εἶχον ἐπὶ καθαιρέσει τινὸς τῶν Ἰουδαϊκῶν
νομίμων προσάψασθαι· καὶ ἐπὶ Τιβερίου μέντοι τὸν αὐτὸν τρόπον,
καίτοι τῶν ἐν Ἰταλίᾳ παρακινηθέντων, ἡνίκα Σηιανὸς ἐσκευώρει τὴν
ἐπίθεσιν. [160] ἔγνω γάρ, εὐθέως ἔγνω μετὰ τὴν ἐκείνου τελευτήν, ὅτι
τὰ κατηγορηθέντα τῶν ᾠκηκότων τὴν Ῥώμην Ἰουδαίων ψευδεῖς ἦσαν
διαβολαί, πλάσματα Σηιανοῦ τὸ ἔθνος ἀναρπάσαι θέλοντος, ὅπερ ἢ
μόνον ἢ μάλιστα ᾔδει βουλαῖς ἀνοσίοις καὶ πράξεσιν ἀντιβησόμενον
ὑπὲρ τοῦ παρασπονδηθῆναι κινδυνεύσαντος αὐτοκράτορος. [161] καὶ
τοῖς πανταχόσε χειροτονουμένοις ὑπάρχοις ἐπέσκηψε παρηγορῆσαι μὲν
τοὺς κατὰ πόλεις τῶν ἀπὸ τοῦ ἔθνους, ὡς οὐκ εἰς πάντας προβάσης
τῆς ἐπεξελεύσεως, ἀλλ'' ἐπὶ μόνους τοὺς αἰτίους—ὀλίγοι δὲ ἦσαν—,
κινῆσαι δὲ μηδὲν τῶν ἐξ ἔθους, ἀλλὰ καὶ παρακαταθήκην ἔχειν τούς
τε ἄνδρας ὡς εἰρηνικοὺς τὰς φύσεις καὶ τὰ νόμιμα ὡς ἀλείφοντα πρὸς
εὐστάθειαν.

[155] How then did he show his approval? He knew that the large
district of Rome beyond the river Tiber was owned and inhabited by
Jews. The majority of them were Roman freedmen. They had been
brought to Italy as prisoners of war and manumitted by their owners,
and had not been made to alter any of their national customs. [156]
Augustus therefore knew that they had prayer halls [*proseuchai*] and met
in them, especially on the Sabbath, when they receive public instruction
in their national philosophy. He also knew that they collected sacred
money from their "first-fruits" and sent it up to Jerusalem by the hand
of envoys who would offer the sacrifices. [157] But despite this he did

not expel them from Rome or deprive them of their Roman citizenship because they remembered their Jewish nationality also. He introduced no changes into their prayer halls [*proseuchai*], he did not prevent them from meeting for the exposition of the Law, and he raised no objection to their offering of the "first-fruits." On the contrary, he showed such reverence for our traditions that he and almost all his family enriched our temple [*hieron*] with expensive dedications. He gave orders for regular sacrifices of holocausts to be made daily in perpetuity at his own expense, as an offering to the Most High God. These sacrifices continue to this day, and will continue always, as a proof of his truly imperial character. [158] Moreover, at the monthly distributions in Rome, when all the people in turn receive money or food, he never deprived the Jews of this bounty, but if the distribution happened to be made on the Sabbath, when it is forbidden to receive or give anything or to do any of the ordinary things of life in general, especially commercial life, he instructed the distributors to reserve the Jews' share of the universal largesse until the next day.

[159] Consequently the whole population of the empire, even if not instinctively well-disposed towards the Jews, was afraid to tamper with any Jewish practice in the hope of destroying it. It was the same under Tiberius, although there was an upheaval in Italy when Sejanus was contriving his attack. [160] For Tiberius realized immediately after his death that the charges brought against the Jews living in Rome were unfounded slanders, fabricated by Sejanus, who wanted to destroy that race completely, because he knew that, should the Emperor be in danger of being betrayed, it would offer in his defence the only, of the keenest, resistence to treacherous schemes and actions. [161] He issued instructions to the governors in office throughout the empire to reassure the members of the Jewish race resident in their cities with the information that punishment was not falling on all but only on the guilty—and they were few in number—and to change nothing already sanctioned by custom, but to regard as a sacred trust both the Jews themselves, since they were of a peaceful disposition, and their Laws, since they were conducive to public order.

Literature: Radice and Runia, *Bibliography 1937–1986*; Runia, *Bibliography 1987–1996*; Schürer, *HJP*, 425; Smallwood, *Legatio*, 23–45.

Comments: For a general introduction, see the introductory comment to No. 138. After eulogies on the Roman emperors Tiberius and Augustus (see Nos. 163, 164), Philo describes their protective treatments of the Jews (§§154–161) beginning with Augustus. This serves as an argument against the Alexandrians' molestation of the synagogues.

§155 The beginning of this section follows the Greek text of Smallwood, *Legatio*, 233–234.... *he*, i.e., Augustus, Roman emperor 31 B.C.E.–14 C.E.... *the large district of Rome beyond the river Tiber*. According to Smallwood (*Legatio*, 234), this district, now called Trastevere, seems to be the only Jewish settlement in Rome known to Philo. The oldest and largest Jewish catacomb (Monteverde, I B.C.E.) is also found here. Josephus reports that there were at least eight thousand Jews in Rome in 4 C.E. (*A.J.* 17.300; *B.J.* 2.80). Perhaps some of the named synagogues mentioned in later Jewish catacomb inscriptions originated in the first century C.E. (Rutgers, *Jews*, 1–49; Barclay, *Diaspora*, 282–319; Levinskaya, *Book of Acts*, 182–85).... *Roman freedmen*. Probably sons of freedmen as well as actual ex-slaves. Freed slaves received either Roman citizenship or rights similar to those enjoyed by Latin colonies. In §157 Philo uses the word "Roman citizenship." That the Jews received money or food at the monthly distributions in Rome (§158) is evidence of their Roman citizenship.... *prisoners*. During the first century B.C.E., thousands of Jewish prisoners had been brought to Rome (in 63–61, 53 and 37–35 B.C.E.).... *their national customs*. In Greek *ta patria*. See comments on No. 138, §43 and No. 162, §7.14.

§156 *they had prayer halls*. Philo uses here the word *proseuchai* for synagogues outside Egypt as in *Legat.* 157 and 371. The formulation implies that there were synagogues in Rome before Augustus.... *met in them*. The Greek text has the active participle of *synienai* "come together." Cf. §157 *synagesthai* (passive voice), "gather, come together, assemble" or "hold a meeting," here translated by "meeting."... *receive public instruction in their national philosophy*. Philo often uses the concept "philosophy" for the exposition of the Mosaic Law in the synagogue meetings (see comments on No. 160, §30 and No. 166, §250). The word is in this context combined with the verb *paideuō*, "train and teach, educate," supplemented by the adverb *dēmosiāi*, "publicly, as a community" (Colson's translation is "as a body"). The Jews in Rome were "trained and taught" together in their ancestral philosophy when they meet in their synagogues.... *sacred money from their "first-fruits."* As God is sovereign and possessor of all things, every Jew had to offer him the firstlings of human males, animals and plants. "First-fruits" (Greek *aparchai*) most often refers to literal portions of the agricultural harvest. Offerings of the first-fruits provided the redemption of the harvest. Public sacrificial ceremonies were performed twice: at Passover (offering of an initial sheaf of barley, Lev 23:10–14) and seven weeks later at Pentecost (offering of bread from the initial wheat harvest, Exod 34:22). Pentecost was called "the day of the first-fruits." The formulation in §156 suggests that the first-fruits were transformed to money in the Diaspora. Therefore, special envoys offered the collected money as sacrifices in the Jerusalem temple. The sum was fixed as an annual tax of a half of a shekel (= two Attic drachmae or two Roman denarii) for all Jewish men over the age of twenty. The Greek word *aparchē* has the literal meaning of "first-fruit" in the Septuagint, but may also have a more general meaning of "(primal) sacrifice, honorary gift." It is used about Augustus' offering in the Jerusalem temple in this section. See also Nos. 100, 101, 108, 110, 120, 194.

§157 *the exposition of the Law.* The Greek text uses the plural form of the word *hyphēgēsis*, "leading, guidance" and the plural form of *nomos*, "law" (see comment on No. 166, §215)....*expensive dedications...regular sacrifices.* In §317 the sacrifice is defined as two lambs and a bull every day. Gentile gifts to the Jerusalem temple were not uncommon. Livia, the wife of Augustus, gave "gold bowls and cups and a number of other costly offerings" to the temple, and Josephus mentions golden wine-vessels as gifts from Augustus and Livia (*B.J.* 5.563). However, Augustus made no attempt to force the imperial cult in its usual form on the Jews, knowing that they would never agree to sacrifice to the emperor. Instead, they could sacrifice to God as a prayer for the Emperor's well-being (see also comments on No. 164, §152)....*the Most High God.* See the comment on No. 162, §46.

§159 *Tiberius.* Roman emperor 14–37 c.e. According to Josephus and Roman historians, he expelled the Jews from Rome in 19 c.e. but allowed them to return later on in his reign....*Sejanus.* Tiberius' personal adviser and co-worker, assassinated in October, 31 c.e. Philo declares that Flaccus had inherited Sejanus' anti-Jewish policy (*Flacc.* 1; Horst, *Flaccus*, 89–91). No other writer in this period, however, mentions imperial hostility toward the Jews at the beginning of the thirties.

§161 *He issued instructions.* Such imperial instructions to different parts of the empire are known from other sources (see the comment on No. 194, §315).

No. 183
Source: *Inscription. JIWE* 2.602 (*CIJ* 1.531)
Date: First to second century c.e.

Dis M(anibus).	
P(ublio) Corfidio	
Signino	
pomario	
de agger	5
a proseucha,	
Q(uintus) Sallustius	
Hermes	
amico benemerenti	
et numerum	10
ollarum decem.	

To the gods of the dead. For P(ublius) Corfidius Signinus, fruiterer from the wall by the prayer hall [*proseucha*]. Q(uintus) Sallustius Hermes for his well-deserving friend; and a number of urns: ten.

Literature: *CIL* 6.2.1281 (no. 9821); Leon, *The Jews*, 152; Smallwood, *The Jews*, 520; Horsley, *New Documents*, 1.118; van der Horst, *Ancient Jewish Epitaphs*, 43; Binder, *Temple Courts*, 114–15, 321; Claußen, *Versammlung*, 115.

Comments: At the present time, this epitaph contains the earliest epigraphic reference to a synagogue in the city of Rome. Its use of the word *proseucha* (l. 6) coheres with literary allusions from the first and second centuries C.E. (Philo, *Legat.* 155 [No. 182]; Juvenal, *Sat.* 3.296 [No. 181]), suggesting this was the normative term for the synagogue in the Roman capital during that era. By the third and fourth centuries, however, the word *synagōgē* would predominate (e.g., *JIWE* 2.96, 169, 189, 194, 562).

The wall mentioned in l. 6 is the Esquiline section of the Servian wall, near the Subura.

3.1.10   *Macedonia*

3.1.10.1   *Beroea*

No. 184
Source: *Literary.* Acts 17:10–12
Date: Ca. 90–110 C.E.

[10] Οἱ δὲ ἀδελφοὶ εὐθέως διὰ νυκτὸς ἐξέπεμψαν τόν τε Παῦλον καὶ τὸν Σιλᾶν εἰς Βέροιαν, οἵτινες παραγενόμενοι εἰς τὴν συναγωγὴν τῶν Ἰουδαίων ἀπήεσαν. [11] οὗτοι δὲ ἦσαν εὐγενέστεροι τῶν ἐν Θεσσαλονίκῃ, οἵτινες ἐδέξαντο τὸν λόγον μετὰ πάσης προθυμίας καθ᾽ ἡμέραν ἀνακρίνοντες τὰς γραφὰς εἰ ἔχοι ταῦτα οὕτως. [12] πολλοὶ μὲν οὖν ἐξ αὐτῶν ἐπίστευσαν καὶ τῶν Ἑλληνίδων γυναικῶν τῶν εὐσχημόνων καὶ ἀνδρῶν οὐκ ὀλίγοι.

[10] That very night the believers sent Paul and Silas off to Beroea; and when they arrived, they went to the Jewish synagogue [*synagōgē*]. [11] These Jews were more receptive than those in Thessalonica, for they welcomed the message very eagerly and examined the scriptures every day to see whether these things were so. [12] Many of them therefore believed, including not a few Greek women and men of high standing.

Literature: As a general reference to commentaries see Barrett, Fitzmyer and Jervell, *Comm., ad loc.* Binder, *Temple Courts*, 292–94; Levinskaya, *Book of Acts*, 157.

Comments: Because of the conflict with Jews in Thessalonica, the Jesus-believers (Greek *hoi adelphoi*, "brethren," i.e., the fellowship of Christ-believers) sent Paul and Silas to Beroea, a large city in Macedonia. Everything that happened in Beroea seems to have been related to the synagogue. Jews in the synagogue welcomed (*dechesthai* "receive, welcome, accept, believe") Paul's message very eagerly. They examined the Scriptures every day, perhaps in the synagogue itself. The Greek word *anakrinein*, "examine carefully, study thoroughly," often used about investigations in courts, is found only here in the New Testament. Paul had interpreted the Scriptures as a witness to Jesus as the promised Messiah. If everything in Beroea was indeed related to the synagogue, the Greek women of high standing and the Greek men mentioned in v. 12 would have been God-fearers or sympathizers of Jewish piety.

3.1.10.2 *Philippi*

No. 185
Source: *Literary.* Acts 16:13–18
Date: Ca. 90–110 C.E.

[13] τῇ τε ἡμέρᾳ τῶν σαββάτων ἐξήλθομεν ἔξω τῆς πύλης παρὰ ποταμὸν οὗ ἐνομίζομεν προσευχὴν εἶναι, καὶ καθίσαντες ἐλαλοῦμεν ταῖς συνελθούσαις γυναιξίν. [14] καί τις γυνὴ ὀνόματι Λυδία, πορφυρόπωλις πόλεως Θυατείρων σεβομένη τὸν θεόν, ἤκουεν, ἧς ὁ κύριος διήνοιξεν τὴν καρδίαν προσέχειν τοῖς λαλουμένοις ὑπὸ τοῦ Παύλου. [15] ὡς δὲ ἐβαπτίσθη καὶ ὁ οἶκος αὐτῆς, παρεκάλεσεν λέγουσα· εἰ κεκρίκατέ με πιστὴν τῷ κυρίῳ εἶναι, εἰσελθόντες εἰς τὸν οἶκόν μου μένετε· καὶ παρεβιάσατο ἡμᾶς. [16] Ἐγένετο δὲ πορευομένων ἡμῶν εἰς τὴν προσευχὴν παιδίσκην τινὰ ἔχουσαν πνεῦμα πύθωνα ὑπαντῆσαι ἡμῖν, ἥτις ἐργασίαν πολλὴν παρεῖχεν τοῖς κυρίοις αὐτῆς μαντευομένη. [17] αὕτη κατακολουθοῦσα τῷ Παύλῳ καὶ ἡμῖν ἔκραζεν λέγουσα· οὗτοι οἱ ἄνθρωποι δοῦλοι τοῦ θεοῦ τοῦ ὑψίστου εἰσίν, οἵτινες καταγγέλλουσιν ὑμῖν ὁδὸν σωτηρίας. [18] τοῦτο δὲ ἐποίει ἐπὶ πολλὰς ἡμέρας. διαπονηθεὶς δὲ Παῦλος καὶ ἐπιστρέψας τῷ πνεύματι εἶπεν· παραγγέλλω σοι ἐν ὀνόματι Ἰησοῦ Χριστοῦ ἐξελθεῖν ἀπ᾽ αὐτῆς· καὶ ἐξῆλθεν αὐτῇ τῇ ὥρᾳ.

[13] On the Sabbath day we went outside the gate by the river, where we supposed there was a place of prayer [*proseuchē*]; and we sat down and spoke to the women who had gathered there. [14] A certain woman named Lydia, a worshiper of God, was listening to us; she was from the city of Thyatira and a dealer in purple cloth. The Lord opened her heart to listen eagerly to what was said by Paul. [15] When she and her household were baptized, she urged us, saying, "If you have judged me to be faithful to the Lord, come and stay at my home." And she prevailed upon us. [16] One day, as we were going to the place of prayer [*proseuchē*], we met a slave-girl who had a spirit of divination

and brought her owners a great deal of money by fortune-telling. [17] While she followed Paul and us, she would cry out, "These men are slaves of the Most High God, who proclaim to you a way of salvation." [18] She kept doing this for many days. But Paul, very much annoyed, turned and said to the spirit, "I order you in the name of Jesus Christ to come out of her." And it came out that very hour.

Literature: As a general reference to commentaries see Barrett, Fitzmyer and Jervell, *Comm., ad loc.* Binder, *Temple Courts*, 290–92; Levine, *Ancient Synagogue*, 109, 293; Claußen, *Versammlung*, 114–20; Runesson, "Water and Worship"; Stegemann, *Synagoge und Obrigkeit*, 211–14; Tellbe, *Synagogue and State*, 234–38.

Comments: From the harbor city of Neapolis, Paul and Silas went up to Philippi, "which is a leading city of the district of Macedonia and a Roman colony" (16:11). The Roman character of Philippi may explain why Luke reports about what happened there. There is no real encounter or conflict between Paul and the Jews in Philippi. Paul and Silas waited for the Sabbath day and then went outside the city to find a synagogue or a place where Jews customarily came together in order to worship (in the open air?). For various reasons, many Diaspora Jewish communities (Delos, Bova Marina, Ostia, Philippi) preferred to have their synagogues outside the city and near a body of water. The word used, *proseuchē*, is a specific Jewish term for place of worship.

They sat down and talked with the women who had come for worship. The only one mentioned is a God-fearer, Lydia from Thyatira. She and her house were baptized, as was later a jailor and his household (16:33). The new fellowship in Philippi, the "brothers" (16:40), is connected to two "houses" in the city, and there is no mention of any Jews becoming believers in Jesus. The apostles were accused because they were Jews who proselytized and disturbed the order of the city with their activities, turning people away from the traditional civic cults (Tellbe).

3.1.10.3 *Thessalonica*

No. 186
Source: *Literary.* Acts 17:1–4
Date: Ca. 90–110 C.E.

[1] Διοδεύσαντες δὲ τὴν Ἀμφίπολιν καὶ τὴν Ἀπολλωνίαν ἦλθον εἰς Θεσσαλονίκην ὅπου ἦν συναγωγὴ τῶν Ἰουδαίων. [2] κατὰ δὲ τὸ εἰωθὸς τῷ Παύλῳ εἰσῆλθεν πρὸς αὐτοὺς καὶ ἐπὶ σάββατα τρία διελέξατο αὐτοῖς ἀπὸ τῶν γραφῶν, [3] διανοίγων καὶ παρατιθέμενος ὅτι τὸν χριστὸν ἔδει παθεῖν καὶ ἀναστῆναι ἐκ νεκρῶν καὶ ὅτι οὗτός ἐστιν ὁ χριστὸς [ὁ] Ἰησοῦς ὃν ἐγὼ καταγγέλλω ὑμῖν. [4] καί τινες ἐξ αὐτῶν ἐπείσθησαν καὶ προσεκληρώθησαν τῷ Παύλῳ καὶ τῷ Σιλᾷ,

τῶν τε σεβομένων Ἑλλήνων πλῆθος πολύ, γυναικῶν τε τῶν πρώτων
οὐκ ὀλίγαι.

[1] After Paul and Silas had passed through Amphipolis and Apollonia,
they came to Thessalonica, where there was a synagogue [*synagōgē*] of
the Jews. [2] And Paul went in, as was his custom, and on three Sabbath days argued with them from the scriptures, [3] explaining and
proving that it was necessary for the Messiah to suffer and to rise from
the dead, and saying, "This is the Messiah, Jesus whom I am proclaiming to you." [4] Some of them were persuaded and joined Paul and
Silas, as did a great many of the devout Greeks and not a few of the
leading women.

Literature: As a general reference to commentaries see Barrett, Fitzmyer
and Jervell, *Comm., ad loc.* Binder, *Temple Courts*, 292–94; Levinskaya, *Book of
Acts*, 154–57; Stegemann, *Synagoge und Obrigkeit*, 226–27; Tellbe, *Synagogue and
State*, 154–57.

Comments: As usual in Acts, Paul first went to the synagogue (cf. Acts 13:5,
14; 14:1; 16:13; 17:2, 10, 17; 18:4, 19; 19:8). The discussion with Jews and
God-fearers (*dialegesthai*; see comment on No. 19) is here clearly connected to
references to the sacred Scriptures. Paul explained the Scriptures (*dianoigein*
"open up, make evident, explain," the same verb as in Luke 24:32) and proved
(*paratithesthai* "show to be true, present evidence of truth, prove") two things:
(1) According to the Scriptures the Messiah had to suffer, die and be raised
up from the dead; and (2) Jesus was this Messiah of the Scriptures. Some Jews
and many Greeks within the synagogue became believers as a result of Paul's
arguments. Soon however, some Jews not accepting Jesus as the Messiah accused
Paul and his co-workers, saying that they advocated customs that clashed with
fundamental values in the Roman imperial ideology (Tellbe).

3.1.10.4   *Stobi*

No. 187
Source: *Inscription. IJO* 1, Macc1 (*CIJ* 1.694)
Date: Second half of second century to first half of third century C.E.

[. . . . . . .]+++
[Κλ.] Τιβέριος Πολύ-
χαρμος ὁ καὶ Ἀχύρι-
ος ὁ πατὴρ τῆς ἐν
Στόβοις συναγωγῆς,   5
ὃς πολειτευσάμε-
νος πᾶσαν πολειτεί-
αν κατὰ τὸν Ἰουδαϊ-

σμὸν, εὐχῆς ἕνεκεν
τοὺς μὲν οἴκους τῷ   10
ἁγίῳ τόπῳ καὶ τὸ
τρίκλεινον σὺν τῷ
τετραστόῳ ἐκ τῶν
οἰκείων χρημάτων
μηδὲν ὅλως παραψά-   15
μενος τῶν ἁγίων. τὴν
δὲ ἐξουσίαν τῶν ὑπε-
ρώων πάντων πᾶσαν
καί τὴν <δ>εσποτείαν
ἔχειν ἐμὲ τὸν Κλ. Τιβέρι-   20
ον Πολύχαρμον [[καὶ τοὺς]]
καὶ τοὺς κληρονόμους
τοὺς ἐμοὺς διὰ παντὸς
βίου. ὃς ἂν δὲ βουληθῇ
τι καινοτομῆσαι παρὰ τὰ ὑ-   25
π' ἐμοῦ δοχθέντα, δώσει τῷ
πατριαρχῇ δηναρίωνι <μ>υριά-
δας εἴκοσι πέντε· οὕτω γάρ
μοι συνέδοξεν. τὴν δὲ ἐπι-
σκευὴν τῆς κεράμου τῶν   30
ὑπερῴων ποιεῖσθαι ἐμὲ
καὶ κληρονόμους
    ἐμούς.

[Claudius] Tiberius Polycharmus, also known as Achyrius, father of the synagogue [*patēr tēs synagōgēs*] in Stobi, having governed all my life according to Judaism, in fulfillment of a vow have indeed donated the rooms to the holy place [*hagios topos*] and the *triclinium* with the *tetrastoa* from my household funds, not touching the sacred monies at all; but the control and ownership of all the upper rooms is to be held by me, Cl(audius) Tiberius Polycharmus, and my heirs for the remainder of our lives. If anyone wishes to make changes to what I have resolved, that person shall give to the Patriarch 250,000 denarii; for so I have agreed. As for the maintenance of the roof tiles of the upper rooms, this will be done by me and my heirs.

Literature: Vulić, "Ancient Monuments," 238–39 (no. 636); idem, "Inscription" (1932), 291–98, idem, "Inscription" (1935), 169–75; Petrović, "Excavations,"

83–84, 135–36; Sukenik, *Ancient Synagogues*, 79–81; Marmorstein, "Synagogue," 373–84; Kitzinger, "Survey," 129–34, 140–46; Hengel, "Synagogen-inschrift," 145–83; *DF* 18–19 (no. 10); Lifshitz, "Prolegomenon," 76–77; Kraabel, "Diaspora Syngogue," 494–97; Poehlman, "Inscription," 235–48; White, *Social Origins*, 2.352–56 (no. 73); Feldman, "Diaspora Synagogues," 597; Fine, *This Holy Place*, 139; Williams, *The Jews*, no. II.7; Runesson, *Origins*, 175; Levine, *Ancient Synagogue*, 270–73; Claußen, *Versammlung*, 199–202; Habas-Rubin, "Dedication," 41–78.

Comments: Serbian archaeologist Joso Petrović discovered this inscription in 1931 on a column found in secondary use within the atrium of a basilica initially identified as the synagogue mentioned in the monument. Forty years later, renewed excavations revealed that the basilica was in fact a Byzantine church built on top of earlier synagogue remains.

The dating of the inscription has been problematic, since it initially relied on two variant readings of the obliterated first line (PIA = 111; TIA = 311). When coupled with calculations based on two different eras (Actian and Macedonian), competing dates of 79 C.E., 163 C.E. and 279 C.E. were proposed. More recent analyses have tended to treat the initial line as unrecoverable, focusing instead on palaeography and the correlation of the inscription with the lower strata of the site remains. This has led to the late second to early third century C.E. date range given above.

The dedication records the donation of several rooms of a house for use as a synagogue, whose main hall is referred to as "the holy place" (*hagios topos*). Other rooms included in the bequest were a *triclinium* or dining room, and a *tetrastoa*, which was likely an atrium.

Cl. Tiberius Polymarchus, the donor, bears the title of "father of the synagoguc" (*patēr tēs synagōgēs*) at Stobi. While this may have carried the sense of *patronus*, it is also possible that the title referenced an active synagogue functionary. This last is perhaps suggested by Polymarchus' expressed desire to dwell with his family in the upper rooms of the building, as well as by the reference to the "sacred monies," which presumably only an officer could access.

The designated fine of 250,000 denarii for breach of the agreement was an exorbitantly high figure that was meant to be taken more as a formulaic prohibition than a literal sum. Some researchers have taken the reference to the Patriarch in line 27 as arguing for a third-century date, since this office probably did not come into prominence outside of Palestine until the time of Judah ha-Nasi (late II C.E.). Yet these positions have also relied upon the tenuous readings of the inscription's first line, which force the researcher to choose between the years 163 C.E. and 279 C.E. When these readings are discarded as unreliable, however, a late second century C.E. dating remains possible.

No. 188
Source: *Archaeological.*
Date: Second half of second century to first half of third century C.E.

Literature: (See No. 187 above); Hachlili, *Diaspora*, 63–66.

Comments: During the renewed excavations of the site in the 1970s, remains were found of the synagogue mentioned in the inscriptions. However, for the earliest phase of the building, these are so few that not much can be deduced from them: paving stones underneath the nave of the later church, an east-west wall, and a threshold stone with marks of burning. Hachlili suggests the dimensions of the building to be 15 × 15 m. The ashes and marks of burning may suggest that the new synagogue was constructed after a limited fire had destroyed parts of the first synagogue.

While these remains marks a spot for where the Polycharmos synagogue once stood, the inscription, of course, remains the most important evidence for the synagogue in Stobi.

3.1.11   *Mesopotamia*

3.1.11.1   *Dura Europos*

No. 189
Source: *Archaeological.*
Date: Second half of the second century C.E.

Literature: Gutmann, *Dura-Europos Synagogue*; Kraeling, *Excavations at Dura-Europos*; Levine, "Dura Europos"; Hachlili, *Diaspora*, 39–45, 72; Levine, *Ancient Synagogue*, 252–57; White, *Social Origins*, 2.272–87 (No. 60); *IJO* III. Nos. Syr81–Syr83.

Comments: Discovered in 1932, the Dura Europos synagogue is most famous for its elaborate wall paintings with scenes from biblical narratives. The synagogue has rightly been referred to as the most complete and important synagogue discovery to date (Levine). The elaborate paintings, however, belong to a second stage in the architectural development of the synagogue, dated to 244/245 C.E.; our upper limit of 200 C.E. compels us to limit the discussion to the first phase of the edifice.

The building stood in the residential area by the western city wall and was constructed in local architectural style with a flat roof and high walls as a private house with a courtyard in the centre surrounded by a number of rooms. The edifice was likely turned into a synagogue sometime between 165–200 C.E.; the original layout of the house was, however, retained. What identifies the building at this stage as a synagogue is the creation of the assembly hall in the south-western part of the complex (room 2). This room, measuring 10.65–10.85 m × 4.60 × 5.30 m, had benches around all four walls and could sit ca. 60 people. Exactly opposite the main entrance to the hall from the courtyard, a semicircular niche, most likely used as a Torah shrine, was located in the western wall.

The purposes of the other rooms are difficult to establish. Room 7, which was connected to the main hall by an entrance, had benches around three walls; this may have been a place for study (cf. similar arrangements in other synagogues, e.g., No. 10). Rooms 4 to 6 may have functioned as living quarters for synagogue officials.

The lifespan of the Dura synagogue was short. Founded in the second half of the second century and renovated in 244/245, it was destroyed in 256 when the Persians attacked the city. The synagogue was so well preserved because it was located near a part of the western city wall that was weak and needed reinforcement. To solve the problem, the Romans built a ramp over the area where the synagogue stood, filling in the edifice. This action inadvertently preserved its treasures for the ages.

3.1.12   *Syria*

3.1.12.1   *Antioch*

No. 190 (= T10)
Source: *Literary.* Josephus, B.J. 7.44–45
Date: *De bello Judaico* consists of seven books and was published in the late 70s. It is possible that the edifice referred to in the passage was constructed in the third or second century B.C.E.

[44] Ἀντίοχος μὲν γὰρ ὁ κληθεὶς Ἐπιφανὴς Ἱεροσόλυμα πορθήσας τὸν νεὼν ἐσύλησεν, οἱ δὲ μετ' αὐτὸν τὴν βασιλείαν παραλαβόντες τῶν ἀναθημάτων ὅσα χαλκᾶ πεποίητο πάντα τοῖς ἐπ' Ἀντιοχείας Ἰουδαίοις ἀπέδοσαν εἰς τὴν συναγωγὴν αὐτῶν ἀναθέντες, καὶ συνεχώρησαν αὐτοῖς ἐξ ἴσου τῆς πόλεως τοῖς Ἕλλησι μετέχειν. [45] τὸν αὐτὸν δὲ τρόπον καὶ τῶν μετὰ ταῦτα βασιλέων αὐτοῖς προσφερομένων εἴς τε πλῆθος ἐπέδωκαν καὶ τῇ κατασκευῇ καὶ τῇ πολυτελείᾳ τῶν ἀναθημάτων τὸ ἱερὸν ἐξελάμπρυναν, ἀεί τε προσαγόμενοι ταῖς θρησκείαις πολὺ πλῆθος Ἑλλήνων, κἀκείνους τρόπῳ τινὶ μοῖραν αὐτῶν πεποίηντο.

[44] For, although Antiochus surnamed Epiphanes sacked Jerusalem and plundered the temple [*naos*], his successors on the throne restored to the Jews of Antioch all such votive offerings as were made of brass, to be laid up in their synagogue [*synagōgē*], and, moreover, granting them citizen rights on an equality with the Greeks. [45] Continuing to receive similar treatment from later monarchs, the Jewish colony grew in numbers, and their richly designed and costly offerings formed a splendid ornament to the temple [*hieron*]. Moreover, they were constantly attracting to their religious ceremonies multitudes of Greeks, and these they had in some measure incorporated with themselves.[14]

---

[14] Translation by Thackeray (LCL).

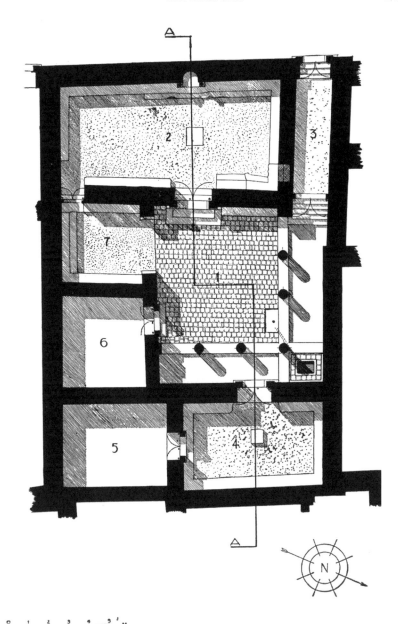

Figure 23. Plan of the first phase of the synagogue

Literature: Williams, *The Jews*, 19; Binder, *Temple Courts*, 264–66; Runesson, *Origins*, 421; Levine, *Ancient Synagogue*, 116–18; Levinskaya, *Book of Acts*, 128–35. See also No. T.10.

Comments: See comments to T.10; cf. the discussion on No. 61.

3.1.12.2 *Damascus*

No. 191
Source: *Literary.* Acts 9:1–2
Date: Ca. 90–110 c.e.

[1] Ὁ δὲ Σαῦλος ἔτι ἐμπνέων ἀπειλῆς καὶ φόνου εἰς τοὺς μαθητὰς τοῦ κυρίου, προσελθὼν τῷ ἀρχιερεῖ [2] ᾐτήσατο παρ' αὐτοῦ ἐπιστολὰς εἰς Δαμασκὸν πρὸς τὰς συναγωγάς, ὅπως ἐάν τινας εὕρῃ τῆς ὁδοῦ ὄντας, ἄνδρας τε καὶ γυναῖκας, δεδεμένους ἀγάγῃ εἰς Ἰερουσαλήμ.

[1] Meanwhile Saul, still breathing threats and murder against the disciples of the Lord, went to the high priest [2] and asked him for letters to the synagogues [*synagōgai*] at Damascus, so that if he found any who belonged to the Way, men or women, he might bring them bound to Jerusalem.

Literature: As a general reference to commentaries see Barrett, Fitzmyer and Jervell, *Comm., ad loc.* Binder, *Temple Courts*, 266–68; Levine, *Ancient Synagogue*, 118; Claußen, *Versammlung*, 98; Runesson, *Origins*, 375–76; Stegemann, *Synagoge und Obrigkeit*, 100–103.

Comments: Damascus, capital of the province of Syria, was a large city with a significant Jewish population that probably required more than one synagogue, as indicated in the text. The author of Acts further presupposes that the High Priest and the Sanhedrin in Jerusalem exercised some power within the synagogues outside Judaea. In the passage, Saul bore letters addressed to the synagogues of Damascus empowering him to exercise disciplinary measures. "Bring" (*agein*) in v. 2 means to arrest and bring people to a place of trial or punishment. In this instance, they were to be brought to Jerusalem for legal proceedings. The Jesus-believing Jews in Damascus probably belonged to those who had fled from Jerusalem as mentioned in Acts 8:1–3. The Jewish term "the Way" refers to the conviction that God's promise of salvation at the end of time (Isa 40) had been fullfilled through Jesus, the Messiah, the Son of God. Saul could not accept this and regarded these Jesus-believing Jews as apostates.

No. 192
Source: *Literary.* Acts 9:19b–22
Date: Ca. 90–110 C.E.

[19b] Ἐγένετο δὲ μετὰ τῶν ἐν Δαμασκῷ μαθητῶν ἡμέρας τινὰς [20]
καὶ εὐθέως ἐν ταῖς συναγωγαῖς ἐκήρυσσεν τὸν Ἰησοῦν ὅτι οὗτός ἐστιν
ὁ υἱὸς τοῦ θεοῦ. [21] ἐξίσταντο δὲ πάντες οἱ ἀκούοντες καὶ ἔλεγον· οὐχ
οὗτός ἐστιν ὁ πορθήσας εἰς Ἰερουσαλὴμ τοὺς ἐπικαλουμένους τὸ ὄνομα
τοῦτο, καὶ ὧδε εἰς τοῦτο ἐληλύθει ἵνα δεδεμένους αὐτοὺς ἀγάγῃ ἐπὶ
τοὺς ἀρχιερεῖς; [22] Σαῦλος δὲ μᾶλλον ἐνεδυναμοῦτο καὶ συνέχυννεν
[τοὺς] Ἰουδαίους τοὺς κατοικοῦντας ἐν Δαμασκῷ συμβιβάζων ὅτι
οὗτός ἐστιν ὁ χριστός.

[19b] For several days he was with the disciples in Damascus, [20] and
immediately he began to proclaim Jesus in the synagogues [*synagōgai*],
saying, "He is the Son of God." [21] All who heard him were amazed
and said, "Is not this the man who made havoc in Jerusalem among
those who invoked this name? And has he not come here for the
purpose of bringing them bound before the chief priests?" [22] Saul
became increasingly more powerful and confounded the Jews who lived
in Damascus by proving that Jesus was the Messiah.

Literature: As a general reference to commentaries see Barrett, Fitzmyer and
Jervell, *Comm., ad loc.* Binder, *Temple Courts*, 266–68; Levine, *Ancient Synagogue*,
118; Claußen, *Versammlung*, 98; Stegemann, *Synagoge und Obrigkeit*, 100–103.

Comments: The wording "the disciples in Damscus" (*hoi en Damaskoi mathētai*)
seems to imply a group of Jesus-believing Jews, but at the same time they
are described as members of different synagogues (see the comments on Acts
9:1–2, No. 191). Luke very seldom describes Jesus as "the Son of God": in
Acts only here and in 13:33 (a quotation of Psa 2:7). The meaning is probably
identical with "the Messiah" in v. 22; both titles come from the Scriptures. Saul
would have argued from the Scriptures in order to prove his claim. "Proving"
(*symbibazein*) normally means "bring together, combine" and also "conclude,
infer" or "show for certain, prove."

3.1.12.3   *Dora (Dor)*

No. 193
Source: *Literary.* Josephus, *A.J.* 19.300–305
Date: *Antiquitates Judaicae* was published 93/94. The event described in the pas-
sage is said to have taken place during the governorship of Petronius, ca. 41 C.E.

[300] παντάπασιν δὲ ὀλίγου χρόνου διελθόντος Δωρῖται νεανίσκοι τῆς
ὁσιότητος προτιθέμενοι τόλμαν καὶ πεφυκότες εἶναι παραβόλως θρασεῖς

Καίσαρος ἀνδριάντα κομίσαντες εἰς τὴν τῶν Ἰουδαίων συναγωγὴν
ἀνέστησαν. [301] σφόδρα τοῦτο Ἀγρίππαν παρώξυνεν· κατάλυσιν
γὰρ τῶν πατρίων αὐτοῦ νόμων ἐδύνατο. ἀμελλητὶ δὲ πρὸς Πούπλιον
Πετρώνιον, ἡγεμὼν δὲ τῆς Συρίας οὗτος ἦν, παραγίνεται καὶ καταλέγει
τῶν Δωριτῶν. [302] ὁ δ᾽ οὐχ ἧττον ἐπὶ τῷ πραχθέντι χαλεπήνας, καὶ γὰρ
αὐτὸς ἔκρινεν ἀσέβειαν τὴν τῶν ἐννόμων παράβασιν, τοῖς ἀποστᾶσι
τῶν Δωριτῶν σὺν ὀργῇ ταῦτ᾽ ἔγραψεν· [303] "Πούπλιος Πετρώνιος
πρεσβευτὴς Τιβερίου Κλαυδίου Καίσαρος Σεβαστοῦ Γερμανικοῦ
Δωριέων τοῖς πρώτοις λέγει. [304] ἐπειδὴ τοσαύτῃ τόλμῃ ἀπονοίας τινὲς
ἐχρήσαντο ἐξ ὑμῶν, ὥστε μηδὲ διὰ τὸ προτεθῆναι διάταγμα Κλαυδίου
Καίσαρος Σεβαστοῦ Γερμανικοῦ περὶ τοῦ ἐφίεσθαι Ἰουδαίους
φυλάσσειν τὰ πάτρια πεισθῆναι ὑμᾶς αὐτῷ, [305] τἀναντία δὲ πάντα
πρᾶξαι, συναγωγὴν Ἰουδαίων κωλύοντας εἶναι διὰ τὸ μεταθεῖναι
ἐν αὐτῇ τὸν Καίσαρος ἀνδριάντα, παρανομοῦντας οὐκ εἰς μόνους
Ἰουδαίους, ἀλλὰ καὶ εἰς τὸν αὐτοκράτορα, οὗ ὁ ἀνδριὰς βέλτιον ἐν
τῷ ἰδίῳ ναῷ ἢ ἐν ἀλλοτρίῳ ἐτίθετο καὶ ταῦτα ἐν τῷ τῆς συναγωγῆς
τόπῳ, τοῦ φύσει δικαιοῦντος ἕνα ἕκαστον τῶν ἰδίων τόπων κυριεύειν
κατὰ τὸ Καίσαρος ἐπίκριμα·

[300] A very short time after this, certain young men of Dora, who set
higher value on audacity than on holiness and were by nature recklessly
bold, brought an image of Caesar into the synagogue [*synagōgē*] of the
Jews and set it up. [301] This provoked Agrippa exceedingly, for it was
tantamount to an overthrow of the laws of his fathers. Without delay
he went to see Publius Petronius, the governor of Syria, and denounced
the people of Dora. [302] Petronius was no less angry at the deed, for
he too regarded the breach of the law as sacrilege [*asebeia*]. He wrote
in anger to the leaders of Dora as follows: [303] "Publius Petronius,
legate of Tiberius Claudius Caesar Augustus Germanicus, to the leading
men of Dora speaks: [304] Inasmuch as certain of you have had such
mad audacity, not withstanding the issuance of an edict of Claudius
Caesar Augustus Germanicus pertaining to the permission granted
the Jews to observe the customs of their fathers, not to obey this edict,
[305] but to do the very reverse, in that you have prevented the Jews
from having a synagogue [*synagōgē*] by transferring to it an image of
Caesar, you have thereby sinned not only against the law of the Jews,
but also against the emperor, whose image was better placed in his
own shrine than in that of another, especially in that of a synagogue

[*synagōgē*]; for by natural law each must be lord over his own place, in accordance with Caesar's decree.[15]

Literature: Binder, *Temple Courts*, 268–69; Bilde, "Synagogue," 20–21; Runesson, *Origins*, 219; Claußen, *Versammlung*, 249–50; Levine, *Ancient Synagogue*, 66–67.

Comments: While we have no archaeological evidence of synagogue buildings from Syria, it is clear from this passage that such buildings did exist (the setting up of a statue requires an edifice in which it could be placed) and could be referred to as "synagogues." One may also note that a temple-like character of the edifice is implied. The incident described occurs after Caligula's failed attempt at introducing his own statue in the Jerusalem temple; the men of Dora are accused of doing the same thing in a synagogue, thus committing "sacrilege." Indeed, the very fact that the image of the emperor is placed in a synagogue building attests to the temple-like character of that building. Cf. Philo's reports of comparable acts in Alexandria against *proseuchai*, and how these events triggered similar attacks on Jewish institutions elsewhere (*Legat.* 346, No. 165).

The letter of Petronius, the first part of which is given here, attests to Roman policy regarding Jewish communal activities and worship. It makes clear that a synagogue building was considered the realm of the God of Israel and that, should another deity be introduced in the edifice, the institution would be destroyed (cf. Levine).

3.2   *General References and Unidentified Locations*

3.2.1   *Literary Sources*

No. 194
Source: *Literary.* Philo, *Legat.* 311–16
Date: Ca. 41–45 c.e.

[311] τεκμηρίοις δὲ ἀφθόνοις πιστώσασθαι δυνάμενος τὸ βούλημα τοῦ Σεβαστοῦ προπάππου σου δυσὶν ἀρκεσθήσομαι. τὸ μὲν γὰρ πρῶτον ἐπέστειλε τοῖς ἐπιτρόποις τῶν κατὰ τὴν Ἀσίαν ἐπικρατειῶν, πυθόμενος ὀλιγωρεῖσθαι τὰς ἱερὰς ἀπαρχάς, ἵνα ἐπιτρέπωσι τοῖς Ἰουδαίοις μόνοις εἰς τὰ συναγώγια συνέρχεσθαι· [312] μὴ γὰρ εἶναι ταῦτα συνόδους ἐκ μέθης καὶ παροινίας ἐπισυστάσας, ὡς λυμαίνεσθαι τὰ τῆς εἰρήνης, ἀλλὰ διδασκαλεῖα σωφροσύνης καὶ δικαιοσύνης ἀνδρῶν ἐπιτηδευόντων μὲν ἀρετήν, ἀπαρχὰς δὲ ἐτησίους συμφερόντων, ἐξ ὧν

---

[15] Translation by Feldman (LCL).

ἀνάγουσι θυσίας στέλλοντες ἱεροπομποὺς εἰς τὸ ἐν Ἱεροσολύμοις ἱερόν. [313] εἶτα κελεύει μηδένα ἐμποδὼν ἵστασθαι τοῖς Ἰουδαίοις μήτε συνιοῦσι μήτε συνεισφέρουσι μήτε διαπεμπομένοις κατὰ τὰ πάτρια εἰς Ἱεροσόλυμα· ταῦτα γὰρ εἰ καὶ μὴ τοῖς ῥήμασι, τοῖς γοῦν πράγμασιν ἐπέσταλται. [314] μίαν δὲ ἐπιστολὴν ὑποτέταχα πρὸς τὴν σὴν τοῦ δεσπότου πειθώ, ἣν Γάιος Νορβανὸς Φλάκκος ἐπιστέλλει δηλῶν τὰ ὑπὸ Καίσαρος αὐτῷ γραφέντα. ἔστι δὲ τῆς ἐπιστολῆς τὸ ἀντίγραφον τόδε· [315] Γάιος Νορβανὸς Φλάκκος ἀνθύπατος Ἐφεσίων ἄρχουσι χαίρειν. Καῖσάρ μοι ἔγραψεν, Ἰουδαίους, οὗ ἂν ὦσιν, ἰδίῳ ἀρχαίῳ ἐθισμῷ νομίζειν συναγομένους χρήματα φέρειν, ἃ πέμπουσιν εἰς Ἱεροσόλυμα· τούτους οὐκ ἠθέλησε κωλύεσθαι τοῦτο ποιεῖν. ἔγραψα οὖν ὑμῖν, ἵν᾽ εἰδῆτε, ὡς ταῦτα οὕτως γίνεσθαι κελεύει. [316] ἆρ᾽ οὐκ ἐναργὴς πίστις ἐστίν, αὐτοκράτορ, τῆς Καίσαρος προαιρέσεως, ᾗ περὶ τὴν τοῦ ἡμετέρου ἱεροῦ τιμὴν ἐκέχρητο, μὴ βουληθεὶς τῷ κοινῷ τύπῳ τῶν συνόδων ἀναιρεθῆναι τὰς τῶν Ἰουδαίων εἰς ταὐτὸ συμφοιτήσεις, ἃς ἀπαρχῶν ἕνεκα ποιοῦνται καὶ τῆς ἄλλης εὐσεβείας

[311] I could demonstrate the intentions of Augustus, your great grandfather, by countless proofs, but I will content myself with two. First, when he discovered that the sacred "first-fruits" were being neglected, he instructed the governors of the provinces in Asia to grant to the Jews alone the right of meeting in the synagogues [*synagōgia*]. [312] He said that these were not meetings [*synodoi*] which had their origin in drunkenness and disorderliness likely to disturb the peace, but were schools [*didaskaleia*] of sobriety and justice for people who practised virtue and contributed their annual "first-fruits," which they used to pay for sacrifices, sending sacred envoys to take the money to the temple in Jerusalem. [313] Secondly, he gave orders that no-one should hinder the Jews from meeting, making their contributions, and communicating with Jerusalem as their custom was. This was the gist of his instructions, at any rate, even if they were not expressed in these words. [314] I append one letter in order to convince you, my lord—a letter from Gaius Norbanus Flaccus in which he made public what Caesar had written to him. Here is a transcript of the letter: [315] 'Gaius Norbanus Flaccus the proconsul greets the magistrates of Ephesus. Caesar has written to me saying that it is a native traditional custom of the Jews, wherever they live, to meet regularly and contribute money, which they send to Jerusalem. He does not wish them to be prevented from doing this. I am therefore writing to you so that you may know that these are his instructions.' [316] Surely this is a clear proof, Emperor, of the policy

which Caesar followed with regard to the respect due to our temple? He did not want the Jews' assemblies, which are held for the collection of the "first-fruits" and for other religious purposes, to be swept away in the same way as the clubs [*synodoi*] were.

Literature: Radice and Runia, *Bibliography 1937–1986*; Runia, *Bibliography 1987–1996*; Schürer, *HJP*, 418, 440; Sterling, "School", 154–55; Smallwood, *Legatio*, 308–11.

Comments: For a general introduction, see the introductory comment to No. 138. When Emperor Gaius Caligula planned to erect a statue in the Jerusalem temple, Agrippa I, grandson of Herod the Great and king over nearly identical territories (37–44 C.E.), appealed to the emperor in the autumn of 40 C.E. and saved the temple from desecration. §§276–329 present Philo's version of Agrippa's memorandum to Gaius. §§311–316 cite Augustus Caesar's protection of Jewish religious liberty in the provinces (cf. *Legat.* §§155–158, No. 182).

§311 *discovered.* Or "had learnt" (Colson) or "heard" (Yonge). Jews in Asia and North Africa had sent deputations to the emperor, reporting negative Gentile actions and attitudes. Augustus' instructions may have been an answer to their complaints.... *the sacred "first-fruits" were being neglected.* See the comment on No. 182, §156. According to these sections, the collection of the first fruits (in form of money) was a very important synagogue activity in the Diaspora. The Jews contributed first-fruits every year (Greek *sympherein* "bring together, collect, contribute," in §313 *syneispherein* "join in payments" and in §315 *pherein chrēmata* "pay money"), commissioning and sending holy envoys (*hieropompoi*) to Jerusalem in order to use the money for sacrifices (Greek *stellein* "send," in §313 *diapempesthai* "send out envoys," and in §315 *pempein* "send").... *the Jews alone.* There seems to have been a general ban on guilds and clubs in the Roman empire. See also "in the same ways as the clubs were" at the end of §316.... *meeting in the synagogues.* The Greek verb is *synerchesthai*, "come together, assemble, meet," and the Greek word for the meeting place, *synagōgion*, "meeting house" as in No. 167, §127 (see also comment on No. 40, §81).

§312 *meetings.* In Greek *synodoi*, one of the words for Roman guilds or clubs, here used in a more general sense. The same word is used in a more technical sense at the end of §316, where it is translated as "clubs."... *schools of sobriety and justice.* See the comment on No. 166, §216.

§314 *Gaius Norbanus Flaccus.* Proconsul of the province of Asia in 24 B.C.E.... *Caesar,* i.e., Augustus. Four other documents similar to the letter to Gaius Norbanus Flaccus are included in Josephus, *A.J.* 16:162–173.

§316 *assemblies.* The Greek word here, *symphoitēsis*, complemented by *eis tauto* "to the same place," comes from *symphoitan*, "go regularly to a place together, go to school together."

No. 195
Source: *Literary.* Philo, *Legat.* 370–71
Date: Ca. 41–45 C.E.

[370] ἐν ἡμῖν δὲ πέντε πρεσβευταῖς σαλεύειν τὰ τῶν πανταχοῦ πάντων
Ἰουδαίων οὐ χαλεπόν; [371] εἰ γὰρ χαρίσαιτο τοῖς ἡμετέροις ἐχθροῖς, τίς
ἑτέρα πόλις ἠρεμήσει; τίς οὐκ ἐπιθήσεται τοῖς συνοικοῦσι; τίς ἀπαθὴς
καταλειφθήσεται προσευχή; ποῖον πολιτικὸν οὐκ ἀνατραπήσεται δίκαιον
τοῖς κοσμουμένοις κατὰ τὰ πάτρια τῶν Ἰουδαίων; ἀνατετράψεται,
ναυαγήσει, κατὰ βυθοῦ χωρήσει καὶ τὰ ἐξαίρετα νόμιμα καὶ τὰ κοινὰ
πρὸς ἑκάστας τῶν πόλεων αὐτοῖς δίκαια.

[370] Was it not hard that the future of all the Jews everywhere should
be at stake in the persons of us five envoys? [371] If Gaius were to
give in to our enemies, what other city would remain quiet? What city
would refrain from attacking the Jews living in it? What synagogue
[*proseuchē*] would be left unmolested? What political right belonging
to those who order their lives according to Jewish traditions would not
be overthrown ? Both the specifically Jewish Laws and their general
rights vis-à-vis each individual city would be overthrown, shipwrecked,
and sent to the bottom of the sea.

Literature: Radice and Runia, *Bibliography 1937–1986*; Runia, *Bibliography
1987–1996*; Smallwood, *Legatio*, 323–24.

Comments: For a general introduction, see the introductory comment to No.
138. At the end of *Legatio ad Gaium*, Philo describes the despair of the Jewish
envoys from Alexandria following their meeting with Caligula (§§368–372).
     §371 On the molestation of the synagogues, see comments on No. 138; on
the deprivation of political rights, see comment on No. 138, §53.

No. 196
Source: *Literary.* Jas 2:2–4
Date: Ca. 60 or ca. 80–100 C.E.

[2] ἐὰν γὰρ εἰσέλθῃ εἰς συναγωγὴν ὑμῶν ἀνὴρ χρυσοδακτύλιος
ἐν ἐσθῆτι λαμπρᾷ, εἰσέλθῃ δὲ καὶ πτωχὸς ἐν ῥυπαρᾷ ἐσθῆτι, [3]
ἐπιβλέψητε δὲ ἐπὶ τὸν φοροῦντα τὴν ἐσθῆτα τὴν λαμπρὰν καὶ εἴπητε·
σὺ κάθου ὧδε καλῶς, καὶ τῷ πτωχῷ εἴπητε· σὺ στῆθι ἐκεῖ ἢ κάθου ὑπὸ
τὸ ὑποπόδιόν μου, [4] οὐ διεκρίθητε ἐν ἑαυτοῖς καὶ ἐγένεσθε κριταὶ
διαλογισμῶν πονηρῶν;

[2] For if a person with gold rings and in fine clothes comes into your assembly[16] [*synagōgē*], and if a poor person in dirty clothes also comes in, [3] and if you take notice of the one wearing the fine clothes and say, "Have a seat here, please," while to the one who is poor you say, "Stand there," or, "Sit at my feet," [4] have you not made distinctions among yourselves, and become judges with evil thoughts?

Literature: As a general reference to commentaries, see Dibelius/Greeven, Mussner and Johnson, *Comm., ad loc.* Binder, *Temple Courts*, 65–66, 499 n. 45; Claußen, *Versammlung*, 68–69; Riesner, "Synagogues", 207–8, Kloppenborg, "Diaspora Discourse", 251–55.

Comments: Many scholars have strongly questioned the relevance of Jas 2:2–4 as a source about the ancient synagogue. Dibelius and Greeven, for example, view this passage as a rhetorical example narrated in a vivid and graphic fashion "without any concern for its reality, and hence, without any consideration for the question of the community in which, or the circumstances under which, this or even something similar could have taken place." Mussner and Johnson, on the other hand, view the verses more concretely: "the reader is transported from the realm of general axioms to the most specific sort of social situation in which those maxims are put to the test." Specifically, the behaviour of the messianic community with respect to the poor is placed into focus in this passage.

The word *synagōgē*, with its possible meanings of gathering, community assembly, community as such, or place of assembly, is probably referring to an assembly of Christ-believers. Christian assemblies could be called *synagōgoi* in the second century (Ignatius, Hermas, Justin). The author uses the word *ekklēsia* with the same meaning in 5:14. Kloppenborg, however, and some others describe the addressees as Jewish communities in the Diaspora, which could include some Jesus-believing Jews. "I suggest that James is bifocal, addressing outside and inside readerships simultaneously" (Kloppenborg). From such a perspective both *synagōgē* and *ekklēsia* in the Letter of James are referring to Jewish fellowships. The example cited in the passage presupposes some sort of fixed seating order in the place where the community met. There seems to have been a raised platform, benches or seats for some, and an open space where one could stand or sit on the floor.

The manuscripts give different alternatives for the words spoken to the poor person: (1) "stand there or sit here below my footstool," (2) "stand or sit there below my footstool," or (3) "stand there or sit below my footstool."

---

[16] While NRSV translates *synagōgē* "assembly" here, given the context, "synagogue" seems to be the better choice of word. See comments below.

Text-critically, the last alternative is to be preferred. The seat near the person speaking is obviously a place of honor. The phrase "made distinctions among yourselves" suggests that the two persons addressed belonged to the community. Yet if they belonged to the community, why would they be referred to their places? The answer is unclear.

CHAPTER FOUR

GENERAL REFERENCES

4.1   *Literary Sources*

4.1.1   *2 Corinthians*

No. 197
Source: *Literary.* 2 Cor 3:14–15
Date: Ca. 57 C.E.

[14] ἀλλὰ ἐπωρώθη τὰ νοήματα αὐτῶν. ἄχρι γὰρ τῆς σήμερον ἡμέρας τὸ αὐτὸ κάλυμμα ἐπὶ τῇ ἀναγνώσει τῆς παλαιᾶς διαθήκης μένει, μὴ ἀνακαλυπτόμενον ὅτι ἐν Χριστῷ καταργεῖται· [15] ἀλλ᾽ ἕως σήμερον ἡνίκα ἂν ἀναγινώσκηται Μωϋσῆς, κάλυμμα ἐπὶ τὴν καρδίαν αὐτῶν κεῖται·

[14] But their minds were hardened. Indeed, to this very day, when they hear the reading of the old covenant, that same veil is still there, since only in Christ is it set aside. [15] Indeed, to this very day whenever Moses is read, a veil lies over their minds

Literature: Furnish, *Comm., ad loc.* Binder, *Temple Courts*, 65.

Comments: A probable reference to the reading of Torah in the synagogues. See comments on No. 33 and No. 174. See also Introduction, n. 14.

4.1.2   *Philo*

No. 198
Source: *Literary.* Philo, *Decal.* 40–41
Date: Ca. 30–45 C.E.

[40] τρίτον, ἵνα μηδείς ποτε βασιλεὺς ἢ τύραννος ἀφανοῦς ἰδιώτου καταφρονήσῃ γεμισθεὶς ἀλαζονείας καὶ ὑπεροψίας, ἀλλ᾽ εἰς τὰ τῶν ἱερῶν νόμων διδασκαλεῖα φοιτήσας χαλάσῃ τὰς ὀφρῦς, ἀπομαθὼν οἴησιν εἰκότι μᾶλλον δ᾽ ἀληθεῖ λογισμῷ. [41] εἰ γὰρ ὁ ἀγένητος καὶ ἄφθαρτος καὶ ἀίδιος καὶ οὐδενὸς ἐπιδεὴς καὶ ποιητὴς τῶν ὅλων καὶ εὐεργέτης καὶ βασιλεὺς βασιλέων καὶ θεὸς θεῶν οὐδὲ τὸν ταπεινότατον

ὑπεριδεῖν ὑπέμεινεν, ἀλλὰ καὶ τοῦτον εὐωχῆσαι λογίων καὶ θεσμῶν
ἱερῶν ἠξίωσεν, ὡς μόνον ἑστιᾶν μέλλων καὶ μόνῳ τὸ συμπόσιον
εὐτρεπίζεσθαι πρὸς ψυχῆς ἀνάχυσιν ἱεροφαντουμένης, ᾗ θέμις τὰς
μεγάλας τελεῖσθαι τελετάς, ἐμοὶ τῷ θνητῷ τί προσῆκον ὑψαυχενεῖν
καὶ πεφυσῆσθαι φρυαττομένῳ πρὸς τοὺς ὁμοίους, οἳ τύχαις μὲν ἀνίσοις
ἴσῃ δὲ καὶ ὁμοίᾳ συγγενείᾳ κέχρηνται μίαν ἐπιγραψάμενοι μητέρα τὴν
κοινὴν ἁπάντων ἀνθρώπων φύσιν;

[40] A third reason is that He wills that no king or despot swollen with
arrogance and contempt should despise an insignificant private person but should study in the schools [*didaskaleia*] of the divine laws and
abate his supercilious airs, and through the reasonableness or rather
the assured truth of their arguments unlearn his self-conceit. [41] For
if the Uncreated, the Incorruptible, the Eternal, Who needs nothing
and is the maker of all, the Benefactor and King of kings and God
of gods could not brook to despise even the humblest, but deigned to
banquet him on holy oracles and statutes, as though he should be the
sole guest, as though for him alone the feast was prepared to give good
cheer to a soul instructed in the holy secrets and accepted for admis-
sion to the greatest mysteries, what right have I, the mortal, to bear
myself proud-necked, puffed-up and loud-voiced, towards my fellows,
who, though their fortunes be unequal, have equal rights of kinship
because they can claim to be children of the one common mother of
mankind, nature?

Literature: Radice and Runia, *Bibliography 1937–1986*; Runia, *Bibliography
1987–1996*; Klinghardt, *Gemeinschaftsmahl*, 251–67; Borgen, *Philo*, 244–45;
Sterling, "School", 154–55; Binder, *Temple Courts*, 134, n. 96, 434–35.

Comments: The book "On the Decalogue" (*De decalogo*) belongs to Philo's
more systematic commentary series on the law of Moses, sometimes called
"The Exposition of the Law." In this treatise he deals with the law-giving
on Sinai and the Ten Commandments. In the first part (§§1–49), he answers
some more general questions, among them why the commandments have the
singular form "thou shalt not…" (§§36–49). The "vast number of myriads of
men" gathered at Sinai could motivate a plural form. As a third answer to this
question Philo says that the use of the singular form is a lesson to the great
not to despise the humblest (§§40–44). Later on, in §§96–101, Philo describes
the activities of the Jews on the Sabbath as a "philosophising" of the Law
without explicitly mentioning the synagogue.

§40 *should study in the school of the divine laws*. According to Yonge, "coming
as a pupil to the school of the sacred laws." The Greek verb *phoitan* means
"go to and fro, resort to a person as a friend/teacher, frequent"; in absolute
form, "go to school"; as a participle "schoolboy." See comment on No. 194,

§316.... *through the reasonable or rather the assured truth of their arguments.* The activity in the synagogue was characterized by reasoned argumentation that resulted in the discernment of truth (*eikoti mallon d' alēthei logismōi*).

§41 *deigned to banquet him on holy oracles and statues...guest...the feast.* All Jews were invited to take part in the teaching of the Mosaic Law in the synagogues. In the next paragraph Philo mentions especially those facing the greatest difficulties or persons of low esteem, such as the destitute, the orphaned, the childless, and those who have suffered the loss of a child (§42). The metaphorical use of banquet for teaching in synagogues may have been related to the custom of conducting after-dinner symposia in an attached dining hall (cf. Josephus, *A.J.* 14:211f., 213, 216, 261; 3 Macc 7:18ff.; Klinghardt, *Gemeinschaftsmahl*, 251–67)....*instructed in the holy secrets.* The Greek verb *hierophanteisthai* means "being a hierophant, being initiated, being instructed in mysteries."

No. 199
Source: *Literary.* Philo, *Opif.* 128
Date: Ca. 40–45 c.e.

[128] Ταῦτα καὶ ἔτι πλείω λέγεται καὶ φιλοσοφεῖται περὶ ἑβδομάδος, ὧν ἕνεκα τιμὰς μὲν ἔλαχεν ἐν τῇ φύσει τὰς ἀνωτάτω, τιμᾶται δὲ καὶ παρὰ τοῖς δοκιμωτάτοις τῶν Ἑλλήνων καὶ βαρβάρων, οἳ τὴν μαθηματικὴν ἐπιστήμην διαπονοῦσιν, ἐκτετίμηται δ' ὑπὸ τοῦ φιλαρέτου Μωυσέως, ὃς τὸ κάλλος αὐτῆς ἀνέγραψεν ἐν ταῖς ἱερωτάταις τοῦ νόμου στήλαις, ταῖς δὲ διανοίαις τῶν ὑφ' αὑτὸν ἁπάντων ἐνεχάραξε, δι' ἓξ ἡμερῶν κελεύσας ἄγειν ἱερὰν ἑβδόμην ἀπὸ τῶν ἄλλων ἀνέχοντας ἔργων ὅσα κατὰ ζήτησιν βίου καὶ πορισμόν, ἑνὶ μόνῳ σχολάζοντας τῷ φιλοσοφεῖν εἰς βελτίωσιν ἠθῶν καὶ τὸν τοῦ συνειδότος ἔλεγχον, ὃς ἐνιδρυμένος τῇ ψυχῇ καθάπερ δικαστὴς ἐπιπλήττων οὐ δυσωπεῖται, τὰ μὲν σφοδροτέραις ἀπειλαῖς τὰ δὲ καὶ μετριωτέραις νουθεσίαις χρώμενος, περὶ μὲν ὧν ἔδοξεν ἐκ προνοίας ἀδικεῖν ἀπειλαῖς, περὶ δ' ὧν ἀκούσια διὰ τὸ ἀπροοράτως ἔχειν νουθεσίαις ὑπὲρ τοῦ μηκέθ' ὁμοίως ὀλισθεῖν.

[128] All this and even more has been stated and philosophized about the seven. For these reasons it has obtained the highest honours in nature, and is also honoured by Greeks and foreigners of the highest reputation who practise the science of mathematics. But it has been especially honoured by that lover of excellence, Moses, who recorded its beauty in the most holy tables of the law and also imprinted it on the minds of his followers. He commanded them after every period of six days to keep the seventh day holy, refraining from all the work required for the pursuit and provision of a livelihood, and keeping

themselves free to concentrate on one thing only, practising philosophy
for the improvement of their character and the examination of their
conscience, which has been established in the soul and like a judge is not
at all bashful about administering rebukes, making use both of threats
that are rather forceful and of warnings that are more moderate. The
former it applies to those unjust deeds which appear to be deliberate,
whereas it uses the latter for involuntary acts done through lack of
foresight, in order that a similar lapse will not happen again.

Literature: Radice and Runia, *Bibliography 1937–1986*; Runia, *Bibliography
1987–1996*; Runia, *On the Creation*, 296–98.

Comments: As a more systematic commentary on the creation accounts in
Gen 1–3, Philo's work *De opificio mundi* belongs to the series called "Exposition
of the Law." Addressing the seventh day, Philo launches into an extremely
long excursus on the number seven (§§89–128). It ends with a reference to
Moses, the lover of virtues (*philaretos*), and his commandment to keep the
seventh day holy (§128). On this day all Jews were to concentrate on only
one thing: "practising philosophy" with the dual purpose of improving their
morals and examining their consciences. On Philo's use of "philosophy" as the
study and practise of the Law (including the use of philosophical knowledge),
see comments on Nos. 160, §30; 166, §215; 168, §61. On the ethical effect
of this "philosophizing" in synagogue meetings, see comments on No. 166,
§216, and No. 168.

No. 200
Source: *Literary.* Philo, *Praem.* 65–66
Date: Ca. 30–45 c.e.

[65] οὗτός ἐστιν ὁ ἀσινὴς οἶκος, ὁ τέλειος καὶ συνεχὴς ἐν ταῖς ῥηταῖς
γραφαῖς καὶ ἐν ταῖς καθ᾽ ὑπόνοιαν ἀλληγορίαις, ὃς ἔλαβεν ἆθλον,
καθάπερ εἶπον, ἡγεμονίαν τῶν τοῦ ἔθνους φυλῶν. [66] ἐκ τοῦδε τοῦ
οἴκου χρόνοις εἰς πολυανθρωπίαν ἐπιδόντος εὔνομοι πόλεις ἐκτίσθησαν,
διδασκαλεῖα φρονήσεως καὶ δικαιοσύνης καὶ ὁσιότητος, ἐν οἷς καὶ ἡ
τῆς ἄλλης ἀρετῆς μεταποίησις μεγαλοπρεπῶς διερευνᾶται.

[65] This is the household, which kept safe from harm, perfect and
united both in the literal history and in the allegorical interpretation,
received for its reward, as I have said, the chieftaincy of the tribes of
the nation. [66] From this household, increased in the course of time
to a great multitude, were founded flourishing and orderly cities, schools
[*didaskaleia*] of wisdom, justice and religion, where also the rest of virtue
and how to acquire it is the sublime subject of their research.

Literature: Radice and Runia, *Bibliography 1937–1986*; Runia, *Bibliography 1987–1996*; Borgen, "Education", 66; Sterling, "School", 154–55; Binder, *Temple Courts*, 134, n. 96, 434–35.

Comments: The book "On Rewards and Punishments" (*De praemiis et poenis*) explores cases of individuals, households or larger groups who have been rewarded for obedience or punished for disobedience. When Philo addresses rewards to households (§§57–66), he mentions the families of Abraham, Isaac and Jacob. Of these, only Jacob's household was rewarded: the twelve tribes eventually expanded into a great nation.

§65 *the household*, i.e. the household of Jacob....*united both in the literal history and in the allegorical interpretation.* More literally, "hold together through the literal contents of the scriptures and through the allegorical interpretations according-ing the deeper sense." Yonge gives the meaning "being continually devoted to the study of the holy scriptures, both in their literal sense and also in the allegories figuratively contained in them."

§66 *schools for wisdom, justice and religion...the rest of virtue.* See the comment on No. 166, §216.... *and how to acquire it is the sublime subject of their research.* In the synagogues, the acquisition of the virtues "is magnificently investigated." The Greek verb is *diereunan.* See comment on No. 160, §31.

No. 201
Source: *Literary.* Philo, *Spec.* 1. 324–25
Date: Ca. 30–45 c.e.

[324] Κοινωνίας δὲ καὶ φιλανθρωπίας εἰσηγητὴς ὢν ἐν τοῖς μάλιστα ὁ νόμος ἑκατέρας ἀρετῆς τήν τε ἀξίωσιν καὶ τὴν σεμνότητα διετήρησεν, οὐδενὶ τῶν ἀνιάτως ἐχόντων ἐπιτρέψας καταφυγεῖν ἐπ᾽ αὐτάς, ἀλλὰ πορρωτάτω σκορακίσας. [325] ἐπιστάμενος γοῦν ἐν ταῖς ἐκκλησίαις οὐκ ὀλίγους τῶν μοχθηρῶν παρεισρέοντας καὶ διὰ τὸ συνειλεγμένον πλῆθος λανθάνοντας, ἵνα μὴ τοῦτο γένηται, προανείργει πάντας τοὺς ἀναξίους ἱεροῦ συλλόγου τὴν ἀρχὴν ποιούμενος ἀπὸ τῶν νοσούντων τὴν θήλειαν νόσον ἀνδρογύνων, οἳ τὸ φύσεως νόμισμα παρακόπτοντες εἰς ἀκολάστων γυναικῶν πάθη καὶ μορφὰς εἰσβιάζονται· θλαδίας γὰρ καὶ ἀποκεκομμένους τὰ γεννητικὰ ἐλαύνει τό τε τῆς ὥρας ταμιεύοντας ἄνθος, ἵνα μὴ ῥᾳδίως μαραίνοιτο, καὶ τὸν ἄρρενα τύπον μεταχαράττοντας εἰς θηλύμορφον ἰδέαν.

[324] But while the law stands pre-eminent in enjoining fellowship and humanity, it preserves the high position and dignity of both virtues by not allowing anyone whose state is incurable to take refuge with them, but bidding him avaunt and keep his distance. [325] Thus, knowing that in assemblies (*ekklēsiai*) there are not a few worthless persons who steal their way in and remain unobserved in the large numbers which

surround them, it guards against this danger by precluding all the unworthy from entering the holy congregation (*syllogos*). It begins with the men who belie their sex and are affected with effemination, who debase the currency of nature and violate it by assuming the passions and the outward form of licentious women. For it expels those whose generative organs are fractured or mutilated, who husband the flower of their youthful bloom, lest it should quickly wither, and restamp the masculine cast into a feminine form.

Literature: Radice and Runia, *Bibliography 1937–1986*; Runia, *Bibliography 1987–1996*; Berger, "Volksversammlung", 171–77.

Comments: Most of the treatise *De specialibus legibus*, "The Special Laws," Book 1, treats regulations about worship (§§66–298). It continues with some exhortations in Deuteronomy (§§299–323) and concludes in §§324–345 with a long allegory on Deut 23:2–7 (LXX, in NRSV Deut 23:1–6). By dividing eunuchs into two categories from the double description in the biblical text (those whose testicles are crushed or those whose penis is cut off), Philo discerns five classes of men symbolized in these laws in Deut 23 and contrasts them to "the scholars and disciples of the prophet Moses" (§345). They are (1) deniers of the Platonic Forms or Ideas, (2) atheists, (3) polytheists, (4) those who rely on the human mind, or (5) those who rely only on the human senses, making gods of them and forgetting the truly living God. The five categories are mentioned again at the end (§344). The Law precluded all these unworthy persons "from entering the holy congregation" (§325) and "naturally banished them all from the holy congregation" (§344). The Greek words *hieros syllogos* (without definite article) could also be translated as "a holy congregation." Philo often returns to this allegorical interpretation of Deut 23 (*Legat.* 3.8; 3.81; *Post.* 177; *Deus* 111; *Ebr.* 213; *Conf.* 144; *Migr.* 69; *Mut.* 204, *Somn.* 2.184, 2.187 and *Virt.* 108), frequently using the word *ekklēsia* and sometimes also *syllogos*.

In Deut 23:2–9, the Septuagint five times contains the simple formulation "he shall not enter into the congregation of the Lord (*ouk eiseleusetai … eis ekklēsian Kyriou*)". Philo uses these words in explicit quotations (*Legat.* 3.81; *Post.* 177; *Deus* 111 and *Conf.* 144), but often has other formulations with "holy/divine assembly/congregation" without the article (*Legat.* 3.81; *Post.* 177 ["from every divine congregation"]; *Deus* 111; *Ebr.* 213; *Conf.* 144; *Migr.* 69; *Mut.* 204; *Somn.* 2.184, 187 [with article in post-position]; *Spec.* 1.325, 344; and *Virt.* 108).

In Deut 23 (LXX), the word *ekklēsia* refers to the people of God, to Israel as a whole. Philo can use *ekklēsia* generally to refer to an assembly (*Abr.* 20; *Spec.* 1.44; *Prob.* 138) or to the congregation at Sinai (*Post.* 143 ["when God is giving laws to His congregation"]; *Her.* 251; *Decal.* 32 ["when the nation, men and women alike, were gathered to an assembly"], and 45). In most cases, however, he uses *ekklēsia* in his allegorical interpretations of Deut 23.

The use of *ekklēsia* and the synonymous *syllogos* in these passages are not very clear, but the best suggestion is that they refer to some form of synagogue fellowship: "Für Philo ist '*ekklēsia*' in seiner Gegenwartsbedeutung vor allem die Zusammenkunft der Gemeinde am Sabbat, und in dieser Institution dürfte sich für das hellenistische Judentum im allgemeinen 'helige *Ekklēsia*' darstellen" (Berger, "Volksversammlung," 173–74). For an additional use of *ekklēsia* as a reference to Sabbath assemblies, see *Bib. Ant.* 11.8 (No. 64).

In *Contempl.* 30, Philo likewise uses the word *syllogos* about the Sabbath meetings of the Therapeutae. Later, Origen interpreted *ekklēsia* in Deut 23 as the Christian church. Philo also combined these passages with hearing the word of God (*Ebr.* 213 ["for what use can he (the 'eunuch') find in listening to holy words"]; *Migr.* 69 [the Law forbids "the son of a harlot to be a listener or speaker in it"]; and *Mut.* 204 ["others who do not hear with honest mind the holy instructions"]). See also *Deus* 111 and *Virt.* 108, cited below (No. 202 and No. 203).

Against such a backdrop, "in assemblies" in §325 (the Greek text has "in the assemblies [*en tais ekklēsiais*]") can refer to assemblies in general or to Jewish assemblies (on the Sabbath) such as the "holy congregation" (*hieros syllogos*). In Philo's view, the Law (Deut 23) had earlier excluded all the unworthy (the five classes mentioned above) from this fellowship.

No. 202
Source: *Literary.* Philo, *Deus* 111
Date: Ca. 30–45 C.E.

[111] ἕτερος δέ τις φιλοσώματος καὶ φιλοπαθὴς νοῦς πραθεὶς τῇ ἀρχιμαγείρῳ τοῦ συγκρίματος ἡμῶν ἡδονῇ καὶ ἐξευνουχισθεὶς τὰ ἄρρενα καὶ γεννητικὰ τῆς ψυχῆς μέρη πάντα, σπάνει κεχρημένος καλῶν ἐπιτηδευμάτων, ἀκοὴν παραδέξασθαι θείαν ἀδυνατῶν, ἐκκλησίας τῆς ἱερᾶς ἀπεσχοινισμένος, ἐν ᾗ [σύλλογοι καὶ] λόγοι περὶ ἀρετῆς ἀεὶ μελετῶνται, εἰς μὲν τὸ δεσμωτήριον τῶν παθῶν εἰσάγεται, χάριν δὲ εὑρίσκει τὴν ἀτιμίας ἀδοξοτέραν παρὰ τῷ ἀρχιδεσμοφύλακι.

[111] But there is a different mind which loves the body and the passions and has been sold in slavery to that chief cateress of our compound nature, Pleasure. Eunuch-like it has been deprived of all the male and productive organs of the soul, and lives in indigence of noble practices, unable to receive the divine message, debarred from the holy congregation [*ekklēsia*] in which the talk and study is always of virtue. When this mind is cast into the prison of the passions, it finds in the eyes of the chief jailer a favour and grace, which is more inglorious than dishonour.

Literature: Radice and Runia, *Bibliography 1937–1986*; Runia, *Bibliography 1987–1996*; Berger, "Volksversammlung", 171–77.

Comments: On Philo's *Quod Deus ist immutabilis*, see the comments on No. 161. The allegory in §§111–116 seems to be founded on Gen 39, where the LXX in 39:1 describes Potiphar as a chief cook and eunuch. Through the last word, this verse is combined with Deut 23:2 (LXX) and Philo's interpretation of the eunuchs there. See No. 201. The eunuch-like slaves of pleasure, prisoners of the passions, are unable "to receive the divine message" (*akoēn paradexasthai theian*). They are separated and cut off from the "holy congregation" (*ekklēsias tēs hieras*), where it is ever the practice to meet (*syllogos*) and talk of virtue (*logoi peri aretēs*). The last sentence could be used as a definition of the prayer halls as Philo describes them elsewhere. *Ekklēsia* and *syllogos* are also coupled in *Somn.* 2.184 and *Legat.* 3.81. The position of the definite article in *ekklesias tēs hieras* could be interpreted as an emphasis on "holy," though the definite nature of the noun could have been added as an afterthought.

No. 203
Source: *Literary.* Philo, *Virt.* 108
Date: Ca. 30–45 c.e.

[108] κἂν εἴ τινες ἐθελήσειαν αὐτῶν μεταλλάξασθαι πρὸς τὴν Ἰουδαίων πολιτείαν, οὐχ ὡς ἐχθρῶν παῖδας ἀσυμβάτως σκορακιστέον, ἀλλÆ οὕτως προσεκτέον, ὡς τρίτην γενεὰν καλεῖν τε εἰς ἐκκλησίαν καὶ μεταδιδόναι λόγων θείων, οἷς θέμις καὶ τοὺς αὐτόχθονας καὶ εὐπατρίδας ἱεροφαντεῖσθαι.

[108] And if any of them should wish to pass over into the Jewish community, they must not be spurned with an unconditional refusal as children of enemies, but be so far favoured that the third generation is invited to the congregation [*ekklēsia*] and made partakers in the divine revelations, to which also the native born, whose lineage is beyond reproach, are rightfully admitted.

Literature: Radice and Runia, *Bibliography 1937–1986*; Runia, *Bibliography 1987–1996*; Berger, "Volksversammlung", 171–77.

Comments: In his explanation of Mosaic laws in *De virtutibus*, "On the Virtues," Philo describes how kindness is to be displayed towards people of different categories: to the Israelites, "the brothers" (§§80–101); to strangers, who are assumed to be proselytes of faith (§§102–104); to the soujorners (§§105–108); and to enemies, women captives, slaves, animals and plants. In the section about the sojourners (*paroikoi*), he refers to Deut 23:7f. (LXX; see No. 201): "You shall not curse an Egyptian, because you were sojourners in his land." The biblical text continues: "If sons be born to them, in the third generation they shall enter into the assembly of the Lord."

This is the background of the formulation in §108. If any of the sojourners wanted to pass over into the Jewish community (*politeia*), they should be invited to the assembly (*ekklēsia*) and receive the divine words (*logoi theioi*). The verbs used are in active form and the two clauses are strongly connected by a "both...and" (*te...kai*). The natives of the land, who were the descendants of God's people, had the right to be instructed in divine words. The verb *hierophanteisthai* means "to be initiated in, to be instructed in." The sojourners received the same right. The formulation is reminiscent of Philo's descriptions of the activities in the prayer halls.

4.1.3   *Acts*

No. 204
Source: *Literary.* Acts 15:21
Date: Ca. 90–110 C.E.

[21] Μωϋσῆς γὰρ ἐκ γενεῶν ἀρχαίων κατὰ πόλιν τοὺς κηρύσσοντας αὐτὸν ἔχει ἐν ταῖς συναγωγαῖς κατὰ πᾶν σάββατον ἀναγινωσκόμενος.

[21] For in every city, for generations past, Moses has had those who proclaim him, for he has been read aloud every Sabbath in the synagogues [*synagōgē*].

Literature: As a general reference to commentaries see Barrett, Fitzmyer and Jervell, *Comm., ad loc.*

Comments: See No. 72.

No. 205
Source: *Literary.* Acts 22:19
Date: Ca. 90–110 C.E.

[19] κἀγὼ εἶπον· κύριε, αὐτοὶ ἐπίστανται ὅτι ἐγὼ ἤμην φυλακίζων καὶ δέρων κατὰ τὰς συναγωγὰς τοὺς πιστεύοντας ἐπὶ σέ

[19] And I said, "Lord, they themselves know that in every synagogue [*synagōgē*] I imprisoned and beat those who believed in you."

Literature: As a general reference to commentaries see Barrett, Fitzmyer and Jervell, *Comm., ad loc.*

Comments: See No. 73.

No. 206
Source: *Literary.* Acts 26:9–11
Date: Ca. 90–110 C.E.

[9] Ἐγὼ μὲν οὖν ἔδοξα ἐμαυτῷ πρὸς τὸ ὄνομα Ἰησοῦ τοῦ Ναζωραίου δεῖν πολλὰ ἐναντία πρᾶξαι, [10] ὃ καὶ ἐποίησα ἐν Ἱεροσολύμοις, καὶ πολλούς τε τῶν ἁγίων ἐγὼ ἐν φυλακαῖς κατέκλεισα τὴν παρὰ τῶν ἀρχιερέων ἐξουσίαν λαβὼν ἀναιρουμένων τε αὐτῶν κατήνεγκα ψῆφον. [11] καὶ κατὰ πάσας τὰς συναγωγὰς πολλάκις τιμωρῶν αὐτοὺς ἠνάγκαζον βλασφημεῖν περισσῶς τε ἐμμαινόμενος αὐτοῖς ἐδίωκον ἕως καὶ εἰς τὰς ἔξω πόλεις.

[9] Indeed, I myself was convinced that I ought to do many things against the name of Jesus of Nazareth. [10] And that is what I did in Jerusalem; with authority received from the chief priests, I not only locked up many of the saints in prison, but I also cast my vote against them when they were being condemned to death. [11] By punishing them often in all the synagogues [*synagōgē*] I tried to force them to blaspheme; and since I was so furiously enraged at them, I pursued them even to foreign cities.

Literature: As a general reference to commentaries see Barrett, Fitzmyer and Jervell, *Comm., ad loc.*

Comments: See No. 20.

4.1.4 *Artemidorus*

No. 207
Source: *Literary.* Artemidorus, *Onirocritica* 3.53
Date: Mid/late second century C.E.

[53] Προσευχὴ καὶ μεταῖται καὶ πάντες ἄνθρωποι προΐκται καὶ οἰκτροὶ καὶ πτωχοὶ λύπην καὶ φροντίδα καὶ τηκεδόνα τῆς ψυχῆς καὶ ἀνδρὶ καὶ γυναικὶ προαγορεύουσι· τοῦτο μὲν γὰρ οὐδεὶς ἄπεισιν εἰς προσευχὴν μὴ οὐχὶ φροντίζων, τοῦτο δὲ καὶ οἱ μεταῖται πάνυ εἰδεχθεῖς ὄντες καὶ ἄποροι καὶ μηδὲν ἔχοντες ὑγιὲς ἐμποδὼν ἵστανται πάσῃ προαιρέσει.

[53] A prayer hall [*proseuchē*] and beggars and all people who ask for gifts, and such as arouse pity, and mendicants, foretell grief, anxiety and heartache to both men and women. For on the one hand no one departs for a prayer hall [*proseuchē*] without care, and on the other, beggars who are very odious-looking and without resources and have nothing wholesome about them are an obstacle to every plan.[1]

---

[1] Translation adapted from Pack.

Literature: Stern, *GLAJJ*, II. no. 395.

Comments: Artemidorus of Ephesus was an interpreter of dreams. Of interest here is the link he makes between the synagogue and beggars, both symbolizing for him a negative sign of coming misfortune. Such an unsympathetic construction of the Jewish institution suggests a negative social relationship between Jews and non-Jews, at least from the perspective of the educated non-Jewish elite. Cf. the similar perspective of Juvenal and Cleomedes (Nos. 181, 208).

4.1.5 *Cleomedes*

No. 208
Source: *Literary.* Cleomedes, *De Modu Circulari* 2.1.91
Date: There is some disagreement regarding when Cleomedes lived, suggestions ranging between the first century B.C.E. and the fourth century C.E. While no certainty can be attained, it seems reasonable to assume a date either in the first or second century C.E. (so Stern, *GLAJJ*, II. 157).

[91] Ἐπεί γε πρὸς τοῖς ἄλλοις καὶ τὰ κατὰ τὴν ἑρμηνείαν αὐτῷ ποικίλως διεφθορότα ἐστί, σαρκὸς εὐσταθῆ καταστήματα λέγοντι καὶ τὰ περὶ ταύτης πιστὰ ἐλπίσματα καὶ λίπασμα ὀφθαλμῶν τὸ δάκρυον ὀνομάζοντι καὶ ἱερὰ ἀνακραυγάσματα καὶ γαργαλισμοὺς σώματος καὶ ληκήματα καὶ ἄλλας τοιαύτας κακὰς ἄτας· ὧν τὰ μὲν ἐκ χαμαιτυπείων ἄν τις εἶναι φήσειε, τὰ δὲ ὅμοια τοῖς λεγομένοις ἐν τοῖς Δημητρίοις ὑπὸ τῶν Θεσμοφοριαζουσῶν γυναικῶν, τὰ δὲ ἀπὸ μέσης τῆς προσευχῆς καὶ τῶν ἐπ᾽ αὐλαῖς προσαιτούντων, Ἰουδαϊκά τινα καὶ παρακεχαραγμένα καὶ κατὰ πολὺ τῶν ἑρπετῶν ταπεινότερα

[91] Since, in addition to other things, his style [scil. Epicuros'] is also a corrupt motley, making use of expressions like "stable states of the flesh" and "hopeful hopes" concerning it, and calling tears "glistening of the eyes" and having recourse to phrases like "holy screechings" and "ticklings of the body" and "wenchings" and other bad mischievous of this kind. One may say that these expressions drive in part from brothels, in part they are similar to those spoken by women celebrating the Thesmophoria at the festivals Demeter, and in part they issue from the midst of the prayer hall [*proseuchē*] and the beggars in its courtyards. These are Jewish and debased and much lower than reptiles.[2]

---

[2] Translation adapted from Ziegler.

Literature: Stern, *GLAJJ*, II. no. 333.

Comments: Cf. comments to Artemidorus (No. 207), especially the connection between synagogues and beggars, revealing a low appreciation of the synagogue on the part of the non-Jewish literate elite. Cf. also a similar comment by Juvenal (No. 181). Note the mention of courtyards as part of the synagogue structure.

4.1.6 *Tacitus*

No. 209
Source: Tacitus, *Historiae* 5.4
Date: The multivolume work *Historiae* was completed ca. 109/110 c.e.

[5.4] Aegyptii pleraque animalia effigiesque compositas venerantur, Iudaei mente sola unumque numen intellegunt: profanos qui deum imagines mortalibus materiis in species hominum effingant; summum illud et aeternum neque imitabile neque interiturum. Igitur nulla simulacra urbibus suis, nedum templis s<ist>unt; non regibus haec adulatio, non Caesaribus honor.

[5.4] The Egyptians worship many animals and monstrous images; the Jews conceive of one God only, and that with the mind only: they regard as impious those who make from perishable materials representations of gods in man's image; that supreme and eternal being is to them incapable of representation and without end. Therefore they set up no statues in their cities, still less in their temples [*templum*]; this flattery is not paid their kings, nor this honour given to the Caesars.[3]

Literature: Stern, *GLAJJ* II. no. 281, p. 43; Runesson, *Origins*, 466; Levine, *Ancient Synagogue*, 128, 480.

Comments: The word *templum*, here used as a term for the synagogue, is paralleled in several (Jewish and non-Jewish) sources that refer to synagogues using temple terminology. While the earlier of these sources may have referred to Jewish temples that offered animal sacrifices, by the second century c.e. when Tacitus wrote, cult centralisation ideology had received widespread acceptance throughout the Diaspora. It may well be, however, that non-animal sacrifices, like incense and vegetable offerings, were not seen as being in opposition to the Jewish law. Even though such institutions should be categorised with synagogues and understood as a type of synagogue, it is possible that temple-

---

[3] Translation by Moore (LCL).

terms used for these institutions also reveal something about the architectural (temple-like) appearance of the buildings (Runesson).

4.1.7 Justin Martyr[4]

No. 210
Source: *Literary*. Justin Martyr, *Dial.* 16
Date: *Dialogus cum Tryphone* was probably authored around the time of the Bar Kochbah uprising (132–135 C.E.), which is mentioned in chs. 1 and 9, or shortly thereafter (Quasten).

[16] καὶ ὑμῖν οὖν ταῦτα καλῶς καὶ δικαίως γέγονεν. ἀπεκτείνατε γὰρ τὸν δίκαιον καὶ πρὸ αὐτοῦ τοὺς προφήτας αὐτοῦ· καὶ νῦν τοὺς ἐλπίζοντας ἐπ᾽ αὐτὸν καὶ τὸν πέμψαντα αὐτὸν παντοκράτορα καὶ ποιητὴν τῶν ὅλων θεὸν ἀθετεῖτε καί, ὅσον ἐφ᾽ ὑμῖν, ἀτιμάζετε, καταρώμενοι ἐν ταῖς συναγωγαῖς ὑμῶν τοὺς πιστεύοντας ἐπὶ τὸν Χριστόν.

[16] Accordingly, these things have happened to you in fairness and justice, for you have slain the Just One, and His prophets before Him; and now you reject those who hope in Him, and in Him who sent Him—God the Almighty and Maker of all things—cursing in your synagogues [*synagōgē*] those that believe in Christ.

Literature: As a general reference, see Barnard, *Justin Martyr*; Chadwick, *Early Christian Thought*; Osborn, *Justin Martyr*; Goodenough, *Hellenistic and Judaistic Influences*; Allert, *Dialogue With Trypho*. Schürer, *HJP* 2.432, 462; Cohen, "Pharisees and Rabbis," 100–102; Levine, *Ancient Synagogue*, 212.

Comments: In ch. 16, Justin attacks the Jews by claiming that they were responsible for the death of Jesus, which in turn resulted in their suffering at the hand of the Romans. The reference to verbal abuse of Christ-believers in the synagogues may suggest that Christ-believers were connected to the synagogues, perhaps even as members. Justin elsewhere discusses such Jewish believers-in-Christ and, contrary to some of his fellow Christians, acknowledges their Jewish interpretation of Christianity to be legitimate (*Dial.* 47). The reference to cursing may allude to the *Birkath ha-Minim*, but it is by no means necessarily the case that ritualized abuse is intended (such as became commonly characterised in later Christian polemic): it may just as well refer to sporadic denunciation of belief in Jesus as the messiah in sermons (cf. below, Nos. 211, 214).

---

[4] All translations of Justin Martyr are by A. Cleveland Coxe. Although *Dialogus cum Tryphone* may have been written in Ephesus (so Quasten), the generalising references to synagogues warrant the inclusion of these passages under the heading General References.

No. 211
Source: *Literary.* Justin Martyr, *Dial.* 47
Date: *Dialogus cum Tryphone* was probably authored around the time of the Bar Kochbah uprising (132–135 C.E.), which is mentioned in chs. 1 and 9, or shortly thereafter (Quasten).

[47] καὶ τοὺς ἀπὸ τοῦ σπέρματος τοῦ Ἀβραὰμ ζῶντας κατὰ τὸν νόμον καὶ ἐπὶ τοῦτον τὸν Χριστὸν μὴ πιστεύοντας πρὶν τελευτῆς τοῦ βίου οὐ σωθήσεσθαι ὁμοίως ἀποφαίνομαι, καὶ μάλιστα τοὺς ἐν ταῖς συναγωγαῖς καταθεματίσαντας καὶ καταθεματίζοντας τοὺς ἐπ' αὐτὸν τοῦτον τὸν Χριστὸν πιστεύοντας ὅπως τύχωσι τῆς σωτηρίας καὶ τῆς τιμωρίας τῆς ἐν τῷ πυρὶ ἀπαλλαγῶσιν.

[47] Further, I hold that those of the seed of Abraham who live according to the law, and do not believe in this Christ before death, shall likewise not be saved, and especially those who have anathematized and do anathematize this very Christ in the synagogues [*synagōgē*], and everything by which they might obtain salvation and escape the vengeance of fire.

Literature: As a general reference, see Barnard, *Justin Martyr*; Chadwick, *Early Christian Thought*; Osborn, *Justin Martyr*; Goodenough, *Hellenistic and Judaistic Influences*; Allert, *Dialogue With Trypho*. Schürer, *HJP* 2.462; Cohen, "Pharisees and Rabbis," 100–102.

Comments: The discussion in ch. 47 concerns the status of Jews who believe in Jesus as the Christ but also adhere to Torah. According to Justin (but contrary to many other contemporary non-Jewish Christians), these Jews would be saved so long as they did not attempt to convince non-Jewish Christians to observe all of the Law. The passage given here again indicates the close relationship between Jews and Christians, to the point where some Jewish communities found it necessary to distance themselves collectively in their synagogues from a belief in Christ.

No. 212
Source: *Literary.* Justin Martyr, *Dial.* 53
Date: *Dialogus cum Tryphone* was probably authored around the time of the Bar Kochbah uprising (132–135 C.E.), which is mentioned in chs. 1 and 9, or shortly thereafter (Quasten).

[53] τὸ δὲ καὶ ὄνον ὑποζύγιον ἤδη μετὰ τοῦ πώλου αὐτῆς ὀνομάζειν τὸ προφητικὸν πνεῦμα μετὰ τοῦ πατριάρχου Ἰακὼβ ἐν τῇ κτήσει αὐτὸν ἔχειν, ἀλλὰ καὶ αὐτὸν τοῖς μαθηταῖς αὐτοῦ, ὡς προέφην, ἀμφότερα

τὰ ζῷα κελεῦσαι ἀγαγεῖν, προαγγελία ἦν καὶ τοῖς ἀπὸ τῆς συναγωγῆς ὑμῶν ἅμα τοῖς ἀπὸ τῶν ἐθνῶν πιστεύειν ἐπ᾽ αὐτὸν μέλλουσιν.

[53] Now, that the Spirit of prophecy, as well as the patriarch Jacob, mentioned both an ass and its foal, which would be used by Him; and, further, that He, as I previously said, requested His disciples to bring both beasts; [this fact] was a prediction that you of the synagogue [*synagōgē*], along with the Gentiles, would believe in Him.

Literature: As a general reference, see Barnard, *Justin Martyr*; Chadwick, *Early Christian Thought*; Osborn, *Justin Martyr*; Goodenough, *Hellenistic and Judaistic Influences*; Allert, *Dialogue With Trypho*.

Comments: Justin here uses "synagogue" metaphorically to designate the Jewish people, a way of talking about the synagogue that became standard in Christian writings of later centuries. Justin, however, contrary to later Christian writings, acknowledges the legitimacy of Jewish Christ-belief and thus avoids the otherwise common polarization between "synagogue" and "Church" as incompatible entities (cf. *Dial.* 134, No. 216 below, and the discussion in the Introduction).

No. 213

Source: *Literary.* Justin Martyr, *Dial.* 72
Date: *Dialogus cum Tryphone* was probably authored around the time of the Bar Kochbah uprising (132–135 c.e.), which is mentioned in chs. 1 and 9, or shortly thereafter (Quasten).

[72] καὶ ἐπειδὴ αὕτη ἡ περικοπή, ἡ ἐκ τῶν λόγων τοῦ Ἰερεμίου, ἔτι ἐστὶν ἐγγεγραμμένη ἔν τισιν ἀντιγράφοις τῶν ἐν συναγωγαῖς Ἰουδαίων (πρὸ γὰρ ὀλίγου χρόνου ταῦτα ἐξέκοψαν), ἐπειδὰν καὶ ἐκ τούτων τῶν λόγων ἀποδεικνύηται ὅτι ἐβουλεύσαντο Ἰουδαῖοι περὶ αὐτοῦ τοῦ Χριστοῦ, ἀναιρεῖν αὐτὸν σταυρώσαντες βουλευσάμενοι, καὶ αὐτὸς μηνύεται, ὡς καὶ διὰ τοῦ Ἡσαίου προεφητεύθη, ὡς πρόβατον ἐπὶ σφαγὴν ἀγόμενος, καὶ ἐνθάδε ὡς ἀρνίον ἄκακον δηλοῦται· ὧν ἀπορούμενοι ἐπὶ τὸ βλασφημεῖν χωροῦσι.

[72] And since this passage from the sayings of Jeremiah is still written in some copies [of the Scriptures] in the synagogues [*synagōgē*] of the Jews (for it is only a short time since they were cut out), and since from these words it is demonstrated that the Jews deliberated about the Christ Himself, to crucify and put Him to death, He Himself is both declared to be led as a sheep to the slaughter, as was predicted by Isaiah, and is here represented as a harmless lamb; but being in a difficulty about them, they give themselves over to blasphemy.

Literature: As a general reference, see Barnard, *Justin Martyr*; Chadwick, *Early Christian Thought*; Osborn, *Justin Martyr*; Goodenough, *Hellenistic and Judaistic Influences*; Allert, *Dialogue With Trypho*. Horbury, "Synagogue Prayer," 299.

Comments: As is evidenced in several first century C.E. sources, copies of the Torah were kept in synagogue buildings, and thus owned communally.

No. 214
Source: *Literary*. Justin Martyr, *Dial.* 96
Date: *Dialogus cum Tryphone* was probably authored around the time of the Bar Kochbah uprising (132–135 C.E.), which is mentioned in chs. 1 and 9, or shortly thereafter (Quasten).

[96] ὑμεῖς γὰρ ἐν ταῖς συναγωγαῖς ὑμῶν καταρᾶσθε πάντων τῶν ἀπ᾽ ἐκείνου γενομένων Χριστιανῶν, καὶ τὰ ἄλλα ἔθνη, ἃ καὶ ἐνεργῆ τὴν κατάραν ἐργάζονται, ἀναιροῦντα τοὺς μόνον ὁμολογοῦντας ἑαυτοὺς εἶναι Χριστιανούς· οἷς ἡμεῖς ἅπασι λέγομεν ὅτι Ἀδελφοὶ ἡμῶν ἐστε, ἐπίγνωτε μᾶλλον τὴν ἀλήθειαν τοῦ θεοῦ.

[96] For you curse in your synagogues [*synagōgē*] all those who are called from Him Christians; and other nations effectively carry out the curse, putting to death those who simply confess themselves to be Christians; to all of whom we say, You are our brethren; rather recognize the truth of God.

Literature: As a general reference, see Barnard, *Justin Martyr*; Chadwick, *Early Christian Thought*; Osborn, *Justin Martyr*; Goodenough, *Hellenistic and Judaistic Influences*; Allert, *Dialogue With Trypho*. Schürer, *HJP* 2.462; Cohen, "Pharisees and Rabbis," 100–2.

Comments: The cursing of Christians in synagogue assemblies is here said to result in the (religio-political) persecution of Christians, since the Romans frequently condemned the latter to death for their faith. As in the above examples, while such condemnations may have been ritualized in the liturgy, the reference may just as well be to anti-Christian diatribes within sermons. In any case, it is clear that Justin thinks such curses took place in the context of synagogue worship.

No. 215
Source: *Literary*. Justin Martyr, *Dial.* 104
Date: *Dialogus cum Tryphone* was probably authored around the time of the Bar Kochbah uprising (132–135 C.E.), which is mentioned in chs. 1 and 9, or shortly thereafter (Quasten).

[104] Καὶ τὸ Εἰς χοῦν θανάτου κατήγαγές με, ὅτι ἐκύκλωσάν με κύνες πολλοί, συναγωγὴ πονηρευομένων περιέσχον με· ὤρυξαν χεῖράς μου καὶ πόδας μου, ἐξηρίθμησαν πάντα τὰ ὀστᾶ μου· αὐτοὶ δὲ κατενόησαν καὶ ἐπεῖδόν με· διεμερίσαντο τὰ ἱμάτιά μου ἑαυτοῖς, καὶ ἐπὶ τὸν ἱματισμόν μου ἔβαλον κλῆρον, ὡς προεῖπον, προαγγελία ἦν διὰ ποίου θανάτου καταδικάζειν αὐτὸν ἔμελλεν ἡ συναγωγὴ τῶν πονηρευομένων, οὓς καὶ κύνας καλεῖ, καὶ κυνηγοὺς μηνύων, ὅτι αὐτοὶ οἱ κυνηγήσαντες καὶ συνήχθησαν οἱ ἀγωνιζόμενοι ἐπὶ τῷ καταδικάσασθαι αὐτόν.

[104] And the statement, "Thou hast brought me into the dust of death; for many dogs have surrounded me: the assembly [*synagōgē*] of the wicked have beset me round. They pierced my hands and my feet. They did tell all my bones. They did look and stare upon me. They parted my garments among them, and cast lots upon my vesture,"—was a prediction, as I said before, of the death to which the synagogue [*synagōgē*] of the wicked would condemn Him, whom He calls both dogs and hunters, declaring that those who hunted Him were both gathered together and assiduously striving to condemn Him.

Literature: As a general reference, see Barnard, *Justin Martyr*; Chadwick, *Early Christian Thought*; Osborn, *Justin Martyr*; Goodenough, *Hellenistic and Judaistic Influences*; Allert, *Dialogue With Trypho*.

Comments: For Justin, "the Jews" were responsible for the death of Jesus, and he adduces support for this conviction from both the Hebrew Bible and the New Testament. The identification of "the assembly of the wicked" (Ps 21:17, LXX) with the synagogue in this passage reinforces this rhetoric through its application to Justin's contemporaries. The passage thus contains the hermeneutical building blocks used in later Christian writings hostile toward Judaism and the synagogue. Cf. the expression "synagogue (*synagōgē*) of Satan" in Rev 2:8–11 and 3:7–13 (Nos. 115 and 111).

No. 216

Source: *Literary*. Justin Martyr, *Dial.* 134
Date: *Dialogus cum Tryphone* was probably authored around the time of the Bar Kochbah uprising (132–135 C.E.), which is mentioned in chs. 1 and 9, or shortly thereafter (Quasten).

[134] ἀλλὰ Λεία μὲν ὁ λαὸς ὑμῶν καὶ ἡ συναγωγή, Ῥαχὴλ δὲ ἡ ἐκκλησία ἡμῶν. καὶ ὑπὲρ τούτων δουλεύει μέχρι νῦν ὁ Χριστὸς καὶ τῶν ἐν ἀμφοτέραις δούλων.

Now Leah is your people and synagogue [*synagōgē*]; but Rachel is our Church [*ekklēsia*]. And for these, and for the servants in both, Christ even now serves.

Literature: As a general reference, see Barnard, *Justin Martyr*; Chadwick, *Early Christian Thought*; Osborn, *Justin Martyr*; Goodenough, *Hellenistic and Judaistic Influences*; Allert, *Dialogue With Trypho*. Cohen, "Pagan and Christian Evidence," 160, n. 5; Claußen, *Versammlung*, 262.

Comments: This is the clearest metaphorical use of "synagogue" for the Jewish people by Justin, who is the first Christian author to apply "synagogue" in this way (Cohen). As noted above (No. 212), however, the polarization between synagogue and church is not absolute. For Justin, Jacob represented Israel, who in turn represented Christ. Thus, "Christ" had married both synagogue (Leah) and church (Rachel). This is a far cry from later medieval representations of "synagogue" and "church," where the former is depicted as either defeated or even executed by the hands of the so-called living crosses (cf. Schreckenberg, *Christian Art*, 64–6). Still, it seems clear that Justin reserves "church" (*ekklēsia*) for non-Jewish Christian institutions, while the synagogue could serve as the home of Christ-believing Jews as well as Jews who did not share this belief. Such a distinction is not evident in earlier sources, where both designations could be used for either Christian or non-Christian (Jewish) institutions (cf. Jas 2:2–4, No. 196, and the discussion in the Introduction).

No. 217
Source: *Literary*. Justin Martyr, *Dial.* 137
Date: *Dialogus cum Tryphone* was probably authored around the time of the Bar Kochbah uprising (132–135 c.e.), which is mentioned in chs. 1 and 9, or shortly thereafter (Quasten).

[137] συμφάμενοι οὖν μὴ λοιδορῆτε ἐπὶ τὸν υἱὸν τοῦ θεοῦ, μηδὲ Φαρισαίοις πειθόμενοι διδασκάλοις τὸν βασιλέα τοῦ Ἰσραὴλ ἐπισκώψητέ ποτε, ὁποῖα διδάσκουσιν οἱ ἀρχισυνάγωγοι ὑμῶν, μετὰ τὴν προσευχήν. εἰ γὰρ ὁ ἁπτόμενος τῶν μὴ εὐαρέστων τῷ θεῷ ὡς ὁ ἁπτόμενος κόρης τοῦ θεοῦ, πολὺ μᾶλλον ὁ τοῦ ἠγαπημένου καθαπτόμενος.

[137] Assent, therefore, and pour no ridicule on the Son of God; obey not the Pharisaic teachers, and scoff not at the King of Israel, as the rulers of your synagogues [*archisynagōgoi*] teach you to do after your prayers: for if he that touches those who are not pleasing to God, is as one that touches the apple of God's eye, how much more so is he that touches His beloved!

Literature: As a general reference, see Barnard, *Justin Martyr*; Chadwick, *Early Christian Thought*; Osborn, *Justin Martyr*; Goodenough, *Hellenistic and Judaistic Influences*; Allert, *Dialogue With Trypho*. Schürer, *HJP* 2.434, 462; Cohen, "Pharisees and Rabbis," 100–102; Claußen, *Versammlung*, 262; Levine, *Ancient Synagogue*, 419.

Comments: The reference to Pharisaic teachers here is somewhat surprising: the mention of *archisynagōgoi* immediately afterwards gives the impression that the former were leaders in the synagogues. It is more likely, however, that Justin reproduces negative stereotypes from the Gospels (although unrelated to first-century synagogue leadership) in order to strengthen his case against the synagogue leadership in his period. As in other passages from this work, Justin refers to the mocking of Jesus in a synagogue context. Here he states that these took place after the prayers when they were allegedly promoted by the synagogue rulers (*archisynagōgoi*), who seem to have functioned as instructors.

CHAPTER FIVE

JEWISH TEMPLES OUTSIDE JERUSALEM

5.1 *Babylonia*

5.1.1 *Casiphia*

No. T1
Source: *Literary.* Ezra 8:17
Date: The reign of the Persian king Artaxerxes II (404–359 B.C.E.)

ואוצאה אותם על אדו הראש בכספיא המקום ואשימה בפיהם דברים
לדבר אל אדו אחיו הנתונים בכספיא המקום להביא לנו משרתים לבית
אלהינו

And I sent them to Iddo, the leader in the sanctuary of Casiphia [*be Kasifia ha-makom*], telling them what to say to Iddo and his colleagues the temple servants in the sanctuary of Casiphia [*be Kasifia ha-makom*], namely, to send us ministers for the house of our God.[1]

Literature: Torrey, *Ezra Studies*, 315–19; Browne, "Jewish Sanctuary"; Menes, "Tempel und Synagoge"; Blenkinsopp, *Pentateuch*, 238; Williamson, *Ezra, Nehemiah*, 117; Binder, *Temple Courts*, 135; Runesson, *Origins*, 404–9.

Comments: In this intriguing passage, a certain Iddo is asked to provide personnel for a rebuilt temple in Jerusalem. Several scholars have argued that the verse refers to a Jewish temple in Babylonia where Iddo was a leading priest. It is clear from 8:15 that Ezra needed Levites for the temple in Jerusalem, and Iddo was to provide them. As is well attested, the term *makom*, which refers to the place where Iddo served, may mean "temple" or "sanctuary" (cf. Binder). The translation of *be Kasifia ha-makom* given here was first suggested by Browne. As is the case with several other terms, such as *proseuchē* and *hieron, topos* (the Greek translation of *makom*) could also refer to the synagogue (Binder, 135–40). That *makom* cannot refer to a synagogue in this verse, however, is evident from the fact that this institution specifically employed "temple servants" (*netinim*), a term used for Levites in the Hebrew Bible.

---

[1] Translation by the authors.

In rendering judgements on the existence of Jewish temples outside of Jerusalem, an important consideration is the degree of cultic centralisation before and during the exile. If, as has been argued, such centralisation occured only after the exile (see Runesson, esp. 426–28 for discussion and literature), Ezra 8:17 could be interpreted as one step towards the implementation of this religio-political program. Here, it is instructive to compare this situation with the evidence from Egypt, where multiple Jewish temples existed in different periods up to 74 C.E., when the Leontopolis temple was destroyed.

5.2 Egypt

5.2.1 *Elephantine*

No. T2
Source: *Papyrus.* Cowley no. 30/Porten B19.
Date: November 25, 407 B.C.E.

1   אל מראן בגוהי פחת יהוד עבדיך ידניה וכנותה כהניא זי ביב בירתא
שלם

2   מראן אלה שמיא ישאל שגיא בכל עדן ולרחמן ישימנך קדם
דריוהוש מלבא

3   ובני ביתא יתיר מן זי כען חד אלף וחין אריכן ינתן לך וחדה ושריר
הוי בכל עדן

4   כען עבדך ידניה וכנותה כן אמרן בירח תמוז שנת {*} דריוהוש
מלכא כזי ארום

5   נפק ואזל על מלכא כמריא זי {אהלה} חנוב זי ביב בירתא המונית
עם וידרנג זי פרתרך תנה

6   הוה לם אנורא זי יהו אלהא זי ביב בירתא יהעדו מן תמה אחר
וידרנג זך

7   לחיא אגרת שלח על נפין ברה זי רבחיל הוה בסן בירתא לאמר
אנורא זי ביב

8   בירתא ינדשו אחר נפין דבר מצריא עם הילא אחרנן אתו לבירת יב
עם תליהם

9   עלו באנורא זך נדשוהי עד ארעא ועמודיא זי אבנא זי הוו תמה תברו
{המו} אף הוה תרען

10   זי אבן {*} בנין פסילה זי אבן זי הוו באנורא זך נדשו ודשיהם קימו
וציריהם

11   זי דששיא אלך נחש ומטלל עקהן {זי} ארז כלא זי עם שירית אשרנא
ואחרן זי תמה

12   הוה כלא באשה שרפו ומזרקיא זי יהבא וכסף ומנדעמתא זי הוה באנורא
זך כלא לקח{ו}

13 ולנפשהום עבדו ומן יומי מלך מצרין אבהין בנו אנורא זך ביב בירתא
וכזי כנבוזי על למצר{ין}

14 אנורא זך בנה השכח ואנורי אלהי מצרין כל מנרו ואיש מנדעם באנורא
זך לא חבל

15 וכזי כונה עביד אנחנה עם נשין ובנין שקקן לבשן הוין וצימין ומצלין
ליהו מרא שמיא

16 זי החוין בוידרננ זך כלביא הנפקו כבלא מן רגלוהי וכל נכסין זי קנה
אבדו וכל נבריו

17 זי בעו באיש לאנורא זך כל קטילו וחזין בהום אף קדמת זנה בעדן זי
זא באיש{תא}

18 עביד לן אנרה שלחן מראן ועל יהוחנן כהנא רבא וכנותה כהניא זי
בירושלם ועל אוסתן אחוה{י}

19 זי ענני וחרי יהודיא אנרה חדה לא שלחו עלין אף מן ירח תמוז שנת
{*} דריהוש מלכא

20 וע{ד?}זנה יומא אנחנה שקקן לבשן וצימין נשיא זילן כארמלה עבידן
משח לא משחין

21 וחמר לא שתין אף מן זכי ועד יום שנת {*} דריהוש מלהוש מלכא
מנחה ולבו{נ}ה ועלוה

22 לא עבדו באנורא זך כען עבדיך ידניה וכנותה ויהודיא כל בעלי יב כן
אמר{ין}

23 הן על מראן טב אתעשת על אנורא זך למבנה בזילא שבקן לן למבניה
חזי בעלי

24 טבתך ורחמיך {זי} תנה במצין אנרה מנך ישתלח עליהום על אנורא זי
יהו אלהא

25 למבניה ביב בירתא לקבל זי בנה הוה קדמין ומחתא ולבונתא ועלותא
יקרבון

26 על מדבחא זי יהו אלהא בשמך ונצלה עליך בכל עדן אנחנה ונשין
ובנין ויהודיא

27 כל י תנה הן עבדו עד זי אנורא זך יתבנה וצדקה יהוה לך קדם יהו
אלה

28 שמיא מן נבר זי יקרבלה עלוה ודבהן דמן כדמי כסף כנכרין | לף
ועל זהב על זנה

29 שלחן הודען אף כלא מליא באנרה הדה שלחן {בשמן} על דליה
ושלמיה בני סנאבלט פ{ח}ת שמרין

30 אף בונה זי עביד לן {כלא} ארשם לא ידע ב{*} למרחשון שנת {*}
דריהוש מלכא

1 To our Lord Bagavahya governor of Judah, your servants Jedaniah
   and his colleagues the priests who are in Elaphantine the fortress.
   The welfare

2 of our lord may the God of Heaven seek after abundantly at all times, and favour may He grant you before Darius the King

3 and the princes more than now a thousand times, and long life may He give you, and happy and strong may you be at all times.

4 Now, your servant Jedaniah and his colleagues thus say: In the month of Tammuz, year 14 of Darius the king, when Arsames

5 had departed and gone to the king, the priests of Khnub {the god} who are in Elephantine the fortress, in agreement with Vidranga who [6]was [5]Chief here, (said),

6 saying: "The temple of YHW the God which is in Elephantine the fortress let them remove from there." Afterwards, that Vidranga,

7 the wicked, a letter sent to Naphaina his son, who was Troop Commander in Syene the fortress, saying: "The temple which is in Elephantine

8 the fortress let them demolish." Afterwards, Naphaina led the Egyptians with the other troops. They came to the fortress of Elephantine with their implements,

9 broke into that temple, demolished it to the ground, and the pillars of stone which were there—they smashed {them}. Moreover, it happened (that the) [10]5 [9]gateways

10 of stone, built of hewn stone, which were in that temple, they demolished. And their standing doors, and the hinges

11 of those doors, (of) bronze, and the roof of wood of cedar—all (of these) which, with the rest of the FITTINGS and other (things), which

12 were there [11]there—[12]all (of these) with fire they burned. But the basins of gold and silver and the (other) things which were in that temple—all (of these) {they} took

13 and made their own. And from the days of the king(s) of Egypt our fathers had built that temple in Elephantine the fortress and when Cambyses entered Eg{ypt}

14 —that temple, built he found it. And the temples of the gods of Egypt, all (of them), they overthrew, but anything in that temple one did not damage.

15 And when this had been done (to us), we with our wives and our children sackcloth were wearing and fasting and praying to YHW the Lord of Heaven

16 who let us gloat over that Vidranga, the cur. They removed the fetter from his feet and all goods which he had acquired were lost. And all persons

17 who sought evil for that temple, all (of them), were killed and we gazed upon them. Morever, before this, at the time that this ev{il} VERSO

18 was done to us, a letter we sent (to) our lord, and to Jehohanan the High Priest and his colleagues the priests who are in Jerusalem, and to Ostanes {the} brother

19 of Anani and the nobles of the Jews. A letter they did not send to us. Moreover, from the month of Tammuz, year 14 of Darius the king

20 and un{til} this day, we, sackcloth are wearing and are fasting; the wives of ours as widow(s) are made; (with) oil (we) do not anoint (ourselves),

21 and wine do not drink. Moreover, from that (time) and until (this) day, year 17 of Darius the king, meal-offering and incence and burnt-offering

22 they did not make in that temple. Now, your servants Jedaniah and his colleagues and the Jews, all (of them) citizens of Elephantine, thus sa{y}:

23 If to our lord it is good, take thought of that temple to (re)build (it) since they do not let us (re)build it. Regard

24 your [23]ob[24]ligees and your friends {who are} here in Egypt. May a letter from you be sent to them about the temple of YHW the God

25 to (re)build it in Elephantine the fortress just as it had been built formerly. And the meal-offering and the incense and the burnt-offering they will offer

26 on the altar of YHW the God in your name and we shall pray for you at all times—we and our wives and our children and the Jews,

27 all (of them) who are here. If thus they do until that temple be (re)built, a merit you will have before YHW the God of

28 Heaven more than a person who will offer him burnt-offering and sacrifices (whose) worth is as the worth of silver, 1 thousand talents and about gold. About this

29 we have sent (and) informed (you). Moreover, all the(se) things in a letter we sent {in our name} to Delaiah and Shelemiah sons of Sanballat gov{er}nor of Samaria.

30 Moreover, about this which was done {all of it} to us Arsames did not know. On the 20th of Marcheshvan, year 17 of Darius the king.[2]

---

[2] Translation by Porten.

Literature: Meyer, "Papyrusfund"; Kraeling, *Brooklyn Museum Aramaic Papyri*; idem, "Elephantine Papyri"; Smallwood, *Jews Under Roman Rule*, 220; Dion, "Synagogues et temples"; Kasher, "Synagogues," 207–8; Frey, "Temple and Rival Temple"; Binder, *Temple Courts*, 233; Runesson, *Origins*, 409–10, 436–41.

Comments: Because the authorities in the Province of Samaria had ignored an earlier letter (Cowley no. 30, l. 29), the present petition was dispatched to Bagavahya, the governor of Yehud/Judah. It requested a letter of recommendation be sent to the Persian satrap of Egypt, Arsames, asking him to allow the reconstruction of the Jewish temple in Elephantine, which had been destroyed as the result of a plot by the local Persian authority, Vidranga, his son, Naphaina, and local Knuhm priests. The Jewish temple probably dates back to the reign of Pharaoh Amasis (569–526 B.C.E.), with the Jews being allowed to continue their cult after King Cambyses of Persia invaded Egypt. While the petition asks that meal offerings, incense, and burnt offerings be resumed in the rebuilt temple, the response (below, No. T3), delivered orally by a messenger,[3] shows that Yehudite authorities recommended the rebuilding of the temple and the carrying out of all its rituals, except animal sacrifices. The letter of the Elephantine Jews to an official, perhaps Arsames (below No. T4), was an attempt to bribe him into allowing the rebuilding of the temple. It confirms that the Elephantine community had accepted the restriction imposed by Bagavahya and Delaiah regarding animal sacrifices.

In order to explain the position of the Yehudite authorities, scholars have pointed to Egyptian or Persian sensitivities, including a possible negative view of animal sacrifices (Meyer; Cowley). However, the best explanation seems to be the introduction of cult-centralisation ideology (Kraeling; Porten; Runesson). For the purposes of the present volume, it is worth noting that the Elephantine Jews were not asked to initiate some sort of synagogue worship: temple rituals, including sacrificial rituals that did not involve animals, were deemed acceptable. This is a strong indication that the origin of the synagogue was not related to the temple cult or the lack thereof.

As Cowley no. 12/Porten no. B45 indicates, the Elephantine temple was rebuilt sometime between 406 and 402 B.C.E. The Jewish colony was removed from Elephantine in the early fourth century, resulting in the temple's abandonment.

No. T3
Source: *Papyrus.* Cowley no. 32/Porten no. B21
Date: Ca. 408 B.C.E.

1 זכרן זי בנוהי ודליה אממרו

2 לי זכרן לם יהוי לך במצרין למֹמֹר

---

[3] Cowley no. 32 is not the letter of recommendation sent to the Egyptian satrap, but a response to the petition sent to the Elephantine Jews.

קדמאָרשם עלבית מדבחא אלה 3

שמיא זי ביב בירתא בנה 4

הוה מן קדמן קדם כנבוזי 5

זי וידרנג להיא זך נדש 6

בשנת {*} דריוהוש מלכא 7

למבניה באתרה כזי הוה לקדמן 8

ומנחתא ולבונתא יקרבון על 9

מדבחא זך לקבל זי לקדמין 10

הוה מתעבד 11

1 Memorandum. What Bagavahya and Delaiah said
2 to me. Memorandum. Saying, "Let it be for you in Egypt to say
   (ERASURE: bef)
3 (ERASURE: to me about) before Arsames about the Altar-house
   of the God of (ERASURE: Heav)
4 Heaven which in Elephantine the fortress built
5 was formerly before Cambyses (and)
6 which Vidranga, that wicked (man) demolished
7 in year 14 of Darius the king:
8 'to (re)build it on its site as it was formerly
9 and the meal-offering and the incense they shall offer upon
10 that altar just as formerly
11 was done.'"[4]

Literature: Meyer, "Papyrusfund"; Kraeling, *Brooklyn Museum Aramaic Papyri*; idem, "Elephantine Papyri"; Smallwood, *Jews Under Roman Rule*, 220; Dion, "Synagogues et temples"; Kasher, "Synagogues," 207–8; Frey, "Temple and Rival Temple"; Binder, *Temple Courts*, 233; Runesson, *Origins*, 409–10, 436–41.

Comments: This is the answer to the petition of No. T2 (above), delivered orally by a messanger; see comment on No. T2 above.

No. T4
Source: *Papyrus.* Cowley no. 33/Porten no. B22.
Date: The letter gives no date, but must have been written shortly after Cowley no. 32 (T3 above), ca. 407 B.C.E., since it responds to requirements in that letter.

---

[4] Translation by Porten.

עבדיך ידניה בר נ[מריה] שמה | 1

מעוזי בר נתן שמה [||] 2

שמעיה בר חני שמה | 3

הושע בר יתום שמה | 4

הושע בר נתון שמה | כל נברן ||||\ 5

סונכן זי ביב בירתא [מ]ה[חס] נן 6

כן אמרן הן מראן [ירח]מן 7

ואנורא זי יהו אלהא זי [לן יתבנה 8

ביב בירתא כזי קד[מן בנ]ה הוה 9

וקן תור ענז מקלו [ל]א ותעבד תמה 10

להן לבונה מנחה [ונסך ... 11

ומראן אודים יעב[ד עלזנה אחר 12

ננתן על בית מראן כ[סף....ואף 13

שערן ארדבן אלוף 14

1 Your servants—
   Jedaniah son of Gem[ariah] by name, 1
2 Mauzi son of Nathan by name, [1]
3 Shemaiah son of Haggai by name, 1
4 Hosea son of Jathom by name, 1
5 Hosea son of Nattum by name, 1: all (told) 5 persons,
6 Syenians who in Elephantine the fortress are herdi[tary-herdi[tary-
   property-hold]ers {sic}—
7 thus say: If our lord [...]
8 and the temple-of-YHW-the-God of ours be (re)built
9 in Elephantine the fortress as former[ly] it was [bu]ilt—
10 and sheep, ox, and goat (as) burnt-offering are [n]ot made there
11 but (only) incense (and) meal-offering [*they offer there*]—
12 and should our lord a statement mak[e *about this, afterwards*]
13 we shall give to the house of our lord si[*lver...and*]
14 barley, a thousa[nd] ardabs.[5]

Literature: Meyer, "Papyrusfund"; Kraeling, *Brooklyn Museum Aramaic Papyri*; idem, "Elephantine Papyri"; Smallwood, *Jews Under Roman Rule*, 220; Dion, "Synagogues et temples"; Kasher, "Synagogues," 207–8; Frey, "Temple and Rival Temple"; Binder, *Temple Courts*, 233; Runesson, *Origins*, 409–10, 436–41.

Comments: See No. T2 above.

---

[5] Translation by Porten.

5.2.2   *Leontopolis*

No. T5 (cf. No. 153)
Source: *Literary. A.J.* 13.62–73
Date: *Antiquitates Judaicum* was published 93/94 C.E. The letter that Josephus claims was written by Onias IV to Ptolemy VI, and which he includes in this passage (13.65–68), dates, if authentic, between 185–145 B.C.E. The temple was probably constructed ca. 164 B.C.E.

[62] Ὁ δὲ Ὀνίου τοῦ ἀρχιερέως υἱὸς ὁμώνυμος δὲ ὢν τῷ πατρί, ὃς ἐν Ἀλεξανδρείᾳ φυγὼν πρὸς τὸν βασιλέα Πτολεμαῖον τὸν ἐπικαλούμενον Φιλομήτορα διῆγεν, ὡς καὶ πρότερον εἰρήκαμεν, ἰδὼν τὴν Ἰουδαίαν κακουμένην ὑπὸ τῶν Μακεδόνων καὶ τῶν βασιλέων αὐτῶν, [63] βουλόμενος αὐτῷ δόξαν καὶ μνήμην αἰώνιον κατασκευάσαι, διέγνω πέμψας πρὸς Πτολεμαῖον τὸν βασιλέα καὶ τὴν βασίλισσαν Κλεοπάτραν αἰτήσασθαι παρ' αὐτῶν ἐξουσίαν, ὅπως οἰκοδομήσειεν ναὸν ἐν Αἰγύπτῳ παραπλήσιον τῷ ἐν Ἱεροσολύμοις καὶ Λευίτας καὶ ἱερεῖς ἐκ τοῦ ἰδίου γένους καταστήσῃ. [64] τοῦτο δ' ἐβούλετο θαρρῶν μάλιστα τῷ προφήτῃ Ἡσαΐᾳ, ὃς ἔμπροσθεν ἔτεσιν ἑξακοσίοις πλέον γεγονὼς προεῖπεν, ὡς δεῖ πάντως ἐν Αἰγύπτῳ οἰκοδομηθῆναι ναὸν τῷ μεγίστῳ θεῷ ὑπ' ἀνδρὸς Ἰουδαίου. διὰ ταῦτα οὖν ἐπηρμένος Ὀνίας γράφει Πτολεμαίῳ καὶ Κλεοπάτρᾳ τοιαύτην ἐπιστολήν·

[65] "πολλὰς καὶ μεγάλας ὑμῖν χρείας τετελεκὼς ἐν τοῖς κατὰ πόλεμον ἔργοις μετὰ τῆς τοῦ θεοῦ βοηθείας, καὶ γενόμενος ἔν τε τῇ κοίλῃ Συρίᾳ καὶ Φοινίκῃ, καὶ εἰς Λεόντων δὲ πόλιν τοῦ Ἡλιοπολίτου σὺν τοῖς Ἰουδαίοις καὶ εἰς ἄλλους τόπους ἀφικόμενος τοῦ ἔθνους, [66] καὶ πλείστους εὑρὼν παρὰ τὸ καθῆκον ἔχοντας ἱερὰ καὶ διὰ τοῦτο δύσνους ἀλλήλοις, ὃ καὶ Αἰγυπτίοις συμβέβηκεν διὰ τὸ πλῆθος τῶν ἱερῶν καὶ τὸ περὶ τὰς θρησκείας οὐχ ὁμόδοξον, ἐπιτηδειότατον εὑρὼν τόπον ἐν τῷ προσαγορευομένῳ τῆς ἀγρίας Βουβάστεως ὀχυρώματι βρύοντα ποικίλης ὕλης καὶ τῶν ἱερῶν ζῴων μεστόν, [67] δέομαι συγχωρῆσαί μοι τὸ ἀδέσποτον ἀνακαθάραντι ἱερὸν καὶ συμπεπτωκὸς οἰκοδομῆσαι ναὸν τῷ μεγίστῳ θεῷ καθ' ὁμοίωσιν τοῦ ἐν Ἱεροσολύμοις αὐτοῖς μέτροις ὑπὲρ σοῦ καὶ τῆς σῆς γυναικὸς καὶ τῶν τέκνων, ἵν' ἔχωσιν οἱ τὴν Αἴγυπτον κατοικοῦντες Ἰουδαῖοι εἰς αὐτὸ συνιόντες κατὰ τὴν πρὸς ἀλλήλους ὁμόνοιαν ταῖς σαῖς ἐξυπηρετεῖν χρείαις· [68] καὶ γὰρ Ἡσαΐας ὁ προφήτης τοῦτο προεῖπεν· ἔσται θυσιαστήριον ἐν Αἰγύπτῳ κυρίῳ τῷ θεῷ· καὶ πολλὰ δὲ προεφήτευσεν ἄλλα τοιαῦτα διὰ τὸν τόπον."

[69] Καὶ ταῦτα μὲν ὁ Ὀνίας τῷ βασιλεῖ Πτολεμαίῳ γράφει. κατανοήσειε δ' ἄν τις αὐτοῦ τὴν εὐσέβειαν καὶ Κλεοπάτρας τῆς

ἀδελφῆς αὐτοῦ καὶ γυναικὸς ἐξ ἧς ἀντέγραψαν ἐπιστολῆς· τὴν γὰρ
ἁμαρτίαν καὶ τὴν τοῦ νόμου παράβασιν εἰς τὴν Ὀνίου κεφαλὴν
ἀνέθεσαν· [70] ἀντέγραψαν γὰρ οὕτως· "βασιλεὺς Πτολεμαῖος καὶ
βασίλισσα Κλεοπάτρα Ὀνίᾳ χαίρειν. ἀνέγνωμέν σου τὴν ἐπιστολὴν
ἀξιοῦντος ἐπιτραπῆναί σοι τὸ ἐν Λεόντων πόλει τοῦ Ἡλιοπολίτου
ἱερὸν συμπεπτωκὸς ἀνακαθᾶραι, προσαγορευόμενον δὲ τῆς ἀγρίας
Βουβάστεως. διὸ καὶ θαυμάζομεν, εἰ ἔσται τῷ θεῷ κεχαρισμένον
τὸ καθιδρυσόμενον ἱερὸν ἐν ἀσελγεῖ τόπῳ καὶ πλήρει ζῴων ἱερῶν.
[71] ἐπεὶ δὲ σὺ φῂς Ἡσαΐαν τὸν προφήτην ἐκ πολλοῦ χρόνου τοῦτο
προειρηκέναι, συγχωροῦμέν σοι, εἰ μέλλει τοῦτ' ἔσεσθαι κατὰ τὸν
νόμον· ὥστε μηδὲν ἡμᾶς δοκεῖν εἰς τὸν θεὸν ἐξημαρτηκέναι."
     [72] Λαβὼν οὖν τὸν τόπον ὁ Ὀνίας κατεσκεύασεν ἱερὸν καὶ βωμὸν
τῷ θεῷ ὅμοιον τῷ ἐν Ἱεροσολύμοις, μικρότερον δὲ καὶ πενιχρότερον.
τὰ δὲ μέτρα αὐτοῦ καὶ τὰ σκεύη νῦν οὐκ ἔδοξέ μοι δηλοῦν· ἐν γὰρ
τῇ ἑβδόμῃ μου βίβλῳ τῶν Ἰουδαϊκῶν ἀναγέγραπται. [73] εὗρεν δὲ
Ὀνίας καὶ Ἰουδαίους τινὰς ὁμοίους αὐτῷ ἱερεῖς καὶ Λευίτας τοὺς
ἐκεῖ θρησκεύσοντας. ἀλλὰ περὶ μὲν τοῦ ἱεροῦ τούτου ἀρκούντως ἡμῖν
δεδήλωται.

[62] Now the son of the high priest Onias, who had the same name
as his father, having fled to King Ptolemy surnamed Philometor, was
living in Alexandria, as we have said before; and seeing that Judaea was
being revenged by the Macedonians and their kings, [63] and desiring
to acquire for himself eternal fame and glory, he determined to send to
King Ptolemy and Queen Cleopatra and request of them authority
to build a temple [*naos*] in Egypt similar to that at Jerusalem, and to
appoint Levites and priests of his own race. [64] In this desire he was
encouraged chiefly by the words of the Prophet Isaiah, who had lived
more than six hundred years before and had foretold that a temple
[*naos*] to the Most High God was surely to be built in Egypt by a Jew.
Being, therefore, excited by these words, Onias wrote the following
letter to Ptolemy and Cleopatra.
     [65] "Many and great are the services which I have rendered you in
the course of the war, with the help of God, when I was in Coele-Syria
and Phoenicia, and when I came with the Jews to Leontopolis in the
nome of Heliopolis and to other places where our nations is settled;
[66] and I found that most of them have temples [*hiera*], contrary to
what is proper, and that for this reason they are ill-disposed toward one
another, as is also the case with the Egyptians because of the multitude
of their temples [*hiera*] and their varying opinions about the forms of

worship; and I have found a most suitable place in the fortress called after Bubastis-of-the-Fields, which abounds in various kinds of trees and is full of sacred animals, [67] wherefore I beg you to permit me to cleanse this temple [*hieron*], which belongs to no one and is in ruins, and to build a temple [*naos*] to the Most High God in the likeness of that at Jerusalem and with the same dimensions, on behalf of you and your wife and children, in order that the Jewish inhabitants of Egypt may be able to come together there in mutual harmony and serve your interests. [68] For this indeed is what the prophet Isaiah foretold, 'There shall be an altar in Egypt to the Lord God,' and many other such things did he prophesy concerning this place."

[68] This, then, is what Onias wrote to King Ptolemy. And one may get at notion of the king's piety and that of his sister and wife Cleopatra from the letter from which they wrote in reply, for they placed the blame of the sin and transgression against the Law on the head of Onias, [70] writing the following reply." King Ptolemy and Queen Cleopatra to Onias, greeting. We have read your petition asking that is be permitted you to cleanse the ruined temple in Leontopolis in Nome of Heliopolis called Bubastis-of-the-Fields. We wonder, therefore, whether it would be pleasing to God that a temple be build in a place so wild and full of sacred animals. [71] But since you say that the prophet Isaiah foretold this long ago, we grant your request if this is to be in accordance with the Law, so that we may not seem to have sinned against God in any way."

[72] And so Onias took over the place and built a temple and an alter to God similar to that at Jerusalem, but smaller and poorer. But it has not seemed to be necessary to write about it dimensions and its vessels now, for they have allready been described in the seventh book of my *Jewish War*. And Onias found some Jews of his own kind, and priests and Levites to minister there. Concerning this temple, however, we have already said enough.

Literature: Frey, "Temple and Rival Temple"; Hayward, "Jewish Temple at Leontopolis"; Delcor, "Le Temple d'Onias"; Steckholl, "Temple of Leontopolis," 55–69; Dion, "Synagogues et temples"; Hengel, "Proseuche und Synagoge," 31–32, 36; Gruen, "Origins," 61; Parente, "Founding"; Bohak, *Jewish Temple in Heliopolis*; Gruen, "Origins," 61; Binder, *Temple Courts*, 234–36; Runesson, *Origins*, 411–14; Richardson, *Building Jewish*, 165–79.

Comments: The Jewish temple in Leontopolis is mentioned in several passages in Josephus (*B.J.* 7.426–36; cf. *A.J.* 12.388, 20.235–37; *B.J.* 1.33) and is discussed at some length in rabbinic writings, where it is accorded limited legitimacy (*m. Menah.* 13.10; *t. Menah.* 13:12–15; *y. Yoma* 6:3, 43c–d; *b. Menah* 109b; *b. 'Avod. Zar.* 52b; *b. Meg.* 10a). Another passage from Josephus (*C. Ap.* 2.10) is also of interest since it mentions several *proseuchai* ("prayer halls") "open to the air" in the area of Heliopolis; some scholars understand this as a reference to multiple temples (for *proseuchē* as a temple term, see Runesson, *Origins*, 429–36).

Archaeological remains of the Jewish temple have been indentified at Tell el-Yehudiyeh, 35 km north of Cairo (for a recent description and discussion, see Richardson, 168–69). As in the case of the Elephantine community, the Leontopolis temple originated in the context of a Jewish military settlement. It was constructed on the site of a ruined Egyptian temple that had been purified for Jewish worship. There is also epigraphic evidence of importance, suggesting an active role of women priests in the cult (Richardson, 174–79).

For the purposes of this catalogue, only the above passage from Josephus is listed, since it contains the earliest detailed description of the temple and its origins. It also offers several important observations for the study of ancient synagogues.

In the first place, the reason given in the letter for the necessity of constructing the temple is that there already existed a multitude of Jewish *hiera* all over Egypt. The author argues that the temple of Onias IV would rid the Jewish communities of the strife and conflict that had erupted from the competing cultic sites and their diverse traditions: Jews would unite around the cult of the God of Israel at Leontopolis.

While the first use of *hiera* in §66 could refer to Egyptian synagogues, some scholars have argued that the term here more likely refers to temples. Two main reasons are given. First, there is an explicit comparison with (non-Jewish) Egyptian *hiera*, and these are surely temples. Second, the Leontopolis temple was to replace other Jewish *hiera*, and competition between synagogues and temples lacks support in the sources, whereas competition between temples is in evidence. In this interpretation, Josephus witnesses to an Egyptian-Jewish cult centralisation.

From the other direction, scholars who hold that *hiera* in §66 refers to synagogues point to comparative material mentioning Egyptian *proseuchai*, which are understood as synagogue references. In addition, they argue that the quotation of Isa 19:19 in Onias' letter alludes to the erection of an Israelite altar (*mizbeah*) in Egypt; if read as a prophecy predicting the erection of the Leontopolis temple, it would suggest a distinction between it and the existing Jewish *hiera*. However, this allusion may also be understood as a reference to a long-standing tradition of sacrificial worship among Egyptian Jews.

Imperial forces destroyed the Leontopolis temple in 74 C.E., a fact that indicates its importance as a Jewish shrine in the eyes of the Romans.

5.2.3   General References and Unspecified Locations

No. T6
Source: *Literary.* Isa 19:19–21
Date: The prophet Isaiah probably began his public career ca. 740 B.C.E. and died sometime in the beginning of the reign of Manasseh, which according to most scholars began 687 B.C.E. The date and unity of the Book of Isaiah has been the object of considerable scholarly debate.

[19] ביום ההוא יהיה מזבח ליהוה בתוך ארץ מצרים ומצבה אצל גבולה
ליהוה [20] והיה לאות ולעד ליהוה צבאות בארץ מצרים כי יצעקו אל
יהוה מפני לחצים וישלח להם מושיע ורב והצילם [21] ונודע יהוה למצרים
וידעו מצרים את יהוה ביום ההוא ועבדו זבח ומנחה ונדרו נדר ליהוה ושלמו

[19] On that day there will be an altar to the LORD in the center of the land of Egypt, and a pillar to the LORD at its border. [20] It will be a sign and a witness to the LORD of hosts in the land of Egypt; when they cry to the LORD because of oppressors, he will send them a savior, and will defend and deliver them. [21] The LORD will make himself known to the Egyptians; and the Egyptians will know the LORD on that day, and will worship with sacrifice and burnt offering, and they will make vows to the LORD and perform them.

Literature: Clements, *Isaiah*, 169–73; Barker, "Isaiah," 513–14; Binder, *Temple Courts*, 235; Runesson, *Origins*, 413–14, 432, 440.

Comments: Cf. the discussion above, No. T5. In a letter Josephus ascribed to Onias IV (*A.J.* 13.65–68), the author uses this verse to legitimise the building of the Leontopolis temple. The historical context in which Isaiah spoke, however, antedates even the earliest dating of the centralisation of Jewish sacrificial cult to Jerusalem by Josiah, ca. 620 B.C.E. Barker discusses this verse in relation to the Elephantine community and suggests a Jewish emigration to Egypt at the time of Manasseh, who, according to the biblical narratives, desecrated the Jerusalem temple. In her view, what Isaiah describes in this passage is a transferral of the Jewish cult to Egypt.

No. T7 (cf. Nos. 153, T5)
Source: *Literary.* Josephus, *A.J.* 13.65–66
Date: *Antiquitates Judaicum* was published 93/94 C.E. The letter that Josephus claims was written by Onias IV to Ptolemy VI, from which the below is a section, dates, if authentic, between 185–145 B.C.E. The temple was probably constructed ca. 164 B.C.E.

[65] "πολλὰς καὶ μεγάλας ὑμῖν χρείας τετελεκὼς ἐν τοῖς κατὰ πόλεμον ἔργοις μετὰ τῆς τοῦ θεοῦ βοηθείας, καὶ γενόμενος ἔν τε τῇ κοίλῃ

Συρίᾳ καὶ Φοινίκῃ, καὶ εἰς Λεόντων δὲ πόλιν τοῦ Ἡλιοπολίτου σὺν τοῖς Ἰουδαίοις καὶ εἰς ἄλλους τόπους ἀφικόμενος τοῦ ἔθνους, [66] καὶ πλείστους εὑρὼν παρὰ τὸ καθῆκον ἔχοντας ἱερὰ καὶ διὰ τοῦτο δύσνους ἀλλήλοις, ὃ καὶ Αἰγυπτίοις συμβέβηκεν διὰ τὸ πλῆθος τῶν ἱερῶν καὶ τὸ περὶ τὰς θρησκείας οὐχ ὁμόδοξον.

[65] "Many and great are the services which I have rendered you in the course of the war, with the help of God, when I was in Coele-Syria and Phoenicia, and when I came with the Jews to Leontopolis in the nome of Heliopolis and to other places where our nations is settled; [66] and I found that most of them have temples [*hiera*], contrary to what is proper, and that for this reason they are ill-disposed toward one another, as is also the case with the Egyptians because of the multitude of their temples [*hiera*] and their varying opinions about the forms of worship.[6]

Literature: See above, No. T5.

Comments: See comment on No. T5. The many Jewish *hiera* are said to exist not only in the area around Leontopolis, but elsewhere in Egypt where Jews live too.

5.3 *Idumea*

5.3.1 *Lachish*

No. T8
Source: *Archaeological.*
Date: Hellenistic period

Literature: Aharoni, *Lachish*; idem, "Excavations in the 'Solar Shrine'"; Arav, *Hellenistic Palestine*, 58; Hengel, "Proseuche und Synagoge," 166; Campbell, "Jewish Shrines", 166; Runesson, *Origins*, 423–24.

Comments: This temple has been identified as Jewish on the basis of its plan, dimensions, and orientation, which are similar to the earlier Jewish temple in Arad (Aharoni). While there is no consensus regarding this identification, the existence underneath of an earlier Israelite temple or *bamah*, dating from the tenth century B.C.E., points in the direction of Aharoni's theory (Runesson). The temple seems to have been destroyed during the Hasmonean expansion of the Jewish state (Arav), as was also the Samaritan temple at Gerizim.

---

[6] Translation by Thackeray (LCL).

5.3.2 *Beersheva*

No. T9
Source: *Archaeological.*
Date: Hellenistic period

Literature: Aharoni, *Beer-Sheba 1*; idem, "The Horned Altar"; Herzog, "Israelite Sanctuaries," 120–22; idem, "Tel Beersheba" in *NEAEHL*, 1, 167–73; Herzog et al., *Beer-Sheba: 2*; Herzog et al., "Location of the Sanctuary," 49–58; Runesson, *Origins*, 425–26.

Comments: The temple in Beersheva is similar in plan and orientation to the Lachish temple and therefore also related to the earlier Arad temple (cf. No. T8 above). It was constructed on top of an earlier Israelite shrine, which included a horned altar. Although Beersheva, like Lachish, came under Idumean rule after the fall of Jerusalem in 587 B.C.E., it is nevertheless mentioned as one of the cities where Jews lived during the Persian period (Neh 11:27). Further, fourth-century ostraca with Jewish names have been found there. Since there is no evidence that the ethnic mix in Hellenistic Beersheva excluded Jews, this structure may serve as an example of a place where Jews continued to worship the God of Israel in a temple setting, rejecting the religio-politically motivated enforcement of cult centralisation in Judaea. This would all change, however, with the Hasmonean annexation of Idumea in 125 B.C.E.

5.4 *Syria*

5.4.1 *Antioch*

No. T10 (= No. 190)
Source: *Literary.* Josephus *B.J.* 7.44–45
Date: *De bello Judaico* consists of seven books and was published in the late 70s. It is possible that the edifice referred to in the passage was constructed in the third or second century B.C.E.

[44] Ἀντίοχος μὲν γὰρ ὁ κληθεὶς Ἐπιφανὴς Ἱεροσόλυμα πορθήσας τὸν νεὼν ἐσύλησεν, οἱ δὲ μετ᾽ αὐτὸν τὴν βασιλείαν παραλαβόντες τῶν ἀναθημάτων ὅσα χαλκᾶ πεποίητο πάντα τοῖς ἐπ᾽ Ἀντιοχείας Ἰουδαίοις ἀπέδοσαν εἰς τὴν συναγωγὴν αὐτῶν ἀναθέντες, καὶ συνεχώρησαν αὐτοῖς ἐξ ἴσου τῆς πόλεως τοῖς Ἕλλησι μετέχειν. [45] τὸν αὐτὸν δὲ τρόπον καὶ τῶν μετὰ ταῦτα βασιλέων αὐτοῖς προσφερομένων εἴς τε πλῆθος ἐπέδωκαν καὶ τῇ κατασκευῇ καὶ τῇ πολυτελείᾳ τῶν ἀναθημάτων τὸ ἱερὸν ἐξελάμπρυναν, ἀεί τε προσαγόμενοι ταῖς θρησκείαις πολὺ πλῆθος Ἑλλήνων, κἀκείνους τρόπῳ τινὶ μοῖραν αὐτῶν πεποίηντο.

[44] For, although Antiochus surnamed Epiphanes sacked Jerusalem and plundered the temple [*naos*], his successors on the throne restored to the Jews of Antioch all such votive offerings as were made of brass, to be laid up in their synagogue [*synagōgē*], and, moreover, granting them citizen rights on an equality with the Greeks. [45] Continuing to receive similar treatment from later monarchs, the Jewish colony grew in numbers, and their richly designed and costly offerings formed a splendid ornament to the temple [*hieron*]. Moreover, they were constantly attracting to their religious ceremonies multitudes of Greeks, and these they had in some measure incorporated with themselves.[7]

Literature: Krauss, *Synagogale Altertümer*, 86–87; Hengel, "Proseuche und Synagogue," 38; Binder, *Temple Courts*, 266; Bilde "Synagoge," 19–20; Runesson, *Origins*, 421, 463–64.

Comments: Krauss and Hengel have suggested that this imposing structure was originally a Jewish temple later transformed into a synagogue. Josephus' use of *hieron* and *synagōgē* in reference to this building certainly implies that it was temple-like. Moreover, the passage indicates that, after Antiochus IV looted the temple in Jerusalem, his successors restored the votive offerings not to Jerusalem, but to the sanctuary at Antioch, which they continued to adorn with votives. If indeed the Seleucid rulers were attempting to create a temple to rival the one in Jerusalem (Krauss; Hengel; cf. the construction of the Leontopolis temple at about the same time), then perhaps this temple followed the same trajectory of transformation into a synagogue as has been proposed for the Egyptian-Jewish institutions (Runesson, *Origins*, 436–59). In any case, by the first century when Josephus writes, this institution was surely functioning in ways similar to other synagogues, and should, at this time, be identified as a synagogue.

5.5   *Transjordan*

5.5.1   *'Araq el-Emir*

No. T11
Source: *Archaeological.*
Date: First quarter of the second century B.C.E.

Literature: Lapp, "Soundings at 'Araq el-Emir"; idem, "The Second and Third Campaigns"; Will, "Recent French Work at Araq el-Emir," 149–58; idem, *Iraq al Amir: le chateau du tobiade Hyrcan*; Brett, "The Qasr el-'Abd"; Arav,

---

[7] Translation by Thackeray (LCL).

Hellenistic Palestine, 107–10; Hengel, *Judaism and Hellenism*, 272–77; Campbell, "Jewish Shrines," 162–63; Frey, "Temple and Rival Temple," 194–95; Netzer, "Pleasure Palace"; Runesson, *Origins*, 418–20.

Comments: The Qasr el-ʿAbd in ʿAraq el-Emir was discovered in 1817 by two British officers. Since then, it has been the object of excavations and a multitude of scholarly studies. Its architecture defies a straightforward identification of the building's purpose. Competing theories have identified it as a fortress, mausoleum, palace, pleasure palace, or temple. Most agree, however, that it was built by Hyrcanus the Tobiad (cf. Josephus, *A.J.* 12.228–234).

The theory that the edifice was a (Jewish) temple has been most elaborately argued by Lapp, who based his analysis on a comparison with Syrian temples. While Lapp's work has received much scholarly support, more recent investigations by Will and Netzer now suggest that the structure served as a manor or pleasure palace.

These two interpretations are the only remaining alternatives today, and both can claim several good arguments in their favour. While no definite answers can be given at this point, the similarities between the Qasr and Syrian temples—and the lack of comparative material for other interpretations of the building's function—argue that the temple-theory cannot yet be abandoned (cf. Arav).

5.5.2   *Unspecified Locations*

No. T12
Source: *Literary.* Josh 22:10–34
Date: Most likely this passage is a priestly, postexilic redaction of an earlier tradition about the altar mentioned in the text.

[10] ויבאו אל גלילות הירדן אשר בארץ כנען ויבנו בני ראובן ובני גד וחצי שבט המנשה שם מזבח על הירדן מזבח גדול למראה: [11] וישמעו בני ישראל לאמר הנה בנו בני ראובן ובני גד וחצי שבט המנשה את המזבח אל מול ארץ כנען אל גלילות הירדן אל עבר בני ישראל: [12] וישמעו בני ישראל ויקהלו כל עדת בני ישראל שלה לעלות עליהם לצבא: [13] וישלחו בני ישראל אל בני ראובן ואל בני גד ואל חצי שבט מנשה אל ארץ הגלעד את פינחס בן אלעזר הכהן: [14] ועשרה נשאים עמו נשיא אחד נשיא אחד לבית אב לכל מטות ישראל ואיש ראש בית אבותם המה לאלפי ישראל: [15] ויבאו אל בני ראובן ואל בני גד ואל חצי שבט מנשה אל ארץ הגלעד וידברו אתם: [16] כה אמרו כל עדת יהוה מה המעל הזה אשר מעלתם באלהי ישראל לשוב היום מאחרי יהוה בבנותכם לכם מזבח למרדכם היום ביהוה: [17] המעט לנו את עון פעור אשר לא הטהרנו ממנו עד היום הזה ויהי הנגף בעדת יהוה: [18] ואתם תשבו היום מאחרי יהוה והיה אתם תמרדו היום ביהוה ומחר אל כל עדת ישראל יקצף: [19] ואך אם טמאה ארץ אחזתצם עברו לכם אל ארץ אחזת יהוה אשר שכן שם משכן יהוה והאחזו בתוכנו וביהוה אל תמרדו ואתנו אל תמרדו בבנתכם לכם מזבח מבלעדי מזבח יהוה אלהינו: [20] הלוא עכן בן

זרח מעל מעל בחרם ועל כל עדת ישראל היה קצף והוא איש אחד לא נוע
בעונו: [21] ויענו בני ראובן ובני גד וחצי שבט המנשה וידברו את ראשי אלפי
ישראל: [22] אל אלהים יהוה אל אלהים יהוה הוא ידע וישראל הוא ידע אם
במרד ואם במעל ביהוה אל תושיענו היום הזה: [23] לבנות לנו מזבח לשוב
מאחרי יהוה ואם להעלות עליו עולה ומנחה ואם לעשות עליו זבחי שלמים יהוה
הוא יבקש: [24] ואם לא מדאנה מדבר עשינו את זאת לאמר מחר יאמרו בניכם
לבנינו לאמר מה לכם וליהוה אלהי ישראל: [25] וגבול נתן יהוה ביננו וביניכם
בני ראובן ובני גד את הירדן אין לכם חלק ביהוה והשביתו בניכם את בנינו
לבלתי ירא את יהוה: [26] ונאמר נעשה נא לנו לבנות את המזבח לא לעולה
ולא לזבח: [27] כי עד הוא בינינו וביניכם ובין דרותינו אחרינו לעבד את עבדת
יהוה לפניו בעלותינו ובזבחינו ובשלמינו ולא יאמרו בניכם מחר לבנינו אין לכם
חלק ביהוה: [28] ונאמר והיה כי יאמרו אלינו ואל דרתינו מחר ואמרנו ראו את
תבנית מזבח יהוה אשר עשו אבותינו לא לעולה ולא לזבח כי עד הוא בינינו
וביניכם: [29] חלילה לנו ממנו למרד ביהוה ולשוב היום מאחרי יהוה לבנות
מזבח לעלה למנחה ולזבח מלבד מזבח יהוה אלהינו אשר לפני משכנו: [30]
וישמע פינחס הכהן ונשיאי העדה וראשי אלפי ישראל אשר אתו את הדברים
אשר דברו בני ראובן ובני גד ובני מנשה וייטב בעיניהם: [31] ויאמר פינחס
בן אלעזר הכהן אל בני ראובן ואל בני גד ואל בני מנשה היום ידענו כי בתו
כנו יהוה אשר לא מעלתם ביהוה המעל הזה אז הצלתם את בני ישראל מיד
יהוה: [32] וישב פינחס בן אלעזר הכהן והנשיאים מאת בני ראובן ומאת בני
גד מארץ הגלעד אל ארץ כנען אל בני ישראל וישבו אותם דבר: [33] וייטב
הדבר בעיני בני ישראל ויברכו אלהים בני ישראל ולא אמרו לעלות עליהם
לצבא לשחת את הארץ אשר בני ראובן ובני גד ישבים בה: [34] ויקראו בני
ראובן ובני גד למזבח כי עד הוא בינתינו כי יהוה האלהים

[1] Then Joshua summoned the Reubenites, the Gadites, and the half-tribe of Manasseh, [2] and said to them, "You have observed all that Moses the servant of the LORD commanded you, and have obeyed me in all that I have commanded you; [3] you have not forsaken your kindred these many days, down to this day, but have been careful to keep the charge of the LORD your God. [4] And now the LORD your God has given rest to your kindred, as he promised them; therefore turn and go to your tents in the land where your possession lies, which Moses the servant of the LORD gave you on the other side of the Jordan. [5] Take good care to observe the commandment and instruction that Moses the servant of the LORD commanded you, to love the LORD your God, to walk in all his ways, to keep his commandments, and to hold fast to him, and to serve him with all your heart and with all your soul." [6] So Joshua blessed them and sent them away, and they went to their tents. [7] Now to the one half of the tribe of Manasseh Moses had given a possession in Bashan; but to the other half Joshua had given

a possession beside their fellow Israelites in the land west of the Jordan. And when Joshua sent them away to their tents and blessed them, [8] he said to them, "Go back to your tents with much wealth, and with very much livestock, with silver, gold, bronze, and iron, and with a great quantity of clothing; divide the spoil of your enemies with your kindred." [9] So the Reubenites and the Gadites and the half-tribe of Manasseh returned home, parting from the Israelites at Shiloh, which is in the land of Canaan, to go to the land of Gilead, their own land of which they had taken possession by command of the LORD through Moses. [10] When they came to the region near the Jordan that lies in the land of Canaan, the Reubenites and the Gadites and the half-tribe of Manasseh built there an altar by the Jordan, an altar of great size. [11] The Israelites heard that the Reubenites and the Gadites and the half-tribe of Manasseh had built an altar at the frontier of the land of Canaan, in the region near the Jordan, on the side that belongs to the Israelites. [12] And when the people of Israel heard of it, the whole assembly of the Israelites gathered at Shiloh, to make war against them. [13] Then the Israelites sent the priest Phinehas son of Eleazar to the Reubenites and the Gadites and the half-tribe of Manasseh, in the land of Gilead, [14] and with him ten chiefs, one from each of the tribal families of Israel, every one of them the head of a family among the clans of Israel. [15] They came to the Reubenites, the Gadites, and the half-tribe of Manasseh, in the land of Gilead, and they said to them, [16] "Thus says the whole congregation of the LORD, 'What is this treachery that you have committed against the God of Israel in turning away today from following the LORD, by building yourselves an altar today in rebellion against the LORD? [17] Have we not had enough of the sin at Peor from which even yet we have not cleansed ourselves, and for which a plague came upon the congregation of the LORD, [18] that you must turn away today from following the LORD! If you rebel against the LORD today, he will be angry with the whole congregation of Israel tomorrow. [19] But now, if your land is unclean, cross over into the LORD'S land where the LORD'S tabernacle now stands, and take for yourselves a possession among us; only do not rebel against the LORD, or rebel against us by building yourselves an altar other than the altar of the LORD our God. [20] Did not Achan son of Zerah break faith in the matter of the devoted things, and wrath fell upon all the congregation of Israel? And he did not perish alone for his iniquity!'" [21] Then the Reubenites, the Gadites, and the half-tribe of Manasseh said in answer to the heads of the families of Israel,

[22] "The LORD, God of gods! The LORD, God of gods! He knows; and let Israel itself know! If it was in rebellion or in breach of faith toward the LORD, do not spare us today [23] for building an altar to turn away from following the LORD; or if we did so to offer burnt offerings or grain offerings or offerings of well-being on it, may the LORD himself take vengeance. [24] No! We did it from fear that in time to come your children might say to our children, 'What have you to do with the LORD, the God of Israel? [25] For the LORD has made the Jordan a boundary between us and you, you Reubenites and Gadites; you have no portion in the LORD.' So your children might make our children cease to worship the LORD. [26] Therefore we said, 'Let us now build an altar, not for burnt offering, nor for sacrifice, [27] but to be a witness between us and you, and between the generations after us, that we do perform the service of the LORD in his presence with our burnt offerings and sacrifices and offerings of well-being; so that your children may never say to our children in time to come, "You have no portion in the LORD."' [28] And we thought, If this should be said to us or to our descendants in time to come, we could say, 'Look at this copy of the altar of the LORD, which our ancestors made, not for burnt offerings, nor for sacrifice, but to be a witness between us and you.' [29] Far be it from us that we should rebel against the LORD, and turn away this day from following the LORD by building an altar for burnt offering, grain offering, or sacrifice, other than the altar of the LORD our God that stands before his tabernacle!" [30] When the priest Phinehas and the chiefs of the congregation, the heads of the families of Israel who were with him, heard the words that the Reubenites and the Gadites and the Manassites spoke, they were satisfied. [31] The priest Phinehas son of Eleazar said to the Reubenites and the Gadites and the Manassites, "Today we know that the LORD is among us, because you have not committed this treachery against the LORD; now you have saved the Israelites from the hand of the LORD." [32] Then the priest Phinehas son of Eleazar and the chiefs returned from the Reubenites and the Gadites in the land of Gilead to the land of Canaan, to the Israelites, and brought back word to them. [33] The report pleased the Israelites; and the Israelites blessed God and spoke no more of making war against them, to destroy the land where the Reubenites and the Gadites were settled. [34] The Reubenites and the Gadites called the altar Witness; "For," said they, "it is a witness between us that the LORD is God."

Literature: Menes, "Temple und Synagoge"; Kloppenborg, "Joshua 22"; Runesson, *Origins*, 417–418.

Comments: This altar was certainly built for the purpose the redactors of the text deny: "burnt offerings and sacrifices and offerings of well-being" (v. 27); an altar built for a reason other than sacrificial rituals would be a contradiction in terms (Kloppenborg). The passage is thus most likely an attempt by priestly circles in the Persian period to "neutralise" evidence of a sacrificial cult dedicated to the God of Israel in an "unclean land" (v. 19). In this view, the existence of the altar in the early Persian period needed to be dealt with ideologically as the cult centralisation was being implemented in Yehud. Since the political authority of the Yehudite leaders at this time did not include the area under discussion, we do not know when the cult was indeed terminated (cf. discussion of Elephantine temple above, No. T2).

While it has been suggested that Josh 22 provides early evidence of synagogue liturgy (Menes), this can hardly be the case since no such rituals are mentioned. In the text, the function of the altar is negotiated into a "witness" of the fact that "the Lord is God" (v. 34). What is at play here is cult centralisation ideology. This process apparently had no implications for the emergence of the synagogue.

BIBLIOGRAPHY

(Abbreviations have been avoided but wherever they occur we have followed Alexander, Patrick H., et al. (eds.), *The SBL Handbook of Style For Near Eastern, Biblical, and Early Christian Studies*. Peabody: Hendrickson, 1999.)

Aharoni, Yohanan. "Trial Excavations in the 'Solar Shrine' at Lachish." *Israeli Exploration Journal* 18 (1968): 157–69.

———. *Beer-Sheba 1: Excavations at Tel Beer-Sheba, 1969–1971 Seasons*. Publications of the Institute of Archaeology, 2. Tel Aviv: Tel Aviv University Institute of Archaeology, 1973.

———. "The Horned Altar of Beer-Sheba." *Biblical Archaeologist* 37 (1974): 2–6.

———. *Investigations at Lachish: The Sanctuary and the Residency (Lachish V)*. Publications of the Institute of Archaeology 4, 5. Tel Aviv: Gateway Publishers, 1975.

Allert, Craig D. *Revelation, Truth, Canon, and Interpretation: Studies in Justin Martyr's Dialogue With Trypho*. Supplements to Vigiliae Christianae, 64. Leiden: Brill Academic Publishers, 2002.

Ameling, Walter, ed. *Kleinasien*. Vol. 2 of *Inscriptiones Judaicae Orientis*. Texts and Studies in Ancient Judaism 99. Tübingen: Mohr Siebeck, 2004.

Applebaum, Shimon. *Jews and Greeks in Ancient Cyrene*. Vol. 28 of *Studies in Judaism in Late Antiquity*. Edited by Jacob Neusner. Leiden: Brill, 1979.

Arav, Rami. *Hellenistic Palestine: Settlement Patterns and City Planning 337–31 B.C.E.* Biblical Archaeology Review International Series 485. Oxford: BAR, 1989.

Atene, Scuola archeologica italiana di. *Annuario della Scuola archeologica di Atene e delle missioni italiane in Oriente*. Vol. 39–40. Rome: Istituto poligrafico dello stato, 1961–62.

Atkinson, Kenneth. "On Further Defining the First-Century C.E. Synagogue: Fact or Fiction? A Rejoinder to H. C. Kee." *New Testament Studies* 43 (1997): 491–502.

Aune, David. *Revelation 1–5*. Word Biblical Commentary 52A. Dallas, Texas: Word Books, 1997.

Avi-Yonah, Michael. "Some Comments on the Capernaum Excavations." Pages 60–62 in *Ancient Synagogues Revealed*. Edited by Lee I. Levine. Jerusalem: Israel Exploration Society, 1981.

Bagnall, Roger S. *Reading Papyri, Writing Ancient History*. London: Routledge, 1995.

Barclay, John M. G. Jews in the Mediterranean Diaspora from Alexander to Trajan (323 B.C.E.–117 C.E.). Edinburgh: T. & T. Clark, 1996.

Barker, Margaret. "Isaiah." Pages 489–542 in *Eerdmans Commenatry on the Bible*. Edited by James D. G. Dunn and Joh W. Rogerson. Grand Rapids: Eerdmans, 2003.

Barnard, L. W. *Justin Martyr: His Life and Thought*. London: Cambridge University Press, 1967.

Barrett, C. K. *The Acts of the Apostles*. A Critical and Exegetical Commentary. 2 Vols. Edinburgh: T & T Clark, 1994, 1998.

Bellen, H. "Συναγωγὴ τῶν Ἰουδαίων καὶ Θεοσεβῶν. Die Aussage einer bosporanishen Freilassungsinschrift (*CIRB* 71) zum Problem der 'Gottfürchtigen'." *Jahrbuch für Antike und Christentum* 8 (1965): 171–76.

Berger, Klaus. "Volksversammlung und Gemeinde Gottes. Zu den Anfängen der christlichen Verwendung von 'ekklesia'." *Zeitschrift für Theologie und Kirche* 73 (1976): 167–207.

Bilde, Per. "Was hat Josephus über die Synagoge zu sagen?" Pages 15–35 in *Internationales Josephus-Kolloquium Brüssel 1998*. Münsteraner judaistische Studien 4. Edited by Jürgen U. Kalms and Folker Siegert. Münster: Lit. Verlag, 1999.

Binder, Donald. *Into the Temple Courts: The Place of the Synagogues in the Second Temple Period*. Society of Biblical Literature Dissertation Series 169. Atlanta: Society of Biblical Literature, 1999.

Bloedhorn, Hanswulf. "The Capitals of the Synagogue in Capernaum: Their Chronological and Stylistic Classification with Regard to the Development of Capitals in the Decapolis and in Palestine." Pages 49–54 and plates XXVIII and XXIX in *Ancient Synagogues in Israel: Third–Seventh Century C.E.* Edited by Rachel Hachlili. Oxford: British Archaeological Reports, 1989.

Boas, Zissu and A. Ganor, "Horvat 'Etri: The Ruins of a Second Temple Jewish Village on the Coastal Plain." *Qadmoniot* 35, 1/123 (2002). Hebrew.

Boersma, Johannes S. Amoenissima Civitas. Block V.ii at Ostia: Description and Analysis of Its Visible Remains. Assen, The Netherlands: Van Gorcum, 1985.

Bohak, Gideon. Joseph and Aseneth and the Jewish Temple in Heliopolis. Atlanta: Scholars Press, 1996.

Bokser, B. M. *The Origins of the Seder: The Passover Rite and Early Rabbinic Judaism*. Berkely: University of California Press, 1984.

Bonnard, Pierre. *L'Évangile selon Saint Matthieu*. Commentaire du Nouveau Testament 1. Neuchatel: Delachaux & Niestlé, 1963.

Borgen, Peder. *Bread from Heaven: An Exegetical Study of the Concept of Manna in the Gospel of John and the Writings of Philo*. Supplements to Novum Testamentum 10. Leiden: Brill, 1965.

———. "Greek Encyclical Education, Philosophy and the Synagogue. Observations from Philo of Alexandria's Writings." Pages 61–71 in *Libens merito. Festskrift till Stig Strömholm*. Edited by Olle Matson. Acta Academiæ Regiæ Scientiarum Upsaliensis 21. Uppsala: Kungl. Vetenskapssamhället i Uppsala, 2001.

———. *Philo of Alexandria: An Exegete for His Time*. Supplements to Novum Testamentum 86. Leiden: Brill, 1997. Paperback edition Atlanta: Society of Biblical Literature, 2005.

Bousset, Wilhelm. *Die Offenbarung Johannis*. Kritisch-exegetischer Kommentar über das Neue Testament 16. Göttingen: Vandenhoeck & Ruprecht, 1906.

Bovon, François. *Das Evangeliium nach Lukas (Lk 1,1–9,50)*. Evangelisch-Katholischer Kommentar zum Neuen Testament III/1. Zürich and Neukirchen-Vluyn: Benzinger Verlag and Neukirchener Verlag, 1989.

Brandt, Olof. "Jews and Christians in Late Antique Rome and Ostia: Some Aspects of Archaeological and Documentary Evidence." *Opuscula Romana* 29 (2004): 7–27.

Brett, M. "The Qasr el-'Abd: A Proposed Reconstruction." *Bulletin of the American Schools of Oriental Research* 171 (1963): 39–45.

Brooten, Bernadette J. *Women Leaders in the Ancient Synagogue: Inscriptional Evidence and Background Issues*. Brown Judaic Studies 36. Chico, Calif.: Scholars Press, 1982.

———. "Female Leadership in the Ancient Synagogue." Pages 213–23 in *From Dura to Sepphoris: Studies in Jewish Art and Society in Late Antiquity*. Edited by Lee I. Levine and Z. Weiss. Ann Arbor, Mich.: Journal of Roman Archaeology Supplementary Series, 2000.

Brown, Raymond E. *The Gospel According to John*. The Anchor Bible 29, 29A. Garden City, NY: Doubleday, 1966, 1970.

Browne, L. "A Jewish Sanctuary in Babylonia." *Journal of Theological Studies* 17 (1916): 400–1.

Bruneau, Philippe. *Recherches sur les cultes de Delos a l'epoque hellenistique et a l'epoque imperiale, Bibliotheque des ecoles françaises d'Athenes et de Rome, fasc. 217*. Paris: E. de Boccard, 1970.

———. "«Les Israelites de Délos» et la juiverie délienne." *Bulletin de correspondance helénique* 106 (1982): 464–504.

———. *Guide de Delos*. 3rd ed. *Sites et monuments/Ecole française d'Athens*. Paris: Ecole française d'Athenes en depot aux Editions E. de Boccard, 1983.

Campbell, Edward. "Jewish Shrines of the Hellenistic and Persian Periods." Pages 159–67 in *Symposia Celebrating the Seventy-Fifth Anniversary of the Founding of the American Schools of Oriental Research (1900–1975)*. Edited by Frank Moore Cross. Cambridge, Mass.: American Schools of Oriental Research, 1979.

Catto, Stephen K. "Does προσευχὰς ποιεῖσθαι, in Josephus' *Antiquities of the Jews* 14.257–8, Mean 'Build Places of Prayer'?" *Journal for the Study of Judaism* 35.2 (2004): 159–68.

———. *Reconstructing the First-Century Synagogue: A Critical Analysis of Current Research* (T & T Clark, 2007; forthcoming).

Chadwick, Henry. *Early Christian Thought and the Classical Tradition: Studies in Justin, Clement, and Origen.* Oxford: Clarendon, 1966.

Chiat, Marilyn Joyce Segal. *Handbook of Synagogue Architecture.* Brown Judaic Studies 29. Edited by Jacob Neusner. Chico: Scholars Press, 1982.

Claußen, Carsten. *Versammlung, Gemeinde, Synagoge: Das hellenistisch-jüdischen Umfelt der früchristlichen Gemeinden.* Göttingen: Vandenhoeck & Ruprecht, 2002.

Clements, Ronald E. *Isaiah 1–39.* The New Century Bible Commentary. Grand Rapids: Eerdmans, 1980.

Clermont-Ganneau, C. "Decouverte à Jerusalem d'une synagogue de l'epoque Hero-dienne." Pages 190–97 in *Syria.* Paris, 1920.

Cohen, Shaye. "Masada: Literary Tradition, Archaeological Remains, and the Cred-ibility of Josephus." *Journal of Jewish Studies* 33 (1982): 385–405.

———. "Pagan and Christian Evidence on the Ancient Synagogue." Pages 159–81 in *The Synagogue in Late Antiquity.* Edited by Lee I. Levine. Philadelphia: The American Schools of Oriental Research, 1987.

———. "Were Pharisees and Rabbis the Leaders of Communal Prayer and Torah Study in Antiquity?" In *Evolution of the Synagogue*, 89–105. Edited by Howard Clark Kee and Lynn H. Cohick.

Collins, John J. *Daniel: A Commentary on the Book of Daniel.* Minneapolis: Fortress Press, 1993.

Corbo, Virgilio C. "L'Herodion de Giabel Fureidis." *Liber Annuus* 13 (1962–63): 219–77.

———. "L'Herodion de Giabel Fureidis." *Liber Annuus* 17 (1967): 65–121.

———. "The Excavation at Herodium." *Qadmoniot* 4 (1968): 132–36.

———. "Gébel Fureidis (Hérodium)." *Revue biblique* 75 (1968): 424–28.

———. "Scavi Archaelogici a Magdala." *Liber Annuus* 24 (1974): 5–37.

———. "La Citta romana di Magdala." Pages 365–68 in *Studia Hierosolymitana in onore del P. Bellarmino Bagatti.* Edited by I. Mancini and M. Piccirillo. Jerusalem: Franciscan Printing Press, 1976.

———. "Resti della Sinagoga del Primo Secolo a Cafarna." *Studia Hierosolymitana* 3 (1982): 314–57.

Cowley, A. *Aramaic Papyri of the 5th Century B.C.: Edited, with Translations and Notes.* Oxford: Clarendon Press, 1923.

Culpepper, R. Alan. *The Johannine School: An Evaluation of the Johannine-School Hypothesis Based on an Investigation of the Nature of Ancient Schools.* Society of Biblical Literature Dissertation Series 26. Missoula, Mont.: Scholars Press, 1975.

Daiches, S. *The Jews in Babylonia at the Time of Ezra and Nehemiah according to Babylonian Inscriptions.* Jews' College Publications. London: Jews' College, 1910.

Danshin, D. I. "Jewish Community of Phanagoria." *Ancient Civilisations from Scythia to Siberia* 3 (1996): 133–50.

Deines, Roland. *Jüdische Steingefässe und pharisäische Frömmigkeit: Ein archäologisch-Historischer Beitrag zum Verständnis von Joh 2,6 und der jüdischen Reinheitshalacha zur Zeit Jesu.* Wis-senschaftliche Undersuchungen zum Neuen Testament. 2. Reihe 52. Tübingen: J. C. B. Mohr, 1993.

Deissmann, Gustav Adolf. *Light from the Ancient East: The New Testament Illustrated by*

Recently Discovered Texts of the Graeco-Roman World. 4th ed. New York: George H. Doran, 1927.

Delcor, M. "Le Temple d'Onias en Égypte." Revue biblique 75 (1968): 188–203.

Dibelius, Martin. *James*. Revised by Heinrich Greeven 1964. Hermeneia. Philadelphia: Fortress Press, 1976.

Dion, Paul E. "Synagogues et temples dans l'Égypte hellénistique." *Science et Esprit* 29 (1977): 45–75.

Downey, Glanville. *A History of Antioch in Syria*. Princeton: Princeton University Press, 1961.

Edwards, Douglas R. "Khirbet Qana: From Jewish Village to Christian Pilgrim site." Pages 101–32 in vol. 3 of *The Roman and Byzantine Near East*. Edited by J. H. Humphrey. Journal of Roman Archaeology Supplementary Series 49. Portsmouth, R.I.: Journal of Roman Archaeology, 2002.

———. "Recent Work in Galilee: A Village and its Region." Paper presented at the annual meeting of the SBL. Washington, DC, November 18–21, 2006.

———. *Religion & Power: Pagans, Jews, and Christians in the Greek East*. New York: Oxford University Press, 1996.

Eilers, Claude. *Josephus and the Evolution of Jewish Privileges*. (Unpublished manuscript; in progress).

Elbogen, Ishmar. *Jewish Liturgy: A Comprehensive History*. Philadelphia: The Jewish Publication Society, 1993.

Evans, Craig A. *Mark 8:27–16:20*. Word Biblical Commentary 34B. Nashville Tenn.: Thomas Nelson, 2001.

Falk, Daniel K. *Daily, Sabbath, and Festival Prayers in the Dead Sea Scrolls*. Studies on the Texts of the Desert of Judah 27. Leiden: Brill, 1998.

———. "Qumran and the Synagogue Liturgy." Pages 404–434 in *The Ancient Synagogue: From its Origin Until 200 C.E.: Papers Presented at an International Conference at Lund University, October 14–17, 2001*. Edited by Birger Olsson and Magnus Zetterholm. Stockholm: Almqvist & Wiksell International, 2003.

Feldman, Louis H. "Diaspora Synagogues: New Light from Inscriptions and Papyri." Pages 577–602 in *Studies in Hellenistic Judaism*. London: Brill, 1996.

Finc, Steven. *This Holy Place: On the Sanctity of the Synagogue during the Greco-Roman Period*. Notre Dame, Ind.: University of Notre Dame Press, 1997.

———. "Non-Jews in the Synagogues of Late-Antique Palestine: Rabbinic and Archaeological Evidence." Pages 234–35 in *Jews, Christians, and Polytheists in the Ancient Synagogue*. Edited by Steven Fine. London: Routledge, 1999.

Fine, Steven, ed. *Sacred Realm: The Emergence of the Synagogue in the Ancient World*. New York: Oxford University Press, 1996.

Fitzgerald, G. M. "Theodotos Inscription." *Palestine Exploration Fund Quarterly Statement* 53 (1921): 175–81.

Fitzmyer, Joseph A. *The Gospel According to Luke*. The Anchor Bible 28, 28A. Garden City, NY: Doubleday, 1981, 1985.

———. *The Acts of the Apostles* The Anchor Bible 31. Garden City, NY: Doubleday, 1998.

Flesher, Paul Virgil McCracken. "Palestinian Synagogues before 70 C.E.: A Review of the Evidence." Pages 27–39 in *Ancient Synagogues: Historical Analysis and Archaeological Discovery*. Edited by Dan Urman and Paul Virgil McCracken Flesher. New York: Brill, 1995.

———. "Prolegomenon to a Theory of Early Synagogue Development." Pages 122–153 in *Judaism in Late Antiquity*, Part III: *Where We Stand: Issues and Debates in Ancient Judaism*. Vol. IV of *The Special Problem of the Synagogue*. Edited by Alan J. Avery-Peck and Jacob Neusner. Leiden: Brill, 2001.

Foerster, Gideon. "Galilean Synagogues and their Relation to Hellenistic and Roman Art and Architecture." PhD diss., Hebrew University, 1972. Hebrew.

————. "The Synagogues at Masada and Herodion." *Journal of Jewish Art* 3–4 (1977): 6–11.

————. "Notes on Recent Excavations at Capernaum." Pages 57–59 in *Ancient Synagogues Revealed*. Edited by Lee I. Levine. Jerusalem: Israel Exploration Society, 1981.

————. "Synagogue Inscriptions and Their Relation to Liturgical Versions." *Cathedra* 19 (1981): 12–40. Hebrew.

————. "The Synagogues at Masada and Herodium." Pages 24–29 in *Ancient Synagogues Revealed*. Edited by Lee I. Levine. Jerusalem: Israel Exploration Society, 1982.

————. "A Survey of Ancient Diaspora Synagogues." Pages 164–71 in *Ancient Synagogues Revealed*. Edited by Lee I. Levine. Jerusalem: Israel Exploration Society, 1982.

————. "Remains of a Synagogue at Corinth." Page 185 in *Ancient Synagogues Revealed*. Edited by Lee I. Levine. Jerusalem: Israel Exploration Society, 1982.

————. "The Ancient Synagogues of the Galilee." Pages 289–319 in *The Galilee in Late Antiquity*. Edited by Lee I. Levine. Cambridge: Harvard University Press, 1992.

————. "Herodium." Pages 618–21 in vol. 2 of *The New Encyclopedia of Archaeological Excavations in the Holy Land*. Edited by E. Stern. 4 vols. Jerusalem: The Israel Exploration Society and Carta, 1993.

Ford, J. Massyngberde. *Revelation*. The Anchor Bible 38. Garden City, NY: Doubleday, 1975.

Fraser, Paul M. "Ἀρχιπροστάτης, ἀρχηιπροστατέω." *Chronique d'Égypte* 26 (1951): 162–63.

————. "Ἀρχιπροστάτης, A Correction." *Chronique d'Égypte* 27 (1952): 290.

————. *Ptolemaic Alexandria*. 3 vols. Oxford: Clarendon Press, 1972.

Frey, Jean Baptiste, ed. *Corpus Inscriptionum Judaicarum*. 2 vols. Vol. 1, rev. ed. 1975. Rome: Poniticio Instituto di Archeologia Christiana, 1936–52.

Frey, Jörg. "Temple and Rival Temple: The Cases of Elephantine, Mt. Gerizim, and Leontopolis." Pages 171–203 in *Gemeinde ohne Tempel: Zur Substituierung und Transformation des Jerusalmer Tempels und seines Kults im Alten Testament, antiken Judentum und frühen Christentum*. Edited by B. Ego. Tübingen: Mohr Siebeck, 1999.

Furnish, Victor Paul. *II Corinthians*. The Anchor Bible 32A. Garden City, NY: Doubleday, 1984.

Garcia Martinez, F., Tigchelaar, E. J. C. *The Dead Sea Scrolls Study Edition*. 2 vols. Leiden: Brill, 2000.

Gerhardsson, Birger. *The Mighty Acts of Jesus According to Matthew*. Scripta Minora Regiae Societatis Humaniorum Litterarum Lundensis, 1978–1979: 5. Lund: CWK Gleerup, 1979.

Gibson, E. L. *The Jewish Manumission Inscriptions of the Bosporan Kingdom*. Tübingen: Mohr Siebeck, 1999.

Goodenough, Erwin Ramsdell. *The Theology of Justin Martyr: An Investigation into the Conceptions of Early Christian Literature and its Hellenistic and Judaistic Influences*. Jena: Verlag Frommannsche buchhandlung, 1923.

————. "The Bosporus Inscriptions to the Most High God." *Jewish Quarterly Review* 47 (1956): 221–44.

————. *Jewish Symbols in the Greco-Roman Period*. 13 vols. New York: Pantheon Books, 1953–68.

Griffiths, J. Gwyn. "Egypt and the Rise of the Synagogue." Pages 3–16 in vol. 1 of *Ancient Synagogues: Historical Analysis and Archaeological Discovery*. Edited by Dan Urman and Paul Virgil McCracken Flesher. New York: Brill, 1995.

Gruen, E. S. "The Origins and Objectives of Onias' Temple." *Scripta Classica Israelica* 16 (1997): 47–70.

Guarducci, M. *Epigrafia greca III*. Rome, 1974.

Guelich, Robert A. *Mark 1–8:26*. Word Biblical Commentary 34A. Dallas, Texas: Word Books, 1989.

Gutmann, Joseph. *The Dura-Europos Synagogue: A Re-Evaluation (1932–1972)*. Missoula: American Academy of Religion, 1973.

————. "Ancient Synagogues: Archaeological Facts and Scholarly Assumpion." *Bulletin of Asia Institute* 9 (1997): 226–27.

Gutman, Shmaryahu. *Gamla: Historical Setting: The First Season of Excavations.* Tel Aviv: Kibbutz Meuhad, 1977. Hebrew.

————. *Gamla: The First Eight Seasons of Excavations.* Tel Aviv: Kibbutz Meuhad, 1981. Hebrew.

————. "The Synagogue at Gamla." Pages 30–34 in *Ancient Synagogues Revealed.* Edited by Lee I. Levine. Jerusalem: Israel Exploration Society, 1982.

————. "Gamla—1983." *ESI* 3 (1984): 26–27.

————. "Gamala." Pages 459–63 in vol. 2 of *The New Encyclopedia of Archaeological Excavations in the Holy Land.* Edited by E. Stern et al. 4 vols. Jerusalem: The Israel Exploration Society and Carta, 1993.

Gutman, S. and D. Wagner. "Gamla—1984/1985/1986." *ESI* 5 (1986): 38–41.

Gutman, S., A. Segal, Y. Patrich et al. "Gamla—1987/1988." *ESI* 9 (1989–90): 9–15.

Gutman, S. and Y. Raphel, *Gamla—A City in Rebellion.* Israel: The Ministry of Defense, 1994.

Habas-Rubin, E. "The Dedication of Polymarchos from Stobi: Problems of Dating and Interpretation." *Jewish Quarterly Review* 102, no. 1/2 (2001): 41–78.

Haber, Susan, "Common Judaism, Common Synagogue? Purity, Holiness and Sacred Space at the Turn of the Common Era." In *Common Judaism Explored: Second Temple Judaism in Context. Essays in Honour of E. P. Sanders.* Edited by Wayne McCready and Adele Reinhartz. Minneapolis: Fortress, forthcoming 2008.

Hachlili, Rachel. *Ancient Jewish Art and Archaeology in the Land of Israel.* Handbuch der Orientalistik, Abt. 7. Bd 1. Abschnitt 2. B. Lief. 4. Leiden: Brill, 1988.

————. *Ancient Jewish Art and Archaeology in the Diaspora.* Handbuch der Orientalistik, Abt. 1, Bd 35. Leiden: Brill, 1998.

Hagner, Donald A. *Matthew 1–13, Matthew 14–28.* Word Biblical Commentary 33A, 33B. Dallas, Texas: Word Books 1993, 1995.

Harland, Philip. *Associations, Synagogues, and Congregations.* Minneapolis: Fortress Press, 2003.

Hayward, Robert. "The Jewish Temple at Leontopolis: A Reconsideration." *Journal of Jewish Studies* 33 (1982): 429–43.

Hengel, Martin. "Die Synagogeninschrift von Stobi." *Zeitschrift für die Neutestamentliche Wissenschaft und die Kunde der älteren Kirche* 57 (1966): 145–83.

————. "Proseuche und Synagoge: Jüdische Gemeinde, Gotteshaus und Gottesdienst in der Diaspora und in Palästina." Pages 157–84 in Tradition und Glaube: Das fruehe Christentum in seiner Umwelt. Edited by Gert Jeremias, Karl G. Kuhn, Heinz-Wolfgang Kuhn and Hartmut Stegemann. Gottingen: Vandenhoeck & Ruprecht, 1971.

————. *Judaism and Hellenism: Studies in Their Encounter in Palestine during the Early Hellenistic Period.* 2 vols. London: SCM, 1974.

Herzog, Z. "Israelite Sanctuaries at Arad and Beer-Sheba." Pages 120–122 in *Temples and High Places in Biblical Times: Proceedings of theColloquium in Honor of the Centennial of Hebrew Union College—Jewish Instituteof Religion.* Edited by A. Biran. Jerusalem: Hebrew Union College—Jewish Institute of Religion, 1981.

————. "Tel Beersheba." Pages 167–73 in Vol. 1 of *The New Encyclopedia of Archaeological Excavations in the Holy Land.* Edited by E. Stern. 4 vols. Jerusalem: The Israel Exploration Society and Carta, 1993.

Herzog, Z., A. F. Rainey and R. Brandfon. *Beer-Sheba 2: The Early Iron Age Settlements.* Publications of the Institute of Archaeology/Tel Aviv University 7. Tel Aviv: Tel Aviv University Institute of Archaeology: Ramot, 1984.

Herzog, Z., A. F. Rainey and S. Moshkovitz, "The Stratigraphy at Beer-Sheba and the Location of the Sanctuary." *Bulletin of the American Schools of Oriental Research* 225 (1977): 49–58.

Holleau, M. "Une inscription trouvée à Broussé." *Bulletin de Correspondance Hellénique* 48 (1924): 1–57.

Horbury, William. "Early Christians on Synagogue Prayer and Imprecation." Pages 296–317 in *Tolerance and Intolerance in Early Judaism and Christianity*. Edited by Graham Stanton et. al. Cambridge: Cambridge University Press, 1998.

Horbury, William, and David Noy. *Jewish Inscriptions of Graeco-Roman Egypt: With an Index of the Jewish Inscriptions of Egypt and Cyrenaica*. Cambridge: Cambridge University Press, 1992.

Horsley, Greg H. R. *New Documents Illustrating Early Christianity: A Review of the Greek Inscriptions and Papyri*. 4 vols. North Ryde, N. S. W.: The Ancient History Documentary Research Centre, 1981–87.

———. "Towards a New Corpus Inscriptionum Iudaicarum?" *Jewish Studies Quarterly* 2 (1995): 77–101.

Horsley, Richard. "Synagogues in Galilee and the Gospels." Pages 46–69 in *Evolution of the Synagogue: Problems and Progress*. Edited by Howard Clark Kee and Lynn H. Cohick. Harrisburg, Pa.: Trinity Press, 1999.

Horst, van der Pieter Willem. *Ancient Jewish Epitaphs*. Kampen, The Netherlands: Kok Pharos Publishing House, 1991.

———. "The Birkat ha-minim in Recent Research." *Expository Times* 105 (1993–1994): 363–68. Also Pages 99–111 in, Pieter Van der Horst. *Hellenism—Judaism—Christianity: Essays of Their Interaction*. Contributions to Biblical Exegesis and Theology 8. Kampen: KokPharos 1994.

———. "Was the Ancient Synagogue a Place of Sabbath Worship?" Pages 8–43 in *Jews, Christians and Polytheists in the Ancient Synagogue*. Edited by Steven Fine. London and New York: Routledge, 1999.

———. *Philo's Flaccus. The First Pogrom:Introduction, Translation and Commentary*. Philo of Alexandria Commentary Series 2. Leiden: Brill, 2003.

Hüttenmeister, Frowald and Gottfried Reeg. *Die antiken Synagogen in Israel: Die judischen Synagogen, Lehrhäuser und Gerichtshöfe*. Wiesbaden: Dr. Ludwig Reichert Verlag, 1977.

Ilan, Z. *Ancient Synagogues in Israel*. Tel Aviv: Ministry of Defence, 1991. Hebrew.

Jervell, Jakob, *Die Apostelgeschichte*. Kritisch-exegetischer Kommentar über das Neue Testament 3. Göttingen: Vandenhoeck & Ruprecht, 1998.

Johnson, Matthew. *Archaeological Theory: An Introduction*. Oxford: Blackwell, 1999.

Kant, Laurence H. "Jewish Inscriptions in Greek and Latin." Pages 671–713 in *Aufstieg und Niedergang der römischen Welt: Geschichte und Kultur Roms im Spiegel der neueren Forschung*. Edited by Wolfgang Haase. New York: W. de Gruyter, 1987.

Kasher, Aryeh. "Synagogues as 'Houses of Prayer' and 'Holy Places' in the Jewish Communities of Hellenistic and Roman Egypt." Pages 205–20 in vol. 1 of Ancient Synagogues: Historical Analysis and Archaeological Discovery. Edited by Dan Urman and Paul Virgil McCracken Flesher. New York: Brill, 1995.

———. The Jews in Hellenistic and Roman Egypt: The Struggle for Equal Rights. Rev. English ed. Vol. 7 of Texte und Studien zum antiken Judentum. Tübingen: J. C. B. Mohr (Paul Siebeck), 1985.

Kee, Howard Clark. "The Transformation of the Synagogue after 70 C.E.: Its Import for Early Christianity." *New Testament Studies* 36 (1990): 1–24.

———. "Early Christianity in the Galilee: Reassessing the Evidence from the Gospels." Pages 3–22 in *The Galilee in Late Antiquity*. Edited by Lee I. Levine. New York: The Jewish Theological Seminary of America, 1992.

———. "The Changing Meaning of Synagogue: A Response to Richard Oster." *New Testament Studies* 40 (1994): 281–83.

———. "Defining the First-Century C.E. Synagogue." *New Testament Studies* 41 (1995): 481–500.

Kitzinger, E. "A Survey of the Early Christian Town of Stobi." *Dumbarton Oaks Papers* 3 (1946): 129–61.

Klinghardt, Matthias. "The Manual of Discipline in the Light of Statutes of Hellenistic Associations." Pages 251–267 in *Methods of Investigation of the Dead Sea Scrolls and the Khirbet Qumran Site: Present Realities and Future Prospects*. Annals of the New York Academy of Sciences. Edited by Michael. O. Wise, et al. New York: The New York Academy of Sciences, 1994.

———. *Gemeinschaftsmahl und Mahlgemeinschaft: Soziologie und Liturgie frühchristlicher Mahlfeiern*. Texte und Arbeiten zum neutestamentlichen Zeitalter 13. Tübingen und Basel: Francke Verlag, 1996.

Kloppenborg, John S. "Joshua 22: The Priestly Editing of an Ancient Tradition." *Biblica* 62 (1981): 347–71.

———. "Dating Theodotos." *Journal of Jewish Studies* 51, no. 2 (2000): 243–80.

———. Kloppenborg, John S. "Diaspora Discourse: The Construction of *Ethos* in James." *New Testament Studies* 53 (2007): 242–270.

Koch, Dietrich-Alex. "The God-Fearers between Facts and Fiction." *Studia Theologica* 60 (2006): 62–90.

Kohl, Heinrich and Carl Watzinger. *Antike Synagogen in Galiläa*. Leipzig: Heinrichs, 1916.

Köster, Helmut. "Τόπος." Pages 187–208 in vol. 8 of *Theological Dictionary of the New Testament*. Edited by G. Friedrich. Grand Rapids: Eerdmans, 1971.

Kraabel, A. Thomas. "Judaism in Western Asia Minor under Roman Rule, with a Preliminary Study of the Jewish Community at Sardis, Lydia." ThD thesis, Harvard University, 1968.

———. "Paganism and Judaism: The Sardis Evidence." Pages 13–33 in *Paganisme, Judaïsme, Christianisme: Influences et affrontements dans le monde antique*. Edited by André Benoit, Marc Philonenko and Cyrille Vogel. Paris: Éditions E. De Boccard, 1978.

———. "The Diaspora Synagogue: Archaeological and Epigraphic Evidence Since Sukenik." Pages 477–510 in *Aufstieg und Niedergang der römischen Welt: Geschichte und Kultur Roms im Spiegel der neueren Forschung*. Vol. 2.19.1. Edited by W. Haase. New York: W. de Gruyter, 1979.

———. "New Evidence of the Samaritan Diaspora has been Found on Delos." *Biblical Archeologist* 47 (1984): 44–46.

———. "*Synagoga Caeca*: Systematic Distortion in Gentile Interpretations of Evidence for Judaism in the Early Christian Period." Pages 219–45 in *"To See Ourselves as Others See Us": Christians, Jews, "Others" in Late Antiquity*. Edited by Jacob Neusner and Ernest S. Frerichs. Chico, Calif.: Scholars Press, 1985.

Kraeling, Carl Hermann. *The Brooklyn Museum Aramaic Papyri: New Documents of the 5th Century B.C. from the Jewish Colony at Elephantine*. New Haven: Yale University Press, 1953.

———. *The Excavations at Dura-Europos: Final Report, 8:1: The Synagogue*. New Haven: Yale University Press, 1956.

———. "Elephantine Papyri." Pages 83–85 in Vol. 2 of *Interpreter's Dictionary of the Bible*. Edited by G. Buttrick. Nashville: Abingdon, 1962.

Krauss, Samuel. *Synagogale Altertümer*. Berlin-Wien: Verlag Benjamin Harz, 1922.

Kroll, John H. "The Greek Inscriptions" in *The Synagogue at Sardis*. Cambridge: Harvard University Press, forthcoming.

Lapp, P. "Soundings at 'Araq el-Emir." *Bulletin of the American Schools of Oriental Research* 165 (1962): 16–34.

———. "'Araq el-Emir." *Revue Biblique* 70 (1963): 411–16.

———. "The Second and Third Campaigns at 'Araq el-Emir." *Bulletin of the American Schools of Oriental Research* 171 (1963): 8–39.

Leon, Harry J., and Carolyn Osiek. *The Jews of Ancient Rome*. Updated ed. Peabody, Mass.: Hendrickson Publishers, 1995.

Leonhardt, J. "Εὐχαὶ καὶ θυσιαί (A 14:260): Opfer in der Jüdischen Synagoge on Sardes?" Pages 189–203 in *Internationales Josephus-Kolloquium, Amsterdam 2000*. Edited by J. Kalms. Münster: Lit Verlag, 2000.

Levine, Lee I. "The Synagogue at Dura-Europos." Pages 172–177 in *Ancient Synagogues Revealed*. Edited by Lee I. Levine. Jerusalem: Israel Exploration Society, 1982.

———. "The Sages and the Synagogue in Late Antiquity: The Evidence of the Galilee." Pages 201–22 in *The Galilee in Late Antiquity*. Edited by L. I. Levine. New York: The Jewish Theological Seminary of America, 1992.

———. "Caesarea's Synagogues and Some Historical Implications." Pages 666–78 in *Biblical Archaeology Today, 1990: Proceedings of the Second International Congress on Biblical Archaeology, Jerusalem, June–July 1990*. Jerusalem: Israel Exploration Society, 1993.

———. "The Nature and Origin of the Palestinian Synagogue Reconsidered." *Journal of Biblical Literature* 115 (1996): 425–48.

———. "Synagogue Officials: The Evidence from Caesarea and Its Implications for Palestine and the Diaspora." Pages 392–400 in *Caesarea Maritima: A Retrospective after Two Millennia*. Edited by Avner Raban and Kenneth G. Holum. Leiden: Brill, 1996.

———. *The Ancient Synagogue: The First Thousand Years*. New Haven: Yale University Press, 2005.

———. "The First Century C.E. Synagogue in Historical Perspective." Pages 1–24 in *The Ancient Synagogue: From its Origin Until 200 C.E.: Papers Presented at an International Conference at Lund University, October 14–17, 2001*. Edited by Birger Olsson and Magnus Zetterholm. Stockholm: Almqvist & Wiksell International, 2003.

———. "The First Century Synagogue: Critical Reassessments and Assessments of the Critical." Pages 70–102 in *Religion and Society in Roman Palestine. Old Questions, New Approaches*. Edited by Douglas R. Edwards. New York: Routledge, 2004.

Levinskaya, Irina. *The Book of Acts in Its Diaspora Setting*. Vol. 5 of *The Book of Acts in Its First Century Setting*. Grand Rapids: Eerdmans Publishing, 1996.

Levinskaya, Irina. Review of E. L. Gibson, *The Jewish Manumission Inscriptions of the Bosporan Kingdom*. *Jewish Quarterly Review* 92 (2002): 507–20.

Lieu, Judith E. "Temple and Synagogue in John." *New Testament Studies* 45 (1999): 51–69.

Lifschitz, Baruch. *Donateurs et fondateurs dans les synagogues Juives*. Paris: J. Gabalda et Cie, 1967.

———. "Notes d'épigraphie grecque." *Revue biblique* 76 (1969): 95–96.

———. *Prolegomenon*. In *Corpus of Jewish Inscriptions: Jewish Inscriptions from the Third Century B.C. to the Seventh Century A.D.* Edited by Jean Baptiste Frey. New York: Ktav Publishing House, 1975.

Linder, Amnon. *The Jews in Roman Imperial Legislation*. Detroit: Wayne State University Press, 1987.

Llewelyn, S. R. *New Documents Illustrating Early Christianity: A Review of the Greek Inscriptions and Papyri Published in 1980–81*. North Ryde, N. S. W.: Ancient History Documentary Research Centre, 1992.

Loffreda, Stanislao. "Ceramica Ellenistico-Romana nel Sottosuolo della Sinagoga di Cafarnao." *Studia Hierosolymitana* III (1982): 273–313.

———. *Recovering Capharnaum*. Jerusalem: Franciscan Printing Press, 1993.

———. "The Late Chronology of the Synagogue of Capernaum." Pages 52–56 in *Ancient Synagogues Revealed*. Edited by Lee I. Levine. Jerusalem: Israel Exploration Society, 1981.

Lüderitz, Gert. *Corpus jüdischer Zeugnisse aus der Cyrenaika*. Beihefte zum Tübinger Atlas des vorderen Orients B 53. Wiesbaden: Dr. Ludwig Reichert Verlag, 1983.

———. "What is the Politeuma?" Pages 183–225 in *Studies in Early Jewish Epigraphy*. Edited by Jan Willem Van Henten and Pieter Willem Van der Horst. New York: Brill, 1994.

Luz, Ulrich. *Das Evangelium nach Matthäus.* 1.–4. Teilband. Evangelisch-Katholischer
    Kommentar zum Neuen Testament I/1–4. Zürich and Neukirchen-Vluyn: Benz-
    inger Verlag and Neukirchener Verlag, 1985, 1990, 1997, 2002.
Magen, Y., Y. Zionit, and E. Sirkis. "Qiryat Sefer: A Jewish Village and Synagogue of
    the Second Temple Period." *Qadmoniot* 33/117 (1999): 25–32. Hebrew.
Magness, Jodi. "A Response to Eric M Meyers and James F Strange." Pages 79–91 in
    Judaism in Late Antiquity, part 3: *Where We Stand: Issues and Debates in Ancient Judaism*,
    vol. 4: *The Special Problem of the Ancient Synagogue.* Edited by Alan J. Avery-Peck and
    Jacob Neusner. Leiden: Brill, 2001.
————. "The Question of the Synagogue: The Problem of Typology." Pages 1–48 in
    Judaism in Late Antiquity, part 3: *Where We Stand: Issues and Debates in Ancient Judaism*,
    vol. 4: *The Special Problem of the Ancient Synagogue.* Edited by Alan J. Avery-Peck and
    Jacob Neusner. Leiden: Brill, 2001.
————. *The Archaeology of Qumran and the Dead Sea Scrolls.* Grand Rapids: Eerdmans,
    2002.
Ma'oz, Zvi Uri. "The Synagogue of Gamla and the Typology of Second-Temple
    Synagogues." Pages 35–41 in *Ancient Synagogues Revealed.* Edited by L. I. Levine.
    Jerusalem: Israel Exploration Society, 1981.
————. "When were the Galilean Synagogues First Constructed?" *Eretz-Israel* 25
    (1996): 416–26.
————. "Synagogue at Capernaum: A Radical Solution." Pages 137–48 in *The Roman
    and Byzantine Near East: Some Recent Archaeological Research.* Journal of Roman Archae-
    ology Supplementary Series 31 Volume 2. Edited by J. H. Humphrey. Portsmouth,
    R.I.: Journal of Roman Archaeology, 1999.
————. "The Synagogue that Never Existed in the Hasmonean Palace at Jericho:
    Remarks Concerning an Article by E. Netzer, Y. Kalman and R. Loris." *Qadmoniot*
    32 (1999): 120–21. Hebrew.
————. "Notes on B. Zissu and A. Ganor's Article in Qadmoniot 123: 'Horvat 'Etri.'"
    Qadmoniot 36/125 (2003). Hebrew.
Marcus, Joel. *Mark 1–8.* The Anchor Bible 27. New York: Doubleday, 2000.
Marmorstein, A. "The Synagogue of Claudius Tiberius Polymarchus in Stobi." *Jewish
    Quarterly Review* 27 (1937): 373–84.
Martin, Matthew J. "Interpreting the Theodotos Inscription: Some Reflections of a
    First Century Jerusalem Synagogue Inscription and E. P. Sanders' 'Common
    Judaism'." *Ancient Near Eastern Studies* 39 (2002): 160–81.
Martola, Nils. "Eating the Passover Lamb in House-Temples at Alexandria: Some
    Notes on Passover in Philo." Pages 521–531 in *Jewish Studies in a New Europe:
    Proceedings of the Fifth Congress of Jewish Studies in Copenhagen 1994 under the Auspices
    of the European Association for Jewish Studies.* Edited by Ulf Haxen. Copenhagen:
    C. A. Reitzel A/S International Publishers, 1998.
Mason, Steve, ed., *Life of Josephus*, Vol. 9 of *Flavius Josephus: Translation and Commentary.*
    Translation and Commentary by Steve Mason. Leiden: Brill, 2001.
Mazur, Belle D. *Studies on Jewry in Greece.* Athens: Printing Office 'Hestia,' 1935.
McKay, Heather A. "Ancient Synagogues: The Continuing Dialectic Between Two
    Major Views." *CR:BS* 6 (1998): 103–42.
————. *Sabbath and Synagogue: The Question of Sabbath Worship in Ancient Judaism.* Religions
    in the Graeco-Roman World 112. Leiden: Brill, 1994.
McLean, B. Hudson. "The Place of Cult in Voluntary Associations and Christian
    Churches on Delos." Pages 186–225 in *Voluntary Associations in the Greco-Roman World.*
    Edited by J. Kloppenborg and S. Wilson. London: Routledge, 1996.
Meiggs, Russell. *Roman Ostia.* 2nd ed. Oxford: Clarendon Press, 1973.
Menes, A. "Tempel und Synagoge." *Zeitschrift für die alttestamentliche Wissenschaft* 9 (1932):
    268–76.

Meyers, Eduard. *Der Papyrusfund von Elephantine: Dokumente einer jüdischen Gemeinde aus der Perserzeit und das älteste erhaltene Buch der Weltliteratur.* Leipzig: J. C. Hinrichssche Buchhandlung, 1912.

Meyers, Eric M. "The Current State of Galilean Synagogue Studies." Pages 127–37 in *The Synagogue in Late Antiquity.* Edited by Lee I. Levine. Philadelphia: American Schools of Oriental Research, 1987.

————. "Synagogue." Pages 251–60 in *The Anchor Bible Dictionary* 6. Edited by David Noel Freedman. New York: Doubleday, 1992.

————. "Nabratein (Kefar Neburaya)." Pages 1077–79 in *The New Encyclopedia of Archaeological Excavations in the Holy Land* 3. Edited by E. Stern. Jerusalem: Israel Exploration Society, 1993.

————. "The Torah Shrine in the Ancient Synagogue: Another Look at the Evidence." *Jewish Studies Quarterly* 4 (1997): 303–38.

————. "The Dating of the Gush Halav Synagogue: A Response to Jodi Magness." Pages 49–70 in *Judaism in Late Antiquity*, part 3: *Where We Stand: Issues and Debates in Ancient Judaism*, vol. 4: *The Special Problem of the Ancient Synagogue.* Edited by Alan J. Avery-Peck and Jacob Neusner. Leiden: Brill, 2001.

Meyers, Eric M. and Carol L. Meyers. "Finders of a Real Lost Ark." *Biblical Archaeology Review* 7 (1981): 24–39.

————. *Excavations at Ancient Nabratein: Synagogue and Environs* Meiron Excavation Project Reports 6. Winona Lake: Eisenbrauns, 2008; forthcoming.

Meyers, Eric M., James F. Strange and Carol L. Meyers. "Second Preliminary Report on the 1981 Excavations at en-Nabratein, Israel." *Bulletin of the American Schools of Oriental Research* 246 (1982): 35–54.

Mimouni, Simon C. "La synagogue 'judéo-chrétienne' de Jérusalem au Mont Sion: Texte et contexte." *Proche Orient Chrétien* 40, no. 3–4 (1990): 215–34.

Moloney, Francis J. *The Gospel of John.* Sacra Pagina Series 4. Collegeville, Minn.: The Liturgical Press, 1998.

Mussner, Franz. *Der Jakobusbrief.* Herders Theologischer Kommentar zum Neuen Testament XIII.1. Freiburg: Herder, 1964.

Naveh, Joseph. *On Stone and Mosaic: The Aramaic and Hebrew Inscriptions from Ancient Synagogues.* Jerusalem: Israel Exploration Society & Carta, 1978. Hebrew.

Netzer, Ehud. "Herodian Triclinia: A Prototype for the 'Galilean-Type' Synagogue." Pages 49–51 in *Ancient Synagogues Revealed.* Edited by Lee I. Levine. Jerusalem: Israel Exploration Society, 1982.

————. "Did the Magdala Springhouse Serve as a Synagogue?" Pages 165–72 in *Synagogues in Antiquity.* Edited by A. Kasher, A. Oppenheimer, and U. Rappaport. Jerusalem: Yad Izhak Ben Zvi, 1987. Hebrew.

————. *Masada. The Yigael Yadin Excavations, 1963–1965, Final Reports.* Vol. 3 of *The Buildings: Stratigraphy and Architecture.* Jerusalem: Israel Exploration Society, 1991.

————. "Le scoperte sotto il palazzo di Erode nella pianura occidentale Gerico riemergono i resti della più antica sinagoga fino a oggi nota." *Archeo* 14 (1998): 32–37.

————. "Floating in the Desert: A Pleasure Palace in Jordan." *Archaeology Odyssey* 2 (1999): 47–55.

————. "A Synagogue from the Hasmonean Period Recently Exposed in the Western Plain of Jericho." *Israel Exploration Journal* 49 (1999): 203–221.

————. "The Synagogue in Jericho: Did it Exist or Not?" *Qadmoniot* 33 (2000): 69–70. Hebrew.

————. *Hasmonean and Herodian Palaces at Jericho.* Vol. 2 of *Final Reports of the 1973–1987 Excavations.* Jerusalem: Israel Exploration Society, 2004.

Nikiprowetzky, V. *Le commentaire de l'Écriture chez Philon d'Alexandrie: Son caractère et sa portée. Observations philologiques.* Arbeiten zur Literatur und Geschichte des hellenistischen Judentums 11. Leiden: Brill, 1977.

Noy, David. "A Jewish Place of Prayer in Roman Egypt." *Journal of Theological Studies* 43 (1992): 118–22.
———. *Italy (Excluding the City of Rome), Spain and Gaul.* Vol. 1 of *Jewish Inscriptions of Western Europe.* Cambridge, New York: Cambridge University Press, 1993.
———. *The City of Rome.* Vol. 2 of *Jewish Inscriptions of Western Europe.* Cambridge, New York: Cambridge University Press, 1995.
Noy, David, Alexander Panayotov, and Hanswulf Bloedhorn, eds. *Eastern Europe.* Vol. 1 of *Inscriptiones Judaicae Orientis.* Texts and Studies in Ancient Judaism 101. Tübingen: Mohr Siebeck, 2004.
Noy, David, and Hanswulf Bloedhorn, eds. *Syria and Cyprus.* Vol 3 of *Inscriptiones Judaicae Orientis.* Texts and Studies in Ancient Judaism 102. Tübingen: Mohr Siebeck, 2004.
Olsson, Birger. *Structure and Meaning in the Fourth Gospel: A Text-Linguistic Analysis of John 2:1–11 and 4:1–42.* Coniectanea Biblica. New Testament Series 6. Lund: C. W. K. Gleerup, 1974.
———. "'All my Teaching was Done in Synagogues…' (John 18,20)." Pages 203–24 in *Theology and Christology in the Fourth Gospel: Essays by the Members of the SNTS Johannine Writings Seminar.* Edited by G. van Belle, J. G. van der Watt and P. Maritz. Bibliotheca Ephemeridum Theologicarum Lovaniensium 184. Leuven: Leuven University Press, 2005.
Olsson, Birger and Magnus Zetterholm, eds. *The Ancient Synagogue From Its Origins Until 200 C.E.: Papers Presented at an International Conference at Lund University, October 14–17, 2001.* Stockholm: Almqvist & Wiksell International, 2003.
Onn, Alexander, Shlomit Weksler-Bdolach, Yehuda Rapuano, and Tzah Kanias. "Khirbet Umm el-ʿUmdan." *Hadashot Arkheologiyot* 114 (2002). Hebrew.
Onn, Alexander and Rafyunu, Y. "Jerusalem: Khirbeth a-ras." *Hadashot Arkheologiyot* 100 (1993). Hebrew.
Osborn, Eric. *Justin Martyr.* Beiträge zur historischen Theologie 47. Tübingen: Mohr Siebeck, 1973.
Oster, Richard E. "Supposed Anachronism in Luke-Acts' Use of ΣΥΝΑΓΩΓΗ: A Rejoinder to Howard Clark Kee." *New Testament Studies* 39 (1993): 178–208.
Overman, Andrew. "Jews, Slaves and the Synagogue on the Black Sea." Pages 141–57 in *Evolution of the Synagogue.* Edited by H. Kee & L. Cohick. Harrisburg: Trinity Press International, 1999.
Parente, Fausto. "Onias III's Death and the Founding of the Temple of Leontopolis." Pages 69–98 in *Josephus and the History of the Greco-Roman Period: Essays in Memory of Morton Smith.* Studia Post-Biblica, 41. Edited by Fausto Parente and Joseph Sievers. Leiden: Brill, 1994.
Pavolini, Carlo. "Ostia (Roma): Saggi lungo la via Severiana." *Notizie degli Scavi di Antichità* 8, no. 35 (1981): 115–43.
Perrot, Charles. "La lecture de la Bible dans le Diaspora hellénistique." Pages 109–32 in *Études sur le Judaïsme hellénistique.* Edited by R. Kuntzmann and J. Schlosser. Paris: Editions du Cerf, 1984.
Pesch, Rudolf. *Das Markusevangelium.* Herders Theologischer Kommentar zum Neuen Testament II.1, II.2. Freiburg: Herder, 1976, 1977.
Petrović, J. "Excavations at Stobi 1931." *Starinar* 7 (1932): 81–86, 135–36.
Pinterović, D. "Da li je u rimskoj kolonii Mursi postojala sinaggoga? (Was There a Synagogue at Mursa?)." *Osjecki Zbornik* 9–10 (1965): 61–74.
———. *Mursa i njeno područje u antičko doba.* Osjeck, 1978.
———. "Mursa za dinastije Severa (Mursa at the Time of the Severi)." *Osjecki Zbornik* 7 (1960): 17–42.
Plassart, André. "La synagogue juive de Delos." *Revue biblique* 23 (1914): 523–34.
———. "La synagogue juive de Délos." Pages 201–15 in *Mélanges Holleaux, recueil de mémoirs concernant l'antiquité grecque.* Paris: Picard, 1913.

Poehlman, W. "The Polycharmos Inscription and Synagogue I at Stobi." Pages 235–46 in vol. 3 of *The Antiquites of Stobi*. Edited by Blaga Aleksova and James Wiseman. Beograd: Macedonian Review Editions, 1981.

Porten, Bezalel. *The Elephantine Papyri in English: Three Millennia of Cross-Cultural Continuity and Change*. Studies in Near Eastern Archaeology and Civilization. Leiden: Brill, 1996.

Pummer, Reinhard. "Inscriptions." Pages 190–94 in *The Samaritans*. Edited by A. Crown. Tübingen: J. C. B. Mohr, 1989.

Rabinovich, Abraham. "Oldest Jewish Prayer Room Discovered on Shuafat Ridge." *Jerusalem Post*, 8 April 1991.

Radan, G. "Comments on the History of Jews in Pannonia." *Acta antiqua Academiae Scientiarum Hungaricae* 25 (1973): 264–78.

Radice, R., and David T. Runia. *Philo of Alexandria: An Annotated Bibliography 1937–1986*. Supplements to Vigiliae Christianae VIII. Leiden: Brill, 1988.

Rajak, Tessa, and David Noy. "*Archisynagogoi*: Office, Title and Social Status in the Greco-Jewish Synagogue." *Journal of Roman Studies* 83 (1993): 75–93.

Ramsay, W. M. *Cities and Bishoprics of Phrygia*. 2 vols. Oxford: B. Blackwell, 1895, 1897.

———. "Deux jours in Phrygie." *Revue des études anciennes* 3 (1901): 272.

———. "Nouvelles remarques sur les textes d'Acmonie." *Revue des études anciennes* 4 (1902): 270.

Rapuano, Yehuda, "The Hasmonean Period 'Synagogue' at Jericho and the 'Council Chamber' Building at Qumran." *Israel Exploration Journal* 51 (2001): 48–56.

Rech, Jason, Alysia Fischer, Douglas R. Edwards, and A. J. Timothy Jull. "Direct Dating of Plaster and Mortar Using AMS Radiocarbon: A Pilot Project from Khirbet Qana, Israel" *Antiquity* 77 (2003): 155–64.

Reich, Ronny. "The Synagogue and the *Miqweh* in Eretz-Israel in the Second-Temple, Mishnaic, and Talmudic Periods." Pages 289–97 in *Ancient Synagogues: Historical Analysis and Archaeological Discovery*. Edited by Dan Urman and Paul Virgil McCracken Flesher. New York: Brill, 1995.

Reinach, T. "Chronique l'orient." *Revue Archéologique Third Series* 12 (1888): 214–26.

———. "L'inscription de Théodotus." *Revue des études juives* 71 (1920): 46–56.

Reynolds, J. M. "Inscriptions." Pages 233–54 in *Excavations at Sidi Khrebish Benghazi (Berenice)*. Edited by J. A. Lloyd. Hertford: Stephen Austin and Sons, 1977.

Richardson, Peter. *Building Jewish in the Roman East*. Waco: Baylor University Press, 2004.

Richardson Peter and V. Heuchan. "Jewish Voluntary Associations in Egypt and the Roles of Women." Pages 226–51 in *Voluntary Associations in the Greco-Roman World*. Edited by J. Kloppenborg and S. Wilson. London: Routledge, 1996.

Riesner, Rainer. "Neue Funde in Israel." *Bibel und Kirche* 46 (1991): 181–83.

———. "Die bisher älteste Synagoge gefunden." *Idea Spektrum*, 28 August 1991 1991, 17.

———. "Synagogues in Jerusalem." Pages 179–211 in *The Book of Acts in Its Palestinian Setting*. Edited by Richard Bauckham. Vol. 4 of *The Book of Acts in Its First Century Setting*. Edited by Bruce W. Winter. Grand Rapids: Eerdmans, 1995.

Robert, L. "Inscriptions grecques de Side." *Revue philologique* 32 (1958): 15–53.

Roitman, Adolfo. *The Bible in the Shrine of the Book: From the Dead Sea Scrolls to the Aleppo Codex*. Jerusalem: The Israel Museum, 2006.

Roth-Gerson, L. *The Greek Inscriptions from the Synagogues in Eretz-Israel*. Jerusalem: Yad Izhak Ben-Zvi, 1987. Hebrew.

———. *The Jews in Syria as Reflected in the Greek Inscriptions*. Jerusalem: Shazar Centre Historical Society of Israel, 2001. Hebrew.

Roux, G. and J. Roux. "Un décret du politeuma des juifs de Bérénikè en Cyrénaïque." *Revue des Études Grecques* 62 (1949): 281–96.

Rowley, H. H. *Worship in Ancient Israel: Its Forms and Meaning*. London: S.P.C.K., 1967.

Runesson, Anders. "The Oldest Original Synagogue Building in the Diaspora." *Harvard Theological Review* 92 (1999): 409–33.

————. *The Origins of the Synagogue: A Socio-Historical Study.* Coniectanea Biblica New Testament Series 37. Edited by Birger Olsson and Kari Syreeni. Stockholm: Almqvist & Wiksell International, 2001.

————. "The Synagogue at Ancient Ostia: The Building and its History From the First to the Fifth Century." Pages 29–99 in *The Synagogue of Ancient Ostia and the Jews of Rome: Interdisciplinary Studies*, ActaRom-4° 57. Edited by Birger Olsson, Dieter Mitternacht and Olof Brandt. Stockholm: Paul Åströms förlag, 2001.

————. "Water and Worship: Ostia and the Ritual Bath of the Diaspora Synagogue." Pages 115–29 in *The Synagogue of Ancient Ostia and the Jews of Rome: Interdisciplinary Studies*, ActaRom-4° 57. Edited by Birger Olsson, Dieter Mitternacht and Olof Brandt. Stockholm: Paul Åströms förlag, 2001.

————. "A Monumental Synagogue from the First Century: The Case of Ostia." *Journal for the Study of Judaism in the Persian, Hellenistic Roman Period* 33 (2002): 171–220.

————. "The Origins and Nature of the 1st Century Synagogue." In the *Bible and Interpretation.* July 2004 (http://www.bibleinterp.com/articles/Runesson-1st-Century_Synagogue_1.htm).

————. "Women Leadership in the Early Church: Some Examples and an Interpretive Frame." *Svensk Teologisk Kvartalskrift* 82:4 (2006): 173–83. Swedish; English summary.

————. "Architecture, Conflict, and Identity Formation: Jews and Christians in Capernaum From the 1st to the 6th Century." Pages 231–57 in *The Ancient Galilee in Interaction: Religion, Ethnicity, and Identity.* Edited by Harold W. Attridge, Dale Martin, and Jürgen Zangenberg. Tübingen: Mohr Siebeck, 2007.

————. "Re-Thinking Early Jewish/Christian Relations: Matthean Community History as Pharisaic Intra-group Conflict." *Journal of Biblical Literature* 127 (2008) forthcoming.

Runia, David T. *On the Creation of the Cosmos according to Moses: Introduction, Translation and Commentary.* Philo of Alexandria Commentary Series 1. Leiden Boston Köln: Brill, 2001.

Runia, David T. *Philo of Alexandria: An Annotated Bibliography 1987–1996 with Addenda for 1937–1986.* Supplements to Vigiliae Christianae LVII. Leiden: Brill, 2000.

Rutgers, Leonard Victor. "Diaspora Synagogues: Synagogue Archaeology in the Greco-Roman World." Pages 67–94 in *Sacred Realm: The Emergence of the Synagogue in the Ancient World.* Edited by Steven Fine. New York: Oxford University Press, 1996.

————. *The Jews in Late Ancient Rome: Evidence of Cultural Interaction in the Roman Diaspora.* Paperback edition. Leiden: Brill, 2000.

Safrai, Shemuel, and Menachem Stern. *The Jewish People in the First Century. Historical Geography, Political History, Social, Cultural and Religious Life and Institutions.* Compendia rerum Iudaicarum ad Novum Testamentum, section 1. Assen: Van Gorcum, 1974.

Saller, Sylvester John. *The Second Revised Catalogue of the Ancient Synagogues of the Holy Land.* Jerusalem: Franciscan Printing, 1972.

Sanders, E. P. *Judaism: Practice and Belief 63 B.C.E.–66 C.E.* London: SCM Press, 1992.

Sanders, Jack T. *Schismatics, Sectarians, Dissidents, Deviants: The First One Hundred Years of Jewish—Christian Relations.* London: SCM Press, 1993.

Scheiber, Alexander. *Jewish Inscriptions in Hungary, from the 3rd Century to 1686.* Leiden: Brill, 1983.

Schreckenberg, Heinz. *The Jews and Christian Art: An Illustrated History.* New York: Continuum, 1996.

Schürer, Emil, Geza Vermes, and Fergus Millar. *A History of the Jewish People in the Time of Jesus Christ.* Revised English ed. 3 vols. Edinburgh: T & T Clark, 1973–86.

Schürer, Emil. "Die Juden im bosporanischen Reiche und die Genossenschaften der σεβόμενοι θεὸν ὕψιστον ebendaselbst." Pages 1.200–225 in *Sitzungsberichte der Königlich Preussischen Akademie der Wissenschaften zu Berlin.* Berlin, 1897.

Schürmann, Heinz. *Das Lukasevangelium.* Herders Theologischer Kommentar zum Neuen Testament III.1, III.2/1. Freiburg: Herder, 1969, 1994.

Schwabe, Moshe. "Greek Inscriptions from Jerusalem." Pages 362–65 in *Sefer Yerusha-layim*. Edited by Michael. Avi-Yonah. Jerusalem & Tel Aviv: Bialik & Dvir, 1956. Hebrew.

Schwartz, Seth. *Imperialism and Jewish Society: 200 B.C.E. to 640 C.E.* Princeton: Princeton University Press, 2001.

Selem, Petar. *Les religions orientales dans la Pannonie romaine, partie en Yougoslavie, Etudes préliminaires aux religions orientales dans l'Empire romain.* Leiden: Brill, 1980.

Shanks, Hershel. *Judaism in Stone: The Archaeology of Ancient Synagogues.* New York: Harper & Row, 1979.

———. "Gamla: The Masada of the North." *Biblical Archeology Review* 5, no. 1 (1979): 12–19.

Sigonius, Carolus. *De republica Hebraeorum libri VII.* Colonie, 1583.

Silber, Mendel. *The Origin of the Synagogue.* New Orleans: Steeg, 1915.

Smallwood, E. Mary. *Philonis Alexandrini Legatio ad Gaium: Edited with an Introduction Translation and Commentary.* Leiden: Brill, 1961.

———. The Jews under Roman Rule: From Pompey to Diocletian. Studies in Judaism in Late Antiquity 20. Leiden: Brill, 1976.

Squarciapino, Maria Floriani. "La Sinagoga di Ostia: Seconda campagna di Scavo." Pages 299–315 in Atti VI Congresso Internazionale di Archeologia Cristiana. Rome, 1962.

———. "Die Synagoge von Ostia Antica." *Raggi* 4, no. 1 (1962): 1–8.

———. "Ebrei a Roma e ad Ostia." *Studi Romani* 11, no. 2 (1963): 129–41.

———. "The Most Ancient Synagogue Known from Monumental Remains: The Newly Discovered Ostia Synagogue in Its First and Fourth Century A.D. Phases." Pages 468–71 in *The Illustrated London News*, September 28 1963.

———. "Die Synagoge von Ostia nach der zweiten Ausgrabungskampagne." *Raggi* 5, no. 1 (1963): 13–17.

———. "The Synagogue at Ostia." *Archaeology* 16 (1963): 194–203.

———. "La Sinagoga di Ostia: Second campagna di Scavo." Pages 299–315 in *Atti VI Congresso Internazionale di Archeologia Cristiana.* Rome: Pontificio Istituto di archeologia cristiana, 1965.

———. "Plotius Fortunatus archisynagogus." *La Rassegna Mensile di Israel* 36 (1970): 183–91.

Steckholl, S. "The Qumran Sect in Relation to the Temple of Leontopolis." *Revue de Qumran* 6 (1967): 55–69.

Stegemann, Wolfgang. *Zwischen Synagoge und Obrigkeit. Zur historischen Situation der lukanischen Christen.* Forschungen zur Religion und Literatur des Alten und Neuen Testaments 152. Göttingen: Vandenhoeck & Ruprecht, 1991.

Sterling, Gregory E. "'The Queen of the Virtues': Piety in Philo of Alexandria", *The Studia Philonica Annual* 18 (2006), 103–23.

———. "'The School of Sacred Laws.' The Social Setting of Philo's Treatises." *Vigiliae Christianae* 53 (1999): 148–64.

Stern, Ephraim. *The New Encyclopedia of Archaeological Excavations in the Holy Land.* 4 vols. Jerusalem: The Israel Exploration Society and Carta, 1993.

Stern, Menachem. *Greek and Latin Authors on Jews and Judaism, Edited with Introductions, Translations and Commentary.* Publications of the Israel Academy of Sciences and Humanities, Sections of Humanities. Jerusalem: The Israel Academy of Sciences and Humanities, 1974–1984.

Steudel, A. "House of Prostration CD XI, 21–XII, 1–Dublicates of the Temple." *Revue de Qumran* 16 (1993): 49–68.

Strange, James F. "Ancient Texts, Archaeology as Text, and the Problem of the First Century Synagogue." Pages 27–45 in *Evolution of the Synagogue.* Edited by Howard C. Kee and Lynn H. Cohick. Harrisburg: Trinity Press International, 1999.

———. "Synagogue Typology and Khirbet Shema': A Response to Jodi Magness." Pages 71–78 in *Judaism in Late Antiquity*, part 3: *Where We Stand: Issues and Debates in Ancient Judaism*, vol. 4: *The Special Problem of the Ancient Synagogue*. Edited by Alan J. Avery-Peck and Jacob Neusner. Leiden: Brill, 2001.

———. "The First Century C.E. Synagogue in Historical Perspective." Pages 37–62 in *The Ancient Synagogue: From its Origin Until 200 C.E.: Papers Presented at an International Conference at Lund University, October 14–17, 2001*. Edited by Birger Olsson and Magnus Zetterholm. Stockholm: Almqvist & Wiksell International, 2003.

Strange, James F. and Hershel Shanks. "Synagogue where Jesus Preached Found at Capernaum." *Biblical Archeology Review* 9, no 6 (1983): 25–31.

Sukenik, Eleazar Lipa. *Ancient Synagogues in Palestine and Greece, The Schwiech Lectures of the British Academy*. London: Oxford University Press, 1934.

Syon, Danny. "Gamla: Portrait of a Rebellion." *Biblical Archeology Review* 18, no. 1 (1992): 21–37.

Taylor, Vincent. *The Gospel According to S. Mark*. 2nd Edition. London: MacMillan, 1966.

Tcherikover, Avigdor, Alexander Fuks, and Menahem Stern. *Corpus Papyrorum Judaicarum*. 3 vols. Cambridge: Harvard University Press, 1957–64.

Tellbe, Mikael. *Paul between Synagogue and State: Christians, Jews, and Civic Authorities in 1 Thessalonians, Romans and Philippians*. Coniectanea Biblica. New Testament Series 34. Stockholm: Almqvist & Wiksell International, 2001.

Thyen, Hartwig. *Das Johannesevangelium*. Handbuch zum Neuen Testament 6. Tübingen: Mohr Siebeck, 2005.

Trebilco, Paul R. *Jewish Communities in Asia Minor*. Society for New Testament Studies Monograph Series 69. Cambridge: Cambridge University Press, 1991.

———. *The Early Christians in Ephesus from Paul to Ignatius*. Wissenschaftliche Undersuchungen zum Neuen Testament 166. Tübingen: Mohr Siebeck, 2004.

Trümper, Monika. "The Oldest Original Synagogue Building in the Diaspora: The Delos Synagogue Reconsidered." *Hesperia* 73 (2004): 513–98.

Urman, Dan and Paul V. M. Flesher. *Ancient Synagogues: Historical Analysis and Archaeological Discovery*. 2 vols. Leiden: Brill, 1995.

Vermes, Geza, and Martin Goodman. *The Essenes. According to the Classical Sources*. Sheffield: ISOT Press, 1989.

Vincent, L. H. "Découverte de la «synagogue des affranchis» a Jérusalem." *Revue biblique* 30 (1921): 247–77.

Virgilio Corbo. *Herodion: Gli edifici della reggia-fortressa*. Vol. 1. Jerusalem: Franciscan Printing Press, 1989.

Vitringa, Campegius. *De synagoga vetere libri tres*. Franequeræ: Typis & Impensis Johannis Gyzelaar, 1696.

Von Gerkan, A. "Eine Synagogue in Milet." *Zeitschrift für die neutestamentliche Wissenschaft und die Kunde der älteren Kirche* 20 (1921).

Vulić, N. "Antički spomenici naše zemlje (Ancient Monuments of our Land)." *Spomenik Srpske kraljesvke akademije* 71 (1931).

———. "Inscription grecque de Stobi." *Bulletin de Correspondance Hellénique* 56 (1932): 291–98.

———. "Inscription grecque de Stobi." *Bulletin de l'Académie des lettres royales Serbe* 1 (1935): 169–75.

Wander, Bernd. *Gottesfürchtige und Sympathisanten: Studien zum heidnischen Umfeld von Diasporasynagogen*. Wissenschaftlich Untersuchungen zum Neuen Testament 104. Tübingen: Mohr Siebeck, 1998.

Weill, Raymond. *La cité de David: Compte rendu des fouilles exécutées à Jérusalem sur le site de la ville primitive, campaigne de 1913–1914*. 2 vols. Paris: P. Geuthner, 1920.

Weinfeld, Moshe. "Synagogue Inscriptions and Jewish Liturgy." *Annual for the Bible and the Study of the Near East* 4 (1980): 288–95. Hebrew.

———. *The Organizational Pattern and the Penal Code of the Qumran Sect*. Göttingen: Vandenhoeck & Ruprecht, 1986.

Weksler-Bdolah, Shlomit, Alexander Onn, and Yehuda Rapuano. "Identifying the Hasmonean Village of Modi'in." *Cathedra* 109 (2003): 69–86. Hebrew.

White, L. Michael. "The Delos Synagogue Revisited: Recent Fieldwork in the Graeco-Roman Diaspora." *Harvard Theological Review* 80 (1987): 133–60.

————. "Synagogue and Society in Imperial Ostia: Archaeological and Epigraphic Evidence." *Harvard Theological Review* 90 (1997): 23–58.

————. *The Social Origins of Christian Architecture*. 2 vols. Harvard Theological Studies 42–43.Valley Forge, Pa.: Trinity Press International, 1996–97.

————. "Reading the Ostia Synagogue: A Reply to A. Runesson." *Harvard Theological Review* 92 (1999): 435–64.

Whittaker, Molly. *Jews and Christians: Graeco-Roman Views*. Cambridge: Cambridge University Press, 1984.

Wieder, N. "The Jericho Inscription and Jewish Liturgy." *Tarbiz* 52 (1983): 557–79. Hebrew.

Wiegand T. and H. Schrader. *Priene: Ergebnisse der Ausgrabungen und Untersuchengen in den Jahren 1895–1898*. Berlin: G. Reimer, 1904.

Will, Ernest. "The Recent French Work at Araq el-Emir: The Qasr el-Abd Rediscovered." Pages 149–58 in *The Excavations at Araq el-Emir*. The Annual of the American Schools of Oriental Research 1. Edited by Nancy L. Lapp. Winona Lake: American Schools of Oriental Research, 1983.

————. *Iraq al Amir: le chateau du tobiade Hyrcan*. 2 vols. Bibliothèque archéologique et historique, 132. Paris: Geuthner, 1991.

Williams, Margaret, ed. *The Jews Among the Greeks and Romans: A Diaspora Sourcebook*. Baltimore, Md.: Johns Hopkins University Press, 1998.

Wischnitzer, Rachel. *The Architecture of the European Synagogue*. Philadelphia: The Jewish Publication Society of America, 1974.

Yadin, Yigael. "The Synagogue at Masada." Pages 19–23 in *Ancient Synagogues Revealed*. Edited by Lee I. Levine. Jerusalem: Israel Exploration Society, 1982.

———— . "Masada." Pages 793–816 in vol. 3 of *Encyclopedia of Archaeological Excavations in the Holy Land*. Edited by M. Avi-Yonah. 4 vols. Jerusalem: Prentice-Hall, 1975.

Yonge, Charles Duke. *The Works of Philo: Complete and Unabridged*. New updated edition. Peabody, Mass.: Hendricksen, 1993.

Zahavy, Tzvee, *Studies in Jewish Prayer*. Lanham: University Press of America, 1990.

Zappa, Giulia Garofalo. "Nuovi bolli laterizi di Ostia." Pages 257–89 in *Terza Miscellanea Greca e Romana*. Edited by G. Barbieri, P. Cavuoto, G. Garofalo Zappa, L. Gasperini, V. La Bua and A. Russi. Rome: Istituto per la storia antica, 1971.

Zevi, Fausto. "La sinagoga di Ostia." *Rassegna mensile di Israel* 38 (1972): 131–45.

ILLUSTRATION CREDITS

Figure 1, page 24. Plan and reconstruction of the Cana public building/synagogue. Courtesy of Peter Richardson.

Figure 2, page 30. Plan of the first century synagogue in Capernaum. After Corbo, "Sinagoga del primo secolo." Copyright by Franciscan Printing Press.

Figure 3, page 31. Reconstruction of the first century Capernaum synagogue. Permission granted from the Visual Bible, Inc.

Figure 4, page 34. Plan of the Gamla synagogue. Courtesy of Danny Syon and Hagit Tahan/Gamla Excavations.

Figure 5, page 35. Photograph of the remains of the Gamla synagogue. Courtesy of Danny Syon/Gamla Excavations.

Figure 6, page 36. Plan of the Herodion synagogue. Courtesy of Ehud Netzer.

Figure 7, page 37. Plan of Horvat ʿEtri. Courtesy of Boaz Zissu.

Figure 8, page 40. Plan of the three phases of the Jericho synagogue. Courtesy of Ehud Netzer.

Figure 9, page 41. Reconstruction of the Jericho synagogue. Courtesy of Ehud Netzer.

Figure 10, page 56. Plan of the Masada synagogue (two phases). Computer drawing by Dieter Mitternacht, based on Ehud Netzer, *Masada*, p. 403.

Figure 11, page 58. Plan of the Modiʿin synagogue. From Alexander Onn et al., "Khirbet Umm el-ʿUmdan." Courtesy of the Israel Antiquities Authority.

Figure 12, page 59. Plan and reconstruction of the first phase of the Nabratein synagogue. From Meyers and Meyers, *Ancient Nabratein*. By permission of the authors, Eric M. Meyers and Carol Meyers.

Figure 13, page 66. Reconstruction of the Qiryat Sefer synagogue. From Magen and Sirkis, "Qiryat Sefer." Copyright by Y. Magen.

Figure 14, page 73. Plan of Khirbeth Qumran, periods 1b–2, by Roland de Vaux. Copyright by the British Academy.

Figure 15, page 74. Reconstruction of room 77 (the refectory) at Qumran by Tanya Slutzki-Greenstein. Copyright by the Israel Nature and Parks Authority.

Figure 16, page 119. Plan of the Aegina synagogue. After Mazur, *Studies on Jewry*, fig. 3. Reproduced in Hachili, *Diaspora*, fig. II.2.

Figure 17, page 132. Plan of the Delos synagogue. Courtesy of Monika Trümper ("Oldest Original Synagogue Building" fig. 3).

Figure 18, page 133. The so-called chair of Moses, Delos synagogue. Photograph by Anders Runesson.

Figure 19, page 144. Plan of the Priene synagogue. After Wiegand and Schrader, fig. 585. Reproduced in Hachlili, *Diaspora*, fig. II.21.

Figure 20, page 227. Plan of the first phase of the Ostia synagogue, by Anders Runesson.

Figure 21, page 228. Reconstruction of the first phase of the Ostia synagogue. Courtesy of Olof Brandt.

Figure 22, page 229. Plan of the second phase of the Ostia synagogue, by Anders Runesson.

Figure 23, page 245. Plan of the first phase of the Dura Europos synagogue. From Kraeling, *Excavations at Dura-Europos*, plan VIII.2; Permission granted from Yale University Press.

LIST OF ABBREVIATIONS

(For abbreviations of ancient texts, see Alexander, Patrick H., et al. (eds.), *The SBL Handbook of Style For Near Eastern, Biblical, and Early Christian Studies*. Peabody: Hendrickson, 1999)

AASA	*Annuario della Scuola archeologica di Atene e delle missioni italiane in Oriente*
CIG	*Corpus inscriptionum Graecarum*
CIJ	Jean Baptiste Frey, ed., *Corpus inscriptionum Judaicarum* (vol. 1, rev. ed.)
CIL	*Corpus inscriptionum Latinarum*
CIRB	I. Struve, ed., *Corpus inscriptionum regni Bosporani*
CJZ	Gert Lüderitz, and Joyce Maire Reynolds, eds., *Corpus jüdischer Zeugnisse aus der Cyrenaika*
CPJ	Avigdor Tcherikover, Alexander Fuks, and Menahem Stern, eds., *Corpus papyrorum Judaicarum*
DF	Baruch Lifshitz, *Donateurs et fondateurs dans les synagogues juives*
GD	Philippe Bruneau and Jean Ducat, *Guide de Delos*
GLAJJ	Menahem Stern, ed., *Greek and Latin Authors on Jews and Judaism*
HJP	Emil Schürer, Geza Vermes, and Fergus Millar, *A History of the Jewish People in the Time of Jesus Christ*, Revised English ed.
ID	*Inscriptions de Délos*
IGRR	*Inscriptiones Graecae ad res Romanas pertinentes*
IJO	David Noy *et al.* (vols. 1, 3), Walter Ameling (vol. 2), eds., *Inscriptiones Judaicae Orientis*
IPE	*Inscriptiones antiquae orae septentrionalis Ponti Euxini Graecae et Latinae*
JIGRE	William Horbury, and David Noy, eds., *Jewish Inscriptions of Graeco-Roman Egypt*
JIWE	David Noy, ed., *Jewish Inscriptions of Western Europe*
JSGRP	Erwin R. Goodenough, *Jewish Symbols in the Greco-Roman Period*
LCL	Loeb Classical Library
LSJ	Liddell-Scott-Jones, *Greek-English Lexicon*
MAMA	*Monumenta Asiae Minoris antiqua*
NEAEHL	Ephraim Stern, ed., *The New Encyclopedia of Archaeological Excavations in the Holy Land*
NRSV	New Revised Standard Version
OGIS	Wilhelmus Dittenberger, ed., *Orientis Graeci inscriptiones selectae*
SB	*Sammelbuch griechischer Urkunden aus Ägypten*
SEG	*Supplementum epigraphicum Graecum*

SIGLA

[ ]	for the restoration of lost text
[?]	for an uncertain restoration of lost text
[[ ]]	for text deliberately erased in antiquity
[[[ ]]]	for the restoration of deliberately erased text
( )	for the resolution of an abbreviation
< >	for the (modern) correction of a mistake or omission in the text
{ }	for text judged to be erroneous
[...]	for lost text where each dot represents a missing letter
[- -]	for lost text where the number of missing letters is uncertain
[- c.4 -]	for lost text where the number of missing letters is estimated
+	for traces of an individual letter that cannot be identified
ạ (dot subscript)	for an uncertain reading of a letter
vacat	for a gap deliberately left in the text
|	for a line division
||	for a division after five lines

INDICES

Numbers refer to source entries, not pages. The Introduction (chapter 1) is not included in the indices.

SOURCES

SUBJECTS AND NAMES

SYNAGOGUE TERMS

GREEK

amphitheatron   131, 132

didaskaleion   166, 168, 194, 198, 200

ekklēsia   201, 202, 203, 216
eucheion   149

hieron   13, 14, 21, 61, 62, 135, 138,
   153, 161, 169, 190, T5, T7, T10
hieros peribolos   138, 143
hagios topos   187

oikos   137

proseuchē   22, 43, 99, 100, 109, 121,
   123, 124, 125, 126, 128, 129, 138,
   139, 140, 141, 142, 143, 144, 147,
   148, 149, 150, 151, 152, 154, 156,

157 (*topos proseuchē*), 158, 159, 163,
   164, 165, 170, 171, 172, 175, 182,
   185, 195, 207, 208, 217
proseuktērion   166

sabbateion   120
semneion   160
syllogos   201, 202
synagōgē   1, 16, 26, 55, 57, 63, 68, 90,
   91, 103, 105, 106, 107, 111, 115,
   126, 129, 133, 170, 187, 190, 193,
   196, 205, 206, 210, 211, 212, 213,
   214, 215, 216, T10
synagōgion   118 (194), 167

thiasos   93, 180
topos   113, 114, 136, 137, 157 (*topos
   proseuchē*), 187

HEBREW

bet hishtahavot   36
bet ha-kneset   44 (*kneset*), 76, 78, 80, 81,
   82, 84, 85, 87

bet ha-Torah   37
bet mo'ed   38
bet ha-midrash   77, 79

LATIN

ecclesia   64

proseucha   181, 183

templum   209

ITALIA

Ostia Rome

Osijek (Mursa)

Stobi

Philippi
Beroea   Thessalonica

MACEDONIA   Pa

Smy
Eph
Corinth   Athens
Aegina   Mi
Delos

Schedia
Alexandria
Xenephyris
Nitriai   Naucratis

Athribis
Leontopolis

Cyrene

Ptolemais   Berenice

EGYPT

CYRENAICA

Arsinoë-Crocodilopolis
Alexandrou-Nesos

Ancient Judaism
and Early Christianity

(Arbeiten zur Geschichte des Antiken Judentums
und des Urchristentums)

———

MARTIN HENGEL *Tübingen*

PIETER W. VAN DER HORST *Utrecht* · MARTIN GOODMAN *Oxford*

DANIEL R. SCHWARTZ *Jerusalem* · CILLIERS BREYTENBACH *Berlin*

FRIEDRICH AVEMARIE *Marburg* · SETH SCHWARTZ *New York*

———

8 J. Becker. *Untersuchungen zur Entstehungsgeschichte der Testamente der zwölf Patriarchen*. 1970. ISBN 90 04 00113 1

9 E. Bickerman. *Studies in Jewish and Christian History.*
   1. 1976. ISBN 90 04 04396 9
   2. 1980. ISBN 90 04 06015 4
   3. 1986. ISBN 90 04 07480 5

11 Z.W. Falk. *Introduction to Jewish Law of the Second Commonwealth.*
   1. 1972. ISBN 90 04 03537 0
   2. 1978. ISBN 90 04 05249 6

12 H. Lindner. *Die Geschichtsauffassung des Flavius Josephus im Bellum Judaicum.* Gleichzeitig ein Beitrag zur Quellenfrage. 1972. ISBN 90 04 03502 8

13 P. Kuhn. *Gottes Trauer und Klage in der rabbinischen Überlieferung.* Talmud und Midrasch. 1978. ISBN 90 04 05699 8

14 I. Gruenwald. *Apocalyptic and Merkavah Mysticism.* 1980. ISBN 90 04 05959 8

15 P. Schäfer. *Studien zur Geschichte und Theologie des rabbinischen Judentums.* 1978. ISBN 90 04 05838 9

16 M. Niehoff. *The Figure of Joseph in Post-Biblical Jewish Literature.* 1992. ISBN 90 04 09556 x

17 W.C. van Unnik. *Das Selbstverständnis der jüdischen Diaspora in der hellenistisch-römischen Zeit.* Aus dem Nachlaß herausgegeben und bearbeitet von P.W. van der Horst. 1993. ISBN 90 04 09693 0

18 A.D. Clarke. *Secular and Christian Leadership in Corinth.* A Socio-Historical and Exegetical Study of 1 Corinthians 1-6. 1993. ISBN 90 04 09862 3

19 D.R. Lindsay. *Josephus and Faith*. Πίστις and πιστεύειν as Faith Terminology in the Writings of Flavius Josephus and in the New Testament. 1993. ISBN 90 04 09858 5

20 D.M. Stec (ed.). *The Text of the Targum of Job*. An Introduction and Critical Edition. 1994. ISBN 90 04 09874 7

21 J.W. van Henten & P.W. van der Horst (eds.). *Studies in Early Jewish Epigraphy*. 1994. ISBN 90 04 09916 6

22 B.S. Rosner. *Paul, Scripture and Ethics*. A Study of 1 Corinthians 5-7. 1994. ISBN 90 04 10065 2

23 S. Stern. *Jewish Identity in Early Rabbinic Writings*. 1994. ISBN 90 04 10012 1

24 S. Nägele. *Laubhütte Davids und Wolkensohn*. Eine auslegungsgeschichtliche Studie zu Amos 9:11 in der jüdischen und christlichen Exegese. 1995. ISBN 90 04 10163 2

25 C.A. Evans. *Jesus and His Contemporaries*. Comparative Studies. 1995. ISBN 90 04 10279 5

26 A. Standhartinger. *Das Frauenbild im Judentum der hellenistischen Zeit*. Ein Beitrag anhand von 'Joseph und Aseneth'. 1995. ISBN 90 04 10350 3

27 E. Juhl Christiansen. *The Covenant in Judaism and Paul*. A Study of Ritual Boundaries as Identity Markers. 1995. ISBN 90 04 10333 3

28 B. Kinman. *Jesus' Entry into Jerusalem*. In the Context of Lukan Theology and the Politics of His Day. 1995. ISBN 90 04 10330 9

29 J.R. Levison. *The Spirit in First Century Judaism*. 1997. ISBN 90 04 10739 8

30 L.H. Feldman. *Studies in Hellenistic Judaism*. 1996. ISBN 90 04 10418 6

31 H. Jacobson. *A Commentary on Pseudo-Philo's* Liber Antiquitatum Biblicarum. With Latin Text and English Translation. Two vols. 1996. ISBN 90 04 10553 0 (Vol.1); ISBN 90 04 10554 9 (Vol.2); ISBN 90 04 10360 0 (Set)

32 W.H. Harris III. *The Descent of Christ*. Ephesians 4:7-11 and Traditional Hebrew Imagery. 1996. ISBN 90 04 10310 4

33 R.T. Beckwith. *Calendar and Chronology, Jewish and Christian*. Biblical, Intertestamental and Patristic Studies. 1996. ISBN 90 04 10586 7

34 L.H. Feldman & J.R. Levison (eds.). *Josephus'* Contra Apionem. Studies in its Character and Context with a Latin Concordance to the Portion Missing in Greek. 1996. ISBN 90 04 10325 2

35 G. Harvey. *The True Israel*. Uses of the Names Jew, Hebrew and Israel in Ancient Jewish and Early Christian Literature. 1996. ISBN 90 04 10617 0

36 R.K. Gnuse. *Dreams and Dream Reports in the Writings of Josephus*. A Traditio-Historical Analysis. 1996. ISBN 90 04 10616 2

37 J.A. Draper. *The* Didache *in Modern Research*. 1996. ISBN 90 04 10375 9

38 C. Breytenbach. *Paulus und Barnabas in der Provinz Galatien*. Studien zu Apostelgeschichte 13f.; 16,6; 18,23 und den Adressaten des Galaterbriefes. 1996. ISBN 90 04 10693 6

39 B.D. Chilton & C.A.Evans. *Jesus in Context*. Temple, Purity, and Restoration. 1997. ISBN 90 04 10746 0

40 C. Gerber. *Ein Bild des Judentums für Nichtjuden von Flavius Josephus*. Untersuchungen zu seiner Schrift *Contra Apionem*. 1997. ISBN 90 04 10753 3

41 T. Ilan. *Mine and Yours are Hers*. Retrieving Women's History from Rabbinic Literature. 1997. ISBN 90 04 10860 2

42 C.A. Gieschen. *Angelomorphic Christology*. Antecedents and Early Evidence. 1998. ISBN 90 04 10840 8

43 W.J. van Bekkum. *Hebrew Poetry from Late Antiquity*. Liturgical Poems of Yehudah. Critical Edition with Introduction and Commentary. 1998. ISBN 90 04 11216 2

44 M. Becker & W. Fenske (Hrsg.). *Das Ende der Tage und die Gegenwart des Heils*. Begegnungen mit dem Neuen Testament und seiner Umwelt. Festschrift für Prof. Heinz-Wolfgang Kuhn zum 65. Geburtstag. 1999. ISBN 90 04 11135 2

45 S. von Stemm. *Der betende Sünder vor Gott*. Studien zu Vergebungsvorstellungen in urchristlichen und frühjüdischen Texten. 1999. ISBN 90 04 11283 9

46 H. Leeming & K. Leeming (eds.). *Josephus'* Jewish War *and its Slavonic Version*. A Synoptic Comparison of the English Translation by H.St.J. Thackeray with the Critical Edition by N.A. Mescerskij of the Slavonic Version in the Vilna Manuscript translated into English by H. Leeming and L. Osinkina. ISBN 90 04 11438 6

47 M. Daly-Denton. *David in the Fourth Gospel*. The Johannine Reception of the Psalms. 1999. ISBN 90 04 11448 3

48 T. Rajak. *The Jewish Dialogue with Greece and Rome*. Studies in Cultural and Social Interaction 2000. ISBN 90 04 11285 5

49 H.H.D. Williams, III. *The Wisdom of the Wise*. The Presence and Function of Scripture within 1 Cor. 1:18-3:23. 2000. ISBN 90 04 11974 4

50 R.D. Rowe. *God's Kingdom and God's Son*. The Background to Mark's Christology from Concepts of Kingship in the Psalms. 2002. ISBN 90 04 11888 8

51 E. Condra. *Salvation for the Righteous Revealed*. Jesus amid Covenantal and Messianic Expectations in Second Temple Judaism. 2002. ISBN 90 04 12617 1

52 Ch.Ritter. *Rachels Klage im antiken Judentum und frühen Christentum*. Eine auslegungsgeschichtliche Studie. 2002. ISBN 90 04 12509 4

53 C. Breytenbach & L.L. Welborn (eds.). *Encounters with Hellenism*. Studies on the First Letter of Clement. 2003. ISBN 90 04 12526 4

54 W. Schmithals & C. Breytenbach (ed.). *Paulus, die Evangelien und das Urchristentum*. Beiträge von und zu Walter Schmithals zu seinem 80. Geburtstag. 2003. ISBN 90 04 12983 9

55 K.P. Sullivan. *Wrestling with Angels*. A Study of the Relationship between

Angels and Humans in Ancient Jewish Literature and the New Testament. 2004. ISBN 90 04 13224 4

56 L. Triebel. *Jenseitshoffnung in Wort und Stein*. Nefesch und pyramidales Grabmal als Phänomene antiken jüdischen Bestattungswesens im Kontext der Nachbarkulturen. 2004. ISBN 90 04 12924 3

57 C. Breytenbach & J. Schröter. *Die Apostelgeschichte und die hellenistische Geschichtsschreibung*. Festschrift für Eckhard Plümacher zu seinem 65. Geburtstag. 2004. ISBN 90 04 13892 7

58 S. Weingarten. *The Saint's Saints*. Hagiography and Geography in Jerome. 2005. ISBN 90 04 14387 4

59 A. Hilhorst & G.H. van Kooten (eds.). *The Wisdom of Egypt*. Jewish, Early Christian, and Gnostic Essays in Honour of Gerard P. Luttikhuizen. 2005. ISBN 90 04 14425 0

60 S. Chepey. *Nazirites in Late Second Temple Judaism*. A Survey of Ancient Jewish Writings, the New Testament, Archaeological Evidence, and Other Writings from Late Antiquity. 2005. ISBN 90 04 14465 X

61 R.T. Beckwith. *Calendar, Chronology and Worship*. Studies in Ancient Judaism and Early Christianity. 2005. ISBN 90 04 14603 2

62 L. Grushcow. *Writing the Wayward Wife*. Rabbinic Interpretations of Sotah. 2006. ISBN 90 04 14628 8

63 T. Landau. *Out-Heroding Herod*. Josephus, Rhetoric, and the Herod Narratives. 2006. ISBN 90 04 14923 6

64 S. Inowlocki. *Eusebius and the Jewish Authors*. His Citation Technique in an Apologetic Context. 2006. ISBN 90 04 14990 2

65 D. Milson. *Art and Architecture of the Synagogue in Late Antique Palestine*. In the Shadow of the Church. 2006. ISBN 90 04 15186 9

66 M. Goodman. *Judaism in the Roman World*. Collected Essays. 2007. ISBN 978 90 04 15309 7

67 S.J.D. Cohen and J.J. Schwartz (eds.). *Studies in Josephus and the Varieties of Ancient Judaism*. Louis H. Feldman Jubilee Volume. 2007. ISBN 978 90 04 15389 9

68 E.J. Bickerman. *Studies in Jewish and Christian History*. A New Edition in English including *The God of the Maccabees*, introduced by M. Hengel, edited by A. Tropper. Two vols. 2007. ISBN 978 90 04 15294 6 (Set)

69 C. Zimmermann. *Die Namen des Vaters*. Studien zu ausgewählten neutestamentlichen Gottesbezeichnungen. 2007. ISBN 978 90 04 15812 2

70 T.M. Jonquière. *Prayer in Josephus*. 2007. ISBN 978 90 04 15823 8

71 J. Frey, D.R. Schwartz & S. Gripentrog (eds.). *Jewish Identity in the Greco-Roman World*. Jüdische Identität in der griechisch-römischen Welt. 2007. ISBN 978 90 04 15838 2

72 A. Runesson, D.D. Binder and B. Olsson. *The Ancient Synagogue from its Origins to 200 C.E.* A Source Book. 2007. ISBN 978 90 04 16116 0